RICHARD BERNSTEIN

ULTIMATE JOURNEY

Richard Bernstein, a book critic for the *New York Times,* served as *Time* magazine's first Beijing bureau chief. At the *Times,* he has been UN bureau chief, Paris bureau chief, and national cultural correspondent. He has written five books, including two other books on Asia: *From the Center of the Earth* and, with Ross H. Munro, *The Coming Conflict with China.* He lives with his wife in New York City.

ALSO BY RICHARD BERNSTEIN

The Coming Conflict with China
(with Ross H. Munro)

Dictatorship of Virtue:
Multiculturalism and the Battle for America's Future

Fragile Glory:
A Portrait of France and the French

From the Center of the Earth:
The Search for the Truth About China

ULTIMATE JOURNEY

玄奘法師像

悠之南行　五十三徳子影西征百二八國

千里跬步僧祇哆栗但有志心胡遠胡傾

弘始荀驂開曆後冀竺梵子文斯軫斯軾

Hsuan Tsang, 603–664 A.D. (The Granger Collection, N.Y.)

ULTIMATE JOURNEY

Retracing the Path of an Ancient Buddhist Monk

Who Crossed Asia in Search of Enlightenment

———◆———

RICHARD BERNSTEIN

VINTAGE DEPARTURES

VINTAGE BOOKS

A DIVISION OF RANDOM HOUSE, INC.

NEW YORK

FIRST VINTAGE DEPARTURES EDITION, FEBRUARY 2002

Copyright © 2001 by Richard Bernstein
Maps copyright © 2001 by David Lindroth Inc.

All rights reserved under International and Pan-American
Copyright Conventions. Published in the United States by
Vintage Books, a division of Random House, Inc., New York,
and simultaneously in Canada by Random House of Canada
Limited, Toronto. Originally published in hardcover in the
United States by Alfred A. Knopf, a division of Random House,
Inc., New York, in 2001.

Vintage is a registered trademark and Vintage Departures and
colophon are trademarks of Random House, Inc.

Library of Congress Cataloging-in-Publication Data
Bernstein, Richard, 1944–
Ultimate journey: retracing the path of an ancient Buddhist
monk who crossed Asia in search of enlightenment /
Richard Bernstein.
p. cm.
Originally published: New York: A.A. Knopf, 2001.
Includes index.
ISBN 0-679-78157-9 (trade paper)
1. Xuanzang, ca. 596–664. I. Title.
BQ8149.H787 B+ (VIII:.x7)
2001045484

Author photograph © Jade Albert

www.vintagebooks.com

Printed in the United States of America
10 9 8 7 6 5 4 3 2 1

To Zhongmei

No ship will ever take you away from yourself.

—Constantine Cavafy

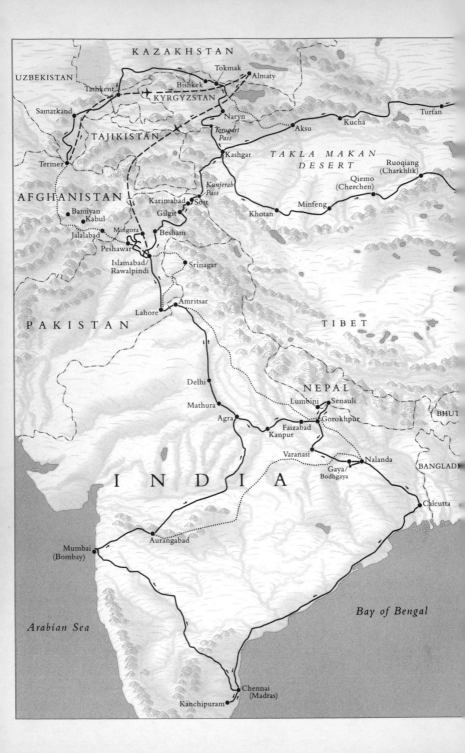

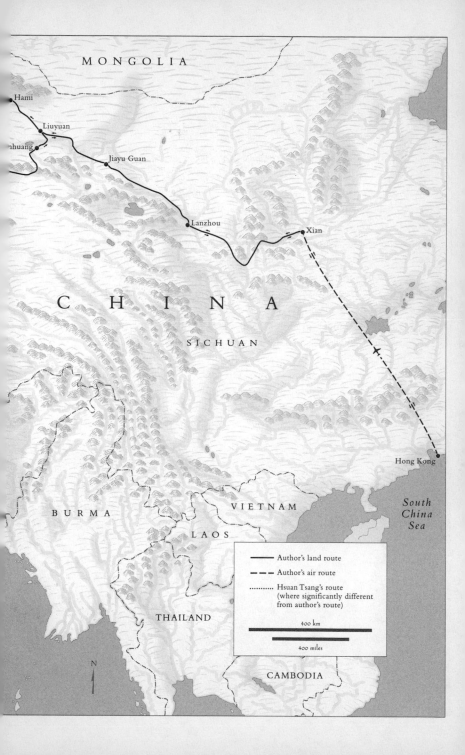

A NOTE ON CHINESE WORDS AND NAMES

With some exceptions, my renderings of Chinese words and names follow the pinyin system, in which, for example, the "sh" sound is rendered with an "x" (as in Xian) and the "chee" sound becomes "qi"—as in Urumqi. The main exception is my main character, the monk himself, Hsuan Tsang, where I follow the previously most common system of romanization known as Wade-Giles. My reasoning was that most other writings about the monk antedate the widespread use of pinyin, and so the Wade-Giles spelling of his name is the one generally recognized. (The pinyin rendition would be Xuan Zang.) And on similar grounds I have used Wade-Giles for certain other historical figures as well, such as the Emperor Tai Tsung.

In a small number of instances, specifically in the citation of passages from Samuel Beal's translations of Hsuan Tsang's works, or of Hui Li's biography of the monk, Chinese words and names appear in Beal's somewhat eccentric system of romanization, distinct from both Wade-Giles and pinyin.

CONTENTS

ULTIMATE JOURNEY

Introduction

My doctrine is to think the thought that is unthinkable, to practice the deed that is not performable, to speak the speech that is inexpressible, and to be trained in the discipline that is beyond discipline.

—The Sutra in Forty-two Sections

A T FIRST, searching for a way to satisfy the common desire to get away from it all, I thought I might teach myself to make Shaker furniture. I owned a small farmhouse in upstate New York that seemed suitable for the purpose, and I started to look at miter saws and chisel sets and flip through do-it-yourself manuals in hardware stores. I imagined myself in the workshop patiently crafting mortise-and-tenon joints while Glenn Gould played unaccompanied harpsichord music by J. S. Bach in the background.

Before I began to build my fantasy woodworking shop, however, I started, as I have before, to scrutinize maps and to think about a trip. Not just any trip, not some two-week sojourn in Italy or even a longer, farther-flung journey to, say, Angkor Wat or Borobudur. I was thinking about a particular trip, one that I had had in mind for a long time but for a variety of reasons (soon to be disclosed) had never undertaken. It was a sort of pilgrimage overland from China to India and back along the route of a Chinese Buddhist monk who went that way in the seventh century in search of the Truth.

The monk's name was Hsuan Tsang, and I think of him as the greatest traveler in history. He is far from a household name in the West, but he is certainly one in the East; in China and India he has had both historic and mythic standing for many centuries. I learned about him a long time ago, so long ago in fact that I don't remember exactly when, but no doubt at some point during the period in my life when I was what is rather grandly called a China expert. I started out in the China field as a graduate student at Harvard, where I studied the Chinese language and Chinese history under the legendary John K. Fairbank. Then, having realized that the academic life was not for me, I went to work for *Time* magazine, which sent me to Hong Kong in the days when that was as close as most Americans could get to China itself. China and the United States normalized diplomatic relations in 1979, and *Time* sent me to Beijing in 1980 to open its bureau there, the first the magazine had had in China since the Communists came to power in 1949.

It was thrilling to be in China in those years, even if the country was still a poverty-stricken police state kept down by the heavy hand of a Maoist dictatorship. China wasn't so much an ordinary country as it was an extraordinary universe, a domain of everything, from architectural ruins to moral-political theater, and because it had been closed for several decades, it was a self-contained universe due for rediscovery. I think it is fair to say that for most of the Western journalists there at the time—many of whom had studied Chinese in school before arriving—China was more a vocation than just another stop in a career as a foreign correspondent. China was all we talked about, China present but also China past, the China whose most powerful leader expectorated into a porcelain spittoon during ceremonies of state and the China of arched marble bridges and the Temple of Heaven.

When the country, under its post-Mao paramount leader Deng Xiaoping, instituted the economic reforms that are now among the wonders of the world, it quickly became clear that the China of old was soon going to vanish, and this created more than the usual amount of antiquarian interest among the relatively small contingent of foreigners who lived in Beijing then. We used to roam the city's antique shops and the small lanes of its ancient neighborhoods. We looked upon the old men with wispy beards walking their finches in cages early in the morning and the tiny ladies with bound feet and black pajamas as relics. And we created a minor cult over certain books that described what the country had been like before we got there, feeling envious of those who had known a far older China than we could know.

One of the books, for example, *The Years That Were Fat* by George N. Kates, described the monuments, the gates, the walls, the temples, the moon-viewing pavilions, the itinerant peddlers and their chants, the streetside operas, and the shadow puppet shows that had already mostly disappeared. Another book, less widely read, but known to a few of us, was *Monkey, or Journey to the West,* a sixteenth-century novel by one Wu Cheng-en. It was the highly fanciful account of an expedition to India made by a Buddhist monk in the company of a five-hundred-year-old monkey of supernatural powers. And some of us knew of the historical monk, Hsuan Tsang himself, whose actual journey to what he called "the West" took place from 629 to 645. The monk's own account of his journey, whose full title is *The Great Tang Chronicles of the Western World,* translated into English in the nineteenth century by a British clergyman-scholar named Samuel Beal, is regarded as one of the great classics of Chinese literature. In India, his chronicle is a major source of information on medieval Indian history. There are hundreds of stories, novels, plays, and operas based on Hsuan Tsang's journey in search of the Truth. There is probably not a single educated Chinese, and there are probably very few educated Indians, who do not know who he was.

Hsuan Tsang went on horseback, on camel-back, on elephant-back, or on foot from the ancient capital of Chang-an (today's Xian) all the way to southern India, a distance of roughly five thousand miles, and then back via a somewhat different route, crossing the harshest deserts and the tallest mountains in the world in both directions. His purpose was to search out what he called the Law, the original classics of Buddhist thought that would enable Chinese Buddhism, a doctrine borrowed from India in a language very foreign to China, to be put on an authentic footing. In other words, Hsuan Tsang wanted to shatter the illusory facade of the world of appearances and penetrate the diamond-hard innermost heart of Reality itself. When he returned to China he wrote, at the express demand of the emperor, about the countries he had visited on his journey, the emperor's purpose being to collect information of potential use in formulating China's military and foreign policies. But while the monk performed that task for his emperor, his concern was with an India that for him stood as the source of supreme wisdom. He went there to achieve the exalted understanding, what he saw as the Ultimate Truth, that alone permits us to achieve the purpose of Buddhism, which is the cessation of otherwise inevitable and inescapable suffering.

That was not my purpose, or at least not what I thought I might achieve. I too wish for a cessation of suffering, and I accept, at least in theory, the Buddhist proposition that the conventional pursuit of happiness leads to endless striving, frustration, and disappointment. But the Ultimate Truth is a more Buddhist thing than a secular non-Buddhist skeptic like me could strive for. What interested me about the monk's great pilgrimage was simply the beauty of his quest and the magnitude of his achievement. It seemed to me that his exploit was even more impressive than that of another figure of enduring fascination for me, Marco Polo, who came along six hundred years later. I take nothing away from the great Italian, but Hsuan Tsang's trip was almost as long and more arduous, and its goal, unlike Polo's, was not riches or renown but wisdom, a benefit for all humankind.

Years ago, a good friend of mine, John Wheeler, a former graduate school roommate who is now vice president of the Japan Society in New York, was talking about the great Buddhist monuments of Asia. At one extremity, he said, is the great Horyuji Temple in Nara, Japan. On the other side are Ellora and Ajanta, about eight thousand miles away in western India. In between are others, including the Mogao Caves at Dunhuang, which had just been reopened to foreign visitors. "Dunhuang stands temporally and geographically midway between Ellora in the west and Horyuji in the east," he said.

That remark stuck with me. The existence of an immensely long strand of Buddhist pearls stretching from the west of India to Japan inflamed my mind. It was magnificent, a great human achievement, the work of thousands of devotees performed over a thousand years. Here was Buddhism, founded by an obscure prince from the North Indian Plain, brought by merchants and monks across thousands of miles of the most forbidding terrain on the globe, and producing one of the most remarkable series of monuments on earth. The Buddha had seen in the Four Noble Truths that the usual strivings of humankind for pleasure and wealth inevitably led to suffering, and that the antidote to that suffering was to understand that the self, as it is normally experienced, was an illusion. An escape from suffering lay not in worldly pleasure, in sex, wealth, or power, but in the quiet cultivation of one's own mind. And here was a simple monk, Hsuan Tsang, traveling the entire geographical-spiritual trajectory that existed up to his time (Horyuji was built a century or so later) and leaving behind him a detailed record of what he saw. I thought of Hsuan Tsang's trip as the ultimate journey along a path over icy mountains and through scorched deserts that was for a millennium the most important thoroughfare of commerce, conquest, and ideas in the world. I thought of it as the road of great events, the greatest event of all being the transmission of the revolutionary doctrine of Buddhism, from India, where it died out, to China, where it flourished, altering the inner lives of hundreds of millions of people. I wanted to go to the same places my pilgrim went, to stand where he had stood, to look at the desert and try to hear the sound of his footsteps echoing down the corridors of time. It is a romantic notion, I know, and maybe it sounds naive, hokey in our cynical age. But when it comes to the history of the spirit, I am a romantic. I believe in paying homage to the figures of the past who conceived the thoughts that have endured, and Hsuan Tsang was such a person. To reproduce his journey would be the trip of a lifetime.

As I say, I was not hoping to find Ultimate Truth. Nor does the literary device often used in the beginning of travel books apply to me, the idea that I was propelled to undertake the lonely rigors of a journey by some grave spiritual or romantic crisis, the collapse of my marriage, the loss of my job, perhaps the death of someone close to me, a life unraveling, falling apart. In truth, my life was not falling apart. I was experiencing no theatrical exigency. My yearning to get away derived from the banal conviction that I had crossed the bourn of fifty, and that some of the things I had promised myself I would do would remain undone if I didn't do them quickly. Along with that conviction came the dread thought that this was it, my life, this and nothing more, until the end, which suddenly seemed less hypothetical than it did when I was less than fifty. Among the things I had promised myself I would do one of these days were reading Proust in his entirety, sailing to Tahiti, writing a historical novel, spending a contemplative year learning to make Shaker furniture—and following the fabled Road of Great Events from China to India and back. One of my predecessors on the China-to-India route, the English writer Peter Fleming, began his classic *News from Tartary* of 1936 with the simplest possible explanation for his travel plans. We traveled, he wrote, "because we wanted to travel—because we believed, in the light of previous experience, that we should enjoy it." That more or less summed up matters for me too, with the important difference that Fleming was twenty-seven when he started his trip and I was twice that age, which made my situation less simple than his. I traveled because I wanted to travel and I thought that I would possibly enjoy it, surely enjoy having done it. Like many men of my age, I was experiencing a kind of quarrel with bourgeois life, bathed in its ease and pleasures but aware too of its smallness and ordinariness, its lack of excitement. Most of us middle-aged men are among that species of routinized, rationalized beings that Max Weber called "specialists without spirit, sensualists without heart." We start out idealists and we end up creatures of habit, more concerned about the state of the lawn than of the spirit. Yes, we say to ourselves, it would be nice to break away for a while, but who would walk the dog?

Working as a book critic for the *New York Times,* I could feel myself glued to a chair, and I wasn't reading Proust. I liked my job, which I regarded as more than a job; it was a privilege. Moreover, I come from a background that does not make it natural for me to take privilege for granted. My father and mother brought up my sister and me on a small chicken farm in a Connecticut town called East Haddam, which wasn't a bad way to get started in life. But I have no doubt that had the opportunities my parents, both of them Eastern European immigrants, made available to me been made available to them, they would have preferred book criticism to collecting eggs and feeding chickens and shoveling manure any old day. I live at that rare nexus of political freedom and material profusion wherein you can actually pay the rent sitting at home pronouncing on the quality of other people's writings. I have my gripes, including the sedentariness of it, but still, my life was pretty good, and I knew it.

The point is, do not expect any stories of personal devastation here, any tales of redemption from grief. Expect rather a story of a man whose biggest problem was an inability, having gotten to a certain point, to get further. This was true of work, where I was in danger of sliding all the way to a suddenly foreseeable retirement age without ever again doing anything physically demanding or adventurous. I liked being a book critic, but I missed getting out and discovering the world, which, when I was younger, is what I thought I would do until I got old.

Then there was love, where I was also comfortably inert. Some years before I began thinking about getting away for a while, I attended a movie screening in New York to write an article for the *Times,* and, looking across the proverbial crowded room, I saw an Asian woman who corresponded to my romantic ideal. She wore a satiny long skirt and a black knit top and she had long hair clipped just beneath the back of her head and allowed to cascade downward to her waist. Her name was Zhongmei Li, and she told me she was a classical dancer who had moved from Beijing to New York a couple of years earlier. We began to see each other, and when I was contemplating Shaker furniture versus the China–India road we were seeing each other still, but in the way that was pathetically habitual for me—without decisiveness on my part. I wanted to move ahead, but something stopped me, as something had stopped me before when I faced other prospects for full romantic attachment (or as this is more directly put, marriage). The result was that I remained what the Talmud calls half a man, a man who had never acquired a wife or had children.

This is such an ordinary problem for so many Talmudically defined half-men in urban America these days that it seems hardly worthy of note. But I am trying to account for myself in these pages, to explain the nature of my two-thirds-of-the-way-through-life malaise, my something-less-than-a-crisis, something-short-of-contentment state of the spirit. There was no danger that I would have a fatal accident while shaving or even that I would knock people's hats off in the fashion of Melville's Ishmael as I roamed the island of the Manhattoes. It was not exactly a drizzly November in my soul, but I did find myself unaccountably moody, difficult to please. I was snapping at the *Times*'s copy editors, who are probably the best copy editors in the world. On getting up in the morning, I was becoming less and less inclined to start reading a book. I couldn't shake off the sentiment that for a former foreign correspondent like myself, who had seen journalistic action in two dozen countries in Europe, Asia, and Africa, being a book critic was a bit like putting myself out to pasture.

It is, of course, unreasonable to expect or demand that daily life, and especially making a living, be an ongoing rhapsody. Yet I was beginning to feel that even the occasional possibility of a rhapsodic moment or two, a modest, occasional touch of the sublime, was eluding me. In addition, despite Zhongmei's welcome presence in my life, I was making no headway in resolving what in the conventional psychobabble is called commitment-phobia. I tried to deal with my normative unhappiness by lying on a couch and draining my brain in the presence of a psychoanalyst. But while the experience did not make me an opponent of Freudian therapy, it seemed an expensive indulgence. Cheaper and maybe more effective to buy a table saw and a drill press and a few books on woodworking, or to pick up a plane ticket to Xian. I knew that if I didn't do one or the other pretty soon, it would be too late. The question was: Which should it be?

My interest in Shaker furniture should not be underestimated. Nor, for that matter, should anyone think that I am especially enraptured by the idea of travel itself. When I was twenty-seven, like Peter Fleming, I wanted to do nothing else. But by the time I contemplated another long trip I had done enough of them to be aware of an almost inevitable disjunction between the romance of travel expectations and the loneliness and hardship of actual travel. A great part of travel, especially to places where you don't know anybody, consists of fatigue and lumpy mattresses and touts who cheat you and dinner by yourself in rooms full of people who are dining together. The Chinese have a saying: The wise man is he who can hear the dogs barking in the next village but has no desire to go there. Perhaps this is the same idea as in Blaise Pascal's celebrated *pensée* about all human evil coming from man's inability to sit quietly in a room.

Making Shaker furniture would be sitting quietly in a room; traveling through Central Asia along the route of a seventh-century Chinese monk would be going to see the dogs in the next village. On the other hand, there is Robert Louis Stevenson, who said, "The great affair is to move." Travel is hard, especially when it involves, as it did for Stevenson, the permanent relinquishment of the place where you belong. But travel that does not lead to that relinquishment can be, despite the reality cited above, the greatest escape from the mundane, from the oblivion of routine, that I know.

I had escaped before—twenty-nine years before, to be exact. In 1970, when I was still a student, I went overland from Paris to India, crossing Turkey, Iran, Afghanistan, and Pakistan on the way. It was the great adventure of my early adulthood, and involved grievous suffering, from homesickness and horniness and dysentery and mouse-sized cockroaches and hard wooden seats and anxiety about money and the solitude of the long-distance traveler. But I became, as it were, a man of the world on that trip, and I set my life on its future course, since it was then that I wrote my first published articles and was able to move, after some delays and false starts and a good deal of wasted time, toward fulfilling my ambition of becoming a journalist and a writer.

Here is where Hsuan Tsang seemed more pertinent than making a Shaker table. What appealed to me about woodworking was what I imagined to be the tranquillity of it, the concentration on the physical object—very different from the sedentary mental work that now occupied my professional days. But I knew that what I really wanted was another experience of foreign climes and distant shores, perhaps my last such experience. To reproduce Hsuan Tsang's journey, and to write my own version of his *Chronicles,* represented an opportunity for me to turn the clock back on myself, to recapture some of the freshness of my earlier years when, anxious and ambitious, I was just starting out. There was nostalgia in this, but there was also a test, a kind of dare that I could fulfill a promise I had made to myself, that I would never, even when I got older, get so settled that unusual adventure would become impossible. Not believing in reincarnation, believing that this is the only time I will exist on the planet, I wanted to go.

AND YET for a long time, I didn't. This was for some years due to the simple fact that the mountain passes one needed to cross to go west from China were closed. They had served merchants, missionaries, pilgrims, diplomats, and armies for millennia, but for the first several decades of Communist rule in China they were shut. This was the case for the northern route through the Ili River Valley between China and Kazakhstan, as it was for the southern route via Tibet to Ladakh in what is now the Indian part of Kashmir; the same for the Oxus River route through the Wakhan Pass (which Marco Polo is supposed to have taken), for the Torugart Pass north of the historic city of Kashgar, for the Kunjerab Pass between China and Pakistan, and for the Bedel Pass to Kyrgyzstan, the pass the monk probably took on his way west.

In 1982, China and Pakistan opened the Kunjerab Pass for commercial traffic, and four years later they began allowing tourists and other travelers to cross between the two countries on that route. That was when I realized that for the first time in decades it was possible to go, as Peter Fleming had, overland from China to India. Still, the Kunjerab Pass was the wrong pass for me. It was not far south of the Wakhan Pass, which the monk took on his return to China, but it was very far from the Bedel Pass, his most likely mountain crossing point on his way west.

Then, in the mid-1990s, China and Kyrgyzstan opened another of the historic east–west crossings, the Torugart Pass, and that made a difference to me. The Torugart Pass, east of the Bedel Pass, is not the route that Hsuan Tsang took, but it covers almost identical terrain. Geographically it was close enough. And the Kunjerab Pass was close enough to Hsuan Tsang's actual return-trip route to make for an authentic reincarnation of his entire journey. In both cases, the geographic and the ethnic terrain would be basically the same as experienced by the monk.

Still I didn't go, or I couldn't go. I had a job, and it was not easy to leave it for the time required for such a long trip. Then, in 1996, a colleague of mine and I wrote a short foreign policy polemic that predicted a long period of conflict and rivalry between the United States and China. The book angered the Chinese authorities, who were just then trying to warm up the Sino-American relationship. Their response was so heated and vociferous that many diplomats and journalists whose opinions I trusted predicted I would never be allowed to travel in China again. The press in China instigated a mini–propaganda campaign against my co-author, Ross H. Munro, and myself, declaring, among other things, that we were white supremacists who had fabricated evidence in our book. Some articles explicitly said that neither of us would ever get a visa to China again. Sure enough, a year or so after the publication of the book when I applied for a visa to travel to Xian and points west, I was turned down at the consulate in New York.

There are two ways to go to China. You can apply for a visa at a consulate, which means filling out a form giving a lot of personal history, your occupation, your place of birth, your previous visits to China. Or you can go to a travel agency in Hong Kong, where, for a somewhat elevated fee, you get a visa, no questions asked. No forms, no disclosures about the books you've written or your past history with China. But because these Hong Kong visas are issued without the approval of the Public Security Bureau in Beijing, there is always the possibility that your name will flash red on the computer screen at your point of entry in China and you will be sent packing. The visa problem was intensified by the fact that I needed to get into China twice to accomplish my purpose, once to begin the journey and again for the return trip via the Karakorum Highway from Pakistan.

Another problem: Whether I could get into China or not, all journalists were banned from what is officially called the Xinjiang Uigur Autonomous Region, a vast stretch of Chinese territory that includes the oasis towns at the edge of the Takla Makan Desert that the monk passed through on his journey. The Chinese were coping with a Muslim independence movement. Terrorists had bombed buses; arrests had been made and executions carried out. And, as is often the case in China, where there is trouble, foreign reporters are banned. In the summer of 1998, two reporters from Taiwan attempting to travel incognito in Xinjiang were picked up by the security police and jailed for a week before being expelled. If Taiwanese journalists were unable to escape detection, how would a sore-thumb Caucasian like me manage in Xinjiang?

Still, at a certain point, as the sports shoe slogan has it, you just have to do it. When I made my first global backpack expedition twenty-nine years before, I had had so much less hesitation. In those earlier times I didn't think so much about potential hazards or try to gather all of the answers to every conceivable question before I departed. Looking back on it, I was amazed at my boldness, and I wondered: Is it one of the characteristics of getting older that you feel you have to have absolute certainty about everything before you put your foot out the door? Life accumulates a kind of weight, like the pound you actually do put on every year. Maybe, I thought, retracing the route of my favorite pilgrim, I would make myself lighter, at least for a time. I asked myself the Existential Question. When I lie on my deathbed, what will I regret more: not having risked running into trouble or not having at least tried to take the Road of Great Events from China to India and back along the route traveled by a seventh-century Buddhist monk who was searching for the Truth?

The answer to that question is that I sent my passport to Hong Kong and got a visa to China through my usual travel agent there. My employers at the *Times* gave me just enough time off to complete the journey. I bought a cheap, nonrefundable round-trip ticket to Hong Kong. I had a six-hour layover there, during which time I bought a one-way ticket on China Northwest Airlines direct to Xian, Hsuan Tsang's starting point. At the last minute, and to my great joy, Zhongmei decided to travel with me for the first Chinese leg of the journey. She wanted to be in Xian to attempt to run interference for me if I ran into trouble with the Chinese bureaucracy. She would fly into China ahead of me and would meet me at the airport after passport control. It was an offer of amazing, eye-opening generosity, an act of love.

The plane from Hong Kong was nicer, newer, more up to international standards than Chinese planes in the days when I lived in Beijing as a journalist. But it still had something about it—a certain stiff formality among the service personnel, the solemnity of the Communist bureaucrats who were my traveling companions—that made me sense I was entering a different world. Going to China was always entering a different world. We took off, and I saw the glistening ribbon of the Pearl River below, and Guangdong Province, a darkening green in the twilight. It had been twenty-seven years since I made my first trip to China in the days when you had to walk across the bridge at Lowu between China and Hong Kong and you went through passport control in a kind of farm shed placed within earshot of a commune pigsty. A lot had changed, most conspicuously the heralded opening of China to the outside world. Whether China would be open to me was what I would find out in just a few hours.

1

How Many Springs Do We See?

THE AIRPORT glowed a feeble orange, and the smell of coal dust hung heavy in the night air. The neon sign above the terminal building saying "Xian," which means "Western Peace," seemed suspended in smoky mist. It is commonplace among frequent travelers to China to exclaim how unrecognizable the country becomes from one visit to the next, and it does. But that dank odor, which comes from soft coal burning under millions of small fires under millions of cooking braziers, doesn't go away. At night in Xian, China smells as it always did.

I walked across the tarmac and headed toward passport control, maintaining a pose of strenuous nonchalance.

A young woman in the blue uniform and red collar stripes of the immigration police hunched over my documents for what seemed a long time, scrutinizing my visa as if she had never seen one before. Then she handed the passport to a similarly attired young man who consulted a computer screen. If there was a blacklist and I was on it, this was the moment when I was going to be caught and my trip was going to end before it even started.

It didn't. The young man handed the passport back to the young woman, who stamped it and gestured me toward the interior of her country. My months of anxiety suddenly collapsed into anticlimax, though as I proceeded to the baggage carousel I neurotically continued to worry that the young man and woman were going to burst out of their booth and come running after me, their red collar stripes bobbing in the gloom, having belatedly discovered that I was the infamous white supremacist author who fabricated his evidence.

Zhongmei was waiting for me on the edge of the pressing crowd outside the customs building, a welcoming glow in the dusty gloom, and as I walked toward her, I could tell that she was relieved to see me. Still, airport reunions, especially in foreign countries, are not cinematic. In China you don't embrace and look lovingly into each other's eyes, though that is what I felt like doing. You clumsily figure out a way for both of you to push through the crowd so you can end up on the same side of the security fence and you talk about such Byronic subjects as the disposition of the luggage and the availability of local transportation. Fortunately for me, Zhongmei had already taken charge and hired a car, a Volkswagen Santana, and a driver, and we drove the dark country road between the airport and Xian.

"Boy, am I glad to see you," I said, looking outside the window and reassuring myself that I was actually in China.

"I'm glad you made it," Zhongmei said, and she smiled. "I was too tired to rescue you if you didn't."

"You might still have a chance to rescue me. It's going to be a long trip."

"Leave it to me," she said. "You're in *my* country now."

Our driver, round and florid and wearing a light gray jacket with a zippered front, turned out to be cheerful and full of local information. As Zhongmei and I surreptitiously held hands in the backseat, she told us that Xian was fifty kilometers from the airport and that the road we were on ended at Yanan, Mao Zedong's onetime revolutionary hideout. I professed interest, and as we passed through the Xian suburbs on the way to our hotel, the Golden Flower Shangri-la, we talked about distances to various places and the improved state of China's roads. The hotel, an ugly glass structure gleaming bronze and gray, was international-class inside. I slept gratefully for ten hours.

Morning brought a whole new atmosphere. It was bright and sunny and the smell of coal dust was gone. Xian was busy. Its main thorough-fares gleamed with new buildings, and in front of the department stores were colorful streamers held aloft by onion-shaped hot-air balloons. We crossed the broad avenue in front of the hotel to the small streets behind, and on Red Flower Lane we had *sha-guo* for breakfast, noodles in broth with pigeon eggs, mustard greens, straw mushrooms, and other delicious unidentifiable things cooked in a clay pot. Dusty apartment houses of rough-baked gray brick lined the lane, and in front of the houses was the usual disorderly row of stands, corrugated metal roofs, and stone braziers holding glowing chunks of charcoal. There was an inordinate number of beauty parlors, many of them called "Hui Gu-niang," which is Chinese for "Cinderella." A man smoking a fat gray cigarette emerged from the public toilet and hitched up his trousers. The waitress who served us the *sha-guo* asked me if I was an Arab.

"Close," I said, responding in my rusty but serviceable Mandarin, "but not exactly."

"Well, what are you?"

"I'm a Buddhist monk," I said.

She laughed. She had one of those flat Asian faces with brick-colored cheeks. China does make one think of bricks. I remembered the previous night the motorized carts piled high with them, driven by men in blue cotton breathing in the black exhaust of their tractor engines.

"You're not dressed like a monk," the waitress said. "Where are your yellow robes?"

"I'm a modern monk."

"No way."

"I'm joking," I said. "I'm an American. But I'm interested in a monk, Hsuan Tsang. Have you heard of him?"

"Tang San Tsang!" the waitress exclaimed. She used the monk's hon-orific, his literary name, the name he is mostly known by in China.

"You should go on the Silk Road," the waitress said. "I've never been there."

"That's a good idea," I said. "Maybe I will."

IN THE AFTERNOON we went to the Old City, the southern corner. It's a district of open-air shops full of jade bracelets, painted fans, stone tur-tles, and temple rubbings, including two famous ones that show the monk on his pilgrimage. In one, he is smiling but slightly stooped under the weight of a very large pack carried on his back, giving him the look of a rugged modern member of the international rucksack brigade. In the other, he is smiling and being carried by a donkey. I bought a copy of each, feeling for the first time a connection between Xian and the man whose journey I had come to reproduce. Zhongmei was looking at painted fans and peacock feathers, both of which figure as props in the dances she performs, and as she did so, a man of about sixty or so appeared from down the street. He was wearing a canvas cap and a wrinkled gray sports coat over a green vest. His teeth were laced together with metal wire. He said he was the director of the Lanzhou Art Museum (Lanzhou was our next destination). There was something too threadbare about him, too dentally impaired, for him to hold such an exalted position. He quivered with a minor dementia. But I didn't doubt that he was a learned man, a gentleman of the old school. He saw our engravings of Hsuan Tsang and told us about him.

"He went to India and many other countries for China. He's very famous," he said.

The scholar put a patriotic gloss on the monk's travels. He traveled *for* China.

The man yanked me by the arm so Zhongmei could take our picture together, and then he sat on the edge of the sidewalk and fumbled in his black plastic satchel for a pen and a flimsy, crepe-thin piece of paper, which, I noted, bore the letterhead of the Lanzhou Art Museum.

"A lot of people are still a little crazy since the Cultural Revolution," Zhongmei whispered to me.

I watched the man write out a poem on the flimsy sheet of paper. His Chinese characters were wobbly and thin, like him, I thought. The Cultural Revolution, which had ended a quarter century before, was fomented by Mao, who fancied himself the Great Helmsman, the Sun in the East, but actually cast a dark light. He put power into the hands of a kind of Lord-of-the-Flies mob of teenagers and urged them to torment their elders, one of whom was probably the man stooped over his poem before us. He would have been in his thirties then, an intellectual and a patriot, and he would have been hounded half to death by the ideological thugs known as the Red Guards. When it was over, Mao sent the teenagers to work on collective farms for a few years, and after the Helmsman died, our friend would have been told it had all been an unfortunate mistake, that he had been wrongly inconvenienced and he was now free to start afresh. Except it would have been too late to start afresh. Persecuted for knowing too much in Maoist China, he would have been left behind for not knowing enough in money-mad, ungentlemanly post-Maoist China. And now he writes out Tang Dynasty poems from memory with a plastic ballpoint pen for the sake of tchotchke-burdened tourists, most of whom (Zhongmei an exception and I partially so) can't read them. After he gave us the poem, he hung on to us in the fashion of a lonely man, trying to detain us as we attempted to make a polite departure.

"You must visit the museum here. You can't visit Xian and not visit the museum. It's an extremely important museum. And you need to go to the Xingjiao Temple. It's where Tang San Tsang is buried."

We edged away. I didn't want to talk too much of Hsuan Tsang. On my first full day in China I continued to imagine being shadowed by agents of the security police. The bricks, I felt, have ears.

Later we read the poem that the man had given us:

> Pear blossoms pale white, willows deep green,
> When willow fluff scatters, falling petals will fill the town.
> Snowy boughs by the eastern palisade set me pondering—
> In a lifetime, how many springs do we see?

Zhongmei, having once been a famous performer in China, has what the Chinese call *guan-xi,* connections. These connections with the Beijing cultural establishment got us a chauffeured car in Xian, a black late-model Audi, to take us to the sights. That afternoon, it took us at unnerving speed on a new divided highway from Xian to the famous Qin emperor's underground army, the thousands of terra-cotta soldiers and horses that were buried with China's first emperor, who died in the third century B.C. It was a useful reminder that when the monk embarked on his trip, Chang-an was already an ancient city with a glorious past.

We looked at the underground army, which the Bureau of Cultural Relics is piecing back together shard by shard beneath a vast industrial roof shaped like an oblong umbrella, testifying to the unbelievable temerity of the first emperor, his utter identification of himself with the nation. I gazed at the rows and rows of rigid terra-cotta foot soldiers and believed they imparted a lesson about recent Chinese history, specifically about the similar temerity of the tyrant Mao, who modeled himself very much on the first emperor.

We drove back to Xian in our official car at more than 160 kilometers per hour (100 mph). There was something strange about going at that speed from a 2,300-year-old archaeological find to a 1,400-year-old Buddhist temple (our next stop was the Big Wild Goose Pagoda, built with imperial patronage by Hsuan Tsang himself). There was also something strange about having two years before been declared an enemy of China in the government-controlled newspapers and being chauffeured around the ancient capital in a ranking apparatchik's car complete with a humorless, duty-bound driver. We hurtled through the disorderly North China Plain, cinder-block walls, sheds, neighborhood brick kilns, corrugated iron roofs, and dusty construction sites all flying by as the car careered forward, the driver blasting away on his horn whenever we overtook a truck or bus. I looked for a backseat seat belt, but there was none. The driver had a seat belt but wasn't using it. Nobody uses seat belts in China. On the plane from Hong Kong two days earlier I had read in the *China Daily* that 86,000 people had died in China in traffic accidents in 1998—this in a country where the vast majority of people never ride in a car.

The divided highway ended and became an ordinary Chinese road, dusty and nondescript, emptying into a strip of open-front shops with dark interiors. A man in a green knit vest was energetically pumping the tires of his bicycle cart while another man, a rare fat man in China, drooped over a stool in the entrance to a food stall and watched. The road was clogged with flatbed trucks and blue-and-white buses. We swerved to avoid a bicycle cart and then surged into oncoming traffic to overtake a row of other vehicles, scattering bicycles and pedestrians trying to cross the road as we did so. Our aggressive progress reminded me that the world is divided into two kinds of countries. There are countries where the cars stop for people and countries where the people stop for cars.

The difference is a philosophical and moral one. In the first type of country, meaning basically the West, the person holding the implement of potential destruction—the car—is charged with the responsibility of protecting others from the very power that he wields. In the second type of country, which includes most of the rest of the world, the person who holds the power deems it only natural that the weaker should make way for him—and the weaker feel the same way. In China, automobiles always have the right of way, because they are bigger. If a woman holding a small child by the hand is halfway across an intersection and a taxi coming around the corner blasts its horn at her, she will stop and back away, pulling her child with her, to enable the taxi to pass, and she will show no anger or annoyance. She might even be grateful that the driver warned her of his imminent passage. There is an analogy to be drawn here with state power. The government and party in China drive a big car; everybody else crosses the intersection at their own risk.

THE BIG WILD GOOSE PAGODA seemed a natural place to establish a connection with the monk. Hsuan Tsang built it in 652 to house the collection of books he had brought back from India, and in the temple's famous pagoda you can still see the carrels where the books were kept. Tourists, mostly Chinese, climbed over the ancient stones and crowded in front of the bronze images of the Buddha. I watched a stout young man in a Snowboarder T-shirt, "Alpine Series," have his picture taken. Here and there, a monk—shaved head, gray robes, cloth shoes, pantaloons tucked into high white socks—scurried by on business. One monk, about four feet tall with smooth cheeks and a shaved head, was sprinkling water over the stones in front of the temple hall with a watering can. I asked him—it wasn't easy to determine his sex—if there was somebody who could talk to me about Hsuan Tsang and explain something about the temple's history. *"Mei-you,"* the monk barked in a baritone. *Mei-you* (pronounced *MAY* with a rising tone and *you,* tonally neutral) means "no," "there isn't any," and it is very often spoken in a bark, or in a manner of brusque bureaucratic dismissal, as in: Is there any hot water in the hotel? *Mei-you.* We bought some incense sticks at a little booth and asked the woman selling them the same question about a guide to the temple's history.

"Mei-you," she said, and returned to her newspaper.

At the entrance to the temple was a group of men wearing yellow hats inscribed with Chinese characters: Ji-yuan Travel Agency.

"Where's Ji-yuan?" I asked. I'm always eager to make conversation.

"Shandong," one of the men replied. I noticed that under his windbreaker was a green vest with the insignia of the Public Security Bureau. He was a policeman from Shandong visiting the pagoda.

"Are you a Buddhist believer?" I asked.

"Yes," he said. "Are you?"

"Um . . . no," I replied.

We burned our incense sticks, and I noticed a monk watching me as I held them in front of me and waved them up and down in the direction of the Buddha image. I was sure that I was revealing myself as a first-timer in this form of religious observance. Maybe this is why, after we dropped some money into the collection box in front of the Buddha and went to the donors book, the monk wouldn't let us sign it.

"You've already given," he said.

"Yes, we've given, so now we want to sign our names," Zhongmei told him.

"No," said the monk. "Since you've already given, there's no need for you to sign."

We let this puzzling statement pass without further argument.

"Do you know of the famous monk Hsuan Tsang?" I asked him.

"Yes."

"Is there anybody here who can tell us something about him and this temple?"

"Mei-you."

We climbed to the top of the pagoda and looked out at Xian and the surrounding countryside, all sitting under a vague mist of industrial smog and Mongolian dust. On one side was a construction site—six new templelike buildings going up. I wondered if Buddhism was on the rise, or just state tourism. Afterward we found a little bookstore in one of the temple annexes and we asked a young monk working there if he had for sale a copy of the Buddhist Association's English translation of Hui Li's biography of Hsuan Tsang. It was a book I had tried to get in New York, but the only version I found was Samuel Beal's original nineteenth-century translation (in which the monk's name is transliterated as "Huien Tsiang"), so brittle and frail that the pages crumbled as I turned them. I fear I'm the last person who will be able to read that copy in the New York Public Library. The monk knew the book we were talking about but the store did not stock an English translation. We did find the Chinese version of the monk's own *Chronicles of the Western World* in four traditionally bound volumes wrapped in a cardboard case. Each volume had a stately indigo cover and finely printed old-fashioned characters—not the simplified characters of the Communist era. I felt a little chill in the back of my neck holding the book in the very place where the monk stored his collection, perhaps the very place where he wrote it.

"Can you read it?" the monk asked me. He had warmed up a bit, dropping his earlier bureaucratic demeanor.

"Not really. I can manage the newspaper but not the literary language."

He nodded knowingly as if to say: I have the same problem.

HSUAN TSANG—or Xuan Zang, or Hiuen Tsiang, or Hiouen Thsang, or Huan Chwang, or even Yuan Chwang (depending on the system used to transcribe Chinese into Roman letters)—was born in 603 in Henan

Province in north-central China. The pronunciation of his name in modern Mandarin Chinese is *"Shyu-ann Dzang."* He came from a family of scholars and officials. One grandfather was the president of the Imperial College of Beijing and, as a consequence, was given the revenues of a town that Beal calls Chow-nan, thereby bequeathing considerable wealth to his descendants. Hsuan Tsang's father was asked many times to take up official posts, but he sensed the decay and decline of the Sui Dynasty, which held power briefly during Hsuan Tsang's childhood, and so he declined these offers. He claimed poor health and lived in retirement instead, presumably thanks to *his* father's Chow-nan bequest—"much to the admiration of his acquaintances," says Hui Li.

Hui Li's life of Hsuan Tsang sounds in places like the life of a Christian saint. At birth, he was "rosy as the evening vapors"; as a boy he was "sweet as the odor of cinnamon or the vanilla tree." He did not join in the games of other children, preferring to study instead. "Although cymbals and drums, accompanied by singing, resounded through the public streets, and the girls and boys congregated in crowds to assist in the games, singing and shouting the while, he would not quit his home," Hui Li writes.

As an adult, he was a tall man, a handsome man, a charming man. "In him were joined sweetness and virtue," wrote a certain Zhang Yue, who, a minister of state in the Tang Dynasty a half century after the Master's death, wrote a foreword to his great book. Certainly he was one of those rare men whose aspirations are somehow different from those of most others. He could have been an official. He could, given his superior intellect, have risen in the bureaucracy of the early Tang Dynasty of the Tai Tsung emperor, who took power after the Sui, and become a model of the upright Confucian magistrate like his illustrious grandfather. But this was not his way. "He considered the limits of life," Zhang Yue writes. His goal was not to establish himself as a man of power but "to cross the ford and escape the world."

Today, fourteen hundred years later, any Chinese person who has been to elementary school knows who Hsuan Tsang was and what he did. But while he was an arresting figure, he was also a complicated one, not easy to know. He was enormously courageous, as he would have to have been to set off by himself on a trip that he knew would take him many years to accomplish. One worshipful contemporary described him as "grave and majestic in bearing" and endowed with "the serenity and brilliance of the Lotus that rises from the midst of the waters." Once, when he was traveling in tropical India, on the Ganges below Allahabad, he and his party were set upon by river pirates, who decided to make a human sacrifice of the Chinese visitor. The monk asked for a few minutes to prepare himself for death. He fell into a trance. A great wind stirred. The river became turbulent. The pirates took fright. They woke him to ask forgiveness. Hsuan Tsang looked up calmly and asked: "Has the moment arrived?" The powerfully affected bandits asked to become his disciples.

I doubt that story is any truer than the stories about the five-hundred-year-old monkey that accompanied Hsuan Tsang to India in Chen Cheng-en's *Wizard of Oz*–like novel. Still, the very existence of a hagiographic and literary legend about Hsuan Tsang confirms his spiritual prowess. He had an aura. He was a prodigy chosen by his teachers for the sort of brilliant philosophical feats of which they felt themselves incapable. He was the kind of person for whom the aforementioned Max Weber invented the word "charismatic" many centuries later. Other people, including, at the end of his life, the supreme ruler of China, Tang Tai Tsung himself, turned to him for wisdom and strength. I doubt that bandits begged to become his disciples, but along his route more than one king pleaded with him to desist from his travels and impart spiritual wisdom to them. He was a master of the discipline of interior mental cultivation in a country whose major philosophy, Confucianism, stressed correct conduct in the world outside. In the whole three thousand years of Chinese history, Buddhism is the only foreign doctrine to have won a following (aside, one might say, from Communism). Hsuan Tsang in this sense was a spiritual revolutionary in two ways. He sought wisdom by cultivating the inner garden and he sought it by traveling afar, and neither of these was the usual route to fame and fortune in his country.

In some ways, certainly to anyone who plows through the entirety of Beal's translation of *Chronicles,* he comes across today as a bit of a pedant, an assembler of vast amounts of what seems now like useless information, like the exact number of monks at a given temple in present-day Pakistan, and whether they were followers of the Big Vehicle or the Little one. He is also superstitious, especially for a deep thinker on philosophical matters, or, more to the point, he recounts as true numerous fantastic stories about the supernatural powers of the Buddha and the Bodhisattvas, the "perfect ones." Still, the record that he kept of his journey was so precise that later explorers, like the indefatigable and intrepid Jewish-Hungarian-English archaeologist and temple robber Aurel Stein, used it to fix the positions of ancient ruins along the Silk Road in Central Asia. He was endlessly curious. When he went to India he noted down everything: the many different names of the country, the units of measure (including, for example, the smallest unit which "cannot be divided further without arriving at nothingness"), the units of time, the divisions of the seasons, the condition of the towns and streets, the nature of the local dress, customs, and languages. He comments on armaments, on intrigue and murder in the various royal courts he visits, on the qualities of leaders and on their subjects, and on whether he found them refined or coarse, honest or mendacious.

When he was still a boy, the serious-minded Hsuan Tsang was introduced to Buddhism by one of his three older brothers, himself already a famous monk. Together the two lived in a monastery in Loyang, China's eastern capital during the Sui Dynasty. Unexpectedly, a royal mandate was issued authorizing the election of fourteen priests who were to be supported out of the public treasury. Even though he was too young to be elected, Hsuan Tsang spent his days near the gate of the Hall of the Candidates. The high commissioner of the monastery noticed him there and was so impressed by him that he went to the board of offices of the institution and asked that the young man be named one of the fourteen. "I fear that neither I nor your excellencies will live to see the day when the soaring clouds shall distill the sweet dew," he said, the sweet dew being a metaphor for the wisdom of the Buddha. "But the illustrious character of this honorable youth will not be eclipsed." It was said that after he had read a book twice, he remembered the entire text. He began to preach and quickly became famous for the clarity and precision of his explanations of the texts. "He thus laid the foundation of his renown," says Hui Li. He was thirteen years old.

The last years of the Sui Dynasty were violent and chaotic, and Hsuan Tsang and his older brother were forced to leave Loyang, which, as Hui Li puts it, had "became a rendezvous for robbers." "The magistrates were destroyed and the body of priests either perished or took flight," he writes. "The streets were filled with bleached bones and the burned ruins of buildings." Unable to get the necessities of life, Hsuan Tsang and his older brother left for the relative calm of the southwest, ending up in a city that Beal translates as "Hsin-tu" but that is almost certainly Chengdu, the capital of present-day Sichuan Province, where, among the large colonies of exiled priests and scholars, the monk's and his older brother's reputations continued to grow.

But even before he was fully ordained as a priest, Hsuan Tsang came to be gnawed by doubts as to the true meaning of certain texts. Exactly which texts he does not say, but it is easy to imagine that many disputes had erupted in China's monasteries over what exactly was meant by certain Buddhist concepts, difficult enough in themselves and perhaps even more difficult when translated in their different ways into Chinese, concepts like "emptiness" and "suchness" and "dependent arising," all of which he would study assiduously once he got to India. For now, our monk only wanted to go to Chang-an—by then the Tang Dynasty had come to power and order had been restored—and study with new masters. When his brother forbade him to leave Chengdu, he left anyway, traveling by boat through the Great Gorges of the Yangtze River dressed as a merchant (the first but not the last time he would leave his abode in secret). After a time at a monastery in Hangzhou, where huge crowds pressed toward him to hear him speak, he eventually arrived in Chang-an and joined a monastery there.

As always, the monk's brilliance soon made him famous. Even allowing for exaggeration in Hui Li's portrayal, he seems to have been a kind of spiritual celebrity, preaching a release from suffering and deliverance from ignorance at a time when unspeakable hardship and disorder were vivid in the popular memory. The most famous sages in Chang-an, the men to whom both the clergy and laity went with questions and mysteries, were named Shang and Bin, whose disciples were "as numerous as the clouds." Hsuan Tsang "persistently inquired of these teachers, and in a moment perceived the deepest truths that they could explain." Buddhist scholarship was in a period of renewal after the generation of war and civil chaos during which things had fallen apart, and the monk was seen as the best of the generation that would restore it fully to its past glory. Hui Li cites the words of the masters Shang and Bin: "You are called to make the sun of wisdom shine again."

And yet certain questions continued to confuse him. Mirroring the pervasive political disorder in which China had been engulfed for several centuries, Buddhism itself was fractured into competing schools of thought. Or, as Chang Yueh puts this state of affairs, "At this time the schools were mutually contentious; they hastened to grasp the end without regarding the beginning. They seized the flower and rejected the reality." Hsuan Tsang listened to this Babel of voices and "was afflicted at heart." There seems little doubt at this point in his life that, though only a bit over twenty years old, he deemed himself a kind of Buddhist savior, his country's greatest religious authority and therefore the man called upon to establish the higher truth. He spoke in lyrical metaphors about Buddhist wisdom—the "sweet dew," "golden mirror," "perfumed palace," "fragrant wind"—whose main goal was to purify the heart and to gain release from the trammels of life and death. But there is also something very this-worldly about the monk, something almost megalomanic in his desire to find the Truth that will release men from desire. Early in his trip, he had long conversations with the king of Gaochang, an oasis kingdom west of the Jade Gate, and in one of those conversations he offered an eloquent testimony of faith and a declaration of the grandeur of his ambition. The monk refers to himself first in the third person, then in the first:

Hsuan Tsang has heard that whoever would traverse the deep expanse of ocean or river must use boat and oar—so those who would rescue the body of living creatures engulfed in ignorance must avail themselves of the Holy Words [of Buddha]. It was for this cause that Tathagata, exercising his great love as of one toward an only son, was born on this much-polluted earth, reflecting in himself the wisdom of the three enlightenments, and, as the sun, illuminating the darkness. The cloud of his love hovered over the summit of the heavens of the universe, and the rain of the law watered the borders of the three thousand worlds. After procuring advantage and quiet, he quitted the world for the state of true peace—and his bequeathed doctrine has spread eastward for six hundred years past.

In agreement with the mysterious character of this doctrine the world has progressed in its higher destiny; but distant people coming to interpret the doctrine are not in agreement. The time of the Holy One is remote from us, and so the sense of his doctrine is differently expounded. But as the taste of the fruit of different trees of the same kind is the same, so the principles of the schools as they now exist are not different. The contentions of the North and South have indeed for many hundred years agitated our land with doubts, and no able master has been found able to dispel them.

Hsuan Tsang owing to his former deserts was privileged at an early date to adopt the religious life, and till he had completed about twenty years, received instruction from his masters. . . . His hand never ceased to examine the different Sacred Books, but notwithstanding all his pains he was never free from doubts, until, wearied with his perplexities, he longed to wend his way to the monastery of the Jetavana [the garden in India where monarchs presented gifts to the Buddha] and to bend his steps to the Vulture Peak [the hill where the first Buddhist congress was held] that he might there pay his adoration and be satisfied as to his difficulties. . . . No anxiety will afflict me lest I should be too late to pay my reverence at the spots where stand the heavenly ladder and the tree of wisdom. . . . And after questioning the different masters and receiving from their mouths the explanation of the true doctrine, I shall return to my own country and there translate the books I have obtained. Thus shall be spread abroad a knowledge of unknown doctrines; I shall unravel the tangle of error and destroy the misleading influences of false teaching. I shall repair the deficiencies of the bequeathed doctrine of Buddha, and fix the aim of the mysterious teachings of the schools.

What exactly were the "doubts" and "perplexities"? Hsuan Tsang's great search for the Truth culminated at the Buddhist university of Nalanda, where he studied with a legendary sage named Silabhadra. But even as he started out across the desert, he probably had in mind not one single problem but several of them, related to the fractured and unstable condition of Chinese Buddhism in the seventh century. One of them stemmed from the fact that few Chinese Buddhists knew the original languages of Buddhism, so that many of the high abstract concepts of Sanskrit ended up being expressed in the very down-to-earth language of China, which is not a good language for abstraction. The concept of perfection, *prajna* in Sanskrit, becomes *yuan* in Chinese, which simply means "round."* Hsuan Tsang complained that important words had been mistranslated, or, as it is put in *Chronicles,* "the phrases of the different regions have been misunderstood on account of the wrong sounds and . . . the words being wrong, the meaning has been perverted." Since he was one of the few Chinese monks who had studied Sanskrit and Pali, the Indian languages in which the Buddhist classics were written, Hsuan Tsang felt that in Nalanda he would learn the original meanings of words and reestablish Chinese Buddhism on a more authentic footing.

Buddhism was powerful in China in the seventh century, and, like Buddhism around the world today, it meant different things to different people. To poets and scholars it was a kind of poetic sensibility, similar in some respects to Taoism, which was an escapist sort of nature worship, a protest against the impositions of human society. The Taoists got tipsy and wrote poetry by the light of the moon, or they practiced breathing exercises aimed at making them immortal. The Buddhists prayed to the various Bodhisattvas, who, rather than achieve nirvana and disappear beyond life and death, stayed around to help the rest of humankind achieve

---

* For this example and other materials on Chinese Buddhism in Hsuan Tsang's era, I am indebted to Arthur Wright, *Buddhism in Chinese History* (Palo Alto, Calif.: Stanford University Press, 1959), and to Kenneth Ch'en, *Buddhism in China: A Historical Survey* (Princeton, N.J.: Princeton University Press, 1964).

enlightenment. Ordinary Buddhist worshippers went to the temple, as they do today. They lighted incense and prayed before an image of their favorite Bodhisattva—perhaps Maitreya, the god of the future, who would summon his followers to heaven to await a better world, or Amitabha, who presided over the western paradise, otherwise known as the Pure Land. Hsuan Tsang's favorite deity was Avalokitesvara, known in Chinese as Guan-yin, the god of mercy, the Bodhisattva you turn to when things go bad.

As a moral philosophy, Buddhism advocated compassion, a dose of which did not hurt in a country as blood-soaked, legalistic, and punitive as China, where enemies of the state, domestic and foreign, were slain in Biblical proportions. During the Sui and Tang dynasties, great monastic leaders arose to found one school or another. Among the most important was what Arthur Wright calls "an intense concentration on individual enlightenment," known as *chan,* the Chinese precursor to what came to be known more widely by its Japanese name, Zen. Its central doctrine was that the Buddha nature was inherent in all things, and that one could achieve it through meditation and introspection. Another widespread and influential sect was founded in the sixth century on Mount Tiantai in eastern China. The Tiantai school was supposed to have distilled the essences of all the various trends of Buddhism into a single true text, the sole path to Enlightenment. The perfect vehicle that could transport men to the far shore beyond mere life and death was the White Lotus of the True Law Sutra, a highly abstruse document that enumerated three levels of truth that were all different and yet all the same.

Three truths that were different and all the same—that's the kind of intellectually playful but also tricky maneuvering that characterizes a great deal of Buddhist theology, which often requires the mind to hold two contradictory statements as true. Mahayana, for example, has a notion of conventional truth and absolute truth, one holding that the self and the world exist and the other that the self and the world do not exist. My theory is that Hsuan Tsang, who was, after all, Chinese and therefore schooled in a very this-worldly, practical reality, was bothered by these antinomies, that their existence was what troubled his mind. There is no question that, like all serious Buddhists, Hsuan Tsang would have believed in two fundamental ideas: one, that the goal of his activity was to find a way out of the world of suffering, and two, that suffering derived from a failure to understand the true nature of things. But the true nature of things is not easy to determine. High philosophical Buddhism is the least religious religion in the world, a religion that does not fall back on some mystical and unknowable, omniscient and all-powerful deity to provide comfort in confrontation with the great mysteries of life—where did we come from? why are we here? what happens to us after we die? why is there evil? why should we be good? Buddhism anticipates existentialism in that it asks us to make our own meaning without God—even if the Bodhisattvas, like Hsuan Tsang's Avalokitesvara have fairly supernatural powers. In going to India, our pilgrim hoped to find many small truths— the answers to specific questions, like the correct meaning of "emptiness" or "perfection." But he hoped also to find a single large truth as well, an Ultimate Truth that would resolve once and for all the true nature of reality.

Hsuan Tsang in this sense fit into his time. As Buddhist theology developed during the first to the seventh centuries, the monastic philosophers of India and Central Asia developed several high-flying philosophical notions about the true nature of reality and the psychology of the mind that perceives that reality. Early Buddhists were content to understand the Buddha's precept that what we grasp at as eternal is really impermanent, that the world we perceive is not the real world, and that our failure to understand this falseness is one of the causes of suffering. But several hundred years later, several Indian philosophers, all revered by Hsuan Tsang, began holding the concept of reality up to a new light, examining it from every angle, turning it upside down. One highly developed school of thought that emerged from this examination was known as Yogacara—the root word *yoga* suggesting deep concentration, highly trained mental discipline. Even before he set out for India, Hsuan Tsang seems to have been a convinced Yogacaran, which meant in essence that he belonged to one of Buddhism's most arcane, rarefied, difficult, and philosophically oriented schools of thought. Yogacara, commonly referred to as the "mind-only school," was a branch of Mahayana Buddhism, the Buddhism of the Greater Vehicle, whose main principle was universal salvation (in contrast with Hinayana, or Lesser Vehicle Buddhism, whose concern was individual salvation). It dealt with questions that didn't come up in Europe until a thousand years later, when René Descartes and the British empirical philosophers arrived on the scene. The Yogacarans, like the followers of other Buddhist schools, asked: Is what we perceive an accurate reflection of a real world, or is it mere illusion? And since whatever we perceive, all of our knowledge, comes to us via the five senses, how can we know whether our perceptions are valid or not? Descartes, of course, concluded that the world exists outside of us and that we can truly come to know this outside world; but the Yogacarans rejected this dualism. Among their first principles was a repudiation of any notion of separation between the self and the world. To the Yogacarans, the world was a beguiling trick and all the objects in it, all of the palpable and impalpable phenomena of life, were mere reflections in the ghostly haze of consciousness, products of mind, dreams within dreams.* To understand the remarkable truth that what you perceived was illusion and that true reality could be understood through deep study and prolonged meditation was to achieve a spiritual release that knew no boundaries of space or time.

As a convinced Yogacaran, Hsuan Tsang would have logically looked to India in his quest for answers. The great university at Nalanda in particular was the leading Yogacara center in the world, whose teachers traced their theological ancestry directly to the school's founders. All Yogacarans faced a fantastic paradox, and it was the effort to resolve that paradox that occupied their deepest thoughts. The Yogacarans believed that all was Mind, both mind itself and the phenomena that we perceive to lie outside of mind—the world out there. But if all is Mind, then isn't that idea mind as well? Or, to put this another way, if everything is illusion, evanescence, a dream within a dream, isn't the truth that all is illusion, evanescence, a dream within a dream, also an illusion? A very modern-day metaphor always pops into my mind as I contemplate this paradox. In the Beatles movie *Yellow Submarine* there is a vacuum cleaner that sucks up everything in sight, everything in the world. This would correspond to the idea that nothing is real, that all is illusion. Then the vacuum cleaner turns in upon itself and sucks itself into nothingness too. The meaning here is that the truth that all is an illusion is also an illusion, that there is a kind of double emptiness, the emptiness of all things and then the emptiness of the doctrine that sees all things as empty.

Not easy, is it? As I traveled, I read books on Buddhist philosophy, translations of the sutras (the teachings of the Buddha) and of the sastras (the commentaries on the sutras), hoping that I too would attain an understanding of what Hsuan Tsang meant when he talked of Enlightenment. The truth is that Buddhism has always appealed to me more as a philosophical matter than a spiritual one, more as wise guidance for the perplexed than religious belief. In matters of the spirit I am a Jew, not a Buddhist, though even there the word "spirit" might be misleading. I

---

* I am paraphrasing the great French scholar of Central Asia René Grousset, whose book on Hsuan Tsang, *In the Footsteps of the Buddha* (New York: Grossman, 1971), has been a major source of information for me in the writing of this book.

come to all religion as a skeptic, essentially a nonbeliever, but, as I like to say of my late father, I am a strangely religious nonbeliever, a devout sort of atheist, attached to the forms of religious ritual, the music, the solemnity of it, the intonation of the word of God, but not to its literal content. My father, born in a Russian shtetl in 1911, was deeply schooled in the Judaic classics, the Torah and the Talmud, in Hebrew and Yiddish, as much probably as Hsuan Tsang was in the Nirvana Sutra and the Sastra of the Great Vehicle, or in ancient Sanskrit and Pali. But my father, especially after he came to the United States at the age of thirteen, rebelled against his own strictly Orthodox father, whose religiosity consisted in a complex set of strict prohibitions. My father was a rationalist, not susceptible to the ancient superstitions. He would have liked to be a writer, or maybe a physicist, and he had the mental equipment for it, but circumstances dictated otherwise, and after he served in the American army in World War II, he became a chicken farmer in East Haddam, Connecticut, where I went to school, in the same building from grade one to grade twelve.

Dad knew his Marx and Gramsci as well as his Dostoevsky and his Sholem Aleichem, whom he read in blue-bound volumes in Yiddish. He quite assertively did not believe in God, or in a heavenly reward, but he went to synagogue on Friday night, fasted on Yom Kippur, led the Passover seder every year with wisdom and humor, and hummed the old Yiddish songs he had learned growing up in Russia. All of his life he gave off a bit of the perfume of the old world, and when he died in 1991 and it fell to me to lead the Passover seder for my family and friends, I felt the stark difference between my father's Jewish authenticity and my shallow amateurism.

Still, I continue to conduct the seder every year, and in other respects, too, I have adopted my father's estranged sort of intimacy with the faith of our fathers. Like him, I am simply not capable of belief in a Supreme Being, but I am familiar with the Hebrew prayers, which move me deeply. I am tied to Judaism by aesthetic sentiment, by respect for the martyrdom of others, and by a sense of history. For me, the Jews are the people of suffering, but Judaism is the philosophy of conscience, highly developed by some of the most acute thinkers of the ages, the redactors of the Mishnah and the Talmud. And Judaism is also the religion of eternity, the oldest extant religion, half a millennium older than Buddhism. I don't believe in eternity; and as I said earlier, I am not convinced by reincarnation either, which is Buddhism's rather sardonic vision of eternity as something not to long for but to escape from. But in the antiquity of Judaism, and in the duration of Jewish conscience, I feel linked to a very long chain, one that stretches all the way back to the beginning of recorded time. In there is my religious meaning. I am my father's son in that neither of us could be casual about an identity that is so old, and for which the ancestors were slaughtered. After all of the centuries and all of the blood, I do not want it to end here, with me.

What of Buddhism, then? Why a Chinese monk instead of a Jewish prophet? Buddhism and Buddhist temples were just part of the scene for me when I began, first when I was a college freshman, to travel to Asia, an agreeable curiosity. I don't believe for an instant that waving incense sticks at a bronze statue of a man sitting cross-legged on a lotus leaf will solve any of my problems. But the tinkling of the bells, the sense of peace, and the composure radiated by that same statue have always appealed to me. The more you look into Buddhism as a system of thought, as a questioning of everything, and as a way of fashioning a systematic alternative to our futile strivings and yearnings, the more Buddhism acquires depth and richness—and the more it resembles Judaism, at least in one important respect. Both Judaism and Buddhism are intellectual religions, requiring not so much acts of faith as the study of the most difficult this-worldly questions. Talmudic Judaism is arguably the most sustained examination of the question of right behavior in history; Buddhism was the earliest and perhaps the deepest investigation into the fatal flaws in the human character, the first doctrine that said, in essence, that the truth shall set you free. Both also entail antiquity and conscience. As I traced the route of Hsuan Tsang, Buddhism never became a religion to me. The religion in which I do not entirely believe is the Jewish religion. The God whose existence I doubt is the God of Abraham, Isaac, and Jacob. But my reverence for Buddhism as a manner of sifting the glitter from the substance, as a means of overcoming the shallowness of the self and of reaching for the tranquil power of the mind, increased. As I have read about Hsuan Tsang's life, I find myself ever more impatient at his devotion to tales of supernatural magic and ever more drawn to his theological purpose. I became convinced that he went to India to resolve the paradox of the Yellow Submarine vacuum cleaner, of the double emptiness. He believed that to perceive so deeply as to plunge beyond that paradox would bring him to an understanding of Ultimate Reality, Absolute Truth.

He set off on his journey in 629, when he was twenty-six years old, having first studied the languages of the countries he would visit. His first traveling companion was a priest from what is now the province of Gansu, who served as his guide. The monk's first major destination was Lanzhou, the capital of Gansu.

He must have been nervous and excited as he took his first steps west, and so was I, and there was an eerie similarity to our situations. Before he left for India, Hsuan Tsang had been informed of an imperial rescript that banned all travel by Chinese west of the Jade Gate. The new emperor, Tang Tai Tsung, was busy consolidating his power, and he did not want any of his subjects venturing beyond the borders of the country, especially into the zones that had once belonged to China but were now under the control of rival, non-Chinese chieftains, Turks, Mongols, and Huns. As for me, it was not very likely that I would run into any trouble in Xian, a major tourist destination where the police were not on the lookout for suspicious foreign travelers. But I would be more conspicuous in Gansu and in Xinjiang, where there were fewer tourists and where journalists were not supposed to go. I too, in my way, was going to be a clandestine traveler hoping not to be discovered. But I was also happy, after all the years of thinking about this trip but doing none of it, finally to be on my way. And now, like the monk, I too had a native guide. I was not alone, and that took a good deal of the edge off of my anxiety.

ON OUR SECOND NIGHT in Xian, we went to the train station to buy our tickets to Lanzhou. There was something phantasmagorical about the scene there. The station was a large, stained cathedral of a building just outside the remaining city walls. There are some Tang-era ruins near Xian, including the Big Wild Goose Pagoda, but the towering crenellated wall strung with delicate lights that stretches perpendicularly away from the station and into the gloaming is the Ming Dynasty Wall, built seven centuries after the era of Hsuan Tsang. It hulks above. It has a mystical and a monolithic aura about it as it erupts upward into the sky and then stretches mighty horizontal wings in both directions.

Inside the station, a man in the green uniform of the Public Security Bureau sat in front of a metal folding table and curtly answered travelers' questions. He shared jokes with a man in a blue uniform with epaulettes who sat beside him. A sign on ticket window number 15 said: "A party member is an advanced model." Zhongmei explained the sign's meaning: The ticket seller at that window is a member of the Communist Party and is therefore supposed to set an example for the other ticket sellers. But that night nobody was there.

A large board on a high wall over the entrance announced the trains for the next day: train number 677, Xian to Tangzhou; number 367, Xian to Korla (our train); 829, Xian to Urumqi, originating in faraway Guangzhou. Opposite was an enormously long placard inscribed on a high wall titled "What you need to know to buy a ticket." The sign presented twelve rules, but we had no time to read them. Outside were rows of food stalls, hot noodles cooking on shiny metal stoves. A sad-looking woman in a dull brown sweater sat on the asphalt selling five-flavored-tea-soaked eggs out of an enamel pan. A sign on the partition of the station esplanade said: "The Old City is our home; cleanliness and sanitation depend on everyone." Alongside the partition were groups of tomorrow's passengers bedding down for an al fresco night. Others sat and smoked or read the newspaper. In the middle of the esplanade two human forms huddled together in sleep.

I realized what it is that makes a Chinese city at night so special. It is the nature of its sound, a muffled roar that is not that of machines or cars or air conditioners but of an enormous number of people, of a million feet scuffing simultaneously on asphalt, a pedestrian shuffle mingling with the sounds of tinny Taiwan music and the occasional radio drama drifting through the public spaces. It is a softer sound than the sound of other cities I have traveled in, a kind of concerto for vocal cords and shoe leather, and it is accompanied by the chiaroscuro of the Chinese night, the frailty of the yellow electric light struggling in the dusky air.

2

Leaving the Ba River Behind

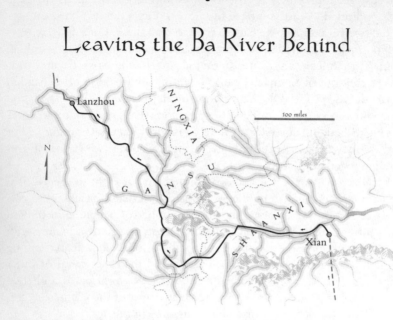

WE HAD two berths in what is called "soft sleeper," which means European-style four-berth compartments. There is usually just one soft-sleeper car per train, placed next to the dining car. Then there are several hard-sleeper cars, in which the berths come in three layers and the furnishings are barer. After that are the hard-seat cars with their square-backed, non-ergonomic benches on which the ordinary Chinese person might go from, say, Guangzhou to Urumqi, in five ass-bruising, back-torturing days. What are the same in all three classes are the toilets, which are slimy and grim. I asked myself at the beginning of my journey what class of train transport the monk would have selected if Chinese trains had existed in the seventh century, and I decided he would have taken soft sleeper. The monk was a hardy traveler, but he accepted comfort on the occasions when he could find it, and he did consider himself a first-class kind of guy. This reasoning was comforting, since I desperately wanted to go soft sleeper myself.

The train lurched out of the Xian station, and I thought of the overused Chinese saying "A journey of ten thousand li begins with a single step." The monk's journey would no doubt have started with an actual step, taken probably by a horse, as he turned from someplace in the vicinity of downtown Xian toward the fabled West—that is, anywhere west of China—where no Chinese monk, and perhaps no Chinese at all, had gone in a century. My own journey began with the turn of an iron wheel, but I had the satisfaction of knowing that no other traveler had undertaken exactly this trip since the monk himself. I was going to be the first person to retrace his steps.

The train lumbered through the Xian suburbs, past the rear precincts of red brick factories and disorderly yards strewn with trucks and cinder blocks, steel reinforcement bars and cable drums. For the first few hours we cut through the flat landscape of the North China Plain and then we entered the Wei River Valley, a corridor of abrupt hills and terraced fields and numberless tunnels cut through the rock. Zhongmei and I sat opposite each other near the window and next to the little plastic-topped table that furnishes every soft-sleeper compartment. Beneath it was an immense red thermos that the service people kept full of hot water, another of those few aspects of China that never change. Zhongmei was reading *Pride and Prejudice,* while I alternated between watching the passing scenery and reading the monk's *Chronicles* in the translation by Samuel Beal, in whom a grudging admiration mingled with racist condescension. Beal's chief interest was India and the history of Buddhism in India, a subject much illuminated by the various Chinese monks who went there over the centuries as pilgrims. And so Beal translated the works of all of the monk-explorers who left behind them written accounts of their journeys, including two who went to India in centuries prior to Hsuan Tsang.

"Never did men endure greater sufferings by desert, mountain, and sea than these simple-minded earnest Buddhist priests," Beal wrote. "That such courage, religion, devotion, and power of endurance should be exhibited by men so sluggish, as we think, in their very nature as the Chinese, this is very surprising, and may perhaps arouse some consideration."

The best-known of these rugged earlier pilgrims was Fa Xien (spelled "Fa-hian" by Beal), who left Chang-an in 399 and returned fourteen years later. Then came Sung Yun, a native of Dunhuang in western China, where the greatest of the Chinese cave temples is situated, who was dispatched by the empress of the Northern Wei Dynasty to India in 518 to collect Buddhist books. Roughly a century after Sung Yun came Hsuan Tsang. He was a close reader of the exploits of his predecessors, and he improved on them. He went to more places, studied longer, and brought back a far more complete record of the existing Buddhist world. Hsuan Tsang showed an almost superhuman, certainly a death-defying, determination to reach his destination. Given the imperial ban on travel beyond the Jade Gate, Hsuan Tsang set off from Xian knowing not only that his journey would be long and arduous but that it would also be illegal and that if he was caught he would be turned back and punished. But this was a man who would be deterred by nothing short of death, and while Beal is surely wrong to be amazed at the durability of such a "simple-minded" man, he is not wrong to wonder that a Chinese of high birth and attainment would endure the hazards of a long journey far away from home.

The simple truth is that except for these monks, the Chinese before the late nineteenth century never went to other countries in search of wisdom. They went as traders in search of wealth, occasionally; they went on diplomatic missions, and on punitive military expeditions. Sad stories are told of the maidens who were sent far from home in order to satisfy the lust of barbarian chieftains, who would then be grateful to the Son of Heaven back in China, since a Chinese princess was the most coveted gift that the Celestial Kingdom could bestow. The men and women who passed through the Jade Gate had no thought of finding anything of intrinsic value in the non-Chinese parts of the world. China was the Middle Kingdom, identical with the civilized world. There was no need to look elsewhere for knowledge or beauty. The Chinese developed no anthropological spirit; the idea that they might understand themselves better if they studied other people carefully and disinterestedly doesn't seem to have occurred to them. They had no disposition to explore for the sake of exploration.

The frequently cited exception to this rule is the famed late-fourteenth-century eunuch admiral Zheng He, who made seven maritime expeditions to the most distant Asian sea-lanes and all the countries on their shores. Zheng was a Central Asian and a Muslim whose family had immigrated to China from Bokhara two hundred years before. He exploited Chinese nautical superiority—compartmentalized hulls; waterproof bulkheads; mechanical steering devices; huge, 440-foot, nine-masted ships—to take flotillas that made the Spanish Armada seem small by comparison all the way to the coasts of India and Africa. But as the historian Frederick Mote writes in his vast history of imperial China, the voyages were probably motivated by the desire of the new emperor, Ming Chenqu, to let the world know that he was in charge in China.* There

---

* Frederick Mote, *Imperial China* (Cambridge, Mass.: Harvard University Press, 1999), pp. 613-17.

was no follow-up to these expeditions, no attempt to collect information on the maritime world or to expand China's natural maritime power.

A century after Zheng He, the Portuguese Prince Henry the Navigator, whose nautical technology was vastly inferior to that of his counterpart in China, systematically dispatched one expedition after another down the coast of Africa in search of new trade routes to India and China. It was the West that sought out China, not self-satisfied, self-sufficient, incurious China that sought out the West. If it had been the other way around, we might all now be speaking Chinese.

The point is that, alone among the billions of Chinese who have inhabited the Middle Kingdom, only the likes of Fa Xien, Sun Yung, Hsuan Tsang, and a few dozen less-recorded others journeyed afar for the sake of wisdom, knowledge, and enlightenment abroad. Hsuan Tsang's *Chronicles* is virtually the only major, systematic study of foreign lands done by a Chinese before the last couple of centuries. If there were doctrinal issues that needed to be resolved, if the search for the Ultimate Truth admitted of obstacles, Hsuan Tsang was a logical self-appointed person to resolve them. In a way, he was a product of his moment in history, a moment when everything was up for grabs in China, politics and theology both. It was a moment when the entire country, recovering from four centuries of civil war, needed men to reestablish both the political order and the theological order. The former was accomplished by a larger-than-life figure named Li Shimin. It fell to Hsuan Tsang to try to reestablish the religious order.

In Hsuan Tsang's early childhood, the Sui Dynasty was in power, having reunified China after about four centuries of fragmentation and war. For reasons that are much discussed among historians, the reunifying Chinese dynasties like the Sui were short-lived, though they paved the way for longer-lived dynasties that replaced them. If, as someone once said, the Russian constitution was absolutism tempered by assassination, China under the Sui was assassination tempered by absolutism. The Sui emperor Wen Di was erratic and violent. He kept the country in a state of constant warfare; within the imperial court, he personally flayed disfavored officials with a bamboo stick until their souls departed from their shredded bodies and were available for reincarnation. He ordered his officials to speak openly, but when he was offended by what they said, he resorted to his punishment baton. He did not inspire affection, not even among his sons, one of whom, in the course of a power struggle with another of his sons, had the emperor murdered so that he could take both his father's favorite concubine and the throne for himself.

In 611, when Hsuan Tsang was eight years old, there were great floods—in Chinese cosmology, always a sign that the emperor has lost the mandate of heaven. The next year, the army suffered a devastating defeat at the hands of the Koreans. A season of drought and pestilence followed. "Those who were strong assembled and became robbers, while those who were weak sold themselves as slaves," the official history reports. A few lines of verse, recalled by the French historian René Grousset, capture the moment:

> Horsemen sheathed in armor
> Surround the imperial capital.
> The snowflakes lie heavy
> Upon the frozen standard.
> The mad voice of the wind
> Mingles with the noise of the drums.*

Into this picture of disorder and devastation enters the man who was on the throne when Hsuan Tsang left for India, a figure whose name at birth was Li Shimin and who is one of the colossal figures of China's history, a kind of Chinese Julius Caesar or Ivan the Terrible. He seems to have been of mixed blood, Chinese and northern "barbarian." He was the second son of Li Yuan, the Duke of Tang, a lazy sensualist who was the commander of an imperial army that put down peasant revolts on behalf of the Sui and defended the frontiers against the Turks. Shimin went into the army at the age of fifteen to begin a military career. Eventually, as the Sui foundered in incompetence, he mounted a devious plot to seize supreme power. He arranged for his temptation-prone father to take a concubine who had been abducted from the harem of the Sui. This was an act of lèse-majesté, which Li Yuan would have been required to pay for with his life. Instead it forced him into rebellion, which succeeded. Emperor Yang Di fled south, where he was murdered in 618, the year Li Yuan formally took the throne as Gao Tsu, the High Progenitor of the new Tang Dynasty. Hsuan Tsang was then fifteen years old and living with his brother at a monastery in Chengdu.

Li Shimin's seizure of power, via the proxy of his father, was only the beginning of a pungent and sanguinary tale of court intrigue and murder that occupied the first few years of the Tang Dynasty, pitting Shimin against his two brothers and his stepmother, the new wife of the emperor.

* Grousset, *In the Footsteps of the Buddha*, p. 3.

In the end, in a kind of shoot-out at the Xuan-men Gate in Xian (then Chang-an), he killed his two brothers, who had schemed repeatedly to have him assassinated. Then, to avoid problems from any pesky pretenders to the throne who might come along later, he took the trouble to have all his brothers' male descendants executed. He also persuaded his father to abdicate in his favor, which made him Emperor Tang Tai Tsung, perhaps the greatest of China's emperors, the de facto founder of a dynasty that was to last for the next three hundred years and to create what was until then the globe's most glittering and advanced kingdom.

Hsuan Tsang and Tai Tsung were only a half generation or so apart, and I have always seen them as representatives of two polar opposites in human nature. This was the case even though they came from similar upper-class backgrounds. They had similar advantages and opportunities. But one was the quintessential hero of the spirit, the other of power. One was dedicated to peacefulness and escape from strife; the other shed blood and made war. In the end, after Hsuan Tsang's trip was over and he had returned to China, the monk and the emperor became close. Hsuan Tsang served as a spiritual counselor to the ruler, who wanted him near as he got old, in return for which he provided protection and funds for the building of monasteries and for the monk's great project of translating into Chinese the documents he had collected in India. One conclusion that can be drawn from this is that Hsuan Tsang was not all that unworldly after all, that he had an eye on practical matters and was not above playing politics when it would serve his cause.

Still, if the monk and the emperor came full circle in their later years, the imperial ban on travel beyond the Jade Gate made them start out on opposite sides of Hsuan Tsang's project. As we know, Hsuan Tsang's trip began as an act of civil disobedience, the monk having left for India clandestinely, illegally, with, at times, the enforcers of the imperial writ hard on his heels.

This made for some excitement as Hsuan Tsang set off from Xian, heading west into the North China Plain, which, in its arid agricultural flatness, probably didn't look all that different from the way it does today. His first destination, Lanzhou, was where China ended and Central Asia began. Beyond it lay the Jade Gate, the guardhouses that stretched into the desert, the endless landscapes of sand and rock where, as the poet put it, "the crescent moon hangs in the void and all that can be seen is wilderness." Beyond the gates lay the oasis kingdoms, most of them controlled by the Turks, many of whom were Buddhist and who therefore gave the renowned monk cordial and respectful receptions. The places immediately beyond the Jade Gate that he traveled to are known now as Hami, Turfan, Kucha, and Aksu, but Hsuan Tsang called them I-gu, Gaochang, Qiu-tse, and Po-lu-jia. About twelve hundred miles to the west was the pass through the Tianshan Mountains that would bring the monk into zones where Chinese writ had never reached. Many more obstacles lay ahead of him, including the Hindu Kush, the Kashmiri Himalayas, the scorched Punjabi Plain, the Yamuna and Ganges rivers, and the steamy heat of the Indian Deccan. Before he was finished, he would engage in a hunger strike, be captured by bandits, be mortally threatened by Hindu priests. He would dine with the Great Khan of the Turks and debate Hindu priests before King Harsha, the monarch of all of northern India. He would study with the greatest Buddhist scholars in the world and write treatises that confounded his theological foes. All that lay in the future. The first task was one of the more hazardous he faced. It was to elude the Chinese enforcers of the imperial prohibition on travel to the West, a task that came very close to costing him his life while he was still at the beginning of his journey.

"MAY I LOOK at what are you reading?" A fellow passenger was speaking to me in English. He was the only other passenger in our soft-sleeper compartment, but I would have noticed him even if there had been many others. He was very tall for a Chinese, well over six feet, as lean as a sapling, with sleepy eyes and black-framed glasses in a style we once called mod. He had struggled into the compartment with a backpack the size of a steamer trunk on his back, wearing Timberland-type hiking boots, black nylon pants, and a tan Banana Republic safari vest festooned with pockets. He gestured toward my copy of Beal and smiled.

The book has an orange cover and a reproduction of one of the famous engraved steles showing the ambulatory monk on his way to the West. I had gotten my Munshiram Manoharlal reprint of the 1884 Beal translation a few years earlier at the Saeed Book Bank ("Book sellers to the nation") in Peshawar, Pakistan, which I had visited on assignment for the *Times* a few years earlier. I did not know enough at the time to ask if Saeed's had the Hui Li biography of Hsuan Tsang, the crumbly volume that I later read at the New York Public Library. But my journey in Hsuan Tsang's footsteps was going to bring me to Peshawar again, so I would try to find the book at Saeed's. And if they didn't have it (they didn't), to try to contact Munshiram Manoharlal itself in New Delhi in the hopes that it would (it did).

"It's *The Great Tang Chronicles of the Western World* by Hsuan Tsang," I replied to the man. "Do you know it?"

"Oh yes!" he said. He was a man of about thirty or so, maybe a bit more. His English seemed textbookish but serviceable. As we talked, he demonstrated a disregard for tenses—in Chinese there are no tenses; past and present are indicated mostly by context—and most of the time he omitted the various forms of the verb "to go." He reached into his bag and pulled out a book of his own. It was a Chinese biography of the monk, complete with maps showing his route through Gansu and Xinjiang.

"Since I this way," he said, skipping "go" for the first time, "I read this."

This astonishing coincidence at first made me worry. So far everything had gone smoothly in China. But it was simply too remarkable that two people traveling in the same train compartment from Xian would be carrying books about the monk, a figure not exactly in the forefront of the collective consciousness. I wondered who this man was who looked like something out of a Chinese version of the L. L. Bean catalogue and whether he was a security officer who knew who I was and what I was doing. I looked at Zhongmei, who betrayed no worry, and I quickly realized that if the security police wanted to nab me, they had no need to infiltrate an agent into my train compartment to catch me in some unwitting disclosure of my identity and purpose.

"You aren't following Hsuan Tsang's route?" I asked.

The man explained that he worked for a travel agency in Beijing and was on his way to Kashgar in the westernmost part of Xinjiang to meet some tourists who were coming over the Kunjerab Pass from Pakistan. He would then accompany them back to Xian along the northern oases of the Takla Makan. He said that his name was Wang Yung, which translates roughly as "Brave King."

"You must know this part of the country well," Zhongmei said.

"Pretty well." A couple of years earlier, Brave King said, he had accompanied a group of Turks who were traveling from Xian to Kashgar. They went the entire distance by camel. "Once they cross Xinjiang," he said, "they take their camels across Torugart Pass into Kyrgyzstan. They all the way back to Turkey."

This was also extraordinary. This person, met accidentally on a train, had gone to the very Torugart Pass where I was going. And he was reading a biography of the monk!

"That sounds like a hell of a trip," I said.

"It takes us six months reach Kashgar," Brave King said. "Camels can only thirty or forty kilometers a day. We camp every night in the Gobi for six months."

"Now that sounds tough," said Zhongmei.

"These Turks terrible," Brave King said. "They get into fights everywhere. That's all they do, fight fight fight. We bring Mongolian camels, but Mongolian camels not strong like Xinjiang camels. Two dic. We buy new camels, Xinjiang camels, but the Turks don't have much money, so they don't want to pay price. They can't speak Chinese. They can't speak English. They fight. They fight in restaurants. They fight in market. They fight camel man who sells them camel. Everywhere they fight."

"But I'll say this," Brave King said. "The Turks are tough and they can eat bitterness. You know the Chinese say *chi ku,* 'eat bitterness.' The Turks eat a lot of bitterness."

The ability to eat bitterness is a sign of a kind of hard virtue in China, a matter of pride.

Brave King continued: "But the Turks are not as good as the Chinese at eating bitterness. You know why? I tell you why. Because the Turks know how to fight, but the Chinese know how to suffer."

We lapsed into silence and looked out our curtained window. We continued to follow the Wei River, narrowed considerably to two shallow streams flowing on either side of a series of mud banks. The valley curved grandly under the hills. We went through a series of sooty tunnels and passed a village tucked into a narrow ledge between the rail bed and the river. It was surprisingly large, row after row of neat stucco houses with handsome gray tile roofs. Where the valley widened, there were broad fields of grain, wheat probably, maybe millet, or sorghum, interspersed with fruit trees and vineyards and vegetable gardens.

While I was observing this rural idyll, we heard a child's voice coming from the corridor outside. Zhongmei, who was taking a nap in the upper bunk, wanted to look. We saw a small boy in blue pants slit at the bottom in the fashion for Chinese children's clothing, accompanied by a woman in a smudged yellow sweater. When Zhongmei leaned down to look at him, her hair, like an ebony shadow, a jet of black silk radiating aromas of frankincense and shampoo, fell into the doorframe. "He's cute," she pronounced. Then she raised her head to go back to her nap, taking the dizzying aroma with her.

• • •

I HAVE A THEORY that I met Zhongmei in China years before we met in New York, or, at least, that I saw her before our New York meeting. It really doesn't matter, and the theory cannot be proven, but I like it because it suggests both the fatefulness of our encounter and its improbability. Early on in my career as a resident journalist in Beijing, I went on an official tour of the Beijing Dance Academy, which chooses dancers from all over China and trains them for national careers. Our guides took us into a drafty rehearsal studio where there were a group of fourteen- or fifteen-year-old girls, slim as blades of grass in their leotards. One of them was crying silently, tears drifting conspicuously down her cheeks even as she held her dance position flawlessly, silently, with no sound of weeping. I remember thinking at the time how unlikely it would be in the West that a teenage girl in such obvious emotional turmoil would maintain that sort of iron discipline, even as she was being observed by a delegation of visiting foreigners. Nearly fifteen years later, when I met the thoroughly grown-up Zhongmei in New York, I told her about my visit to the Beijing Dance Academy and my memory of that weeping girl. She decided that the girl might well have been she, since she was a student at the academy then. She would have been about fourteen years old. She cried often, she told me.

She is from the far northeast of China. The Soviet border was visible from her village across the Amur River in Heilongjiang Province, the North Dakota of China. Her father, a former Red Army soldier during the Communists' march to victory, had been sent there with his unit to open up the barren land and to build Chinese towns. A little clue to a familial resoluteness that I've often seen in Zhongmei is provided by the experience of her mother, who was in Shandong Province, about one thousand miles to the south. She had been told simply what unit her husband was in and what province, and that it was permissible for her to join him. She had no money. There was no public transportation available to her. So she walked, the entire distance, begging for food along the way and carrying the two young children she had then (Zhongmei came later) on a balancing pole over her shoulder.

When Zhongmei was eleven, her older sister saw a notice in the *People's Daily,* the Communist Party newspaper, that the Beijing Dance Academy was holding its annual auditions in Beijing. Zhongmei, who liked to dance but had had no formal training, wanted to go. Her parents refused. To send a daughter to Beijing from northern Heilongjiang represented a considerable expense to them. Zhongmei went on a hunger strike until they relented. She went, staying at the home of an army friend of her father's. She was one of twelve girls chosen for that year's class out of about twenty thousand who auditioned.

She then spent six unhappy years at the academy. All the other girls were from urban areas, and more sophisticated and more affluent than she was. On Sunday, the only full day off from school, the routine was to go as a group to Tiananmen Square and take turns buying popsicles, but Zhongmei never went, because she didn't have enough money to buy a round when her turn came up. Zhongmei, in talking about that period, during which, she says, she never smiled, stresses the enormous prejudice against rural people, peasants. She was seen as so hopelessly out of place at the elite academy that one of the main teachers refused to allow her to take her regular dance class, making her sit on the floor and watch the other girls instead. Zhongmei made a deal with the night watchman. Every morning at four o'clock, two hours before the mandatory wake-up, the watchman pulled a string that dangled from the second-story window of the girls' dormitory. The other end of the string was tied around Zhongmei's wrist. Every morning for six years she practiced two hours in the dance studio by herself while her classmates slept. She's like that. She's not her mother's daughter for nothing. When she graduated, it was the general consensus that she was the best female dancer in her class, and there is proof of that. China, like most Communist countries, had national competitions in just about every activity—music, acrobatics, diving, and dance among them. No dancer had ever won first prize more than once. Zhongmei won four years in a row.

She came to the United States in 1991 with a scholarship to get a master's degree in a dance teaching program at Dallas Baptist University, some members of which she had met during an international festival in Hong Kong. She stayed in Dallas for three months and decided it wasn't for her. She didn't speak a word of English, but she nonetheless figured out a way to come to New York to study modern dance at the Martha Graham School, and then at the Alvin Ailey Company. She had been a star performer in China, a regular on national television, earning a salary higher than a university professor's, but for three years she lived in a maid's room in New York, looking after an aging member of her host family and doing light housework in exchange for room and board.

When I met her at that fateful movie screening and asked her what she did, she naturally told me she was a dancer. I remember thinking: That's nice, a dancer, thinking of her the same way as I might think of a waitress who described herself as an actress. Not that it mattered. I knew that I hoped to see her again and I didn't care if she was a dancer or an accountant. But then she invited me to a rehearsal of a program she was preparing for an out-of-town show. I sat on a rickety wooden stool in a dingy Soho loft and watched her as she danced in front of me, the music pouring out of a little portable tape player. She was astonishing, brilliant, a goddess. She had only shortly before created her own dance company, to perform Chinese classical dance for American audiences, and she was about to do several programs at the Joyce Theater in Manhattan, importing her former classmates at the Beijing Dance Academy to perform with her. So I don't know if she was the girl I saw weeping in the studio all those many years before, but she was the kind of girl who would have kept going through the distress. She is a slender wisp with willpower of steel. And though I know how it happened, it will never cease to amaze me that a girl from a state farm in Heilongjiang and a Jewish boy from a chicken farm in Connecticut would end up riding a train together in western China retracing the steps of an ancient Buddhist monk.

AT THE END of the afternoon we were still in the valley of the Wei River, still going through tunnels smelling of coal smoke. We passed through station after station, each of them a crumbling concrete platform with a masonry terminal building and small clots of passengers clutching plastic satchels and rushing toward the hard-seat cars. We pulled into Tianshui. Alongside us was a green wagon marked "Guangzhou–Urumqi," and I had some thoughts about the vast extent of China, humid, semitropical Guangzhou being two thousand miles from arid Urumqi. At each town a predictable tableau presented itself: a clutch of people, some on bicycles, some on donkey carts, others on motorcycles and scooters, a large number on foot, their faces looking up at the train windows catching a glimpse of me as I tried to catch a glimpse of them.

Beyond Tianshui, the hills flattened out under a hazy sky and slowly gave way to green agricultural fields interspersed with tombstones. Zhongmei and I went to the dining car while Brave King voluntarily stayed behind to watch the bags. I had by now accepted that he was a tour guide whose interest in Hsuan Tsang was a happy coincidence, not a Public Security Bureau deception.

We ordered *gongbao* chicken (chunks of chicken sautéed with peanuts, vegetables, and red pepper) and some sautéed spinach with rice. In the front of the wagon, one of the serving women was accusing a man of trying to pass her a counterfeit fifty-yuan note. That seemed bad enough, but things got worse when the man demanded his note back and the waitress refused to give it to him. Instead, she summoned security, which soon arrived in the form of a stout man with fat, veinous cheeks and a blue uniform. The policeman took the counterfeit bill and demanded that the man produce his ticket for inspection. The man looked poor. He wore sagging gray trousers and a threadbare blue jacket. He refused to show his ticket. The policeman smacked him across the face with a closed fist. The man's knees sagged for a moment, but he stayed upright. He surrendered his ticket. The policeman ordered him to sit in the dining car, and he chose a seat just opposite us, his hangdog expression taking away my zest for our meal.

"He wants his money back," Zhongmei said. "But since it's counterfeit the waitress won't give it to him."

"Fifty yuan is a lot of money for him," I said. "It's a week's wages."

"Somebody gave him a counterfeit bill, and now he's stuck with it," Zhongmei said.

"What are they going to do with him?"

"I think they're waiting for the next station and they'll turn him over to the police. His ticket is probably fake too."

"Maybe we should give him fifty yuan," I said. I was thinking that that is what the monk would have done, winning merit, showing compassion. The prince who many reincarnations later would become the Buddha gained merit by turning himself into a fish to feed hungry peasants.

"Don't do that. The police will start asking you all sorts of questions if you do," Zhongmei said.

We ate quickly and returned to our compartment. Outside it was dark. Brave King told us a joke about a female crab who wanted to marry a male crab who only walked straight. One day she saw such a crab and she married him. But the next day, she saw that he walked crooked.

"I married you because you walked straight," the female crab said.

"But I can't drink that much every day," her husband replied.

We laughed. Then we readied our bunks and lay down. I continued to read Beal's translation of Zhang Yue's foreword to the *Chronicles,* where he describes the early part of the monk's journey through these same brown hills, probably past the same brown stream:

He took his staff, dusted his clothes, and set off for distant regions. He left behind him the dark waters of the Ba River; he bent his gaze forward; he then advanced right on to the Tsungling Mountains.

The Tsungling Mountains still lay ahead of us, but the Ba River (which I assumed was today's Wei River) was already behind. I lay sleepless as the train clattered and rocked. It stopped frequently, and when it did the silence of the Chinese countryside filled my ears. It struck me as a great emptiness, like the Buddhist emptiness, a dark void on the earth. I listened to it and tried to imagine villages and fields and a monk wending his way slowly along a river heading for distant mountains. And then the train would seem to come alive and begin to creak and rumble onward again.

We woke up in the morning to a semirural landscape of brown suburban villages, sheds, and smokestacks against the horizon. We went to the dining room in our usual two shifts and ate cold fried eggs with warm rice porridge. When we got back to our compartment, we asked Brave King his plans. He would stay overnight in Lanzhou and resume his train ride the following day. Was he in a hurry? we wondered. No, he said. He'd be happy to spend the time with us, if we liked. We said we would be happy for his company. As the train pulled into the platform, we had now become a journey to the West for three.

3

The Fugitive Monk

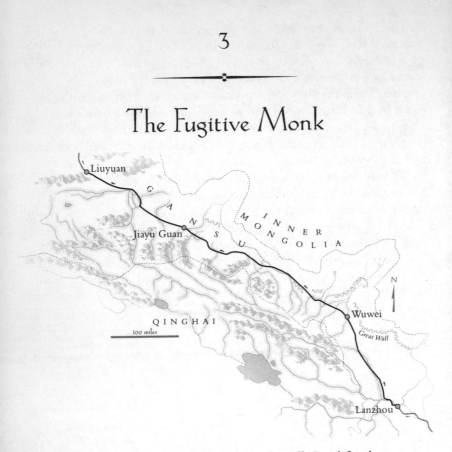

LANZHOU WAS the first major city on the Silk Road for the caravans leaving Xian, about three hundred miles to the southeast. It is on the Yellow River, whose name is a poetic idealization of muddy brown. It is an ugly river, a mud-colored gash. Lanzhou is like Xian except rawer, more under construction. I had been here seventeen years before, and I remembered a much smaller, more Central Asian town with a vast Muslim market full of meat stalls with slaughtered lambs and burlap bags of nuts and spices. Now Lanzhou is a big, chaotic city with a stronger Chinese imprint. Along the main street, there was one big construction site after another, glassy buildings going up, buildings sheathed in sleek surfaces, post-Communist Bauhaus. Zhongmei went off to visit the local dance company while Brave King and I went to a market street for an early lunch. Ordering the food stall owners around like a pasha, he had them bring various dishes from various stalls to our table. There was a very fine steamed chicken; there was spiced lamb on skewers; there were noodles in soup with *jie-lan,* which translates as Chinese broccoli but is much better than broccoli.

"Have you had *yang-tou?*" Brave King asked.

"*Yang-tou?* You mean lamb's head?"

"Yes."

"Well, I've had veal's head, in France. It was pretty disgusting, actually."

"When we get to Hami we can have lamb's head," Brave King said.

He was becoming my guide.

Leaving the food stall, we saw a group of men in white skullcaps and long coats and decided to follow them. It was obvious that they were Muslims and were going to pray, and we wanted to know where the mosque was. They entered a straight and narrow road marked with a banner at its entrance: "A designated civilized street," it said. The road ran between a long row of buildings sealed off from the street by high walls and a railroad embankment along which the occasional freight train made an ear-splitting, earth-quaking passage. We passed Dr. Wang Yanbang's "Internationally Famous Acupuncture Clinic," a square cement-and-tile box sitting on a single-story pedestal. Ahead of us I could hear the muezzin declaring *Allah 'u Akbar,* "God is Great." In front of the clinic, a whimpering boy of perhaps thirteen or fourteen was being reprimanded by a man pushing a bicycle cart. It seems that the boy had run into the cart on his bicycle.

The men in long coats disappeared around a bend, and we walked quickly trying to catch up. As we turned the corner we could see a minaret in the form of a Chinese pagoda with a half-moon and a star on top of it, a cultural hybrid if ever there was one. We followed the men into the courtyard of a mosque. They went into a concrete side room and performed their ablutions and afterward went into the mosque to pray. Outside, a small man in a ragged coat and cloth shoes stared at us and smiled stupidly. Most of the others glanced at us expressionlessly, not hostile but not friendly either, used to the occasional camera-toting tourist.

We took a taxi to the major Buddhist temple in Lanzhou, the Wu Qian Shan, Five Springs Mountain. A sign on the back of a taxi urged everyone to "be a civilized angel." The taxi, a Xia-li, a tiny Chinese-made vehicle reminiscent of an old Fiat with a metal security cage between the front and back seats, was driven by a woman who wore black satiny gloves, a purple knit jersey with large black buttons running halfway up her sleeves, and spandex pants. Her shoulder-length hair was dyed a light brown. She picked us up going the wrong way on a street with a median divider, and I was glad that she had come along and glad also that she was quite capable in the constant contest of wills that is driving on China's anarchic streets.

"There are a lot of us," she said, when I told her I had never seen a woman taxi driver in China before. "We've lost our jobs in factories, where we weren't making any money anyway, so we drive taxis."

At the temple entrance was a placard. "Starting from today, starting with yourself, starting with the small things—don't use bad language, don't spit just anywhere, don't throw garbage on the streets, don't destroy public property," and so on. Among the stories featured on the front page of the *Lanzhou Evening News* was an article entitled "200 Cities and Towns in Gansu Province Show the Media That the Propaganda Battle for Civility Is Off to a Good Start." The newspaper reported, "Yesterday, the provincial committee's propaganda bureau held a special meeting to announce that the curtain has been raised on our province's first advanced-model propaganda battle to build up the spirit of civility." The movement "is under the unified direction of the committee to build up the spirit of civility and the provincial committee's propaganda bureau. Competitions will be organized and the work units and individuals who best exemplify the spirit of civility will be awarded prizes and their names published in special books and newspapers."

This campaign for civility was very interesting in its way. When I lived in China, the most common slogan was "Strive for Ever Greater Victories." Since then, the Communist Party has turned from an organization that imposes revolutionary ardor to one that asks people to be clean and nice and not to spit (an admonition, I conclude from anecdotal evidence, not widely heeded). Now it's the Propaganda Bureau for Civility, the Reverend Commissar.

It was May Day, a national holiday, and Wu Qian Shan, which is on a hill above the business section of the city, was jammed with tens of thousands of people, filling the pathways leading up to the shrine and filling an esplanade that leads back to the center of the city. Inside the main courtyard, a monk stood in front of the impressive Buddha image and alternately banged a large iron pot and shooed visitors away from an offering table on which the pot was placed. The Scowling Buddha, I named this monk. In front of a kind of temple office were a group of old men, including one with a pockmarked nose who wore a blue serge suit, an open-necked blue shirt, and a blue knit vest.

"I'm following the route that Hsuan Tsang took to India," I announced to the assembled elders.

"Yes?" said the man in blue.

"Are you familiar with Hsuan Tsang?"

"Yes."

"Did he come to this temple?"

The man confidently assured me that he couldn't have come to this temple because he didn't come to Lanzhou. To come to Lanzhou would have required crossing the Yellow River, and in those days it was impossible to cross the Yellow River. I expressed skepticism over this reasoning.

"There was no bridge," the man insisted. Others around him muttered their agreement.

"There were boats," I said.

"No, there weren't any boats either," the man said. "Hsuan Tsang came from Shaanxi. He went to Tian Shui, Long Xi, Ling Tao, and Yung Jing."

Later, when I looked at the map, I saw that that route would have brought Hsuan Tsang across the Yellow River fifty miles or so west of Lanzhou. It is a possible route, even if it too would have achieved the impossible river crossing. But Hui Li notes that the monk "came to Lanzhou and stopped there one night." So I stopped there one night too. I asked the man in the blue suit how he knew Hsuan Tsang's itinerary.

"From books," he replied.

"Which books?" I asked.

"That I don't remember," he said.

Leaving the temple, we saw an old monk. He had what seemed to me wrinkles of wisdom radiating from his eyes.

"You know the famous monk Hsuan Tsang?"

"No," the monk said, and hurried on his way.

I didn't know whether this was the Ignorant Buddha or just the Buddha Who Didn't Want to be Bothered.

We got on the train for Jiayu Guan, four hundred miles to the northwest, at 8:30 p.m.

IN THE MORNING, after another night of jostled sleep, we were in the Takla Makan Desert, a vast brown pebbly plain under a chalky sky. There were power lines and the Qilian Mountains to the south, more power lines and the Black Mountains to the north, but the mountains were mere suggestions against the misty horizon. Twenty minutes out of Jiayu Guan, the landscape turned to a fine gravel-colored powder. Low hills to the south looked like the eroded leftovers of something that had once been grand but was no longer. To the north of us industrial chimneys erupted on the horizon, each emitting a thick geyser of gray smoke. Jiayu Guan is a city of heavy industry, the guidebook says; it is named after the nearby Jiayu Pass, which was one of the historic gateways to the West, though less famous than the Jade Gate, another such gateway farther west. The city makes cement. A chill had crept into the train compartment, and when we disembarked, it was raining, tiny drops raising puffs of dust on the dry ground.

It turned out that Brave King had a friend with a car in Jiayu Guan, and he met us at the station. We asked him if he knew a good noodle shop for lunch.

"I know just the place," he said, and we raced through the pebbly landscape into town.

The patron of this modest establishment, where we ate noodle soup with beef and hot pepper sauce, was one of those overly friendly types, eager to do his bit for mutual understanding among the peace-loving people of the world.

Zhongmei asked him if he had a paper napkin.

"Yes," he replied in English to demonstrate his command of that language.

"Oh, you speak English!" I said ingratiatingly.

"A couple of years ago I saw two Americans on the street who were looking for something and they said something about the post office," he began to tell us, speaking Chinese. "But my English was so bad I didn't understand the words 'post office,' so I sent them to a government building, not the post office. By the time I realized what 'post office' meant, it was too late. They were already angry. And when I pointed out the post office, they didn't trust me enough to go there. I felt so bad I decided to learn English right then and there, and so I did."

"Well, it was really the Americans' fault," I said, ingratiating myself again. "They should learn Chinese."

"I want to invite you to try some special Chinese dishes," the patron said. He was sitting in a chair next to a tiny girl in a stained gray jacket. On the wall were large pictures, one of them showing a Western breakfast, large glasses of orange juice, and plates of bacon and eggs, another a still life of fruit and cheese and two glasses of white wine. We agreed to the invitation and said we would be back at seven-thirty. The man noticed the little notebook that I always keep with me. It was on the table, open, next to my bowl of noodles.

"Are you a spy or something?" he asked, looking at me, and just like that the mood changed. The restaurant owner was a dark-complexioned man in a purple jacket, and he was smoking a thick Chinese cigarette. His stare was level and hostile.

"If you think I'm a spy," I said, "don't tell me any secrets."

"Well, if you're a spy, I'm a public security officer," he said. He leaned back against the wall and blew a vapor of smoke toward the ceiling. "What are you doing in Jiayu Guan, anyway?"

"He's very interested in Chinese history," Zhongmei said while I silently chastised myself for my impetuous Chinese and my conspicuous little notebook.

"Yeah, well, he can be interested in history all he wants, but if he's one of those Americans stirring up trouble for China, we have ways of dealing with him."

"Nobody's stirring up any trouble," said Brave King, trying to smooth things over.

"The Americans are stirring up trouble," the restaurant owner shouted, while the small girl in the stained jacket looked on with surprise in her eyes. I kept on eating my noodles, wanting to finish and get away. "They think they can control us, tell us what to do, threaten us. America wants to stop China from being strong. But they can't, and you know why they can't? Because America is a paper tiger." The man laughed; he was demented. He continued to stare at me and I continued to eat my noodles. The hot sauce made my nose run. Sweat dripped from my forehead and trickled under my armpits.

The Chinese have an expression, *aiguo fenzi,* "a love-country element," "an ultrapatriot." Clearly we were in the presence of such an element, and while I knew rationally that he had no power to cause any trouble, my imagination laid out a disastrous sequence of events. I recalled a bit of recent history. In Beijing after the Tiananmen massacre in 1989, a man on the street was filmed by ABC News telling how he'd seen Chinese soldiers shooting at people; he mimicked a man sweeping the field with an automatic rifle. The footage wasn't even broadcast. The Chinese internal security service had picked it up from the unedited satellite upload and decided to make a negative example of the man. He was declared a criminal for spreading counterrevolutionary rumors. He fled Beijing. A day or two later he was captured when two women in Shijiazhuang, south of Beijing, recognized him from his television image. These love-country ladies reported him to the police, and he was seized and filmed, looking bruised and terrified, recanting his ABC testimony, which nobody in China had seen anyway.

I didn't think there was a good chance that I would really be arrested, but I did think it not beyond the bounds of the possible that our formerly friendly restaurant owner would go to the police and report a suspicious Chinese-speaking foreigner going around Jiayu Guan writing things down in a little notebook. The police would listen with a certain skepticism to the restaurant owner's story; but you never know.

I am always wary in countries where there is no rule of law, no defense lawyers to assure your rights are respected, nothing to curb the power of the authorities. I knew a man in China in the early 1980s who was studying economics at the university and every once in a while would call me to get together. I gave him a code name so he would never have to use his real name on the phone, and we always agreed in advance on our next place to meet. A few years later, the student, now a businessman in Los Angeles, came to New York and looked me up. He told me a remarkable story: Immediately after my departure from China, he was suddenly and without explanation put in prison for three days, and then, also without explanation, released and sent home. When he arrived there, three agents of the Public Security Bureau were waiting for him with a request. Since he had known me, they told him, he would be in a good position to befriend the man who was about to replace me in the bureau in Beijing and to report to them on his activities. The man refused, denying that he knew me, whereupon the police played nine separate tape recordings of conversations I had had with him using his pseudonym. They showed him photographs of the two of us on street corners, in parks, standing next to my car.

Earlier than that, in 1979, during the intense period of public agitation around the so-called Democracy Wall, where free speech was transiently allowed, I was able to make contact with the members of the leading unofficial magazine being published at that time. I put on a worker-blue Mao-style jacket and a blue short-brimmed cap in an effort to disguise my foreignness, and I was taken late one afternoon through a maze of narrow alleys to the home of Liu Qing, the magazine's editor. A few months later, Liu was arrested and put on trial for "counterrevolutionary" offenses—most important, the publication in his magazine of the statement that the dissident Wei Jingsheng had made at his trial a few months before. But meeting with foreign reporters was also a counterrevolutionary offense, and in this regard, one of the pieces of evidence used against Liu, he told me more than a decade later, after he had served out his sentence and been released, was a photograph of me sitting with him and his friends in the living room of his house. It had been taken through the window from the alley outside. So, while it is true that things have changed in China and that, in any case, I was probably being paranoid about my run-in with the restaurant owner in Jiayu Guan, I am not inclined to underestimate the ability of the police to keep watch on the foreigners in their midst.

Maybe, I thought, the Jiayu Guan Public Security agents, having nothing else to do, would go to the hotel and look at my registration there and then they would check with the Public Security Bureau in Beijing, which would dig up its file on me, and then I would be cooked. I would be accused of being a journalist impersonating a Buddhist pilgrim for the purpose of collecting information on the décor of noodle stands in western Gansu Province. My pilgrimage would come to an end.

AFTER WE LEFT the restaurant, we visited a remnant of the Ming-era Great Wall. It begins at a point a few miles outside of Jiayu Guan and steeply climbs a few hundred yards into the Black Mountains. You pay two dollars and walk up to the top. I appreciated the significance of the view. To the west and south stretches the desert, which continues, broken by several rugged chains of mountains, all the way to the Himalayas, which form a vast half-circle around Chinese Turkestan, hemming it in from the south, the west, and the north. Xinjiang was for a thousand years one of the great perpetually contested crossroads of the world.

The Mummies of Urumchi, a book by Elizabeth Wayland Barber,* recounts how the settlers of the eastern parts of Xinjiang were, from the evidence of the mummies, Caucasians. They spoke a now extinct language called Tokharian, and they used woven cloth that bears similarities to that of the Celtic peoples an unimaginable distance to the west. Barber's interesting conclusion is that the Celts, more particularly the Irish and Scots, and these early inhabitants of Xinjiang, whose mummified remains you can see in the museum of Urumqi, once belonged to the same tribe, which probably originated someplace north of the Caspian Sea. At some point it divided into two branches. One branch went to Ireland and Scotland; the other inaugurated the Road of Great Events. It made its way slowly across the Central Asian steppe, then crossed the mountain passes to the Tarim Basin, where it established a civilization inside the oases. The ghostly, grinning, desert-dry corpses of the Tokhar-

---

* Elizabeth Wayland Barber, *The Mummies of Urumchi* (New York: W. W. Norton & Company, 1999), pp. 131–45.

ians are being uncovered at archaeological sites all the way from Khotan on the southwestern edge of Xinjiang to the very east.

As I say, I appreciated the spectacle. I was at the same time telling myself how ridiculous it was to be nervous about the encounter in the restaurant a short time before. And it *was* ridiculous. But then I saw three uniformed policemen walking on the wall in our direction, and I was sure they were coming for me. The policemen, recognizable as such in their grass-green uniforms with the red collar tabs, plodded slowly up the wall in our direction. I stood at the top of the wall and watched them laboring upward, leaning forward as the stones got steeper. They followed us all the way to the top of the wall and, when we headed down, all the way down. They laughed and took pictures of one another posing against the brown emptiness of the desert background, and that was that.

"JIAYU GUAN" MEANS "the pass" or "gate at Jiayu," and it is the name of the town where we stayed and also of a nearby ancient border post, one of the official points of entry and exit between China and the countries to the west. Hui Li doesn't mention the Jiayu Guan. He speaks of the Yumen Guan, the Jade Gate, the ruins of which are about one hundred miles southwest of the gate at Jiayu, near the present-day city of Anxi. In fact, over the centuries, the exact locations of the passes shifted from one place to another. There are several passes with different names that were used as the border crossing during different dynasties. Passes of the same name can be found in different spots. The gates themselves were allowed to fall into ruins when new ones were built farther to the east or the west. The current Jade Gate is southwest of Dunhuang; the one that existed in the monk's time is now buried under a manmade lake. But wherever the gates were, they had the same basic architecture and served the same purpose. They would be placed on the desert plain in between the mountain ranges. A detachment of troops would be stationed there and along nearby watchtowers keeping an eye on the plain itself, so that no caravans or other travelers could pass unobserved on either side of the border post.

There is a thick accumulation of poetry and legend about the passes, marking as they did the frontier between the inner country, China, and the barbarian territory outside. The poems are about the sadness of exile, for beyond the gate is where enemies of the state, failed generals, and disgraced prime ministers were sent, for a term of years or for life, and, of course, there are the legendary beauties carried on palanquins to give some desert satrap a reason not to raid the settled areas of China. The day we were at the gate at Jiayu, a bicycle, a surrealist prop, stood on its kick-stand while beyond it the desert stretched purple and brown into infinity. What the generals and emissaries and princesses saw was just that, an infinity of pebbles and exile.

The historian Owen Lattimore has described the relationship between China and the territories beyond the gate in his classic work *Inner Asian Frontiers of China*.★ When the empire was weak, the men on horse-back, the Turks, Mongols, and Huns, would conquer it. When China was strong, it drove the invaders back over the passes, its great armies chasing them beyond the Great Wall all the way to the Persian kingdoms of Bactria and Fergana. The early heroes of Chinese history are the diplomat-soldiers who got the barbarians out of the Tarim Basin or made alliances with some in order to defeat others.

A lot of this history pitted the Chinese against a people they knew as the Hsiung-nu, who later became known in Europe as the Huns. René Grousset, the great French historian of Central Asia, says they were a Turkic-Mongol people, nomads, who spread out in several tribes from eastern Siberia. The men were mounted archers who wore long pants and boots rather than the robes of the sedentary Chinese. It was to meet them in the field of battle that China itself moved from the heavy chari-ots that were used in their civil wars to mobile cavalry. It was the threat of the Hsiung-nu, the most powerful of these Turkic-Mongol tribes, that impelled the first Chinese emperor, the cruel Qin Shi Huang Di, to build the Great Wall.

Even so, the Huns settled inside the wall. In the second century B.C., they laid siege to the Chinese capital of Taiyuan, and the emperor saved himself and his realm by resorting to sexual diplomacy. He gave a Chinese maiden—poets have subsequently referred to her as "the poor partridge"—to the Hun ruler, known to the poets as "the Wild Bird of Mongolia." In 138 B.C., the emperor Wu Di sent a diplomat-soldier named Zhang Qian over the Pamir Mountains to present-day Uzbekistan in an attempt to form an alliance with the Scythian people who had set-tled there after being defeated by the Huns. Zhang was captured by the Huns and held for a decade. When he finally reached the Scythians, they turned down his offer of a balance-of-power alliance. They were happy with things as they were and wanted to fight with the Huns no longer. When Zhang Qian got back to China, traveling with the one companion who had survived out of the hundred he started out with, he reported on

★ Owen Lattimore, *Inner Asian Frontiers of China* (New York: Oxford University Press, 1989).

the existence of rich civilized lands in the west—Fergana, Samarkand, Bokhara, and India. It was the first time the Chinese learned that there were great civilized populations beyond the ring of barbarous tribes that hemmed them in on the surrounding steppe. It became Chinese policy to clear a road through the Tarim Basin so that trade and diplomatic relations could be carried out with these peoples. A century or so later, a Macedonian trader named Maes Titianos sent agents to reconnoiter the passes through desert and mountain to China. The information that he gleaned was used by the Greek geographer Ptolemy, who named the places between Antioch in modern Syria and China. The West thus discovered China, Seres, and named the wondrous product that was carried by the caravans from there after it. The Silk Road came into existence.

Around the time of Maes Titianos, during the Later Han Dynasty of the first and second centuries A.D., another strong emperor ascended the throne and sent a general, Ban Chao, one of the great military leaders of all time, to the Tarim Basin to defeat the Huns once and for all. He waged a series of ferocious battles from Khotan, Kashgar, and Yarkand in the west to Kucha, Turfan, and Hami closer to China. "He who does not enter the tiger's den will never catch the cubs," he said. "To eliminate war by waging war—this was the conduct of the most glorious rulers." He cut off thousands of heads as he attempted to make the world safe for silk. "He accomplished glorious exploits in faraway countries," the official Chinese history says. "All of these realms without exception offered the marvelous riches of their lands, or they turned over hostages that were precious to them. Bareheaded, walking on hands and knees, [these hostages] turned toward the East to pay homage to the Son of Heaven."[*]

The Silk Road ran from Xian to the Jiayu Guan, and at Dunhuang it split into two branches. One followed the oases that lay on the northern edge of the Tarim Basin, the other followed the southern oases. The way west was either over the Tianshan Mountains into what is now Kyrgyzstan or over one of several passes in the High Pamirs to present-day Afghanistan or Pakistan. Hsuan Tsang took the northern route on his way to India, the southern route on his way back. He serves as a reminder that the routes opened and safeguarded by tens of thousands of Chinese troops over the centuries were not for commerce, diplomacy, and warfare alone. They were also the routes used by the men who brought spiritual revolution to China, the solace and philosophical depth of Buddhism.

* René Grousset, *The Empire of the Steppes: A History of Central Asia* (New Brunswick, N.J.: Rutgers University Press, 1970), pp. 42–46.

．　　　　．　　　　．

THE GATE AT JIAYU itself is about ten miles into the Gobi, west of the present-day industrial town. It consists of high walls and watchtowers and heavy gates, one on the east and the other on the west. Now the place is a site for tourists doing the Silk Route. You buy a ticket; you read the sign that announces a prohibition on video cameras; you walk through a sequence of fortified spaces past the souvenir shops and the signs asking you to protect the environment. What you see is not the Tang Dynasty gate but a Ming reconstruction of a thousand years later, with some major recent repairs. At the western gate, which looks out over an impressive expanse of desert, you pay an additional fee (about fifty cents) for the right to pass through the gate. You get a passport in facsimile brush calligraphy, stamped with the red seal of an imaginary general of the Tang Dynasty, giving you permission to pass to the west. A man dressed in a shabby period costume and chinked full-dress armor rides an ancient white donkey out of the gate and poses for pictures, holding aloft a curved sword.

"Hsuan Tsang didn't come here," he announced to us from atop his docile mount, and this was true. Our monk, after all, was escaping from China so that he could collect the Law in India. He was an illegal emigrant. "He went through there," the horseman said, pointing to a rugged set of hills to the north. The locals call them the Black Mountains. "It's very rough up there, very dangerous, but it was the only way for him to go."

"Ask him how long it took," I said to Zhongmei. Having been declared a spy in the noodle shop, I wasn't going to risk speaking Chinese here at the gate of the empire.

"Two years," the man said.

He was wrong. Hsuan Tsang doesn't say how long he spent skirting the Jiayu Guan, but since it took him only a year or so to reach India, he was a lot less than two years in the Black Mountains. Still, as I gazed over the western desert, I found it reassuring that this fake frontier guard who posed for pictures for tips was cognizant of the humble monk who did not pass this way fourteen hundred years ago.

WE GOT ON the train the next day in the early afternoon. The Qilian Mountains glimmered spectrally in the south, rising sixteen hundred feet above the flat brown carpet of dry grass and gravelly desert. The ruins of guard towers, misshapen obelisks of mud and straw, extended west. The desert colors ranged from ocher yellow to rusty red. There were gullies and ravines and dry riverbeds, and here and there an oasis, a mud-brick village and some trees. We passed the Yumen train station, and I noted another of those propaganda signs urging more civil behavior on the 1.2 billion Chinese: "It is not enough to change only on the inside; both the inside and the outside must change."

We arrived in Liuyuan, which was our destination for the night. "Liuyuan" means "willow garden."

"There are no willows in the Willow Garden," I said, observing the brown treelessness around.

"It's the dream," Zhongmei said. "Sometimes you name things after what you don't have."

We stayed at the Huitong ("Shiny Bronze") Guesthouse, which had private bathrooms and hot water from nine to eleven in the evening. The town itself was plain and listless, a wide main street lined by noodle shops and a few larger buildings faced with square white tiles. We ate at a Xin-jiang restaurant and had an excellent lamb dish and a bottle of Xiliang ("West Cool") beer. Taking our postprandial stroll near the hotel later, we came across a little alley. There we found a large billboard advertising the tourist spots of Anxi County. The map included a twisting blue line that marked the route of the monk in this area.

During his single night in Lanzhou, the monk met with a group of mounted men who agreed to show him the way to Liangzhou, the next major city on his route. Liangzhou is now known as Wuwei, and it is a place of no particular distinction—except perhaps that the famous bronze Flying Horse of Gansu was discovered there in recent times, and that there is a seventh-century pagoda built in honor of Kumarajiva, a monk of Central Asia who translated the Mahayana classics from Sanskrit into Chinese in the late fourth century. In the seventh century, Liangzhou was a major intersection, nearly the last such intersection on the western extremity of the empire. Travelers from as far away as Tibet and the coun-tries to the west met and mingled there, as did the occasional pilgrim on his way to the great temples of Dunhuang and the more occasional pil-grim going to India.

Arriving there, the monk, whose fame was already considerable, was asked by priests and laymen eager to gain some benefit from his visit to explain the Nirvana Sutra and other Buddhist mysteries, and this he did with his usual brilliance and clarity. Those who listened to him, Hui Li says, "offered jewels and precious things, as they bowed down and uttered the praises of the Master." They gave him "white horses without number" to help him on his way, and then they returned to their several countries spreading the word that the Master of the Law was about to go westward to seek truth in the country of the Brahmans, the Indian priests.

This intelligence was flattering to the monk, but it was almost his undoing. Hui Li explains the Tang emperor's prohibition on travel beyond the borders: "At this time, the administration of the country was newly arranged, and the frontiers did not extend far. There were severe restrictions placed on the people, who were forbidden to go abroad into foreign parts." The governor of Liangzhou, Li Daliang, heard of the presence of the priest from Chang-an whose intention was to travel to the western regions. He summoned the monk before him and ordered him to return to Chang-an. The evidence is that the monk offered no verbal resistance to this order and may even have given the impression that he would obey it. But he found allies among other renowned Buddhist believers from west of the river, and they found disciples who promised to conduct him in secret past the Jade Gate and to the West.

From this point on, Hsuan Tsang became a figure of the shadows. He hid during the day and traveled at night, like a fugitive, a smuggler, a member of the resistance, helped by those he met who shared his beliefs.

He made it to Guazhou, west of Liangzhou, and there a sympathetic local governor gave him provisions. He asked about the road west and was told that he would have to cross a difficult river at the head of which was the Jade Gate. Beyond the gate to the northwest were five signal towers spaced about twenty miles apart. "In the spaces between them there is neither water nor grass," the monk was told, and this filled him with "anxiety and distress." The fugitive monk was therefore "sad and silent" as the time passed and he contemplated his uncertain situation. As he did so, agents from Liangzhou arrived in the city bearing a warrant issued to all governors of the provinces and the districts ordering the arrest of the monk on sight. The governor of Guazhou accordingly summoned him to the seat of government and imperial administration and asked him if he was the person named in the warrant.

We can imagine the monk's dilemma here. If he denied his correct identity, he risked compounding the offense of illegal departure from China with the additional offense of perjury, and the officials of that era had severe ways of dealing with perjurers. But if he admitted the first offense, he would be arrested and sent back to Chang-an. So he said nothing.

"The Master ought to speak the truth, and your disciple will make some plan for you to escape," the magistrate said.

It needs to be remembered that Buddhism at this time was the dominant religion of China and that its adherents were everywhere, including inside the high ranks and the lower echelons of the Chinese bureaucracy. The monk must have realized at this point in his interrogation that he was in the presence of a member of the club, a clandestine disciple, a secret sharer, a brother. And so he admitted who he was and what he hoped to do. The magistrate tore up the arrest warrant and told the monk to depart in haste, for both their sakes.

Once I had an experience reminiscent of the religious clandestinity of the far reaches of China during Hsuan Tsang's era. In 1982, I went to Urumqi, the capital of Xinjiang, to write an article for *Time*. In those days, Urumqi and the ancient Silk Road oasis of Turfan were the only places in Xinjiang open to foreign visitors. I stopped at a market stall to buy a bowl of yogurt, and the woman tending the stall asked me if I was a Catholic. I told her I wasn't. She said that she was. I was surprised by this. During the time of my visit to Xinjiang, China was in the process of restoring limited freedom of religion, so it was natural for any journalist to try to visit Catholic and Protestant churches, Buddhist temples, and Islamic mosques being restored after the depredations of the Cultural Revolution. And so I had asked my officially provided minder if there were Catholics or a Catholic church in Urumqi. She had assured me quite authoritatively that there were not. But the yogurt seller told me that there was a church, and she told me how to get there.

I found it behind a gate opening between high mud-brick walls down a long, narrow alley. A couple of dozen people were busy refurbishing what had clearly been an old Catholic church fallen into disrepair. While many churches were being restored in China then, the work could only be done after the religious community agreed to abide by an important condition. All of the religious establishments, Protestant, Roman Catholic, Muslim, and Buddhist, had to belong to what were called "Patriotic Associations," which meant in the case of the Catholics that they could have no connections with the Vatican. They could practice the rites, celebrate the Eucharist, observe Easter and Christmas, but their priests were appointed by a Chinese Catholic Church that was ultimately supervised by the Chinese Communist Party. I was warmly greeted by the Catholic carpenters and masons of Urumqi who brought me to see the church and introduced me to the priest. Since my guide didn't know about the church, I asked the priest if the Patriotic Church in Beijing knew of their activities. It was a stupid question, but you have to understand that in China in those days, anybody conducting open activity was assumed to be doing so with official approval, and it was an act of ordinary politeness for a foreigner to take for granted their participation in the Great National Endeavor. But in this case, my question only elicited an embarrassed shuffling, a collective lowering of heads.

"Are you a Catholic?" the priest finally asked me, breaking the silence.

"No," I said, "but I believe in religious freedom."

The priest then put his partial liberty into jeopardy by asking: "What good would it do us to inform the Patriotic Association of our existence here?"

I understood. I looked the priest in the eye sympathetically. Here in Urumqi, where heaven was high and the emperor far away, I had discovered a branch of the underground Catholic Church, an underground church, moreover, whose existence was being tolerated by the local authorities. For surely if I had discovered this place after three days in Urumqi, the Public Security Bureau knew about it also.

The priest beckoned me to follow him, and he took me to a building adjacent to the church. It had a low ceiling and an earthen floor and it smelled of wet stone. Inside were two men with parchment skin, frail bones, opaque eyes, and wisps of white beard. They were the oldest-looking living human beings I had ever seen. The priest told me that both of them had been imprisoned since the 1950s and had been released a short time before on condition, of course, that they desist in their practice of the Roman Catholic faith. Refusing that condition, they took refuge in this western foothold of the underground church, where they were harbored and provided with sympathy. We talked briefly. It was a long time ago and I don't remember much of what was said, except when one of the priests, looking up at me with a soft smile, told me:

"They couldn't take it away from me."

"What couldn't they take away from you?" I asked.

The priest looked at me for a long time.

"My faith," he said.

I tiptoed away, vowing that I would not expose the church to official punishment by writing about it in *Time*. But I did tell one person, a Chinese-American photographer and friend, Liu Heung Shing, who had accompanied me on my trip. Liu, agreeing that he would not disclose anything about the church, went to visit it the next day. But he was received coldly and told to leave. Somehow, possibly because of some police spy inside the church, or possibly because my minder had looked into my whereabouts during our brief period of separation, the authorities had learned about my visit, and they had warned the Urumqi Catholics against welcoming any more foreigners into their midst. They were willing to tolerate this Roman Catholic exception, but only on condition that it remain unknown to the outside world.

THE SITUATION of the Urumqi Catholics in 1982 was not all that different from that of the Buddhist monk of the seventh century, who also defied the decrees of the newly constituted central government of the newly constituted Tang Dynasty and who found officials who abetted his criminal enterprise. But even though Hsuan Tsang received help along the way from those who believed the Four Noble Truths, his anxieties did not abate. He was still far from the end of Tang jurisdiction, and he faced new problems. Remember, since Lanzhou he had been accompanied by two Buddhist novices who had vowed to see him past the Jade Gate. But when the monk reached Guazhou, one of the novices turned away and returned to his home in Dunhuang, and while the other remained, the monk could see that he was too old and frail for a rigorous journey through the desert. He sent him home too, and so was now left without a guide.

Hsuan Tsang prayed to the image of Maitreya, the Bodhisattva of the future. He heard about a priest named Dharma who in a dream saw the monk sitting on a lotus flower and traveling on it toward the west. "Dreams are vain and deceptive," the monk, who believed that the world was illusion, declared, but nonetheless, this particular dream led him to nurture renewed hope. Then, out of nowhere, a "foreign person," a man who wore the aspect of the lands beyond the Great Wall, came to the temple to worship Buddha. This man saw the monk, understood his holiness, and walked around him three times in a show of respect. Our Master of the Law asked him his name, and the man replied that it was Bandhu. The monk noted that this new acolyte was strongly built and respectful in manner. He confided his plans to him and asked his help. Bandhu readily agreed to escort the monk beyond the five signal towers and to put him on the road to Hami, the first of the independent Buddhist kingdoms to the west.

The next morning, when they met again, Bandhu introduced the monk to a strange old man, also a foreigner. He had a gray beard and he rode a skinny red horse and he tried to dissuade the monk from undertaking his journey, citing the difficulty of the road, the evil spirits that lived there, the inescapable hot winds that blew there, and the sand-streams that stretched forever.

"Numbers of men traveling together, although so many, are misled and lost," the man said, adding that Hsuan Tsang, traveling alone, was almost certain to share their fate. "How can you accomplish such a journey?" he asked.

The monk's reply was that he was determined to reach the Western world in order to seek out the great Law, and that if he failed to reach the land of the Brahmans, it wouldn't matter if he died en route.

"If you must go, sir, ride this horse of mine," the old man said. (Hui Li in his account of the monk's crossing of the Chinese desert does not say what happened to those white horses without number that were given to him by the grateful merchants and priests of Liangzhou.) "He has gone to and from I-gu some fifteen times. He is strong and knows the road." In the seventh century, I-gu was near where Hami is today.

And so Bandhu and the monk were off, traveling by night. When they reached the river, they saw the Yumen Guan in the distance. Bandhu made a bridge of a tree trunk, branches, and some sand, and the two were able to cross at the river's narrowest point. Having done so, the exhausted travelers spread their mats on the sand and went to sleep. In the middle of the night, the monk awoke and saw Bandhu creeping toward him, knife in hand. Hsuan Tsang sat up and prayed to the Bodhisattva Avaloki-tesvara, the god of mercy. The tableau that emerges from this incident is pregnant with iconic images. On the one side is the treacherous servant, knife in hand; on the other, the holy man, praying to an invisible god; around them is the desert and darkness; in the near distance, perhaps sil-houetted against the night sky, is a tower representing a hostile and un-forgiving authority. We do not know exactly why—perhaps it was the nearness of that authority, perhaps the mere sight of the holy man in prayer—but Bandhu turned around and left the monk unharmed.

At dawn the monk and his guide talked. The guide recited the dangers of the route. There were still five imperial watchtowers west of the Jade Gate, built to catch exactly such clandestine travelers as might attempt to evade the reach of the emperor's prohibition. "Between the Jade Gate and the fifth watchtower there will be no water," Bandhu said. "Only after the fifth tower will there be water, which we will have to get at night, in secret. If at any place along this route we are perceived, we are dead men." Then, having recited the dangers of the journey, Bandhu showed more signs that he was not as enthusiastic as he had seemed only a short time before to conduct the monk to Hami. "Wouldn't it be better to turn back and be at rest?" he advised.

The monk of course rejected this counsel, and after a few more li— one li is equal to about a fifth of a mile—he was not surprised when Bandhu refused to go any farther. For the sake of his family, Bandhu said, he did not want to risk transgressing the laws of his country. He left the monk to fend for himself.

"And now alone and deserted," Hui Li writes, "he traversed the sandy waste; his only means of observing the way being the heaps of bones and the droppings of horses." Hallucinations afflicted him. He saw hundreds of horsemen dressed in fur and felt. Camels appeared in the desert and disappeared. "Then fresh forms and figures changing into a thousand shapes appeared, sometimes at an immense distance and then close at hand, and then they dissolved into nothing." But Hsuan Tsang heard voices crying out of the void saying, "Do not fear; do not fear." After eighty li, he saw the first watchtower and a pond beneath it. But as he was filling his water vessel, probably a gourd or a bag made out of goatskin, an arrow whistled toward him and grazed his knee. He had encountered the armed might of the empire after all, even here beyond the Jade Gate. He turned himself in. The captain of the watchtower, like everybody else, tried to persuade the monk to turn back, offering personally to lead him to Dunhuang. "There is a master of the law there called Chang-kiau who reveres men of virtue and honors the priesthood; he will rejoice to see you."

Needless to say, Hsuan Tsang refused this offer, frankly telling this sympathetic official that there was no point in studying with any priest in China. For years the most eminent priests had, without exception, come to seek *him* out for instruction. "I may boldly say," he boldly said, "that I am the leading authority of the time. If I wished for further renown and encouragement, should I seek a patron at Dunhuang?"

The next morning, the monk continued on his way, armed with an introduction to the captain of the fourth watchtower given to him by the captain of the first. He arrived at night, and when he went to get water at a nearby spring he had another close call with an imperial arrow. As at the first watchtower, this was followed by his surrender and then a welcome from the captain of the tower, who gave him a place for the night and fed his horse. After the Master of the Law had eaten, the captain took him aside and warned him not to approach the fifth watchtower. The guards were "rude and violent and some mishap may befall you if you go there," the captain said. He proposed an alternate route, about one hundred li to the Ye-ma ("Wild Horse") Spring, where he would be able to get water.

Hsuan Tsang plunged into the desert. "There are no birds overhead and no beasts below; there is neither water nor herb to be found," he later told Hui Li. As he went, he kept the goblins away by reciting the Prajna-paramita-hridaya Sutra, the Sutra of Perfected Wisdom, otherwise known as the Heart Sutra, the peerless mantra that banishes fear and suffering. It is the highest expression of the idea of an Ultimate Reality compared to which all things are empty. "Form is no different from emptiness, emptiness no different from form; form is emptiness and emptiness is form," we can imagine Hsuan Tsang chanting to himself as he wandered, small and alone, under the yellowing sky. He thought again of Avalokitesvara, the Bodhisattva, the Enlightened Being, who postponed his own escape from the world of birth and death in order to help suffering creatures achieve Enlightenment first. It was Avalokitesvara who, looking down from the Vulture Peak, saw that the five constituent parts of the self, the five heaps, are empty. Form, feelings, perceptions, impulses, and consciousness are all equally marked with emptiness. They neither exist nor do not exist; they can be neither attained nor annihilated. "This is why in emptiness there are no forms and no sensations, perceptions, volition, or consciousness, no eye, ear, nose, tongue, body, or mind, no form, sound, smell, taste, touch, or object of mind. . . . Because there is nothing to be attained, the mind of the Bodhisattva, by virtue of reliance upon the Perfection of Wisdom, has no hindrances, and therefore, no terror or fear; he is far removed from error and delusion, and finally reaches nirvana. . . . Gone, gone, gone beyond, gone altogether beyond, O what an awakening!"*

When Hsuan Tsang had gone one hundred li, he was unable to find the Wild Horse Spring. No matter—he was traveling with a water vessel with enough water for one thousand li. But then as he raised this heavy vessel to take a drink, it slipped from his hands and spilled on the desert floor, its precious contents wetting the pebbles and soaking into the sand. The monk had no choice but to continue on his way toward Hami, but the winding road confused him and he was unable to figure out the direction. For a moment, he thought about retracing his steps and returning to the fourth watchtower, but he quickly remembered his vow to accept

*Edward Conze, *Buddhist Wisdom Books: The Diamond and the Heart Sutra* (London: Mandala, 1988), pp. 99–124.

death rather than take a single step back toward the east. He invoked the god of mercy and headed toward what he hoped was the northwest.

"The view was boundless," says Hui Li. "There were no traces either of man or horse, and in the night the demons and goblins raised fire-lights as many as the stars; and in the daytime the driving wind blew the sand before it as in the season of rain." Still, even though the monk drank nothing for four nights and five days, "his heart was unaffected by fear." He lay down on the sand and said a prayer: "Hsuan Tsang in undertaking this journey does not seek for riches or worldly profit, he desires not to acquire fame, but only for the sake of the highest religious truth does his heart long to find the true Law." He continued praying through the middle of the night, when suddenly a cool breeze swept up, refreshing the monk and enabling his exhausted horse to stand.

He went on for ten more li and then his horse started off in another direction, resisting all efforts by the monk to return him to what he thought was the correct path. After several more li, the amazed monk saw several acres of green grass. It was not a mirage. He dismounted to let the horse graze and advanced on foot for several more li. A few steps brought him to "a pool of water, sweet, and bright as a mirror." Clearly, he felt "that this water and grass were not natural supplies, but undoubtedly were produced through the loving pity of Bodhisattva, and it is a proof of his guileless character and spiritual power."

4

The Ghost Town

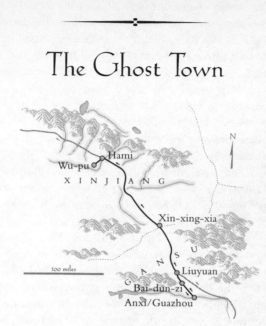

Aurel Stein once followed the monk's route across the desert. Stein, born in Hungary, educated at Oxford, one of history's great archaeologist-travelers, lived for years in a cottage in Kashmir, from which he set off on his expeditions to Xinjiang. In fierce competition with the other legendary explorers of the Silk Road, the Swede Sven Hedin and the German Baron Alfred Von Le Coq, he unearthed buried cities, cut out cave-temple frescoes and statuary, and sent them to England via horse and camel across the desert. He is viewed as a villain in China today—a despoiler of ancient treasures, an intruder, an imperialist thief— and he was. But in the first decades of the century when Stein undertook his expeditions, no Chinese authority was evincing much interest in the ruined Buddhist monuments of the Silk Road. Today they are glorious emblems of the Road of Great Events, but when Stein uncovered them and took them away, they were being either neglected by the local authorities or vandalized by crooks.

After tracing Hsuan Tsang's journey, Stein wrote up the results of his findings in the *Geographical Journal* of November 1919 in his usual sober, uninflected language. He began his expedition in Anxi, just southeast of Liuyuan, a town that he found "scarcely more than a straggling street within a big enclosure of crumbling walls." From there he recapitulated the monk's journey, using the indications in Hui Li's biography as his guide, stressing the difficulties that a man traveling alone in the seventh century would face, attributing the monk's sightings of ghosts and goblins to the mirages that, Stein says, "are common here." Stein rode horses and camels, and, accompanied by his usual team of bearers and guides, he used the archaeological evidence to determine the locations of three of the five watchtowers that were of concern to the monk. He measured the distances between them to see if Hsuan Tsang's readings of distance and direction were correct.

He found the first watchtower at a place called Bai-dun-zi and the fourth at Ma-lian-jing-zi, these being the two where Hsuan Tsang received help from Buddhist believers among the frontier guards. The fifth signal tower was at Xin-xing-xia on the present-day border between Gansu and Xinjiang. Beyond the fifth signal tower is a great desert all the way to Hami, about 120 miles away. The monk, as we have seen, skirted the fifth tower, where he was told the guards would be hostile, and at that point got lost in the desert, finding water only when he let his horse choose the route. Stein even identified the place to which the monk wandered in his four-day near-death experience. He finally found water, Stein believed, in a place called Chang-liu-shui, which is 106 miles from the fourth watchtower at Ma-lian-jing-zi, a long way to trek in the Takla Makan without food or water.

The monk's story of desert survival might have lent itself to exaggeration, especially if Hsuan Tsang wanted to create an image of heroism for posterity. But having traced the same route, Stein determined that the monk's desert crossing "seems actually to have happened, and is recorded by Hui Li the way in which the Master of the Law himself is likely to have told it."

WE GOT UP EARLY to do our own retracing of Hsuan Tsang's crossing. Liuyuan was even more forlorn in the early morning than it had been the night before. The night before, Brave King had flagged down a taxi whose driver, deciding he didn't want to go all the way to Hami for the hundred dollars we were offering, sent a friend with a Volkswagen Santana to take us instead. The long, single main street, which began at the railroad station and ended at the desert, was gray and shuttered. Motorcycle rickshaws with green-windowed passenger compartments clustered at the entrance to the market, the drivers blowing thick plumes of cigarette smoke into the heavy air. We went to a tiny general store to buy a couple of water jars in which Zhongmei and Brave King would make tea. I noticed under the glass of the display case, locked up as if they were pieces of jewelry, tubes of Crest toothpaste and bars of Safeguard soap—a sign of Procter & Gamble's market penetration.

The only restaurant serving breakfast was small and close and crowded, so we took off for the edge of town and amid the brick shacks that abutted the desert found a warehouselike noodle shop alongside a gasoline station. Amazingly, Brave King knew the owner. "I came a couple of years ago with the camels," he reminded the owner, who instantly remembered the band of Turks and their Chinese guide.

The restaurant was a truck stop alongside the two-lane Trans-Xinjiang Highway, which was laid out across the sand from Anxi in the east to Hami and beyond in the west. We ate our noodles in the company of a dozen or so truck drivers who slurped and smoked and chewed on raw garlic cloves, and then we were off in our Volkswagen, plunging down the undulating tar road toward Anxi. The gray landscape, speckled with yellow and black, seemed scoured and pounded as if by giant sledgehammers. Black conical hills gave way to a pebbly plain scored with dry riverbeds and gullies. About twenty miles southeast of Liuyuan is Bai-dun-zi, identified by Stein as the site of the first of the Tang Dynasty watchtowers, and sure enough, a few hundred yards off the road we saw some remains, an imposing L-shaped ruin made of layered mud and straw overlooking a spring-fed pond.

Was it the very watchtower where the monk was grazed by an arrow and then helped by a sympathetic captain of the guard? There was little else in Bai-dun-zi, no stores or habitations, but there was a humble, low-slung little museum that looked from the outside like a farm shed. We paid our entrance fee and got taken on a tour. In one wing was photographic history of the Communist Fourth Route Army's losing battle against the Muslim Xinjiang warlord Ma Bufang. In 1936, the beleaguered Communists, trying to escape the Kuomintang's military encirclement campaigns, fled through the Jiayu Pass and into this territory, where they were outnumbered and defeated in a struggle that created martyrs to their cause and became part of their heroic legend. There were pictures of Fourth Route Army soldiers, including several who had been so badly beaten before being executed that they were barely recognizable as human beings.

The other wing of the museum contained a fanciful artistic rendering of the monk's desert crossing stretching frescolike on the walls. Here was our monk dressed as a Central Asian merchant and wearing a black beard, slipping through the Liangzhou Pass. Here he was grimacing as soldiers threw ropes over his neck in an attempt to force him back to China; but then there was the sympathetic local official who gave him a laissez-passer to Guazhou. We saw him in his flowing robes kneeling at a waterhole in front of the first watchtower being shot at by the guards within—and so on, the whole story all the way to the heaven-sent well at Chang-liu-shui. We asked where the first watchtower was, and our guide told us, pointing in the direction of the ruin we had seen on the other side of the road, "Why, it's right there, outside."

"That's it? The original tower?" I asked.

"Yes."

"How do you know it's the original tower? How do you know it wasn't thrown up fifty years ago?"

"They didn't build things like that fifty years ago. It's an important Tang Dynasty relic."

Of course, we walked over to see it, threading our way along a curving embankment between swampy fields. The tower itself rose above a clear, cold spring-fed pond, which, if this was indeed the first watchtower, would have been the very place where the monk was getting water when an arrow grazed his leg. We stood inside it and looked over the desert. It had a commanding view of the surrounding desert, a good thing for a watchtower, and its construction of mud layered with straw was the Tang Dynasty method. According to the historical record, the watchtowers were spaced about a hundred li, or twenty miles, apart, starting with the Yumen Gate. The Yumen Gate in the early Tang Dynasty was near present-day Anxi, which is about twenty miles southeast of Bai-dun-zi, which, in turn, is one hundred miles from Xin-xing-xia. The directions and distances accorded perfectly.

We got back into the car and drove to Guazhou, which, according to the map, is just outside the larger town of Anxi, a single straggling street in Stein's time but an important garrison for the Chinese army today. After some wandering, we were directed by some farmers to what they said was the wall surrounding ancient Guazhou. We went down a long dirt track lined with thick rows of desert poplars. The track ended at the gates to a chemical factory, the gates themselves cut into a high, mis-shapen earthen wall that stretched grandly out in both directions.

"This would have been the North Gate," a man standing there told us.

"Are these Tang Dynasty ruins?" I asked him.

"I'm not sure," he replied.

Anyway, they had the look of a Tang-era wall, made entirely of layers of baked mud and straw and constructed layer by layer, so we could see the lines of stratification. Whether this was the actual Tang Dynasty wall or some later structure, we seemed to have found the very place whence the monk set off into the desert, the treacherous Bandhu by his side.

We hit the road again, driving back toward Bai-dun-zi roughly along the route that the monk would have taken to the first watchtower. The road continued to the northwest through the unvarying landscape of dirt and rock, gullies and dry riverbeds, stone mesas, cones of black coal dust, everything dry, treeless, and severe. Brave King pored over his Chinese map of Gansu Province, his glasses slipping down his nose, but he was unable to find Chang-liu-shui, where the monk finally found water, and it wasn't on my English maps either. Two hours later, we arrived in Xin-xing-xia (written by Stein as "Hsin-hsing-hsia"). This is where the fifth watchtower stood in the Tang Dynasty. Now it is two rows of truck stops on either side of the Trans-Xinjiang Highway. This is the border between Gansu and Xinjiang. We chose a Muslim restaurant—a few wooden tables, white plastic tablecloths, and the usual concrete floor—and ate lamb stew, *gongbao* chicken, and sauteed *youcai,* a kind of spinach. We asked the restaurant owner if she had beer available.

"Muslims don't drink alcohol," she said, "but we're running a business here."

"I was here before," Brave King said, "with the camels."

"Oh," said the woman. "That was you!"

We got to Hami two hours later, and it seemed veritably metropolitan compared to Liuyuan. Our stolid and stalwart driver, silent until then, dispensed with some Han Chinese wisdom about the various people, Chinese and non-Chinese, who make up the local population. "The Uigur people are full of sweet words but they have knives in their hearts. The Hui-tzu people"—ethnic Chinese Muslims—"have gentle hearts but small eyes. The Han people have sharp tongues but kind hearts." Whatever the inhabitants' moral characteristics, they have left little in the way of an architectural stamp. Hami is your cookie-cutter Chinese town, though cleaner—a few broad avenues, a heroic statue or two at the main intersections, propaganda slogans exhorting more civilized behavior. There wasn't much to do there, no important Buddhist monuments to visit, no ancient ruins inside the town itself. The town gives its name to a deliciously sweet melon, *hami-gua,* but when we were there, they were out of season. Hami is a new town with a public park dominated by a full-scale model of the Arc de Triomphe, complete with heroic Napoleonic friezes.

For dinner Brave King led us to his favorite spot in Hami, the night market, where we sat at one stall and ordered from several—the now familiar spiced lamb on skewers, a clay hot pot, rice cooked with carrots, a barbecued fish, sweet sticky rice balls for dessert. The owner of our stall couldn't believe that Zhongmei and Brave King were Chinese.

"You're Japanese, right?" he said.

"Come on," said Brave King. His Banana Republic–Timberland attire led his own people often to take him for a Japanese, which to him was like an Arab being taken for a Jew, a Muslim for a Serb. "I'm Chinese, of course."

"Really, what are you?" the stall owner asked again.

He was a round, direct, friendly man, maybe about sixty years old, not Chinese but a member of one of the country's minorities, a Muslim with a broad, round face and large oval eyes. Zhongmei insisted she was Chinese. She called him Lao Bo, "Elder Uncle," as in "Lao Bo, can we have some more tea please?" She called the fat, friendly woman in the red and black sweater who ran the next stall Da Ma, "Big Mother."

"Well, you're different from the other Chinese," the man said. "The others aren't so polite to us, and it's pretty rare that they actually talk to us."

"Now I know why they don't believe we're Chinese," Brave King said ruefully. "We're too nice."

We had no hotel reservation, but eventually we found a lodging called the Electricity Hotel, which was new and smart and demanded double the usual price for Zhongmei and myself, because I was a foreigner.

"That's our rule for foreign guests," the smiling woman at the reception desk said when Zhongmei protested.

In China these days the old practice of charging foreigners two to four times what the local people pay is slowly disappearing. When I lived in Beijing, everything—plane and train fares, hotels, restaurant meals—was more expensive for foreigners, which was both annoying and somehow acceptable, given that foreigners had a kind of separate but superior life in China, not to mention much more money than local people. By now, train and plane fares are the same, as are hotel rates in the big cities, but here in the more remote regions of the country, the hotels still had different prices. It made Zhongmei apoplectic.

"Look," she told the hotel manager, who came by to see what the argument was about, "I'm coming back to China after so many years and I'm embarrassed, humiliated, ashamed, mortified to have to pay the foreign guest price. Why should foreigners have to pay more? The room is the same, exactly the same."

The manager relented. We saved a few dollars. That was not the only advantage of the Electricity Hotel, whose brochure contains this description: "It is a comprehensive three star hotel with luxurious decoration and including staying, dinning, funning, shopping."

Settled into our room, we watched a program on local television about a little girl named Maomao who, because her parents had hoped for a boy, had been thrown into a garbage dump. Things like that happen in China, where the one-child-only population control policy gives couples only one shot at having a boy. Maomao also had something wrong with her hip and needed expensive medical treatment, another reason she was discarded. But Maomao was pulled out of the garbage by a nurse who found her there. Her bad hip was treated surgically. Her story was shown on television every day until an anonymous letter was sent to the television station identifying the parents. When confronted by the authorities, the couple admitted that Maomao was theirs, and, showing sufficient remorse for what they had done, they went unpunished. The tearful mother and the contrite father were shown at length on the program. Experts in the law were interviewed saying, "A child is not a possession of the parents to be disposed of like a television set."

HUI LI SAYS that even after Hsuan Tsang found water in the desert, "the dangers and difficulties through which the Master of the Law passed cannot be recounted in detail." The monk had now left China proper, and while he didn't make too much of that fact, he did demonstrate a certain yearning for his homeland. He speaks of staying at a temple where three Chinese priests greeted him, including one old man who cried: "How could I have hoped at this time ever to see again a man of my own country?" Hsuan Tsang embraced him. He too was moved to tears.

The monk spent a few weeks in what he called I-gu, recovering from his desert ordeal. We wanted to leave quickly, but when we got up in the morning, we learned that there was no train to our next destination, Turfan, until midnight. So the question arose: What to do in a place where there is nothing to do? I had heard about the ruins of an ancient city, Wu-pu, which is not mentioned by the monk or by his biographer but seems in the Tang Dynasty to have been a center of Buddhist worship.

The local people knew of a collection of desert ruins at a place near Wu-pu that they called Mogui Cheng, or Demon Town, and their advice was not to go there.

"It's very dangerous," the hotel manager told us. He had become very cordial since Zhongmei's victorious outburst the day before. "You'll need two jeeps. One to pull out the other when it sinks into the sand." He continued: "The deputy mayor of Hami went there last year and he got lost in a terrible sandstorm and almost didn't make it back." The manager was a short man dressed in a dark blue suit, crisp white shirt, and tie. His voice took on an ominous edge. "Strange things happen there. Some people who went there disappeared. It's impossible to go."

Brave King then remembered reading a book that tells of a Ming or Qing Dynasty rebel army that went to Mogui Cheng. There was a sandstorm in the desert. The wind whistling through crevices in the ancient walls of the city was like voices that summoned the soldiers, each of them by their names. The soldiers turned to follow the voices, and then they disappeared into the unknown. The entire army vanished.

I expressed skepticism about the veracity of that account. "How, if the entire army vanished, would we know the story of the voices calling the soldiers by name?" I asked.

"Well, strange things happen that science can't explain," Zhongmei said. "In each dynasty they've been afraid of this place. People don't believe that people have disappeared there, so they go, and they disappear too. Maybe it's because they get buried by sand and that's why they disappear. It's not ghosts. Or maybe these stories about people disappearing are just what local people tell each other, but it's really not true. Then again, there was the deputy-mayor who almost died there. He made it back but people say he was lucky. We don't know exactly the story, but that's why as soon as you asked people about Mogui Cheng they gave you a funny look."

Still, the hotel manager, at my insistence, contacted a jeep driver who said he would go to Mogui Cheng if another jeep would go too. The driver said it was too dangerous to go in only one car. The friendly manager located another vehicle, a Beijing Jeep—a well-known brand in China since Jeep began manufacturing there about a decade ago—which soon arrived. But then the first jeep was delayed, until it turned out that the driver wouldn't go even with a second jeep in the entourage. Evidently when asked for his services, he had been too polite to refuse outright but was hoping that his conditions would not be met. Then it turned out that the hotel assistant manager—a tall, young, very thin man also in a blue serge suit, crisp white shirt, and tie—had been to Mogui Cheng and lived to tell the tale. This emboldened the manager himself to volunteer to accompany us. He would drive the required rescue jeep himself, he said, and he scurried down the street. A while later he returned driving an Isuzu four-wheel-drive truck.

We bought a case of bottled water and some biscuits and we were off in the Beijing Jeep, followed by the hotel manager in his Isuzu. We stopped for gas. The Isuzu whizzed by to get a steel cable to be used for the expected jeep rescue operation. "There's a factory down there," our driver said, waving his hand down the road, which I noted was called Number Two Electric Road. To the north, the Tianshan Mountains glinted with snow; they disappeared in a chalky haze, then reappeared. To the south was the brown stony plain and then . . . nothing, a vertical wall of gray haze covering the horizon. Having gotten gas, we zoomed down the Trans-Xinjiang Highway for a few miles until we were well outside of Hami, then turned south onto Er-pu (Second Pu, *pu* meaning "village") Road. We turned again at a long mud wall emblazoned with an advertisement for a medication that promised to end drug addiction in six days.

After a few miles we came to Wu-pu (Five Pu), where a woman I hadn't seen before got out of the Isuzu. She was an employee of the hotel who turned out to be a Uigur from this very village. The manager had enlisted her to find a local guide to show us the way to Mogui Cheng. Eventually two men arrived, wearing baggy wool pants and short-brimmed hats, and they joined the hotel manager, the Uigur woman, and the assistant manager in the Isuzu. Our party had grown to nine, leading our driver to grumble, "We don't need all these other people. We could have come here ourselves."

"You're not afraid?" I asked him.

"What's there to be afraid of?" he said.

"Sandstorms. Ghosts. Voices that whisper your name and lure you to annihilation."

"Nah," said the driver.

We careered through Wu-pu, which was a pleasant village of high mud walls, grape trellises, fruit trees, wheat fields, donkey carts, and long rows of slender poplars whose leaves showed their silvery undersides sparkling in the breeze. We passed a mosque. I saw a man plowing a field with an iron plow drawn by two donkeys. Women wearing scarves and long dresses of many colors walked on the road, squeezing to the side as our driver blasted away on his horn, Chinese-style. Young girls wore flaring skirts and knit blouses. Boys sat on the backs of donkey carts driven by their fathers. At the edge of the village were strange structures made from mud bricks spaced in such a way as to leave a rectangular air hole for every actual brick. They are the rooms in which the grapes are dried to make raisins. It takes about fifty days.

Mogui Cheng was twenty miles into the desert down a track that was half pulverized earth, half sand. The manager's Isuzu, our putative rescue vehicle, got mired three times in the sand, and each time it took our Beijing Jeep, the steel cable, and all the men in the party pushing to free it. After a few miles, we came to the remains of a sculpted animal, a large, long-necked animal peering eerily out of empty eyes into the desert. It could have been a crouching camel or a turtle—our local guides said a camel. We continued on our way, passing some impressive eroded remains of what had once been mighty ramparts, still easily fifty feet high and one-third as thick. Another few miles brought us to more such ramparts and the remains of numerous other structures, an Ozymandian scene that could easily have inspired rapturous nineteenth-century-type ruminations about the traces of perished grandeur. The members of our expedition got out of their vehicles and spent an hour clambering over ancient walls and temples and gazing across the empty stretches of desert to the south and the diamond-dusted Tianshan Mountains in the other direction. I wondered if the ancient cities excavated by Aurel Stein hadn't looked something like this when he was first brought to them by his local guides.

Judging from the remaining walls, the city now known as Mogui Cheng must have been at least a square mile. It had high towers that dominated the plain below and no doubt an imposing entry gate surmounted by curved-roof pavilions and battlements. In the Tang Dynasty, of course, there had been water here, a river perhaps, springs fed by the melting Tianshan snow. Several thousand people had probably lived in the town. It had been a vibrant place where melons grew, silk was traded, and the finer points of Buddhist theology were intensely debated. And it must have seemed to its inhabitants over the centuries that it would be that way forever.

ON THE WAY BACK, we stopped in Wu-pu to drop off our Uigur guides and the woman from the hotel. We stopped in the village center, where a dusty bus with no windows drew up to discharge its load of workers coming home from Hami at the end of the day. It's not often that two jeeps with a foreigner stop in town, so my presence there attracted a group of young men, happy and noisy and full of good humor.

They asked me where I was from, and I told them.

AMIRICA, one of them wrote in the dust coating the fender of the jeep. This prompted other inscriptions: MONIKA was written with a nervous giggle. It was the time of the White House sex scandal, and here on the sere rim of the Tarim Basin they were well informed about it. Then somebody wrote a version of the name of the most famous American in China: MIKELJORDAN. And then the second most famous: GEORGE-KLINTON. I was about to explain the mistaken conflation of the first name of the first president with the last name of the forty-second, but before I could do so, a young, shy-looking man in a white cotton shirt and blue trousers came from the back of the crowd and wrote CHESS in the dust.

"Chess?" I said.

"Do you play chess?" the man asked me. We spoke Chinese in the land of this man's ancestors. He was a Uigur, so it was a foreign language to us both.

"Yes, I know how to play," I said.

"Fischer, Spassky," the man said.

"That was a long time ago," I said, remembering that Bobby Fischer and Boris Spassky had their match in the Philippines in the 1970s.

"I have a book with every game," he said, ignoring me.

I wanted to tell him about Karpov, Kasparov, and the unbeatable IBM computer called Deep Blue. He seemed to be out of date.

"Come to my house and we'll play a game," he said.

I looked at the others, the hotel manager and his assistant especially.

"I don't think we have time for that," I said. "I'm sorry. If we had time, I'd love to play."

The man looked at me silently.

"How did you get interested in chess?" I asked him.

"From the newspaper," he said. "Fischer and Spassky. I love chess. Chess is deep. I have a book on Fischer and Spassky. I've played every game." He looked at me. The other young men and boys looked at both of us.

"He plays chess," one of them said. The others smiled indulgently.

"Why don't you come to my house and we'll have a game."

"I really wish I could, but we've got to get back before nightfall," I said.

"You know," said the young man, leaning forward confidentially and speaking in a low voice, "in this entire village, among all these people, during all this time, the only one who cares about chess, the only one, is me."

BACK IN THE JEEP on the way to Hami, I told Brave King that I was disappointed Mogui Cheng hadn't lived up to its terrifying legend.

"Seems pretty safe," I said.

"Well, yes, but if there was a wind, you wouldn't be able to see a thing, and there's no water. It would be easy to get lost, and to die," he pointed out.

And surely too, it is easy to dismiss the talk of ghosts and demons as peasant superstitions, which, of course, they are. But it's easy to be rationally unafraid when you have two four-wheel-drive vehicles and an entourage of nine and it is a calm afternoon in early May. If you were traveling alone on an old red mare as the monk was when he arrived in I-gu after his travails of the desert, the ghosts and demons would seem very real. This was a landscape of many strange forms and formations, of grotesque shapes rising out of the sand, a scary place to be alone at night, thirsty and lost. Even with our vehicles, we needed local guides to take us to this place in the desert sea. How easy it would be traveling alone here fourteen hundred years ago to be terrified by nonexistent ghosts and demons, whose natural habitat would be a place where no plant grew and no creature could survive. How consoling it would be to pray to Avalokitesvara, or to recite the Heart Sutra as the monk did when Bandhu abandoned him on his way to Hami.

"And therefore one should know the prajnaparamita as the great spell, the spell of great knowledge, the utmost spell, the unequaled spell, the allayer of all suffering, in truth, for what could go wrong. By the prajnaparamita has this spell been delivered: Gone, gone, gone beyond, gone altogether beyond, O what an awakening!" Amen.

5

The Long Dead

W E SPENT A fitful night on the hard sleeper to Turfan inserted into our close-together berths like chinchillas in cages, while the train rumbled and rambled along the desolate edge of the Takla Makan. The monk had a fitful journey too. He left I-gu after having recuperated from his desert ordeal, but then he almost died from the unwanted kindness of the next ruler he encountered along his route. This was the king of Gaochang, the ancient city on the eastern outskirts of present-day Turfan, who, having heard of the celebrated monk's arrival in I-gu, sent emissaries, including several of his ministers mounted on horses, to escort Hsuan Tsang into his royal presence. It took six days to cross the desert to Pih-li. There the tired monk wished to stop for the night, but his escorts urged him on despite the onset of dark, telling him that there were several relays of horses up front and that if they hurried they could reach Gaochang before the following day.

Hsuan Tsang obeyed, even leaving behind the red horse on which he had ridden since Guazhou, the one that had saved him in the desert. At midnight, the procession reached Gaochang, where the king himself came out to meet him. We know from cave-temple wall paintings what the scene must have looked like. The members of the court dressed in flowing robes belted at the waist; they had curving mustaches and flowing

83

beards and high conical headdresses held in place with silk chinstraps. The ladies, who included the queen, were resplendent in their brocades, their bangles, their jade pins, bracelets, and hairpieces. A thousand faces glowed in the light of a thousand torches that illuminated the desert poplars and the peach and apricot and almond trees, while all around the opaque night stretched to the horizon. The excited monarch, who identified himself as "your disciple," told the monk that he was so happy at the prospect of his arrival in his capital that he had been unable to sleep or eat.

By the time respects were paid, including those of the queen and dozens of maidservants, it was close to dawn. The monk begged permission to rest, which the king reluctantly granted him, leaving behind several eunuchs to wait on him during what was left of the night. The monk, having left a land where he was distrusted and his departure hindered, had arrived in the great swath of territory where Buddhism held sway and where he would be not just welcomed but revered. It held sway, moreover, because of the active support of kings and khans who held power, kings and khans who seem to have showered honors on the monk. Hsuan Tsang did not refuse them.

GAOCHANG IS ABOUT thirty miles east of Turfan, a major destination these days for the tourists traveling on the Silk Road. Its elevation of five hundred feet below sea level is the lowest in China. It is a furnace, the hottest place in Chinese Turkestan. Grape trellises arch over some of its streets, and young people play pool late into the night at tables set out next to soft-drink stands. We rented bicycles whose brakes didn't work and pedaled through the midmorning heat to the tourist sites nearest town, including the eighteenth-century mosque and minaret known as the Sugong Tower. The tower was built by one Suleiman to honor his father, one Eminhoja, who, according to the tourist brochure, "achieved brilliant exploits in safeguarding state unity." The tourist brochure, in a spasm of patriotic correctness, stressed the national goal of keeping far-flung territories populated largely by non-Chinese (including, of course, Tibet) within the Chinese fold. Suleiman had allowed himself to become a vassal of the Qianlong emperor, and he was duly rewarded with dancing girls from his harem (this part of the deal is not mentioned in the brochure), while being given funds for the construction of the tower and mosque. The tower is an impressive cylinder 120 feet high and tapering toward the top so it looks like an immense bullet pointed at the sky. It is built of bluish bricks that have faded to brown and are arranged in triangles and wavy patterns, rhombuses, and four-petal flowers.

The next day we went to the Bezikelik Grottoes, my first Buddhist cave temples of the journey, carved into a barren cliff within a superheated moonscape of rust-colored hills known as the Flaming Mountains. The grottoes were built during the course of the fifth and sixth centuries, paid for by wealthy merchants eager to earn merit in the next life and whose portraits often stand in a special corner of the caves that they sponsored. The paintings are not the best preserved among the Chinese cave temples; the best caves are in Dunhuang, which the monk visited on his return trip. On the trip to Bezikelik, we heard the first of the many tirades we were to hear about Aurel Stein, who cut out some of the best frescoes and packed them off to London, where they can now be seen in the British Museum. But even though they are minor, the Bezikelik frescoes have an extraordinary patina to them, a blend of green and ocher and burnt yellow that gives the portraits of the Buddha and his disciples a gentle kind of radiance, as if they were illuminated from someplace within the wall behind. Like those in other caves, from Ajanta in India to Dunhuang itself, many of the frescoes are devoted to telling what are known as the Jataka stories, the hundreds of edifying tales of the Buddha's previous lives, his many earlier incarnations during which he earned the merit necessary to become the Buddha. The Jataka stories are full of acts of self-sacrificing, suicidal generosity of the sort you can show only if you are confident of the truth of reincarnation—like the king who, to feed his hungry people, threw himself into a river and turned himself into an edible fish. Then there is the philosophical story of the animals and the monk all answering the question "What is the most painful thing?" "Hunger," answered the deer; the snake said, "Poison"; the pigeon said, "Sexual desire"; and the bird replied, "Thirst." Said the monk: "Living is the most painful thing. To live is to suffer."

LATER WE WENT to the Turfan Municipal Museum, where the main attraction is a collection of mummies dating from the sixth to the eighth century. Among them is a woman estimated to have been about thirty when she died, probably during childbirth. I looked carefully at her supine figure, spread out inside a glass case like a patient etherized upon a table, at her mouth twisted into a grimace and at her unnerving open eyes. Her hair is combed into a bun, though some strands have spilled out of the grasp of her ancient clasp. Strips of red cloth have been draped discreetly over her private parts by the museum curators, who evidently wanted to banish any prurient thoughts from the prying eyes of her admirers. Her skin is shriveled but intact, her hands are together over her chest, her face is ghostly.

She casts a spell, this woman. There is a kind of dark magic about her, as there is about all mummies, those most compelling of all relics. Mummies have a kind of sanitized horror about them. They are corpses, but they are so old that they have become abstracted and therefore less creepy than a fresh corpse would be. I wondered if she had living descendants, which she probably did, and that led me to wonder what it would be like actually to see the dead body of a person you know to be a distant ancestor. It is one thing, after all, to see pieces of pottery or frescoes painted on the walls of a cave, or even a photograph. It is another to gaze at an actual human being, a person who breathed and thought and who looks the way you might look in a thousand years or so, if you are buried in dehydrating sand. This woman under glass lived roughly around the time of the monk; she might have been a humble subject of the very king of Gaochang who honored him, one of the crowd of town-dwellers who came out late at night and saw him by the torchlight. I am traveling this route in part because I seek to make some kind of connection with the traveler of centuries ago, and the sight of this still intact and recognizable individual helped to forge the link.

The past, after all, links us to the great panorama, the vast theater of human striving. It makes us all related. It forms what Kafka, speaking of a smaller, more constricted, more tribal past, called the circle of blood. It gives us something big to belong to. And so, to gaze upon eyes dried like raisins that may actually have beheld the monk was to give the past I was seeking to reincarnate a kind of immanence, a humanoid concreteness. Suddenly a person, rather than words on a page, was on the scene. And while I understand, of course, how unlikely it is that the woman before me actually saw my monk, the possibility that she did gave her desiccated, crusty cadaver talismanic power. I stared at her for a very long time, and as the afternoon wore on in dusty, torrid Turfan where she passed her days fourteen hundred years and seventy generations ago, I felt her benignly mysterious emanations.

That night, as always, Brave King led us to the night market for dinner. It occupied an open esplanade outside the movie theater. A large banner strung over a nearby street said, "It is Everybody's Responsibility to Pay Taxes According to the Law." The culinary theme was Uigur, decidedly carnivorous, un-Buddhist. There were enormous pots of lamb tripe and lamb lung, lamb tongue and lamb feet, the last of them gristly objects stewed in hot pepper sauce; there were whole basins of lamb heads, their teeth bared and grinning ghoulishly. We ordered some pieces from a side of lamb coated in a red marinade and grilled over coals, and we ate them with soup noodles and warm beer. We bought watermelon for dessert and ate it while strolling, spitting the seeds onto the ground. The esplanade was filled with the sound of music, specifically "Into the Desert" by a singer named Ablajan (all the rage in Turfan) and "The One I Love" by Shirali, both blasting simultaneously over competing record-store loudspeakers.

I watched as an old woman dragging behind her several cardboard boxes, one placed inside the other, came to the watermelon stand and asked for a slice. The watermelon peddler cut one with his long, curved knife and held it out to her, but when she heard the price, one yuan, or about twelve cents, she muttered the word *gui,* "expensive," shook her head, and walked away, her boxes cutting grooves in the dust behind her. I caught up with her and asked if I could buy her a slice. She seemed unsurprised by this foreign devil speaking Chinese, but she shook her head no and thanked me for my kindness. I told her not to stand on cere-mony, that it was a hot night and some cool watermelon would surely hit the spot. But the woman shook her head again in dignified refusal, thanked me again, and continued on her way, leaving me in melancholy contem-plation of age and poverty. To have lived a long, hard life, and not even to have the minor consolation of a slice of summer watermelon for pen-nies—I have thought about that woman often since then.

The next day we went to the ruins of Gaochang, about thirty miles east of Turfan, not far from the Bezikelik Grottoes, with which the ancient city was spiritually connected. A cave temple needed several basic ele-ments, most important a sheer limestone cliff into which to carve the caves and a stream running alongside it to sustain the small, permanent settlement of artisans who devoted years to carrying out the donors' com-missions. Gaochang had water but no cliffs, while Bezikelik had cliffs as well as water but only the narrowest strip of farmable land. Gaochang was flat, and it stretched under the iron-hot sky for several kilometers. It is so big that you need to hire a donkey cart to see what is left of the watch-towers and granaries, the dwelling places and the devotional towers of the tens of thousands of people who lived there. It is a very old city, founded by the emperor of the Han Dynasty, who needed a place to house the troops he sent to secure the western frontiers. When the monk arrived there in 629 or 630, it was in the last years of one of its several periods as an independent kingdom. Before Hsuan Tsang had finished his return journey, Li Shimin had already annexed it and made it the capital of the Tang Western Prefecture. Now it is the sort of ruin that might inspire a poet to some plaintive verses about the palaces of pleasure crumbling to dust, the flowers turning to weeds and the butterflies playing no more. But in its day it was one of the great Central Asian kingdoms with all the pretensions and vanities of power.

Its king was called Qu Wencai, and as we will see when we examine his later fate, he was a bullheaded man who brought tragedy upon himself. In Hui Li's version of Hsuan Tsang's account, he was a devout and hospitable ruler, but he was also a monarch and had monarchical expectations. He commissioned a certain Master Kwo Tong Wang, eighty years old, to request that the Master of the Law give up his idea of traveling to the West and stay instead in Gaochang. Days later, the king himself renewed this request, and when Hsuan Tsang reverently declined the invitation, the ruler let it be known that he would be obeyed. This conversation between two men of the seventh century, which Hui Li reproduced more or less verbatim, has a rhetorical elegance to it that makes it worth repeating.

"I have already commissioned the Master Tong to confer with you and request that you remain here," the king said. "What, sir, is your intention?"

The Master replied: "To request that I remain here is surely an act of goodness on the part of the king, but truly my heart cannot consent."

During his travels to China in the era of the Sui Dynasty, the king replied, he had met many renowned priests. "My heart felt no affection for them," he said. "But from the time I heard the name of the Master of the Law my body and soul have been filled with joy, and my hands have played and my feet have danced. Let me persuade you, sir, to remain with me here. I will provide for your wants to the end of my life, and I will undertake that all the people of my realm shall become your disciples, if, as I hope, you on your part will instruct them. . . . I pray you accede to my desire and earnest request and do not think of going on your journey to the West."

The monk wondered aloud how he, "a poor and solitary priest," could acknowledge the king's generosity. But then he continued:

I undertook this journey not with a view to receiving religious offerings. Grieved at the imperfect knowledge of religion in my native

land, and the poor and defective condition of the Sacred texts, and being myself agitated by doubts as to the truth, I determined to go and find out the truth for myself. Hence at the risk of my life I have set out for the West, to inquire after interpretations not yet known. My purpose is that the sweet dew of the expanded law shall not only water Kapila [an ancient Buddhist mountain kingdom in present-day Afghanistan], but that the mysterious words may also spread through the regions of the East. The thought of finding my way through the mountains and my earnest desire to seek a friend of illustrious ability, this has, day by day, strengthened my purpose; why then would you cause me to stop midway? I pray your majesty to change your mind, and do not overpower me with an excessive friendship.

The monarch replied like a lover who refused to be spurned: "I am moved by an overpowering affection toward you; and the Master of the Law must stop here and receive my religious offerings. The Tsungling Mountains may fall down, but my purpose cannot change."

"Your august majesty in days gone by has prepared an excellent field of merit, and so has become a ruler of men," the monk replied. "Not only are you the preserver and sustainer of your subjects, but you are also the protector of the doctrine of Buddha. It is only reasonable, therefore, that you should support and disseminate it. How is it that you are now opposing that end?"

The king insisted that it was precisely because he had no teacher and guide that he would detain the Master of the Law, "in order that he may convert the ignorant and foolish." But the monk continued to refuse to remain behind in Gaochang when the great search for the truth in the West remained unachieved.

In the face of this stubbornness, the king colored with anger. Stretching his hand out beyond his sleeve, he said, "I have a different way of deciding this question, sir! If, sir, you still think you can go when you like, I will detain you here by force and send you back to your own country. I recommend that you think this over; it will be better for you to obey."

The Master answered: "Hsuan Tsang has come here for the sake of the great Law, indeed! And now I have met with one who opposes me. But you have power only over my body. Your Majesty cannot touch my will or my spirit."

The king pressed food on the monk from his own provisions, and this seems to have given Hsuan Tsang an idea. Sitting in what Hui Li calls "a grave posture," meaning, presumably, with his back straight and his legs crossed in front of him, the monk refused to eat or drink for three days. It may have been the first use of the hunger strike as a form of political suasion in history. And it worked. On the fourth day, the king saw that the monk was becoming faint. He felt shame and sorrow and he actually bowed before the fasting pilgrim and said: "The Master of the Law has free permission to go to the West! I pray you, take a slight morning meal." The two men, as a sign of good faith, went to the temple together and prayed there. The monk was free to go, on one condition: that on his return journey he sojourn in Gaochang for three years. Hsuan Tsang agreed.

With the confrontation ended, relations between monk and monarch became cordial and respectful once again, full of flowery language and expressions of mutual obeisance. The king made clothing suitable for the cold weather that lay ahead—face coverings, gloves, and leather boots. He gave the Master one hundred gold ounces and what Beal translates as "three myriads" of silver, as well as five hundred rolls of satin and taffeta that would last for twenty years, the expected duration of the monk's journey. He assigned him twenty-four servants and thirty horses and gave him a letter of introduction to the khan of the kingdom that lay ahead: "The Master of the Law, a friend of your humble servant, desires to search for the Law in the country of the Brahmans. I beseech the Khan to be kind to him, as he has ever been kind to me, his humble servant."

If nothing else, we get from these exchanges a sense of the courtliness, the elaborate rituals of humility, that governed discourse in the seventh century, at least among khans and Masters of the Law. Hsuan Tsang thanked the king profusely. "All acknowledge your profound virtues and are obliged to you for your condescending qualities, and in addition, your respect for learned men and your love for erudition exhibit themselves in your loving attention to their advantage."

With that the monk took his leave. The king, bringing along his priests and his ministers, accompanied him for a few miles, then they "embraced with tears," so that as the monk, now surrounded by his impressive escort, more like a soldier than pilgrim, headed west through the Turfan Depression, the cries and groans of the court of the king of Gaochang echoed off the obdurate red stones of the Flaming Mountains and dissipated in the baking air of the Takla Makan.

A DYNASTIC HISTORY of the third century A.D. has it that in the first year of the Yuan-shou era—namely, 2 A.D.—a Chinese official named

Jing-lu received from the ambassador of the Scythians the oral transmission of the Buddhist scriptures. It is not clear if this verbal teaching of the Law took place in Scythia, which extended from modern Afghanistan to central India, or in China. Wherever it was, it is the first indication in the historical record of China's contact with Buddhism. A half century later, during the Later Han Dynasty, Prince Ying of Chu, the half brother of Emperor Ming, is recorded as having held a vegetarian banquet for the Buddhist laymen and monks who lived in his kingdom. That is the first recorded mention of a Buddhist community in China.

It makes sense that Buddhism would have come from the Scythians. Remember that in the second century B.C. the Chinese emissary Zhang Qian went to their kingdom in Bactria, and when he returned to China he reported on the existence of rich and advanced civilizations west of the Pamirs. All during the Han Dynasty there was trade between the Scythians, known to the Chinese as the Yueh-chih, and China. The Scythian merchants who accompanied the caravans over the mountains and across the Tarim Basin were Buddhists themselves, and they would have been able to get rest and nourishment at the Buddhist monasteries set up all along the route, making donations to show their gratitude and to earn merit. At some point, missionaries joined this caravan route, bringing with them the texts that promised salvation. And as they did so, the road between India and China became a spiritual as well as a commercial route, an avenue of an idea that would survive and flourish in China and then Japan long after it had died out in India itself.

It took Buddhism a long time to acquire a missionary impulse. For the first two centuries after the death of the Buddha, the doctrine did not spread very far. Then, in the middle of the third century B.C., the third king of the Mauryan Dynasty, the great Ashoka, after whom numberless Indian hotels and restaurants have been named, adopted Buddhism, and, much as Constantine did with Christianity in the Roman Empire several centuries later, he made it the official religion of all of India. Throughout the kingdom, he had pillars erected to demonstrate his piety, and these Ashoka Pillars are still among the main tourist sites in India. More important for our purposes, Ashoka sent missionaries to the surrounding territories—to Ceylon in the south, Gandhara and Kashmir in the north.

Meanwhile, the Scythians, having been expelled by the Huns from their original home in northwest China, settled in Bactria, present-day Afghanistan. The Scythians supplanted the Greeks who had ruled there since the time of Alexander, spreading their influence, including their Hellenic styles of painting and sculpture. During the second and first centuries B.C., the Scythians—who had rejected Zhang Qian's offer of an anti-Hun alliance—expanded south all the way to Mathura and Benares and so became the rulers of all of northern India. Their most historically important king was Kanishka, who converted to Buddhism sometime in the first century A.D. and, like Ashoka before him, encouraged its propagation. Buddhism had thus become the official religion of the entire region from the Ganges to the Oxus, from India to Gandhara, Kashmir, and Bactria. From there missionaries certainly went to the Tarim Basin, especially Khotan and Kucha, the two most important kingdoms on the edges of the desolate Takla Makan, one on the southern caravan route, the other on the northern route. Any traveler going from China to the West or from the West to China would have to pass through one or the other of these two strategic Buddhist kingdoms.

Buddhism did not always have an easy time in China, where it often rested uncomfortably on the Confucian bases of society. The Chinese culture of the Han Dynasty was a very pragmatic, this-worldly one, oriented toward the network of social relations that were emblemized at the top by the emperor himself. Confucianism, which took official hold in China during the Han Dynasty, stressed the proper relations of emperor to subject, father to son, husband to wife. The proper observance of these relations ensured that the kingdom would remain in harmony with the cosmos itself. The spheres of Heaven, Earth, and Man were united in the figure of the Son of Heaven, the ruler. The very ideogram for "king," the Chinese word *wang,* consists of three horizontal lines, representing the three spheres, joined by a vertical one. The emperor performed rituals that were as closely prescribed as the rituals of the ancient Hebrews in the Temple of Solomon. These rituals, performed to music, ensured the proper balance among Heaven, Earth, and Man. A cadre of superior men was trained in the six classic texts that contained the wisdom passed down from the great rulers of the past.

Part of the arrangement required the emperor to suppress deviant doctrines, and the historical record is full of bitter attacks on Buddhism as Confucian officials urged the emperor to strike against it. "By their vain dreams," a Tang official wrote in a memorial to the emperor, "they induce simple souls to pursue an illusory felicity and inspire them with scorn for our laws and for the wise teachings of the ancients."

In truth, it seems something of a miracle that Buddhism became the most important religion in China, a country that seemed in many ways inhospitable to it. It should be remembered, after all, that with the exception of Marxism in the twentieth century, no other idea from the barbarian territories outside the Middle Kingdom ever succeeded in taking deep hold in China, and Buddhism in its early Indian forms was about as alien a concept as it would be possible to imagine there. It stressed a universal ethic of spiritual salvation, while the emphasis in China was on the ties of family and state.

As Arthur Wright notes in his book *Buddhism in Chinese History,* Buddhism consisted of abstract, often paradoxical statements whose main proposition was that things are not what they seem. The perceived world is not the real world. The pursuit of worldly goals leads to suffering. Attachment to the self brings pain. Buddhist philosophy elaborated a complicated and sophisticated metaphysics, and metaphysics was alien to the practical Chinese mind, oriented not toward such matters as the nature of ultimate truth but toward formulas for regulating society. For the Chinese person, whose main goal was prosperity for himself and his family, earned by becoming an official of the state, and whose favorite pastimes were to dally with his concubines and write poems, the Buddhist renunciation of all attachments must have seemed useless and defeatist. The earliest sutra to be translated into Chinese was probably the Sutra in Forty-two Sections, which stresses the pain that arises from passion. "People cleave to their worldly possessions and selfish passions so blindly as to sacrifice their own lives for them," it says. "They are like a child who tries to eat a little honey smeared on the edge of a knife." The early translations from Sanskrit included instructions on mental concentration as a way of overcoming the passions—handling lust, for example, by going to the cemetery and concentrating on the corpse in its various stages of decomposition, not the sort of thing that a Chinese ancestor worshiper is likely to do. Buddhism taught the doctrine of emptiness, the idea that a deep sort of ecstasy was to be found by meditating on the notion that reality is existent and nonexistent at the same time—also not an idea to be immediately apprehended by the more literal Chinese mind.

But, of course, every society has its needs for escape, practical and philosophical. There is labor, suffering, disease, death, and grief. There are mysteries that cannot be resolved. There is the need for mystical or just drunken relief. In China, Taoism was the native creed that emerged to take care of those needs. Taoism emphasized a spontaneous liberty from the conventions and trammels of Confucian society. Its stress was on the balance of natural forces and on nonstriving, on the wisdom to do nothing. Superficially, foreign Buddhism and native Taoism did bear some similarity. Wright mentions that some Buddhist concepts were at first translated into Taoist terms. The Sanskrit word *dharma,* for example, which means the teachings, the body of Buddhist knowledge, was translated as *tao*, the Taoist word for "the way"—as in the mystical first line of the Tao Te Ching, "The way that can be known is not the true way." But Taoism was always a credo of individual escapism from the collective conformity of Chinese life; it was never a universalist doctrine of spiritual salvation. Poets sat naked in their huts, drank rice wine, and wrote poems about their own tipsiness, like these lines from the great Du Fu:

With sad songs, sometimes self sorrow;
Drunken dancer—for whom should I be sober?

The Taoists considered the paradoxes of Chuang-tzu (Am I a man who dreamed he was a butterfly, or am I a butterfly dreaming that he is a man?), they took elixirs and mind-altering drugs, and they practiced breathing exercises in an effort to achieve immortality. But they never elaborated an entire system of psychology and epistemology aimed at elucidating the illusory nature of all experience. Buddhism encompassed more than Taoism; it was a system, a bureaucratic one as well as an intellectual one, and it promised benefits to anyone who practiced it, even without imbibing rice wine while gazing at the moon. When the airtight Confucian world of the Han Dynasty weakened around the first century of our era, Buddhism filled unmet spiritual needs. Even then, the Taoists tried to compete with the growing influence of Buddhism by developing a doctrine known as the conversion of the barbarians. It held that Lao-tzu went to India, where he converted the barbarians and became the Buddha.

In 311, we have seen, the Huns sacked the eastern Chinese capital at Loyang, and a few years later they occupied Chang-an itself, putting an end to Chinese control of China for the next three centuries. The early missionaries from Bactria, Gandhara, and Kashmir concentrated on converting the barbarian rulers to Buddhism, which they did by convincing them of its magical properties. It is not recorded how, but one of the most successful of these missionaries, one Fo-tu-deng of Kucha, made a brilliant blue lotus flower spring out of his begging bowl, thereby so impressing the illiterate and ignorant Hunnish king that he became an ardent patron of Buddhism. That patronage meant a kind of church-state union in the foreign-controlled dynasties. The various governments authorized a clerical establishment that was responsible for creating and supervising schools and monasteries. In the Northern Wei Dynasty, one of the longer-lasting and culturally flourishing of the foreign kingdoms of northern China, the emperor became the Buddha incarnate. The Indian doctrine, which had by now been better translated into Chinese, linguistically disentangled from Taoism, was so well established that when the Sui and Tang ruled a newly united and newly Chinese China they did not reject Buddhism as a pernicious foreign doctrine. They used it to win favor and consolidate their rule, establishing themselves at the top of what Wright calls a kind of Caesaro-papist Buddhist church.

A key figure in the domestication of Buddhism was Kumarajiva, whom Wright calls the greatest translator in history. Kumarajiva had an Indian father and a Kuchan mother, a princess, who became a nun when her son was seven years old and took him to faraway Kashmir to study with the greatest Buddhist masters of the era. Originally a Theravadin, a follower of the Lesser Vehicle, Kumarajiva continued his studies in Kashgar, where he became a convert to Mahayana Buddhism, especially the concept of *sunyata,* the notion of "dependent origination," that all is contingent, that objects are void and have no self-existence. He spent the next twenty years at home in Kucha, where his fame grew, eventually reaching China through the report of a Chinese monk. The emperor of the dynasty of the moment, which historians call the former Qin Dynasty, asked that he come to Chang-an, which Kumarajiva was willing to do. But on his way he was detained in Liangzhou by a non-Buddhist chieftain, until, finally, the emperor in Chang-an sent an expeditionary force to free him.

So did Kumarajiva arrive in Chang-an in 401, and until his death he served as the "Grand Preceptor" of an enormous translation project involving thousands of monks and scholars. He translated the Amitabha Sutra, the basic text of the Pure Land school in China; the Perfection of Wisdom Sutra was completed in 404; later came translations of the Treatise in One Hundred Verses, the Treatise on the Middle and the Treatise on the Twelve Gates, the Lotus of the Good Law, the Sutra Spoken by Vimalakirti, the Sutras on the Ten Stages, and the Treatise on the Completion of Truth. The most important of these treatises advanced the philosophy of the great Indian philosopher Nagarjuna, who was in turn the predecessor of Hsuan Tsang's heroes, Vasubhandu and Asanga, the creators of the Yogacara doctrine.

The going gets a bit heavy here. Nagarjuna consolidated the philosophical structure of Mahayana Buddhism through the idea that since all things are preceded by causes and conditions, nothing has independent reality—the notion of dependent origination referred to above. "Nothing comes into being, nor does anything disappear" was Nagarjuna's most celebrated epigram. "Nothing is eternal, nor has anything an end. Nothing is identical, or differentiated, nothing moves hither, nor moves here nor moves anything there."

In other words, our fierce attachment to the world of phenomena, to the accumulation of things, to the pleasures of the senses, is an illusion from which suffering is continuous and inevitable. How un-Chinese an idea that is, and yet Kumarajiva anchored it in a set of translations that acquired the status of classics in China. Never has history seen a deeper cultural transmission. With Kumarajiva and the thousand monks he supervised, Buddhism became irrevocably Chinese. And when, two hundred years after Kumarajiva's death, our lone illegal pilgrim headed off from Turfan in the direction of Kucha itself, his mind burned with a universe of ideas whose perfection required only the completion of what the Indian-Kuchan translator—in Chinese eyes, a barbarian in the service of a barbarian chief—had already done. It had made it seem indistinguishable from a homegrown product, as Chinese as Confucius, calligraphy, or poems about the light of the moon.

6

The Bombing of Belgrade

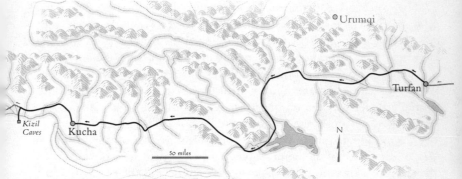

THE MONK PRESSED on to Kucha, which was the major Buddhist kingdom on his route, and so did we, riding a little red Xia-li to the station, about an hour's drive, for the overnight train from Turfan. It was midafternoon. The desert was a metallic brown. The Tianshan Mountains to the north glimmered an iridescent blue. Our driver was a thickset young man with a sparse mustache who had a disconcerting habit of hugging the median line and then, just as a truck would materialize out of the shimmering asphalt ahead, turning to talk to the always affable Brave King beside him. "Shit, that was close!" I would exclaim as the car wallowed in a passing truck's aftershock and the two young men in the front seat talked calmly about the new tollgate visible up ahead. As we approached it, the car veered off the main road and over a gravel embankment. We bounced onto a side road that ran parallel to the highway, and while we bounced the driver explained to Brave King that only the local people knew how to avoid the toll this way.

"Now you know!" Brave King exclaimed, turning to me. "If you come to Turfan again, you won't have to pay toll!"

"I'll remember that," I said.

We arrived at the train station and realized that we had left Zhongmei's video camera case in the lobby of the hotel in Turfan. We had half an hour before our train left, and the hotel was a thirty-minute taxi ride away. Brave King sprang into action. He found a telephone and called the hotel.

"Yes!" he said, it's a black camera case.

"Yes!" he said, it has a red stripe.

He was told a man with that bag over his shoulder was walking out of the hotel.

"Well, stop him! He's stealing it!"

The hotel did stop the man and recover the case. Brave King and Zhongmei went into the Railroad Office Tower, where we were supposed to pick up our tickets, while I watched the bags outside. We were overlooking a square abutting the train station on one side, the post office and police station on the other, and the bus station in the middle. Alongside were some restaurants, empty of customers in these afternoon hours, with metal tables set out on the concrete esplanade in front of them. As I stood there, a woman in a white blouse with seagulls printed on it came over to me and gestured in an entreating, plaintive sort of way for me to take a seat at one of the empty tables. I worried that the woman was on the edge of destitution, but I declined anyway, and then watched as a younger woman wearing a red sweater appeared from the restaurant holding a bowl of noodles; emerging behind her was a small boy in a kind of Osh Kosh b'Gosh pair of overalls grasping a long green cucumber in his small hand and nibbling at its end. Behind him was a man wearing the standard white shirt, blue pants, and plastic sandals—most likely the son or son-in-law of the entreating older woman. The noise coming from the station square was tremendous, shattered orchestral music blasting over loudspeakers on one side, a radio melodrama with powerfully amplified static blasting forth from the other. Train announcements coming from the station crackled over the square. Buses filled with bearded Uigurs and smooth-skinned Chinese ground out of the station, leaving behind plumes of black exhaust and the smell of half-combusted diesel fuel.

Eventually Zhongmei appeared holding our train tickets. Brave King volunteered to wait for the missing bag and, if the hotel taxi came after the train's departure, to get the next train and rejoin us in Kucha. I argued with insincere vociferousness against this plan, saying that if the bag didn't arrive, all three of us could wait for the next train. But the next train wasn't until midnight, and we knew from earlier inquiries at the ticket office that only hard seats were available on it. Fortunately for me, this was a matter of "face" for Brave King, who had taken on the role of Chinese host to a visiting stranger. He stayed behind at the railway ticket office while Zhongmei and I went to get on the train. She persuaded the clerk at the railway ticket office to help us with our bags, and, treating us like visiting celebrities (or, more accurately, treating Zhongmei like a visiting celebrity), he loaded himself up with our bags and labored under them through the waiting room, out to the platform where our long green train was already waiting, and onto our soft-sleeper car. I stared guiltily at the hard-seat carriages of the sort that Brave King would ride if the missing bag made him take the midnight train, at the many faces staring out from within their dim and dingy interiors. Zhongmei told the smitten young man from the ticket office just to leave the bags on the floor, we would handle them ourselves, even as he strained and grunted to put them in the storage area next to the upper berth.

As Zhongmei and I settled in, taking out books to read, I realized that I had been a passive observer of the events of the half hour or so just past. Brave King had become the fixer, the intermediary between me and the details of making arrangements. I began to wish that he could continue on the journey all the way to India with me, like the monkey of supernatural powers who went with Hsuan Tsang. As for Zhongmei, she and I were reversing our usual roles. In America, she was the foreigner, the exile, the person who made grammatical mistakes and was not just unknowing but unknown, who needed me to call American Express to question a charge, or to explain the parts of the movie that she hadn't understood, or to check the spelling on a letter she was writing to a grant-giving institution. In China, she was self-assured, full of savoir faire, virtually all-knowing. I was the one who needed help.

The minutes ticked by and the train began to move. Brave King materialized at the door, smiling, his face flushed, his mountainous backpack (which reminded me of the monk's in one of the famous Xian rubbings) peeking over his head, Zhongmei's camera bag in his hand.

"You made it!" Zhongmei said.

"Thank you very much," I shouted.

"It was nothing," he panted.

KUCHA IS a Uigurization of Qiuci (pronounced *Cheeoh-tse*), which is still the Chinese name given to the almost negligible ruins of the ancient city. "The air is soft, and the manners of the people honest," Hsuan Tsang wrote of the place. "The style of writing is Indian, with some differences. They excel other countries in their skill in playing on the lute and pipe." The king, he noted, was a man of limited intellect ("his wisdom being small"), so the kingdom was ruled by a powerful minister. But much of the monk's account of Kucha is devoted to a savory tale involving a former king, his younger brother, an Othello-like act of suspiciousness, and a Buddha-like gesture of redemption.

The former king—the monk provides neither his name nor his era—decided that he wished to "pay homage to the sacred relics of the outer world." What this means is not entirely clear, though probably, like Hsuan Tsang himself, the king wished to travel to the Buddhist holy places in India. In any case, he did wish for a leave of absence, whereupon he entrusted the affairs of the empire to his younger brother. This latter person then "mutilated himself," the monk says, meaning he cut off his genitals so that he could "avoid any rising of passion." This extraordinary act is also unexplained by our storyteller, but presumably it means that the younger brother wanted to forestall any future suspicion that, during the king's absence, he played around in the harem. He put the relevant body parts into a golden casket that he laid before the king.

"What is this?" the king asked.

"On the day of your majesty's return home, I pray you open it and see."

You will be able to guess what happened next. There were mischief-makers at court who, upon the king's return, said, "The king's deputy, in his absence, has been debauching himself in the inner rooms of the women." The king was angry, but then, of course, the brother had him open the golden casket, revealing its contents.

"You now have proof of my foresight," he said.

The king, Hsuan Tsang writes, "was filled with the deepest reverence and strangely moved with affection." He gave the brother the run of the palace, including its inner chambers.

There are several odd aspects to this story. The king, for one, was enough of a Buddhist to wish to pay homage to the sacred relics, and at the same time enough of a king to maintain a harem. No Buddhist renunciation of desire there. The king in this sense seems to foreshadow the celebrity Buddhism that has emerged in America today, the movie-star Buddhism of privileged audiences with the Dalai Lama one day followed by flashbulb-popping appearances with yet another starlet the next. Why did the story appeal to the monk? Possibly because it had the same basic theme as the Jataka stories, the theme of self-sacrifice to the point of amputation. The prince gave his arm so a tiger might eat; the brother cut off his member so he could be true to the trust that was placed in him—even if he was also striking a kind of preemptive blow against his enemies.

The story, as told by the monk, also has a redemptive ending.

One day, the younger brother saw a herdsman who was preparing to geld five hundred oxen. Moved to sympathy for the oxen, the brother, who knew about gelding, raised money and precious jewels to save the herd from the knife. "In consequence of this act of love," the monk writes, "he recovered by degrees from mutilation." As a consequence, says Hsuan Tsang, "he ceased to enter the apartments of the women." Here's an absurdist paradox. As long as the man's penis is missing, he can visit the harem; as soon as he has a penis again, he can't. The story, apparently very satisfying to the monk, would better suit our own ironical sensibilities if the brother had hidden the miraculous recovery of his genitals from his brother and spent many delicious hours making love to the king's favorite concubines. But irony was not within the monk's interpretive vision. His age was a sincere one. The younger brother's willingness to renounce pleasure and to be good was what moved him, not the Catch-22 illogic of his condition.

We arrived in Kucha from Turfan early in the morning and checked into one of the seedier hotels of our trip. Kucha in general more fit the image of an old Central Asian oasis town than just about any other of my destinations in China, which seemed to be divided into two general categories: gleaming, antiseptic new towns with wide avenues and white-tiled buildings, and disheveled red-brick industrial, mining, or oil towns, workers' camps in the desert. But Kucha was neither. Kucha was gray, sleepy, indolent. Its low-slung buildings shaded by white poplars were built mostly of the whitewash-covered baked earth of the pre-gleam, pre-ceramic-tile Communist era. Men with forked beards sat on donkey carts and surveyed the passing scene. The market was redolent of dried apricots, sesame, cardomom, anise, chili, freshly ground black pepper, red pepper, walnuts, and almonds. A man in a long white beard and knit skullcap stood in front of eighty-eight bags of herbs serving them to customers with a long-handled ladle. Freshly killed lambs, their flyspecked carcasses coated with layers of white fat, hung from iron hooks in front of the butcher stands, and behind them men sat at little tables eating *la-tiao-zi,* "pulled" noodles covered with stew.

We went about ten miles into the desert to the Zhao-gu-li Temple, the dust pouring through the floorboards of our hired car and leaving a powdery red-brown patina on our hair and skin. Zhao-gu-li is the ruin of a pagoda that belonged to one of the most important monasteries on the Road of Great Events. It is an amazing sight. Red sandstone mountains cut east and west through the desert just to the north of it. The green of an oasis, looking like the roughened felt top of a billiard table, was visible just below them. The desert itself is a kind of burnt pink stretching under a smoky sky from the red mountains on one side to a flat horizon on the other. A hot wind whistled overhead and kicked up eddies of dust around us. To the east of us and across a dry riverbed was the ruin of another pagoda, a vague pyramid silhouetted against the mountain.

Before leaving in the morning, I had read the monk's description of a pair of what he called monasteries (Beal's translation is "convents," meaning possibly that their occupants were nuns, not monks) in a place near Kucha that Beal transliterated as "Chau-hu-li." They were "close together on the slope of a mountain, but separated by a stream of water," the monk wrote. This had to be the same place, a fourteen-hundred-year-old ruin that was flourishing when Hsuan Tsang was here. On this very spot! From Bai-dun-zi to Gaochang to Zhao-gu-li, there are still traces of the monk's passage. They seemed important to me; they provided a sense of connection, a continuity. They made the monk concrete rather than abstract, somewhat in the same way that the mummified remains of that woman in the Turfan museum had.

But that satisfied feeling was soon swept away by a kind of melancholy, by the scene's very desolate beauty and the sense that the passage of time had brought a kind of death to this place. I found myself nostalgic, thinking of things temporally or geographically very distant. The monk, Zhao-gu-li, my own origins, all blended together in a single melody whose motif was vanished time and lost places. On the chicken farm where I grew up there used to be a few small bungalows where summer guests would stay. There was a large vegetable garden alongside an old New England barn that we had converted into a coop for "layers," as we called our egg-producing hens. Standing at the end of a large grassy field was what we called the New Coop, which my father had built and which contained the modern elements of egg farming—namely automatic feeding and watering troughs that considerably reduced the labor involved in providing for the chickens' needs. Down the road a way was an immense and very beautiful apple and peach orchard, the trees planted in straight rows descending a long hillside that offered a grand view of a broad reach of the Connecticut River below.

We sold the farm when I was thirteen, and my parents moved to another town during my university years, so I had almost no reason to go to East Haddam after I finished school there. I forgot about it. I wasn't nostalgic about it then. It was just the place where, as Andre Aciman wrote about Alexandria, Egypt, his place of origin, I first dreamed about other, more thrilling places. But a few years ago I went to have a look, hoping to experience some powerful sensation by visiting the scene of my childhood dreams and fears, maybe to recapture the time lost as it were, to inhale the fragrance of memory along with the pollen-laden air.

I remembered one stormy night when I lay in bed in our farmhouse frightened by the sound of thunder, the walls groaning, the branches of the maple outside my window illuminated in the phosphorescent glare of the lightning and looking as if they were about to be torn away, and my father reassuring me that the house had survived storms like that for a hundred years, so there was no possibility that it would come crashing down around us. Years later, the house was still there and in good shape, occupied by a young professional couple who were renting it from an absentee owner. But the rest was crumbling. One of the bungalows, the one we had called the Green Bungalow, where a Polish hired hand named Stanislaus lived with his wife, had been torn down, and the others were dirty and empty. The garden was overgrown, the barn had become derelict, the other chicken coops were sagging and filled with the rusting hulks of abandoned cars, and the New Coop had collapsed altogether into a rectangular pile of debris, shingles, and two-by-fours, and rusted feed hoppers that had once nourished the birds that nourished us. Down the road the orchard still commanded its beautiful views of the river valley, but the trees were untended, thickened with age, infertile, silent witnesses to the time when we used to sneak in to steal an apple or a peach or two, brush them on our sleeves, and eat them, the juice running down our chins.

It is easy to be sentimental about this, though generally I am not sentimental about old places. The farm stirs a kind of melancholic affection in me. It was the place where, especially in the summers, my grandparents, my uncles and aunts, and my cousins gathered, and where we went for long walks through fields and woods with our dog rambling nearby. The farm also conferred a touch of exotic distinction when I told people about it in the cities where I later lived—Hong Kong, Beijing, Paris, New York. But I was often lonely on the farm and I was awkward in school, where I was viewed as a strange Jewish bird by my classmates. I was a good chess player, like my friend from the village of Wu-pu near Hami, and I dreamed of the literary life, but those attributes didn't count for much at the Nathan Hale–Ray High School in Moodus, Connecticut, whose claims to fame were its high school soccer and basketball teams, of which I was not a star member.

The farm is also the place that I associate with secure times that preceded a less secure, more anxious period for my family. My parents sold the farm after a losing battle with falling egg prices, and for about three years after that we lived in something close to poverty, in a four-room rented house pressed up against the main road just outside of town; we used to have to keep the bedroom shades drawn to avoid feeling like fish in an aquarium. For a couple of those years, my parents ran a laundry in a neighboring town called Deep River, washing the linens for the little hotels and guesthouses that were scattered around the area. I remember once my mother, with me in tow, delivered some laundered, folded towels to one such hotel, but the proprietor was unhappy. There weren't enough towels, and my mother told him that she wouldn't be able to deliver more until the next day. The man stared at her silently, turned around, and walked away, his hunched back an insulting rebuke to my mother. I felt like murdering him, and I felt the frustration of knowing that I could not carry out my wish. I felt sorry for my mother, which was the worst feeling of all. The truth is that she did not feel sorry for herself, and anyway, our conditions improved when my father began working for a farmers' organization that produced feed for chickens and marketed eggs. The laundry, happily, burned down one night, the fire the result of some faulty wiring, and we collected insurance money.

The point is that I never saw returning to East Haddam as a return to some period of lost wholeness. And yet, when I saw the wrecked coops and the overgrown garden and the bare choirs of the apple and peach trees, I was filled with melancholy. The time passes, and where once there was a real-life struggle, now there is a rotting heap of building materials. And down the road there are antique shops, and young urban professionals wearing Banana Republic jeans and Nike shoes with those check marks on them who know nothing of what happened in this place before they arrived.

I wondered: If Hsuan Tsang could return to the Zhao-gu-li Temple, what would he think of the ruin it is now, compared to what it was once like? He was impressed by what he saw. In his *Chronicles,* he speaks of a statue of Buddha "richly adorned and carved with skill surpassing that of men." The occupants of the convents, he writes, "are pure and truthful and diligent in the discharge of their duties." He finds a jade stone of a yellowish-white color, shaped like a seashell, on whose surface "is a foot trace of Buddha, one foot eight inches long and eight inches or so in breadth; at the expiration of every fast-day it emits a bright and sparkling light."

Standing at the temple, I imagined one of these truthful and diligent nuns watching from the balustrade as our pilgrim appeared over the horizon. He would have emerged over the hill just on the other side of the riverbed, going first on the far side of the riverbed to the east convent. Then he would have crossed the river. Perhaps it was shallow enough to ford, or maybe there was a ferry. Thousands of people lived near this oasis. It was a major Buddhist center allowed to fall into ruin when Buddhism itself disappeared from Central Asia. The monk would have ridden his horse over the pebbly concourse that stretched between the riverbed and the western convent. He would have arrived from Turfan after about 350 miles of desert at another way station, knowing, even as he did so, that he had only covered a small part of his journey, that India still lay an uncountable number of li to the west. He would have held a fan in one hand, a begging bowl in the other; his face would have been encrusted with sand, the skirt of his robe swept back by the wind, his eyes firmly planted on his destination.

ON OUR WAY BACK to Kucha across the desert, we stopped in a large village and presented ourselves at a house, chosen more or less at random. We were unannounced and certainly uninvited, but the family there lived up to the Uigur reputation for hospitality. The woman of the house received us in her courtyard of swept earth as if she had been expecting us all afternoon and led us into a large reception room, where we sat on a long raised brick platform covered with rugs. Her husband sat on the edge of the platform and looked at us. He was bearded and wore a jacket of rough wool. The rugs, it turned out, had been made by his daughter, who soon appeared with tea. She seemed impossibly young to have woven such a large quantity of rug, but when asked if she was indeed the weaver, she shyly said yes, she was. She had on a dark purple dress and a red headscarf, and she was sweetly pretty, demure. In the corner I noticed a stir. A young man—he turned out to be the husband of the rugmaker—had been sleeping along the far wall. He sat up looking slightly nonplussed. Well, what would your reaction be if you were napping in your living room and awoke to find a group of Uigur tribesmen sitting on the sofa?

The Uigurs, who spoke to us through the driver, a Chinese-speaking Uigur, informed us that the family was about to sit down to lunch and invited us to join them. This we declined, not wishing to eat this family out of house and home. But Brave King, speaking to the driver, was made to know that declining the invitation would be an insult. Our logic was that since we weren't invited, we should go without causing any further disturbance. "No," said Brave King. "Their logic is that since they didn't invite us, we have to be very careful to do what they want. If we don't eat, they'll think we think their food isn't good enough for us." We stayed, of course, and ate a plate of beef stew served in a single dish with four spoons and a plate of rice—one for each of the three of us and one for our driver. The stew was tender and aromatic. As we ate, the father of the family began to talk—about pigeon blood.

"You put it behind your joints and lie in the sun," he said, "and you get better right away."

"It's a common cure in the countryside," said our driver, not explaining exactly how we got on to this subject but being helpful anyway. "These people work harder than their bodies can stand, so they are always looking for cures."

"Just behind your joints," the householder repeated, tapping his elbows and his knees, "and you lie in the sun."

THE NEXT DAY we were eating lunch at a little restaurant down the main road from our hotel when a news bulletin came on a television set placed in a corner. Slowly I became aware that the room had become silent and that all eyes were on the newscast. During the air campaign against the Serbian dictator Slobodan Milosevic, the United States had bombed the Chinese embassy in Belgrade. The clientele watched intently as a parade of Chinese from all walks of life came on the air to denounce the United States, to declare that the attack was intentional, and to demand a vigorous retaliation. Just what I needed. I felt conspicuously like a citizen of my country as the program continued, but nobody looked at me. They knew how I was feeling.

That night, Zhongmei, who never stopped amazing me with the quality of her connections, talked by phone to some friends who were well placed in the government in Beijing. She learned what the Chinese television had not reported: that the American consulate in Chengdu had been sacked and burned and some Americans had been beaten by angry crowds on the streets of Beijing and Xian. How the crowds knew that their victims were Americans and not, say, Canadians or Germans, was never explained. In any case, I did not feel endangered. Kucha is far from Beijing, and besides, the majority of the population in Kucha is Uigur, not Chinese—though I was in no position to assess the extent of nationalist feeling among the Uigurs.

The Chinese certainly were whipping up anti-American sentiment over the incident. There was not even a hint of a possibility in that lunch-time broadcast or in the many broadcasts that ensued that the bombing might have been an accident, a miscalculation. It was the old China, the China that I knew from my years of residency here, the Stalinist-Maoist China whose propaganda bureau used its total control over the media to arouse nationalist feelings with a distorted version of events and to feed it incessantly to the public. It confirmed my longtime sense that a sort of wounded antiforeignism simmers just below the surface in China and can explode at any time. On the other hand, it was rather incredible that of all the embassies in the former Yugoslavia, the United States had bombed the Chinese one. Given the recent tension in the media and the tendency of many in Congress to denounce China as the new totalitarian menace, it was not illogical from the Chinese standpoint to think deliberation was more likely than accident. For the first time I felt a bit awkward about traveling with Brave King. Would he share the resentment against the United States being encouraged by the media?

"I'm sorry about what happened," I told him as we walked from the restaurant back to the hotel.

"There's going to be war," said Zhongmei.

"No, there won't," I said. "At least I don't think there will be. There might be some hard feelings, but I don't think there will be war."

"You don't think it was on purpose?" Brave King said. "You don't think the United States wanted to scare us?"

"No, I really don't," I said. "The United States has no interest in making a billion Chinese people, including you, angry at us."

"Well, China has to do something now," Zhongmei said. "The embassy was bombed and people were killed. They can't just do nothing."

"But what are they going to do, bomb New York?" I said.

"Well, anyway," Zhongmei said, "I think it's dangerous for you. You could be attacked."

"I think I'll be okay," I said. "I don't think anybody will attack me here."

"You never know what can happen," Zhongmei replied. "There is a lot of anger, and some people have been attacked already."

"Don't worry about that," said Brave King. "If anybody attacks him, he'll have to attack me first."

Later Zhongmei and I stayed up late and talked. As things turned out, she would be leaving me in Kucha, so we had only one more day and a night together before we would see each other again in New York. Originally our plan had been for her to go with me as far as Kashgar, but it turned out that the return plane schedule from there would force her to miss an important appointment in Beijing, so Kucha would have to be her last stop. In two days, when Brave King and I went westward to Aksu, she would take the train east back to Turfan and from there would make her way to Beijing. That was why she was so worried about my safety— because she wouldn't be there if something bad happened.

Among the people she called during the trip was a friend of hers in Beijing who was a ministerial-level official. She called him at every one of our stops to get a name or two from him of people in the local branch office of his ministry in case we ran into trouble. She wanted to have an important name to drop in case the Public Security Bureau questioned me and discovered my identity. They wouldn't let me continue on my way, she told me, but they wouldn't do anything worse than send me home. "I can't do much," she said, "but if somebody high up says you're his friend, at least no harm will come to you."

I was uneasy about the news of the bombing of the Belgrade embassy, but, maybe with excessive optimism, I didn't think it would cause me any serious inconvenience. It was strange; for months, years, I had imagined that it would be impossible for a foreigner like me to travel in Xinjiang without being stopped by the security authorities along the route and made to answer a few questions about who I was, but now that my route had been more or less smooth for a couple of weeks, being in Xinjiang felt normal, unexceptional. I didn't feel invulnerable exactly; I felt wary, but also that if something was going to happen it would have happened already, and that I was going to get through.

Zhongmei, on the other hand, was visibly worried, and I realized as we spoke that in my self-absorption I had failed to understand just how fraught with subtle difficulties the trip was for her. After all, she was a Chinese woman traveling with a foreign man in China, a place where the average person does not look especially kindly on romantic or erotic relations between local people and foreigners, where people tend to assume some sort of corruption in the relationship, that money is being exchanged, that there is some immorality involved, some yielding by the Chinese girl to the illicit enticements of the foreign man. Zhongmei told me that she was happy to be traveling with me. She wanted me to see her country. It was the first time we had undergone a difficult trip together, and she felt that we had formed a good team. But she was nervous that something would go wrong, and she was at least occasionally embarrassed.

"When we go into the dining car on a train I'm watching the other people, wondering who they are," she said. "I see that they're looking at you, and I don't know if it's just because you're a foreigner, or because they're angry to see us together, or because the Security Bureau is watching you."

"I think it's because I'm a foreigner," I said.

"I'm not so sure," she said. "Anyway, it makes me nervous. I feel responsible for you."

When we checked into hotels, she told me, she noticed the surprise on the faces of the reception desk clerks when they learned we were sharing a room. "It bothers me when I have to take out my American passport and show it to them," she said. "I'm Chinese. Why should I have to show an American passport? But if I don't show them my passport, they'll keep fighting with me." In China, only foreigners are allowed to stay in the same room together if they're not married. Chinese people wouldn't be allowed to do that. "And," Zhongmei continued, "when I take out my passport, I know that they feel bad too, because they're embarrassed they showed what they thought of me."

"I know what I would think if I saw a Chinese woman traveling with a foreign man," she told me once. "I would feel that she's not a good girl. I would feel that she wants something from him, so I know that's what people are thinking when they see me with you. I don't really care usually, but sometimes it bothers me."

And now, just when we were parting company, she had to worry about possible consequences for me of the Belgrade bombing. Suddenly it was doubly fortunate that we had met Brave King, and that he had become my guide and our friend. His resourcefulness was enormously reassuring. His presence would make me look like a wealthy private traveler who had hired a local guide. Zhongmei told me to be sure not to have too much conversation with ordinary people as I continued the trip, and above all not to speak Chinese to anybody. "You never know who you're talking to," she said. "Just look at that guy in the restaurant"— meaning the restaurant owner in Jiayu Guan. "Finally I was feeling relaxed," she said, "having some noodles, and we're all talking and having a good time not worried about anything, and the next thing he's saying you're a spy."

"I thought it was over," I said.

"I've been nervous all along," Zhongmei said. "I just didn't want you to see it. I wanted you to concentrate on the trip and not have to worry."

"It doesn't seem like much just to say this," I said, "but I appreciate how complicated this is for you, and I especially appreciate that you decided to come with me."

There was a moment of slightly awkward silence. Neither of us knew exactly what to say.

"I'm sorry you have to turn back now," I said. "I was hoping we could get all the way to Kashgar together."

"Why can't you look more Chinese?" she said. "Everything would be easy if you looked Chinese."

"I am what I am."

"A foreign devil," she said.

"Yes," I said, "I can't help it."

"It's not your fault," Zhongmei said.

We laughed and went to sleep.

THE NEXT MORNING at breakfast there were two men from Chicago in the hotel restaurant poring over maps and Silk Road brochures and talking about desert roads. They were dressed in the best of Abercrombie & Fitch, and had that lean and toughened look of ex-marines. I'll call them Dan and Bill; Dan was a bit older and seemed to be in charge. They were in lawyering and real estate, and members of the Chicago Explorers Club pioneering a desert route through Xinjiang.

"We're goin' mostly by jeep," Dan said. "Got all the permits an' everything, plus a Chinese police escort to keep us outta trouble."

"Did you hear about the bombing of the Chinese embassy?" I asked them.

They hadn't.

"I guess it doesn't matter for us," Dan said finally. "We're gonna be out in the middle of nowhere anyway."

I asked them where they were going.

"We're leaving for . . . what's the name of that place? . . . Aksu in the morning. Then we're cuttin' through the desert from Aksu to Khotan by four-wheel-drive. Far as we know we'll be the first foreigners to do that. It's gonna be two days and two nights in the desert. Then we're goin' to Kashgar from Khotan and then we're goin' over . . . what's the name of that thing? . . . the Kunjerab Pass to Pakistan."

Dan asked me about my itinerary, and I told him.

"What do you do back home?" he asked.

I saw Brave King standing nearby and felt I had to lie.

"Real estate investment," I said. With a bit of sophistry on my side I could argue that that wasn't a lie. I own my apartment in Manhattan. I dream about my apartment appreciating so much in value that I'll be able to sell it and live in some modest dwelling by the ocean, writing full-time rather than pursuing the far more hectic daily journalism I do now.

"Well," Dan said, "we got a lot of stuff to do to get this show on the road. Maybe we'll see you in Aksu or someplace." And he and Bill were off.

THAT DAY WE went to the Kizil Caves, more completely known as the Kizilgahaha, the Thousand Buddhist Caves, another of the great Buddhist complexes on the China-India road, more important than the Bezikelik Grottoes. We drove for an hour through a phantasmagorical Xinjiang landscape. It was as though towering, jagged rock outcroppings had been levered on their side so the lines of stratification were slanted nearly vertical rather than the usual horizontal. The caves are along one side of a curving cliff looking down on a verdant oasis. The frescoes, like those near Turfan, tell the Jataka stories and other useful parables, like the one about the hunter who lost his hands when he killed a bear that had saved his life, and the prince who threw himself off a cliff so a starving tiger could feed on his dead body.

We spent several hours at the caves, which are in a state of damaged magnificence. Many of the eyes of human figures in the frescoes were gouged out by fanatical Muslims who swept through here in the eleventh century and were rigorous adherents of the Koranic injunction against graven images. The brochure helpfully informed us that there are 130 intact caves containing some five thousand square meters of murals, painted from the third through the seventh century. It is not certain that Hsuan Tsang came here. He does not mention the Kizilgahaha, but if he did he would have happened upon a vivid and cosmopolitan scene—hundreds of artisans from as far away as the Swat Valley in Pakistan recording the exploits of the Buddha as well as scenes of daily and religious life.

We know from the caves themselves and from the archaeological record a good deal about the desert kingdom then called Qiuci. Racially and culturally it was essentially an Indo-European place whose inhabitants spoke a version of Tokharian, which, as we have seen, was related to ancient Celtic. Kucha represented a rich cosmopolitan mixture, geographically very close to the powerful Turks who straddled the mountains to the north, but culturally linked to Persia, Gandhara, and India. It was not Chinese at all, though Emperor Tai Tsung was to impose his control within a few years.

Many of the greatest paintings and sculptures of the Kizil Caves illustrate the forms of what the art historians call Greco-Buddhist, the styles that were transmitted by the Hellenic civilization that descended from Alexander the Great's conquest of Bactria and Gandhara. In the caves at Kizil—and in the museums in Berlin and London where many of the best works from Kizil were taken—you see images of Zeus transformed into images of Brahmans and Bodhisattvas. You see the same sort of classical drapery that you would see on a Roman statue. There is one cave at Kizil depicting a company of knights that, the French explorer René Grousset maintains, could have escorted Hsuan Tsang from Turfan to Kucha. "What a surprise to discover here people of a Western race with pure oval faces, long straight noses and strongly arched eyebrows," Grousset writes. "We know them right down to the last detail of their fashions in dress, right down to their favorite colors."* Grousset's opinion is that Kucha, which he calls "this little Persia in the heart of the Gobi," was a "chivalrous society" whose knights and sense of pageantry make it appear very close to the medieval West.

We even know such homely details as the names of the songs that Hsuan Tsang would have heard as he visited the royal court—like "The Jade Girl Hands the Cup Around" and "The Flower Contest." We know the costumes that the musicians wore: turbans of black silk, robes of purple with embroidered sleeves and matching trousers. The ladies of Kucha are shown in the Kizil frescoes wearing close-fitting bodices and narrow sleeves and long skirts that flare at the hem. We know what Hsuan Tsang would have seen in the bazaar, the silks and spices, the dried grapes and apricots, the jade hairpins, the porcelain, the musical instruments, the embroidered borders that the women sewed onto their flaring skirts. The men wore blue caps with fur trim and long gray jackets edged with blue and gathered at the waist with garnet belts.

What we see in the frescoes, Grousset reminds us, was soon to disappear, since Kucha and the other Indo-European cultures of what is now Chinese Turkestan were engulfed by a Turkish invasion a few decades later. So Hsuan Tsang's visit there has a valedictory quality. The king he encountered was named Swarnatep, which means "Golden Rod" in the Tokharian language, and his foreign policy consisted of maintaining good relations with Tang China, to whose new emperor he sent gifts of horses. Our pilgrim gives him credit for being a devout Buddhist, though the monk did not have much respect for the Hinayana theology practiced there. In the first of what would be many fractious theological encoun-

* René Grousset, *In the Footsteps of the Buddha*, p. 54.

ters along his route, Hsuan Tsang met one Mokshagupta (a very Indian name), who was Swarnatep's spiritual adviser and a philosophical real-ist. He believed that the world we perceive actually exists, while, as we know, Hsuan Tsang took it to be purely a product of the mind. When they met, Mokshagupta complained to Hsuan Tsang that Mahayana phi-losophy was a latecomer that had been irreverently and unjustifiably imposed on the original doctrine of the Buddha himself, who had said nothing about the phenomenal world being a mere dream within a dream. The Mahayana books, he declared, "contain only erroneous views" and were not studied by "true disciples of the Buddha." Hsuan Tsang flew into a rage. We see him here at his most dogmatically unpleasant. "The Yoga Sastra," he said, referring to the principal Mahayana classic, "was expounded by a sage who was an incarnation of the Bodhisattva Maitreya. In calling it today an erroneous book, have you no fear of being cast into a bottomless pit?"

Despite this difference of opinion, King Swarnatep, anxious, it would seem, not to offend a visiting Chinese dignitary, ceremoniously sent Hsuan Tsang off after a visit of sixty days. He provided him with a full caravan of servants, camels, and horses and brought along to the city a large delegation of monks to wave to him as he began again the long trek west.

THE CHINESE MEDIA continued to hammer away on the Yugoslavian bombing. Every afternoon and every evening on television, workers, sol-diers, students, and housewives were shown making declarations of fealty to the motherland in this hour of crisis and vowing to work harder to make the country stronger. One night there was extended footage of the top Chinese leaders visiting a hospital where some of the wounded in the embassy attack were brought for treatment. Zhongmei kept calling her friends in Beijing to get the latest news and rumors—that the American embassy had been attacked by a stone-throwing mob while the police stood idly by (true); that several Americans were in critical condition after being assaulted on the streets of Chongqing, Wuhan, and Guangzhou (false); that Americans were leaving China en masse (true); that Ameri-cans arriving in the country were being turned back at the border (false). Brave King spoke to the head office of his travel agency in Beijing and was told that many scheduled tour groups were canceling their plans. Now he was worried that the group he was going to meet in Kashgar would fail to show up.

"I don't think it's a good idea to go to Aksu by train," Zhongmei said.

"He'll be okay," Brave King said. "I'll protect him."

"You can't protect him if a huge crowd of people wants to get him," Zhongmei said.

"The deputy minister of public security made a speech on television yesterday and he said that foreigners in China should be protected," Brave King said. "There's no more danger. Nobody's going to get him."

I wanted to believe that, but I wasn't entirely convinced. The paradox, which even the monk would have appreciated, was that I used to be worried about getting into China; now, visualizing my remote position on the map, seeing myself surrounded by potentially hostile territory that stretched for thousands of miles in every direction, I was worried about getting out.

"All it takes is a few angry people," I said.

"I'm angry too," said Brave King, "but you had nothing to do with it."

"The Americans who've been beaten up didn't have anything to do with it either," I said.

"It's going to be all right. Nobody will do anything after the speech on television yesterday."

"You're angry?" I said.

Brave King's jaw muscles worked.

"Of course. I'm a Chinese."

"But it was an accident," I said.

"You think it was an accident?" Brave King said. He had been thinking about our conversation the day before. "I don't believe that with all that technology the Americans could have an accident like that."

"It doesn't matter," Zhongmei said. Clearly she had continued to think about the situation since our conversation in the hotel room the night before. "I think you should fly to Beijing right away and then leave for Hong Kong."

"He doesn't have to do that," said Brave King. He reminded Zhongmei that the airport in Kucha was closed, which was the reason she was taking the train back to Turfan.

I listened to the discussion and briefly considered leaving China right away, but I decided against it for two reasons. First, leaving China, which involved first taking a train from Kucha to Urumqi, where I could get on a flight to Beijing, exposed me to the same danger as staying in China, which involved taking the train from Kucha to Aksu. Second, and more important, I was here, and I didn't feel the danger was great enough to require me to leave. I am not brave; I have left places when I thought I might run into serious trouble. But I have also stayed when other people were leaving. In 1989, right after the Tiananmen massacre in Beijing, tourists and businessmen suddenly decamped, leaving just the reporters behind to rattle around in empty hotels. The reporters stayed because it was their job to stay, but also because they knew that the authorities didn't want anything bad to happen to them. The same situation, I felt, prevailed in China after the Belgrade bombing.

"I'm not going to give up the trip now," I told Zhongmei. "I've come too far to turn back now. And anyway, something tells me things are going to turn out okay."

7

The Horror of Home

T<small>HE MOON</small>, a yellow wafer, hung in the dusty air when we left the hotel early the next morning. The headlamps of the Xia-li taxis driving to the station threw vaporous shafts into the gloomy dawn. Zhongmei, whose train wasn't until late in the afternoon, came to see us off. She got on the train with us and helped us settle into our compartment. Nobody took notice of me. There were no denunciations of America or pledges to work harder to make China stronger, just a crowd of recently awakened people shuffling sleepily to their next destination.

The time for the train's departure came, and Zhongmei and I said goodbye in the drafty space above the car coupling. Then she stepped down to the platform and walked away with that unself-consciously jaunty stride of hers, her hair swaying like an irregular pendulum behind her back. "Be careful" were her parting words. In a few days, Brave King and I would also go our separate ways, he back to Beijing in the company of his American tour group, I over the Torugart Pass to the Kyrgyz Republic.

Suddenly, like a candle in a dark room, an intense longing to cling lovingly to my hearth lit up in my heart. I watched Zhongmei disappear down the platform and into the gloomy hall of the station building, and the contradictions of my nature wrote themselves large in my head. But I think I can report that the balance, finally, was shifting. Perhaps when this trip was over I could stay at home and be wistful about travel, rather than travel and be wistful about home. It is said about Peter Fleming, the author of the classic *News from Tartary,* in which he recounted his 1935 trip of almost a year, mostly on foot and on horseback, from Peking to New Delhi across Chinese Turkestan and over the Pamir Mountains, that once he got home, he lived happily ever after in a house in Surrey and never left again. But when he traveled, he did it with a disregard for discomfort that I take as a model to emulate. He celebrated his twenty-eighth birthday while trekking across Xinjiang with Kini Maillart, and on that day he describes a tough walk, heavy sleet, and a meal of antelope, rice, and curry that he claims sardonically to have been sumptuous. "And we both thanked heaven that we were not celebrating somebody's birthday at the Savoy," he writes.

I understood that. To be on the mountain was uncomfortable, but it was also to be free, unencumbered, without obligations; it was death-defying, exciting, life on the Nietzschean edge. I have a friend who was in what was called the pacification program in Vietnam during the 1960s. After the war, he lived in Tokyo, then Hong Kong, then Bangkok, then Hong Kong again, but couldn't bring himself to go back to California. There were many like him in Asia in those days, hacks and photographers and former spooks who hung around the Foreign Correspondents Club and reminisced about "Nam." I thought of them as the you-can't-go-home-again brigade, and the spiritual malaise that they suffered as the horror of home. "Once you've flown over a burning village in a helicopter and taken enemy fire from the ground," my friend told me, "you can never go back." The horror of home. It is the dread that home, so romanticized in poetry, so idealized in the imagination, is humdrum, safe, boring, a denial of the more romantic possibilities of life. But my friend did go home eventually, and he married and had children. Peter Fleming too. He must have decided that the Savoy wasn't so bad after all.

I have lived in my undramatic way on the edge between loneliness on one side and the horror of home on the other. Many years before my journey on the Road of Great Events, I left Cambridge, Massachusetts, where I was a graduate student in Chinese history at Harvard, and where I had a girlfriend of the sort you brought home to meet Mom and Dad and, if you weren't like me, you married. But I was like me, and I therefore left her to go to Paris, where my goal was to become a French-speaking man of the world. I lived by myself in a little room in the Fifteenth Arrondissement, where eventually I got a letter from my girlfriend telling me she wasn't putting up with me and my uncertainty anymore. It was goodbye, and who could blame her? I put her letter in a box, and after my year was up and my man-of-the-worldism sufficiently advanced, I started to travel. I went overland (and over sea) to India, via Italy, Greece, Turkey, Iran, Afghanistan, and Pakistan. Here and there, of course, I met fellow travelers, including some memorable ones. In Bombay I wrote my first ever published article and thus inaugurated my career in journalism. In Kerala in the south of India I met a young woman whose parents managed a tea plantation in the Western Ghaut Mountains and I spent a happy week with her and them. One day some snake charmers came and found two cobras under the porch, and even though upon inspection by my friend's savvy father the cobras turned out to be defanged, meaning that the charmers had planted them before they found them, it was thrilling nonetheless. I traded a shirt for the gourd that one of the snake charmers had made into the flute with which he charmed the snakes. I wrote an article about that too—my second published piece. My career was blossoming.

But mostly I was by myself, gamely pushing ahead. Why? Because I wanted to see the world and I wanted to do so untrammeled and unconnected so that whatever might happen could happen. I've done that at other times too. When I went to open up the *Time* bureau in Beijing, there was a woman in the picture then too, but I never asked her to go to China with me. That failure was more reflex than thought, but the reflex was to see somebody else as circumscribing the adventure, drawing a circle in barbed wire around it. As a result, I missed my girlfriend and was lonely a lot of the time in China. There were a lot of dispiriting Sundays there, but I never asked her to join me. Well before that, on my post-student adventure from France to India, I saw young couples traveling together. I was envious of them and at the same time I knew that I could have traveled in the same way if I had chosen to do so. But I repudiated permanent company, or, more accurately, I was propelled away from it by some force I didn't understand. Permanent company was too much like staying home, and home to me was commitments, and commitments were things that quite literally gave me a sensation of choking, like a gob of something greasy and gristly that I had somehow to swallow.

My manner of living had its rewards, many of them, and I'm not sorry

I didn't do things differently, but it also brought me a kind of grief. I wanted to be free, but I wasn't exactly a happy vagabond either. There was one moment in particular. It was in a cheap hotel room in Singapore, where there was a rat in the corner and immense water bugs hanging upside down from the ceiling beams. I had arrived there one night from Bangkok on my way to Indonesia, and suddenly and unexpectedly I simply broke down. I wept. I felt the loneliness and what seemed to me my inability to bring it to an end wrap themselves around me like boa constrictors and squeeze the spirit out of me. I have rarely felt that bad since. But the loneliness returned again and again, self-imposed, brought on by my compulsion to keep all of my options open. I was for many years unable to do or to be otherwise.

I thought about this as the day dawned in Kucha and the train began its slow exit from the station. Zhongmei had gone, and I hoped she was already back at the hotel for a bit more sleep. I thought about how she had been waiting for me in Xian, standing outside the airport exit pressed against the security rope by the crowd behind her and waiting to see me. She was fairly optimistic that I would make it through passport control and that I would appear there with my luggage. But she was well aware of the possibility that I could be taken into custody, put in some hotel room for the night, and sent to Hong Kong on the first flight in the morning. And then she would have come all the way to Xian for nothing. She came anyway. She had equipped herself with a letter from some official she knew in Beijing that she hoped might help her get in to see me wherever the vigilant border guards would have taken me to spend the night. I walked down the train corridor to my compartment fully aware of how lucky I was to have her.

I won't say that I had an epiphany right there and then. For a long time, I had been thinking about making a life with Zhongmei, and when I did so the horror of home turned into something very different. Something was changing, and perhaps that moment on the train in Kucha standing between the soft-sleeper car and the dining car was when the knowledge of the change first came to me in clear and unambiguous form. The change was that nothing was pushing me to be a solitary figure anymore, that I didn't have to be what the Chinese call a *gan-gwer,* a bare stick, an old boy, a lonely bachelor. Now I had Zhongmei and I didn't want to lose her. Sitting in the compartment, Brave King sitting opposite me, and watching the early-morning scenery of the Xinjiang Uigur Autonomous Region go by, I realized that once this trip was over, I would try my best no longer to take my voyages alone.

· · ·

THE TRAIN ARRIVED in Aksu a little after noon, and we spilled out into bright, steaming sun. Workmen were busy building a new railroad station, so the normal chaos of a Central Asian train arrival was intensified by the disorder of a construction site. Cars, trucks, taxis, buses, and donkey and horse carts were all jammed together trying to merge into the single lane that left the station precincts. A traffic cop stood in the middle of it all and made futile gestures with his arms. Drivers blasted away on their horns with lusty good humor.

Hsuang Tsang stopped briefly in Aksu and then went directly west, crossing the Pamir Mountains at a point, known these days as the Bedel Pass, which the Chinese government has closed to traffic. I would therefore have to go on to Kashgar, where the monk went only on his return journey, and from Kashgar I would go north over the Torugart Pass into the Kyrgyz Republic, rejoining Hsuan Tsang's route in the northern part of Kyrgyzstan. I knew that a special permit from the Ministry of Public Security was required to go to the Torugart Pass, and I was duly equipped with one, obtained with the help of a Chinese friend—and what the friend had called a "facilitation fee," a very large one—even before I had arrived in China. There was no passenger train from Aksu to Kashgar, only a freight train, so we would have to go by public bus.

"What is it, about four hundred kilometers to Kashgar?" Brave King asked our taxi driver.

"Are you kidding? You've got close to five hundred kilometers." The driver had to shout so loud over the cacophony of horns and jackhammers that it hurt my ears.

"I think it's four hundred," Brave King said.

"You can think what you want, but it's five hundred."

"Where's the bus?" Brave King screamed.

"It's right there," the driver screamed back, pointing to a few dilapidated vehicles on the side of the road.

"Well, it's five hundred," Brave King said to me confidentially. "That's hard. Once I from Ili to Urumqi by bus. Seat very hard. Road very jump. Trip many hours. After I arrive, I am very painful."

Finally we made it out to the main street. Aksu, which I had imagined to be a crumbling Turkestani backwater redolent of ancient Central Asia, turned out to be a big, gleaming town bristling with new construction. It didn't have much charm, but it was bright, especially by comparison with dark and battered Kucha. It had a desert cleanliness to it and the newly remodeled Friendship Hotel had a welcome smell to it, like a new car. Still, I was restless in Aksu, anxious to get moving toward Kashgar, to get out of Xinjiang before some alert policeman questioned me and discovered that I was a journalist traveling in an area where journalists were banned. My mood was not improved when Brave King and I took a taxi to the town center in search of a late lunch. We found a place called Kuai-Tsan, "Fast Food," which was like one of those Panda restaurants you see at American airports. We ordered at the counter. Food was placed into a plastic dish. I sat down and immediately made the unpleasant discovery that someone had spilled tea or Coke or something into the molded plastic seat, where it had made an inch-deep puddle. My backside was soaked. I quickly ate my lunch and got up.

"How bad is it?" I asked Brave King. I was thinking of the impression my sodden bottom would make on the Aksu-ites, how silly I looked.

Brave King took a look. "It's bad," he said helpfully. "It's very bad."

I got a taxi back to the hotel and ran into the Chicago adventurers standing in the lobby in a bad mood. They were supposed to have left on their cross-the-trackless-desert expedition early in the morning. I began to explain my disaster, but they were too preoccupied with their own to listen.

"I'm ready, the jeeps are ready, but there's nothin' in them," Dan said. He spoke like George C. Scott in the movie *Patton,* using the first person singular pronoun to refer to the entire army. "They were supposed to have gotten supplies yesterday but they didn't for some goddamn reason and I don't know what the hell is goin' on."

"Does it matter that much if you leave a day later?" I asked.

"It does matter," Dan said. "I gotta go today so I can make it to Kashgar in time for the Sunday market, and after that I've got four days to do the Karakorum. I got a flight outta Pakistan on Thursday, and if I'm late for that I'm up shit creek."

A Chinese helper stood nearby. He turned out to be the police escort Dan had spoken about when we met in Kucha.

"Why don't you see if you can get your Uigurs down there right now, so's I can get this show on the road," Dan said to the policeman.

The three of them walked briskly out the door and I turned to my room to deal with my soaking pants.

BRAVE KING AND I went to the bus station, which turned out not to be where the taxi driver said it was but inside an impressive, orderly building elsewhere in town. The woman ticket-seller never took her eyes off her newspaper as Brave King asked her questions about times and prices. But we did learn that the bus for Kashgar would leave at one the next afternoon and take ten hours and that the price for Brave King would be forty-seven yuan (about five dollars) and exactly twice that amount for me.

"Why is the price more for foreigners?" Brave King asked the ticket-seller.

She glanced up at him for just a second and then returned to her newspaper.

The next day when we came back, we bought tickets from a different ticket-seller and paid only forty-seven yuan for each, which we experienced as a small victory for the principle of fairness. Our bus was a soft sleeper, which meant that it had two levels of couchettes, though they would have been an additional eighty yuan for the two of us. You can, in other words, recline for the entire journey to Kashgar if you want to. We didn't want to. We took seats perched just above the doorwell. Then a ticket-taker came on board, and, pointing to me as if I were a piece of excess baggage, she told Brave King that my ticket was ninety-four yuan, not forty-seven. The ticket-taker had a look on her face of remote, bored indifference, the standard configuration of the remote, bored, indifferent Chinese functionary. There is something banally chilling about it. She was a person who followed orders and then went home to relax. In any case, we were denied our victory, but we were on our way to Kashgar, the westernmost city in China, the most non-Chinese place in the current Chinese empire, the gateway to all of the major mountain crossings along the Road of Great Events, the city of intrigue where Britain and Russia once spied on each other's consulates, where a Muslim dancer-cutthroat named Yakub Beg threatened the empire, where Genghis Khan and Tamerlane made conquests on their way to China itself. You get the point. Kashgar is redolent with the aroma of historical romance. A few weeks before, when I thought I might be stopped by immigration officials in Xian, the very word "Kashgar" sang to me of impossible romance, and now I had a mere ten-hour bus ride before arriving there. I was excited.

The bus pulled out at about one-thirty, half an hour late, squeezing through the metal gates of the Aksu bus station. Most of my fellow passengers seemed to be Chinese. In the upper bunk just behind me was a soldier with his wife, who was nursing a baby. Above and across from them was a man with a pockmarked face wearing a dark blue shirt buttoned to the throat. He was carrying a Makita precision saw in a cardboard box. A middle-aged woman who smiled at me when she got on the bus was in the seat in front of the door opposite the driver. As we headed down the clogged road west we began to pick up other passengers, mostly hirsute Uigurs in coarse wool jackets who bargained with the conductor over the ticket price. Some got the price they wanted and got on, some didn't.

At three-thirty we stopped at a roadside food stall for lunch. It was gaily decorated with a red-and-blue-striped canopy with red cloth trim, but Brave King and I took a look into its dark and smoky interior and decided against it. Diarrhea is the great comi-tragic enemy of the traveler, especially the foreign traveler unused to the local microbes—even if the better, more elegant travel writers rarely refer to this affliction. More than once already on this trip, I had had to scurry around in urgent search of a Xinjiangese toilet. Brave King and I had paid for our roasted lamb in the Turfan night market with close inspections of a large percentage of the Xinjiang public toilets available on that short stretch of the Road of Great Events. The word in Chinese is *cesuo,* pronounced, spat out, as "TSEH-swo." It is almost onomatopoetic. The TSEH-swo consist of narrow rectangles cut into a cement or brick floor over which you squat (sometimes with another person squatting over the adjacent rectangular hole) while the flies buzz your ass. Two hours out of Aksu with eight hours to go to Kashgar, with nothing but desert all around and no toilet on the bus, I took a longing look at the skewers of spiced lamb that the local restaurateurs were asking me to eat, and I declined. I bought some dry Tianjin biscuits, which were quite good actually, and ate a few of them with bottled water.

While we sat on the bus in front of the food stall a curious Uigur from a bus going in the other direction got on and tried to make conversation. He said something in Uigur and looked at me expectantly. I hazarded a reply.

"America," I said.

"America!" he repeated. He gave a thumbs-up and repeated, "America!" He said something else in Uigur and waited for my reply.

"Kashgar," I said.

"Kashgar!" Another thumbs-up.

I pointed at my watch and said with rising intonation, "Kashgar?" The man counted the hours and pointed to 1 a.m.—two hours later than scheduled. Then he turned to Brave King sitting next to me and said in Chinese, "Japan?"

"No, I'm Chinese," Brave King sighed. It had happened again. Anyway, he and the Uigur began to converse in Chinese, which the Uigur spoke with a heavy accent. In general, I didn't want to arouse curiosity about myself, and I particularly didn't want to do so just after the United States had bombed the Chinese embassy in Belgrade. Americans who speak Chinese are almost invariably journalists, academics, diplomats, or spies. They are rarely New York real estate investors. So, while I remained quiet, Brave King and the Uigur chatted, first about the Uigur's occupation—he was a trader in goat skins—then about how many children they had—Brave King none, the Uigur, who was forty-six years old, six. He had started having children when he was twenty, he said, and his wife was sixteen. He had two grandchildren. He beamed.

"You have to start early or your juice is no good anymore," he said. Then he asked Brave King how old I was. While I meditated silently on my bottled water, Brave King and the Uigur settled on about fifty for me, pretty close. I was hoping he wouldn't ask me how many children I had. Another six to zero would have been too lopsided a score.

"What is he?" the man asked.

"He's a businessman," Brave King replied, truthfully as far as he knew.

"He's a bomber!" said the man with the pockmarked face and the Makita saw. "He bombs Chinese embassies!"

I pretended not to understand, but the atmosphere suddenly seemed chilly. The man was smiling, but his stare was hard.

"He makes bombs to drop on China," he said, still smiling, maintaining a face of studied innocuousness. Just a joke. No offense. Still pretending not to understand, I asked Brave King for a translation, and when he gave me one I waved my hands in denial, smiling also, and realizing at the same time how silly my gesture was. I was actually bothering to assure a man on a bus in Xinjiang that I didn't manufacture bombs for the American air force. I was eager for the friendly Uigur to leave, which he did in haste when his bus was about to pull away.

We left at four-thirty, grinding down the corrugated asphalt. We were on China Route 302, the road that goes all the way from Shanghai to Kashgar, the same road we had been on from Liuyuan to Hami, though here there were no kilometer markers, no tollgates, no median markers. Here was just a narrow, corrugated, tooth-loosening, bowel-jarring two-lane strip through the desert. The road was heavily traveled, mostly by oil tankers and open-backed blue trucks carrying rolls of cable, chunks of coal, bags of grain, slabs of stone. I looked at the truck drivers as we overtook them, doing so in the Chinese fashion, with constant blasts of the horn. They were swarthy men with mustaches, expressionless, dusty, stoical, heroic. We passed through small settlements—a few mud-brick hovels, a food stall with a little white cooler in front, a boy riding on a donkey cart driven by his father, a mangy camel, a conical bonfire in a field surrounded by standing figures, the smell of garbage burning, and behind it all a flat domain of pebbles and dry earth stretching to the barren hills beyond.

At about seven o'clock there was suddenly a strong odor of gasoline, and the driver stopped for a repair, neatly replacing a section of the fuel line by bending a piece of copper tubing into the proper shape. It took close to an hour, the driver swearing as he twisted the tubing with a pair of pliers. "I told the boy at the station to check this damn bus, but he didn't," he said. "I thought everything was okay, but it wasn't." While the driver fixed the fuel line, the passengers roamed the edge of the desert or sat on their haunches by the side of the road. I noted that the roamers were the ethnic Chinese, the haunch-sitters were Uigurs. I did some roaming, some squatting. At eight we were under way again, and I watched as the sky grew dark blue, then smoky gray, and then dark gray, and the hills in the distance were slowly enveloped in darkness.

There was a weightiness to this bus ride, I felt, a kind of eventful monotony. The drivers—a Chinese alternated every two hours or so with a Uigur—worked hard, shifting, swerving to avoid rocks, slowing down when the road abruptly disappeared and the bus crunched onto gravel and stone and then bumped with the sound of shearing metal onto the road again. By ten it had gotten very dark and the headlights of oncoming vehicles looming up from great distances ahead seemed to come almost from the horizon. You saw the light, but then it took a long time for the vehicle originating it to reach us. The oncoming lights strangely obliterated the foreignness of my situation. Riding a cantankerous bus across the glaring Takla Makan Desert from Aksu to Kashgar brought no memories with it, but it did bring something familiar, a sense of life redux translated to someplace else.

We have all driven on some country road at night speeding through a tunnel of darkness and feeling the anxiety of those headlamps appearing ahead of us and pointing menacingly in our direction. For some strange reason I remember the nocturnal school buses of my youth, driving home from basketball games held in the opposing team's gym, the bus churning noisily through the winding roads of southeastern Connecticut, going home from small towns the names of which were important in my school years but are almost forgotten now. The bus would be quiet on the way home, the countryside dark except for those alarming moments when the road was suddenly lit by a passing car, high beams on a little bit too long, blinding you for just a second. In China on the road to Kashgar, the custom seemed to be to travel on low beams and then switch to high about fifty feet away from the oncoming vehicle, or to flash them on and off before roaring by.

I wasn't good at basketball. It was the great agony of my youth, the reason I didn't get the girls, I thought. Chess and literary ability were not sexual attractions at my high school. I tried hard and I was tolerated on the team, but I mostly played in practice, not much in competition when the cheerleaders, who were also on the bus, shouted the other players' names and the crowd cheered their exploits. And so the bus ride home held no satisfaction for me, rather a sense of unease, of failure, of dislocation, the powerful, secret conviction that I ought to be someplace else, and those knives of light that moved like searchbeams in the Connecticut night found out my nonbelonging. This is perhaps the hidden affliction of all travelers, the reason that the writers among them conceal their discomfort, their suffering, their dysfunctional bowels, their loneliness, the long stretches of tedium they experience en route. They don't belong, and so they have to pretend always to be having fun, enjoying where they are. I wondered if the monk's colossal journey, undertaken to find the Law, wasn't in some part motivated by the nonbelonging of a man of no power at a time when savage power was shifting from one hand into another. That is what I was thinking now on the Road of Great Events thirty-five years after my meager career as a basketball player came to its quiet end, as our bus passed a roadside cluster of brick shacks in a placed called Su-gun. A question occurred to me: Would I be here at all if I had been better at basketball—if one of the pretty Irish girls who led the cheers belonged to me, would it ever have occurred to me to come to China?

At about eleven o'clock, the Chinese driver—who was resting, having turned the wheel over to the Uigur, who drove more slowly, more carefully—told us we had about one hundred kilometers to go, about two hours. I thought about Zhongmei, who was by now on a train going through the night in the opposite direction to Turfan, where she was supposed to arrive in the morning. Then she had to pick up new tickets at the railroad office above the bus station, wait all day, and board another train for Liuyuan, arriving at 4 a.m. Then she had to find a bus or a taxi for the two-hour trip to Dunhuang, where she was to meet a group from the Ministry of Culture that would have special access to caves normally closed to visitors. I worried about her arriving in seedy Liuyuan at 4 a.m. Brave King told her not to take a taxi but to get a public bus. "A woman at that hour with a taxi driver," was all he said.

Zhongmei has a long history with Chinese trains, especially from when she was a student in Beijing. The dance academy used to close twice a year and the students would be obliged to go home. But all of the other girls lived in Beijing itself or in other big cities that were easy to get to. Zhongmei had to go two nights and three days (or was it three nights and two days?) to Baoyuan in northernmost Heilongjiang Province. She went hard-seat but she never got a seat. She slept on the floor under a seat. Even now in soft-sleeper class on Chinese trains the toilets are no bargain, but in those days the toilets in hard-seat class were crowded with passengers who couldn't find seats in the cars, so there was no going to the bathroom in any case. She had to change trains in Harbin late at night, and that required a wait of several hours, but passengers were not allowed to wait in the station itself. Zhongmei remembers roaming streets that were so cold she began to lose the feeling in her feet. Once she tried to go into a hotel to sit in the lobby, but she was chased away. She was twelve years old. While the normal mood in the school was festive as vacation approached, she was filled with dread at the prospect of another train ride and the frigid nocturnal wait.

After graduating, she performed for five years with Beijing's leading company, and she was its star. She knew everybody. She was invited to banquets by senior Communist Party bureaucrats. She traveled and performed abroad. She appeared on television in the annual Chinese New Year's special, the closest the country has to an Academy Awards program, watched by hundreds of millions. She knew movie directors and movie stars. Visiting businessmen from Hong Kong and Thailand courted her and promised her a life of riches and ease if she would marry them, or be their mistress. In 1991, when her five years of mandatory service to her company in China were over, she came to the United States. She struggled to start her own dance company. She's still struggling. She's another nonbelonger, another traveler. I see us on the map of the Xinjiang Uigur Autonomous Region, two points of light moving away from each other like asteroids in the void. We have moved away from each other before. I know that I don't want to move away from her anymore. The juice is getting too old.

We arrived in the Kashgar bus station at 1 a.m., just as my Uigur friend had predicted, not bad given the roadside repair, the blockages along the way, the pitch-and-roll detours, the sand blowing across the highway. We got into the taxi of a very angry taxi driver who poked his head out the window and started swearing loudly at a car blocking his way. Then he swore at other, unseen things, like the Communist Party, for example, whose members, he told us, go to banquets every night while he, one of the common people, possessing one of the "old hundred surnames," couldn't earn enough to make ends meet. It is said in China nowadays that you can say anything as long as you say it in private, and the taxi driver's tirade would seem to be proof of that.

"They fired me," he yelled at us and at the starry void above, "after twenty years as a truck driver. Actually, they didn't fire me. I quit. But it was the same thing. Because they made you pay commissions, see? And the commissions they made you pay were more than the income you could make with your truck. You know what I mean? They knew it, but they took the commissions anyway, and then they sat on their asses and drank tea and read the newspaper and waited for the day to end. It's a fucked-up system. You work your balls off for twenty years and what do you get? You get a fucking Xia-li taxi that's hardly big enough for you to squeeze your body into and you fucking have to drive eighteen fucking hours a day in order to fucking survive while the state pays these fucking Communist bureaucrat bastards for having meetings and banquets. You drive and they meet and eat and then they tell you you have to pay taxes when you don't have enough fucking money to buy a fucking bowl of noodles in the fucking market."

The man was so excited he didn't see another taxi alongside and almost veered into it. What he saw was the other taxi almost veering into him, so he started swearing at the other driver, and when the other driver didn't apologize, he began driving alongside it and threatening to bash into him and knock him off the fucking road. We told him to take it easy.

"Safety first," said Brave King cheerfully.

"Don't worry," the furious driver said, forgetting the other taxi, which fled down a side road. "I've been driving for twenty years and I've never had an accident."

Speak no evil. We sped down a broad avenue lined by white poplar trees and after a few more minutes approached a traffic circle just outside the gates of our hotel. Our car darted ahead of another Xia-li taxi that was just then pulling away from the curb. We were the only two cars in an empty place that could have accommodated hundreds of tiny vehicles like ours. But our driver, not seeing the other car, cut short across the circle and made for the hotel entrance. The two cars crashed. The back door on Brave King's side crumpled, but he was unscratched. We got out. We paid our driver the twenty yuan we had agreed upon at the bus station and took our bags out of the car and slipped into the hotel as he harangued the other driver for his stupidity and carelessness.

We hadn't eaten since breakfast, except for a few biscuits and some water, and even though it was nearly 2 a.m., we went out in search of some noodles.

"I've been here before," Brave King said. "I know a strange place we can get some instant noodles."

We went to a low-slung building at the back of the hotel courtyard. It was adorned with a curving, dark purple neon sign that said "Sauna." Two women sat on a couch in the foyer. They wore flimsy blouses and close-fitting sheaths with slits up the leg. One of them was pretty in a concupiscent sort of way. The sauna sold plastic bowls of instant noodles, and we bought two of them. I looked at the women while Brave King made the purchase and they looked back at me. Our noodle purchase completed, we turned to leave.

"Don't you want to stay and have a bath?" one of the sheathed girls, but not the pretty one, said to me. Her voice was husky. Or maybe it was just the perfume of her dress.

For a very brief moment I considered it, a bit of consolation after the dusty travail of the bus trip.

"Maybe another day," I said, and we walked out into the loud rustle of the wind in the poplar trees.

Kashgar. I had imagined Xinjiang to be filled with suspicious, identity-paper-checking agents of the Public Security Bureau, but I had not showed my passport to anyone other than a train conductor since immigration in Xian. I had made it.

8

The Torugart Pass

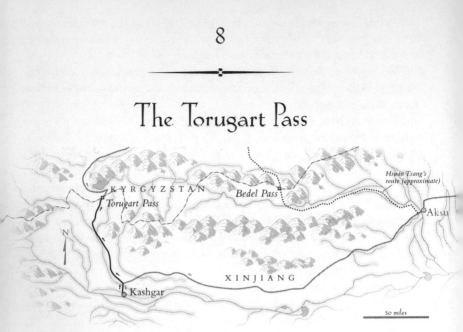

W E SPENT THE DAY looking into travel to Kyrgyzstan over the Torugart Pass, and the messages were mixed. Across the street from the Seman Hotel, where both Brave King and I got rooms, there is a place called John's Café—"Your Home Away from Home on the Silk Road"— which serves bad Western and good Chinese food at outdoor tables to the backpack brigade. A man there, a foreigner sipping instant coffee and eating an omelet, told me that you can't cross over the Torugart Pass. He had a pencil-thin beard running from ear to ear and under his throat. He wore a T-shirt that said "Captain Morgan's Parrot Bay." Nearby, Uigur boys were playing pool on rickety tables. A stream of men with heavy beards and those Pakistani long shirts and billowy pants carried briefcases out of an adjacent hotel and walked briskly down the street.

"I went up there," Captain Morgan said. "You can't do it." He had a South Commonwealth accent, possibly South African.

"What do you mean, you can't do it?" I asked.

"They turned me back. It's only open to Chinese and Kyrgyz people. Foreigners fuck off."

"Well, I have a permit. It's strange that they gave me a travel permit if they don't let you cross the border."

"You have a permit?"

"You need a special permit."

"Fuck."

Brave King and I asked taxi drivers if they would take me. They said they were only allowed to go as far as the Chinese station, but the station is a hundred kilometers from the actual border. Somebody mentioned a bus that goes all the way from Kashgar to Bishkek, which is the Kyrgyz capital, about 460 miles away, and we got a good half-day walking tour of Kashgar looking for this bus (or a ticket office, or an information bureau). We never found it. John's Café, it turned out, had e-mail service, so we sent a message to a tour operator in Bishkek asking advice about how to go from the Kyrgyz border, once I got there, to Bishkek. We were told there were occasional taxis but the drivers knew that travelers crossing the border had no alternatives, so they charged as much as five hundred dollars for the trip to Bishkek. There was no reply from the Kyrgyz tour operator. Even if you do manage to get to the border, somebody told me, there is a twelve-mile gap to the Kyrgyz customs station and there is no transportation between the two.

"I think no problem for foreigners," Brave King said. "Turkish camel men go that way. Then again, they have letter, Turkish president to Jiang Zemin." Jiang Zemin is the president of China and the general secretary of the Communist Party, and therefore the most powerful man in China. "I guess they are special."

"Anyway, I don't happen to have any camels," I said.

"We could get you some."

"Some? All I need is one."

"You need one camel for yourself and at least one more camel for water and food and probably another camel for your bags, plus you have to have camel man to take care of camels and camel man needs one for himself and one for supplies."

"So that's five camels."

"You need extra camel in case one dies. Many Turkish man's camel die."

"How much does a camel cost?"

"Only a few hundred dollars each." Brave King smiled. "Also you need the special permission to cross border by camel, from China and probably from Kyrgyz side too."

"How long would that take?"

"Oh, probably a few months. You have to go Beijing apply for permission."

"I think I'll take a pass on the camels."

Brave King next met a friendly clerk at the Seman Hotel who told him that he had a Kyrgyz friend, a trader, who had the right to drive straight through from Kashgar to Bishkek and that I could hitch a ride with him. We went to visit the hotel clerk.

"How much?" I asked.

The Kyrgyz trader wanted six hundred dollars. I declined the offer. The reception clerk accepted my decision with good grace and, trying to be helpful, told me that I could go to the border and hitch a ride on a truck to Bishkek for about one hundred dollars. I was enthused. But trucks don't drive straight through to the border. Goods to Kyrgystan are taken on Chinese trucks, off-loaded at the border, and put on Kyrgyz trucks for the rest of the journey. When I sought details on this, asking, for example, whether I would find a Kyrgyz truck at Chinese customs, or whether the trucks would be at the actual border, or at Kyrgyz customs, and, if they were at Kyrgyz customs, how I would manage the 112 kilometers to there from Chinese customs (to which I could take a taxi from Kashgar), the answer was a little vague.

"I guarantee it," the reception clerk said.

"You guarantee what exactly?"

"I guarantee no problem."

"Have you ever sent any foreigners this way before?"

"Last year there was an Englishman."

"One Englishman?"

"Yes."

Well, that's not very many Englishmen, I thought, but it's something.

I decided to take my chances on the truck, but then, walking past the Chinibagh Hotel, I noticed an office of the China International Travel Service, the official government tourist agency. In my experience living in China (in the dark days when it was mandatory for foreigners to arrange all domestic travel through the CITS) I found this organization to be dependably expensive, obstructionist, and inefficient. Inside the office was a tall, slim Tajik named Luyik who spoke English with something close to a Midwestern accent.

"Can you arrange transport from Kashgar to Bishkek for me?" I asked.

"No problem," Luyik said. He had a permit to escort foreign visitors past the Chinese customs station all the way to the actual border gate in the mountains. There, he said, he could arrange for me to be met by a jeep sent from Bishkek by an outfit called Dostuck Trekking. I asked if I could camp one night at the Tash Rabat, a high valley about a hundred kilometers over the Kyrgyz border.

"No problem," Luyik said. It was the new China.

The estimate was pricey, but less than the price being demanded by the Kyrgyz trader friend of the hotel reception clerk. Anyway, they know when they've got you in places like Xinjiang and Bishkek. I agreed. The only problem was that it was Thursday. I couldn't leave the next day, and the border was closed on the weekend, so the earliest I would be able to go was Monday.

I had seen a sign in the hotel lobby advertising a *qi-gong* massage service. It would eliminate your fatigue and illnesses. "Please have a connection with the savicing-desk lady in the hotel and make a Pre-engager!" the sign said.

"Let's make a pre-engager to go to the border on Monday," I told Luyik.

KASHGAR IS a Central Asian city being engulfed by Chineseness. In the market, there is very little in the way of Uigur culture left. There are, however, tourist knives and mandolins and sheepskin hats. And there is a large night market where on one side of the street the food is Chinese and on the other it is Uigur, meaning mostly lamb shishkebab served with pieces of thick round bread. "The old things are disappearing," Brave King said. He remembered being here three years before with his camels and Turks and there were still people wearing Uigur fashions on the street, and Uigur tailors in the market. Now there are plastic sandals and that shiny gray gabardine that Chinese bureaucrats make into pants and suits.

Often when traveling in Asia I have the feeling that I was born too late. Having been in China for the first time in 1972 and having lived there from 1980 to 1982, I feel at least that I caught a few glimpses of the last remains of the old China. Beijing in the early 1980s was an overgrown north Chinese village, decorated with some of the most lavish and opulent imperial monuments on the globe. It was a place through which farmers herded their sheep late at night, and where, in the old alleys near the Drum Tower, a man might be playing a two-string *er-hu* outside his gated courtyard home at night. Half the people you saw in Beijing, wandering across the traffic-free streets, were peasants; the other half were bureaucrats. Now Beijing is a big, anonymous, featureless international city with no peasants and no nocturnal sheep, but many businessmen and traffic jams worthy of Paris or New York. You are more likely now to hear the *er-hu* played in the New York subway than in an alley in Beijing.

Kashgar is a small Beijing in the making, but it has been like that for only a short time. As the westernmost city of China, it has China's most exotic history. Behind the Seman Hotel, where I stayed, is the old original building of the Russian consulate, a single-story gray-brick place with old wainscoting and European murals where you can almost hear the samovar hissing on the heavy mahogany table. The British consulate, presided over for a quarter century by a Chinese-speaking Eurasian diplomat named George McCartney, was in the Chini Bagh, the Uigur expression for "Chinese Garden" and now the other—socialist-style—Kashgar hotel (where my new friend Luyik had his office). McCartney's first trip to Kashgar came in the 1890s when he accompanied the legendary explorer-soldier Francis Younghusband on an exploration of the High Pamirs, where the current borders of China, Afghanistan, and Pakistan meet. Younghusband was one of the most famous practitioners of the Great Game, the hundred-year contest for influence between Russia and Britain conducted in the Central Asian countries from Turkey to Chinese Turkestan.

Kashgar was one of the minor prizes in the Great Game. In 1865, Yakub Beg, who had once been a dancing boy in his hometown of Khokand (in current-day Uzbekistan), led a small army over the Pamirs and seized the Chinese-controlled oases. Yakub was a Tajik, which meant that he spoke Persian, and he controlled the desert all the way to Urumqi, a thousand miles east of Kashgar, which was his capital. The histories of this event depict him almost as a racial stereotype, the wily Oriental despot. One imagines him in a labyrinthine palace with a well-stocked harem sending tax collectors to all of the oases under his control and living luxuriously off the tribute. In 1868, a British tea merchant from Kashmir named Robert Shaw crossed the Karakorum Mountains from Ladakh and was received by Yakub in his palace. Shaw's purpose was to sell tea in Kashgaria, which is what Yakub called his desert kingdom. But the "wily" leader was playing a bigger game, making promises first to the British, then to the Russians.

Someplace else in Kashgar during Shaw's visit was Mirza Shuja, who was one of the Indian spies sent out by the British, usually in the guise of Buddhist pilgrims, to map the empire's borderlands. Shuja was being held chained to a log by Yakub Beg. The British viceroy in Calcutta had banned English officials from traveling in Central Asia for fear that if they were murdered or taken prisoner, the British would be unable to retaliate—bad for the indomitable colonial reputation.

A third person in Kashgar was just such an Englishman, however, an explorer-adventurer named George Hayward. After Shaw's initial meeting with Yakub, during which the emir of Kashgaria had called the Englishman his brother (the two men spoke directly to each other in Persian), all three were under one form or another of arrest, in three separate places.

Yakub was using the time to see if he could get formal recognition of his new country from the Russians. When St. Petersburg proved too timid, he summoned Shaw and told him he wanted to send an emissary to India. This resulted in the release of all three men, Shaw, Shuja, and Hayward, who climbed back over the mountains together to Ladakh. Shaw and Hayward received a hero's welcome. Shuja was quietly received back into the Indian secret service. But three of the four actors in this little Kashgar drama came to a bad end. Shuja was murdered in Bokhara while on another mission. Hayward was killed by a tribal leader near the Darkot Pass in northern Kashmir while on his way to explore the Pamirs. Yakub Beg died in Kashgar, possibly poisoned, after a Chinese military expedition seized back the Takla Makan oases in 1877.*

Kashgar is now a Chinese city with a strong underlayer of Muslim and Uigur culture. The main Uigur-like institution is the Sunday market, where farmers meet in a huge esplanade behind the covered market to buy and sell sheep, goats, horses, donkeys, mules, camels, and cows. Sure enough, when I went there I found Dan and Bill, who told me they had almost gotten lost in their desert crossing but had been saved by Dan's handheld GPS, his Global Positioning System monitor, the modern traveler's indispensable guide to navigation. Around us were four women from France taking pictures through lenses as big as thermos bottles. Here and there above the sea of black-topped Uigur heads you could make out blond Scandinavian coiffures. It's safe to say that every foreigner in Kashgar comes to the Sunday market to watch the local people transact their business. Brave King told me that the Uigur handshake is a bargaining tool. The buyer taps his offering price into the palm of the seller in such a way that other potential buyers will not know the size of his bid. Surveying it all was a Chinese policeman in a green uniform sitting at a desk and looking over the registration forms that all the market participants had signed.

"I'm headin' into a dust storm," Dan told me, getting back to his desert crossing, "and I can see the driver doesn't know where the road is. I tell our guide there, 'We're goin' north,' but the driver doesn't believe me. If I didn't have my GPS, I'd still be roamin' around out there."

---

* Peter Hopkirk, *The Great Game: The Struggle for Empire in Central Asia* (New York: Kodansha International, 1992), pp. 321–38.

Brave King and I wandered from the animal market area to the food market area nearby. Tangles of meat sat on donkey carts covered by towels in turn covered by flies. The meat-sellers removed the towels to show the quality of their product underneath and gestured at us to buy some of it. There were enamel basins of severed lambs' heads, basins of lambs' feet, basins of tripe. Nearby, soup was being cooked in large iron cauldrons set over brick fireplaces. Chunks of meat were being roasted on skewers placed over charcoal braziers. I overheard an American tourist in a plaid flannel shirt talking to a local guide.

"I tell you what," he said. "You eat as much of this lamb head as you want." (Urged on by Brave King, I had tried it at the night market in Hami and suffered diarrhea all the next day.) "But for me, you find me a live lamb. I want to watch as they cut its throat and let it bleed to death. I want to see them carve it up and make a nice rack of lamb out of it. I want them to keep the flies off it and to have it on the fire within fifteen minutes. *Then* I'll eat it."

KASHGAR WAS under construction. Narrow lanes were being torn up and replaced by broad, straight avenues with names like West People's Road, a name that has few associations with the Uigur culture. West People's Road intersects with Liberation Road, wider than the Champs Elysées. Nearby we saw an Internet club, a shallow storefront lined with computers glowing with Windows and Yahoo.com. Much of this is the product of simple modernization, not a Chinese imposition. There is no reason why Uigurs should do without the Internet. But so much of the atmosphere of Kashgar has resulted from pure Sinification: the broad, arrow-straight avenues to the "National Defense" bases guarded by People's Liberation Army soldiers standing at attention, their bayonets fixed; the socialist-Bauhaus architecture; the office of the party committee; the cement rectangles where the Chinese immigrants live.

During my long weekend in Kashgar, television reports continued the propaganda campaign about the American bombing of the Chinese embassy in Belgrade. Factory workers, soldiers, students, and small entrepreneurs stood in front of the camera and declaimed their anger at the United States, their support of the Communist Party, and their vow to work even harder to make China stronger. That was the national news. Then came the local Xinjiang news: workers, farmers, students, and small entrepreneurs shown in front of the camera expressing their anger, pledging their support, vowing to work harder, and all the rest. The message to the Uigur and other non-Chinese inhabitants of the Xinjiang Uigur Autonomous Region was that in moments of crisis they belonged to the national effort. The message was: You can do what you want. You can go to the mosque; you can teach your children Uigur in school; you can study Arabic and bow to Mecca five times a day; you can get rich in private enterprise; if you are Uigur or Kyrgyz or Tajik, you can have two children in the city and three in the countryside (if you are Chinese, wherever you are, you can have only one child). Just don't mess in politics; don't complain that there's not enough autonomy, or about the growing number of Chinese settlers in your midst; above all, don't even think about independence, and be patriotic when we ask you to be.

The message was important because in the past several years there have been a small number of terrorist incidents in Xinjiang, especially in Urumqi but in Kashgar also, engineered by Muslims demanding independence. This is the reason the entire autonomous region had been declared off limits to foreign journalists. The Chinese understand that foreign reporting on explosions in public buses and in market squares will engender more such explosions, since among the gods of the independence forces is international publicity. The foreign press would also report on Chinese counterterrorism measures, like torture, imprisonment without trial, summary executions. The overall result would be another headache for Beijing, which is bothered enough already by human rights groups complaining about unjust imprisonment in China and the treatment of Tibetans. Allowing the news to be reported from Xinjiang would discourage tourism and foreign investment. So Beijing bans the foreign press. As far as I know, I was the first foreign journalist in Kashgar in several years, but my purpose was not to try to ferret out independence activists by asking questions at the mosque.

Brave King told me that when his Turkish camel drivers arrived in Kashgar they managed, without his knowledge, to interview the brother of an outspoken Uigur nationalist who lived in Turkey. Several months later, the interview was aired on Turkish television, and then Brave King, as the Turks' official guide, was called into the Public Security Bureau for questioning. They suspected him of having helped the Turks get in touch with the independence advocate's brother.

"I tell them," Brave King told me, "I didn't do it. I know nothing. I don't know how they find this guy. I never see them. I not with all of them every minute. I keep diary. I put everything in diary. The Public Security reads diary. There is nothing about this guy in diary. I never meet him. I don't know him. I spend one month talking with policemen. Finally they believe me."

"What happened to the brother?"

"Oh, he must be in jail," said Brave King. "Or maybe he is dead."

There were no signs of dissent among the Uigurs or anybody else while I was in Xinjiang, but when I got home I read in the *New York Times* about one Rebiya Kadeer, a fifty-three-year-old woman from Urumqi. Her husband lived in Oklahoma City, and from there, speaking on Radio Free Asia, he had supported Uigur nationalism and criticized Chinese government policy in Xinjiang. Ms. Kadeer played no role in her husband's political activities. Still, in the fall of 1999, she was invited to have dinner with some visiting American congressional staffers. On her way to the dinner, she was arrested, and she has not been seen since. In March 2000, according to members of her family, she was put on trial and sentenced to eight years in prison.

On Monday, Brave King, Luyik, and I got in a jeep and set off for the border. Farmland surrounds Kashgar for several miles, the fields radiating outward from the city center in an irregular green circle. The roads are lined by tall stands of white poplar whose leaves flash like silver coins in the breeze. Suburban villages are surrounded by high mud walls. Tractor carts pounded along the side of the road. Bullocks waved their heads in that mazy motion of theirs, heavy heads sweeping low over the ground. People stared as the jeep went by.

Beyond the oasis was a terrain of ridges and dry gullies. Snowy mountains gleamed in the sunlight—the Tianshan in the north, the Pamirs in the south. The terrain here is similar to that farther east where the monk would have crossed. He is laconic in his description of the first of several difficult mountain crossings on his long journey. But for him, from just west of Aksu all the way to Samarkand in present-day Uzbekistan, he would have faced one forbidding range after the other, a distance of about twelve hundred miles, most of it on foot carrying the heavy overhanging backpack that is pictured on the famous Xian stele.

"Crossing a stony desert, we come to the Ice Mountain," the monk writes after setting off from Aksu. "Both hills and valleys are filled with snowpiles, and it freezes in both spring and summer; if it should thaw for a time, the ice soon forms again. The roads are steep and dangerous, the cold wind is extremely biting, and frequently fierce dragons impede and molest travelers with their inflictions." The monk offers some odd rules of the high road: "Those who travel there should not wear red garments nor carry loud-sounding calabashes. The least forgetfulness of these precautions entails certain misfortune. A violent wind suddenly rises with storms of flying sand and gravel; those who encounter them, sinking through exhaustion, are almost sure to die."

Exactly how red clothes and noisy calabashes could cause such misfortunes, we do not know. Beal speculates that the monk may have believed that the color red might have angered the dragons that caused these storms of flying sand and gravel. Calabashes are gourds used for carrying water. Maybe when they froze and burst they made a loud noise, like the report of a rifle, and that might have been thought to cause avalanches among the "snowpiles." We must accept this as a mystery. In his *Chronicles,* the monk does not speak of the suffering his party experienced crossing the Tianshan Mountains, but he spoke of it to Hui Li, who goes into some detail: The monk and his escort spent seven days in the Tianshan, where they endured fantastic hardship. "Twelve or fourteen of the company were starved and frozen to death." Larger numbers of oxen and horses were lost. The monk, who came from the North China Plain, speaks with awe of the height of the mountains, but he does not enjoy their beauty. He complains that they are "steep and dangerous." "The frozen glaciers reach to the sky and mingle with the clouds, making a spectacle so bright that one cannot gaze at it for more than an instant. Great slabs of ice lie athwart the road." Moreover, "the wind and the snow driven in confused masses make it difficult to escape an icy coldness of body though wrapped in heavy folds of fur-lined garments. When one is desirous of food or sleep, there is no dry place to be found for a halt; the only way is to hang the pot for cooking, and to spread the mat on the ice for sleeping."

There were other dangers. One night, the monk's party slept alongside a stream where they had met some foreign merchants who, "coveting an early sale of their merchandise, privately went forward in the middle of the night. Scarcely had they gone ten li when they met a band of robbers who murdered every one of them. And so, when the Master of the Law and the others came to the place, they found their dead bodies there, but all their riches gone." They passed on, "deeply affected with the sight." Eventually, the monk arrived at what he calls the Great Qing Lake, *qing* being the Chinese word for "blue" or "clear." The lake is the Issyk Kul, in what is now northern Kyrgyzstan. Here, finally, he was geographically and culturally beyond the range of all Chinese influence, in a place where Chinese power had never been and would never extend. His host was a man he calls "the great Khan of the Turks." He wore a green satin robe and his loose hair was bound up with a long silk ribbon. The khan was surrounded by troops "all clothed in furs and fine-spun garments; they carried lances and bows and standards and were mounted on camels and horses. The eye could not match their number." The monk, in other words, had, after about 2,800 miles of arduous travel, reached "the West."

WE PASSED a police checkpoint about twenty miles outside of Kashgar and were almost turned back there when it turned out that our driver hadn't paid his automobile tax. There was a long discussion, which I watched from the car, Luyik and the driver shuffling through papers, the policeman looking at them. The policeman had the English word "CHECK" in large letters emblazoned on the back of his uniform. Nearby, a stand of white poplars rustled in the warm breeze. Finally, Brave King got out of the car and pleaded with the policeman, asking to be let through on the grounds that we were being met at the border and our plans would go awry if the driver was forced to turn back to Kashgar. The policeman relented.

A half hour farther, through a harsh terrain of sandstone gullies and cliffs, we came to the Chinese customs station. The propaganda sign in Chinese characters read: "Strengthen the Border; Strengthen National Defense." The South African at John's Café had told me that I couldn't go through here, and, while I knew I could, I expected the official Chinese establishment to be in some windblown forlorn place suggestive of rugged inaccessibility and remoteness. It is windblown and forlorn, but how remote it was can be suggested by the presence just ahead of me of a tour group of retired Americans, mostly from Florida. There were about fifteen of them, exhibiting that cheery affability of Americans, which contrasted with the grim officiousness of the three officials who were laboriously strengthening the border by giving the Americans' passports and visas long and meticulous examinations, lasting perhaps five minutes each. You never know when some retired schoolteacher from Fort Lauderdale on an organized prepaid tour might threaten the national defense by leaving China on a visa with his middle initial given incorrectly. But finally the senior citizens passed on and it was my turn to hand my passport and my permit to cross the Torugart Pass through the open window and into the wooden box where the immigration officials sat.

The first passport-checker looked at it and handed it to the second passport-checker, muttering something that I couldn't hear.

"Where did you get your visa?" the second one asked. The tone was decidedly suspicious. I pretended not to understand and waited for Luyik to translate.

"In Hong Kong," I answered.

This border control officer was young and intense. I could just imagine the hours of political study he had sat through in one of those bureaus in China where the local party secretary holds sway. He was well schooled in the depredations that the imperialist powers had visited upon his country. He had been among those to rise and take a stand against the most recent such depredation, the American bombing of the Chinese embassy in Belgrade. He looked at the visa stamp for a long time. Several times he leafed through the entire passport inspecting my onward visas to Kyrgyzstan, Uzbekistan, Pakistan, and India. He scrutinized the passport picture, all the while glancing up at me as if comparing my face with my picture feature by feature.

"There's no duration of stay indicated on this visa," he said. "How long did they say you could stay in China?"

Again I waited for Luyik's translation.

"I think they told me thirty days," I said.

He took another long look at the visa and then at the Torugart permit. My mouth went a bit dry. The problem with the Hong Kong travel agency visas is that they don't look exactly like the visas issued in consulates or other normal visa-issuing agencies. They don't, for example, have a duration of stay. Surely passport control officers know that people get visas from Hong Kong travel agents because they might have trouble getting them elsewhere—or do they?

"You came to China on April 27," the visa officer said.

"Yes."

"You have thirty days."

"Yes, I think so."

"The date on your Torugart permit is June 1," he said.

"Yes, I suppose it is."

The young soldier pierced me with a schoolmarmish stare. "How many days are there between April 27 and June 1?"

"Thirty-three," I said.

"And your visa is for thirty days," the soldier said.

I understood. He felt that by getting a permit to go through the Torugart Pass on June 1, I had shown an intent to overstay my visa. Again, speaking through Luyik, I tried to explain: When I had asked for the permit several months before, I hadn't known exactly when I would be getting to China or exactly when I would be leaving, so June 1 was kind of a guess. I had had no intention of staying longer than thirty days in China, and since today was only May 18, I hadn't.

"Your permit is for June 1, not May 18."

"Aha," I said. "But the permit means I can cross the border any day up to June 1. It doesn't mean I have to cross exactly on June 1, does it?"

Apparently it did. Brave King, who had nothing to do with any of this, who had only accompanied me here as a gesture of friendship, began to speak through the window. It was a misunderstanding, he said, smiling ingratiatingly. I had never seen him so deferential. I stood quietly, studiously nonchalant. Brave King kept on talking in respectful tones. He knew what he was doing. The passport control officers decamped en masse for a backroom. After about five minutes, the young man who had done the talking came back and took his elevated seat. Scowling at me, he seized his chop, pressed it into his inkpad, and pounded it with a loud report onto the appropriate page of my passport. Then he waved me forward.

IT WAS ANOTHER hour in the jeep past the sprawling customs yard and up a winding road to the border itself. A soldier in a green camouflage uniform carrying an AK-47 assault rifle checked my passport midway into a broad pebbly plateau. Patches of dirty snow lined the road, mirroring cleaner patches of cloud hanging in the pale blue sky. Brown overgrazed hills stretched out on either side. The late-afternoon sun bore down powerfully and tussled with a chill wind that blew up from the other side of the border. We passed on to the border itself, where a few more soldiers in camouflage stood alongside a high arched gate to the left of which the red flag of China stood out stiffly in the wind.

A border guard got into the jeep at the checkpoint and rode with us to within one hundred or so yards of the gate. A couple of trucks could be seen squeezing through it and then heading our way. I asked if I could take a picture, and the guard said no. Then Brave King, putting on his you're-the-boss demeanor, reasoned with him. "This foreign guest has come a long way to be here and he wants to just take one picture for his memory." The soldier relented. He actually smiled. Brave King got out of the jeep while I took a shot of the border gate. Then Luyik took a picture of the two of us. We said goodbye, vowing to meet each other again when I returned to Beijing. We embraced. I shouldered my bag and my computer and labored the last few meters to the gate, and stepped through it.

9

Genghis Khan's Ancestors

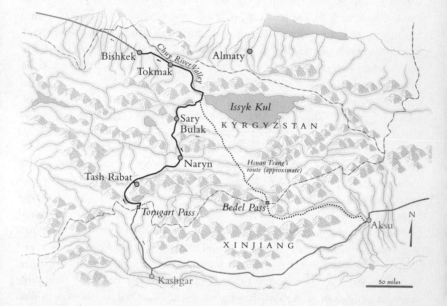

Sasha, dispatched by Dostuck Trekking, as Luyik had promised, was waiting at the other side of the gate, along with Andrei, the driver. "Sit down," Sasha said, and pointed to a muddy Land Rover marked "Bristol, England." Sasha had a round face, blue eyes, and a small blond mustache. The Land Rover was pulled off the side of the road just down a brief grade from the China–Kyrgyzstan border marker.

"Nice car," I said.

"Fifteen years old," Sasha said with a shrug, and we were off, bumping down a dirt track to the Kyrgyz Republic customs and immigration center. This was a cluster of desolate cement buildings with a watchtower and barbed wire, leftovers from what Sasha called "the broke Soviet Union," by which he meant the "broken-up" Soviet Union. Sasha was immediately likable and friendly, and he tried hard. His English was also far better than my Russian, so I wasn't complaining, but it did have a tendency to slide midway through a sentence into a swampy terrain of guess-at-able-only phonemes.

The barbed wire stretched as far as the eye could see along a dirt path parallel to the mountains, parallel to the border with China. In one of his books, the Polish journalist Ryszard Kapuscinski makes sense of the borderland barbed wire of the old Soviet Union. "You will not escape here; you will not get away," is its message. You are in a world of "deadly seriousness, orders, and obedience."* In fact, Kyrgyzstan is known as the most democratic of the former Soviet Central Asian republics. Customs and immigration were tedious and cumbersome, and the formalities took place in a series of rooms that would make Alcatraz seem cozy, but there was a certain relaxed quality to it that contrasted with the more recently experienced Chinese touchiness and suspiciousness.

For me the striking thing about this border was not that there was barbed wire, but that we were four thousand miles from Moscow and three thousand from Beijing, and the languages spoken on either side of this border in the mountains were Russian and Chinese. The distances illustrate the extent of the Russian and Chinese zones, which, despite the disintegration of the Soviet Union, were still pressed tightly against each other here, scratching their backs on that perfect emblem of twentieth-century totalitarianism, barbed wire. When a man named Wang handed me over to a man named Sasha, it seemed as though both the Chinese and the Russian were demonstrating the achievement of a kind of manifest destiny. Both had spread their names and their zones of control to the point where there was simply no room to spread any more. In so doing, they had engulfed dozens of other peoples, the Kyrgyz included, but also Uigurs, Kazaks, Tajiks, Mongols, and others who still live on either side of the great Sino-Russian divide. It wasn't always like that. When Hsuan Tsang crossed into what is now Kyrgyzstan, he entered into the great domain of the Mongol-Turks, an already powerful nomadic people who were later to give the world such conquerors as Genghis Khan, Tamerlane, and Babur, a direct descendant of Tamerlane who was the first of the Mogul kings of India. But for now, Russia and China are like sumo wrestlers standing gut to gut in a small circle with very little place to push each other.

We waited an hour and a half behind a checkpoint at customs because we arrived just before two in the afternoon and lunchtime is one to three at the Kyrgyz border. While we waited, a soldier in camouflage with an

* Ryszard Kapuscinski, *Imperium* (New York: Vintage Books, 1995), p. 46.

AK-47 assault rifle slung over his shoulder sauntered out through the gate and began climbing the grassy hill opposite us.

"What's he doing?" I asked Sasha, wondering if we were about to witness a cross-border excursion by a Kyrgyz guerrilla.

"Maybe hunt marmot," Sasha said. We had seen a marmot lumbering across the tundra as we drove down from the border. It looked like a cross between a woodchuck and a prairie dog. "Kyrgyz national dish," Sasha said, and he and Andrei burst into laughter.

Sure enough, the soldier lay down on his belly and began crawling forward. Then, propped on his elbow in an infantryman's firing position, he raised the AK-47 and tattered the earth opposite him with bullets. He scrambled up and advanced forward, but when he got to the place where the enemy should have been lying dead, no marmot was there.

"Ran into hole," Sasha commented. "Too bad; him without lunch." He and Andrei roared with laughter again.

Meanwhile, Sasha got down to business. He took out a well-worn Russian map of Kyrgyzstan and began showing me the various routes of the Silk Road across the border from China. "One branch such named northern route begin Bedel Pass," he said. That was the one that the monk took but was now closed. "Nothing there," Sasha said. "No road." Then there was the route from the Torugart Pass north to Naryn and then to the Chuy River Valley and Bishkek. That was the route we were going to take, with an overnight stopover at an old stone caravansary that was used by merchant caravans a century ago. Sasha's finger traced yet a third route:

"Another branch such named south direction go from Torugart Pass, then descend to valley of Arpa River, then go to Fergana mountain range and to Osh." Sasha gave me the names of the major mountain ranges in Kyrgyzstan, the height of Victoria Peak, the country's highest mountain (something over 24,000 feet), and the depth of the permafrost in the Torugart range, where we were. Finally, we were off through the border checkpoint down a gravel road inside the barbed wire and through a valley that was abundant with marmots, clusters of horses, and the occasional motheaten camel. We drove for an hour before turning off the road, crossing a shallow stream, and ascending a parallel valley. Fifteen kilometers later we were at Tash Rabat—"Means 'Stone Town,' " said Sasha. There was the old stone caravansary along with a small white house, two Kyrgyz yurts, many shaggy yaks, and a valley of breathtaking beauty and grandeur running up to a snow-covered ridge.

I took a long walk up the valley floor, wary of the yaks, which, though very large, were wary of me. My feet crunched on the dry grass, making a sound like eggshells breaking. Jackdaws wheeled overhead. A marmot, on hind legs in front of his hole, startled me when it screeched a warning. The yaks looked on, curious that I was so jumpy. I saw some horses farther up the side of the valley and headed for them. That brought me over the rise behind the caravansary, and I sat down for a while to survey the scene. To the east, the valley rose up through a steep gorge to a high, snow-covered bluff. Behind me the horses, whose legs were tethered, whinnied as if apprehensive about something. The earth was cold and the breeze carried with it the breath of the eternal frost. I had a woolen shirt on over a T-shirt and a cotton shirt, and I was wearing a light jacket that I had bought in the department store in Xian (Yalu Fashion, it was called), all of which would be only barely adequate for what promised to be my sole cold night of the trip. On either side of me darkening mountains rose up to block out one-third of the sky. I could see Venus over the one in front, Mars behind. Directly below was the caravansary and beyond that the two yurts of my Kyrgyz hosts and their little wooden house.

The man of the house, and the owner of the yaks and the horses and of a bright red Russian motorcycle, was Jergalbek. When we arrived he greeted me warmly, taking both of my hands in his. He spoke Russian with Sasha and Andrei and Kyrgyz with his wife, whose name was Torsun, and they had a small daughter of six or seven who, after a period of shyness, began to flirt with me and by evening's end had fallen into my arms. Jergalbek had a fine, narrow, wizened face and a mustache. He wore a heavy green coat and black trousers and the soft, conical hat of the Kyrgyz mountain people. Torsun was ruddy and round and wore a forest-green dress with a flowered apron and embroidered slippers. Nothing was explained to me, but it was clear that Sasha had an arrangement to bring here the occasional foreign visitor looking for a scenic stopover on the route from the Chinese border to Bishkek. Only I would sleep in the yurt. It was a kind of initiation. All the others had done it already, and, that being the case, they were going to sleep in the house, where the coal-burning stove would keep them nice and warm.

While Sasha made dinner and Andrei tended to the Land Rover, I sat alone in the modest living room of what was a kind of bed-and-breakfast in the At-Bashy Range. On the wall was a picture of Jergalbek and Torsun, taken, I surmised, on their wedding day. Jergalbek in particular showed a touch of foppishness on this putative wedding day, his hair combed at a rakish slant over his forehead. Another photograph showed him in a naval uniform. There is probably no place on earth farther from the sea than Tash Rabat. I wondered how he had gotten from the sea to here, or, more likely, from here to the sea and back again. Then again, Iowa is also far from the ocean, but no doubt there are Iowans in the United States Navy.

We ate macaroni and drank three shot glasses of vodka each. It grew dark. I went outside and looked at the sky. Venus was still glowing on the one side of the valley, Mars on the other. The mountains were hulking shadows. The air was still and cold. I saw the Big Dipper, which seemed to salute me from some familiar place, and thought of the last lines of a Chinese poem known to every Chinese schoolchild: "I raise my head and look at the light of the moon; I lower my head and think of my native land."

THE MONK DIDN'T go through this valley, but he must have spent many nights in some similar valleys as he trekked across what is now Kyrgyzstan. The poem about looking at the moon hadn't been written yet— it was composed by the great Tang Dynasty poet Li Bo a century or so later, and expresses the poignant dilemma faced by the Chinese magistrate sent to administer a faraway country, the man torn between duty and the warmth of home. The Chinese are very sentimental about home. They are always writing about the moon and the faraway loved ones who might at that moment be looking at it. "Tonight when the moon is over Fuzhou/ She will be watching all alone in her room" are the first two lines of a poem by Du Fu, another of the immortal Tang versifiers. Historically, until recent decades, the Chinese didn't show an exploratory spirit; they didn't bother to climb Mount Everest because it was there, or participate in races to be the first to reach the South Pole. They didn't bother, as did Burton and Speke and the Royal Geographical Society, about the source of the Nile, or even of the Yangtze. When they left home, it was almost always out of economic necessity, as it was for the thousands who came from Tayshan County in Guangdong Province to build the American transcontinental railway.

There is a Talmudic expression: The wise man is he who is contented with his lot. It applies well to China but not to the West (and not to the Jews), which has been guided by a kind of creative discontent, a yearning to see what lies beyond the horizon and to be the first to get there. I am in the latter tradition, or else I wouldn't have found myself sleeping in a yurt in Tash Rabat, but, like Du Fu, I look at the moon and think of those back home looking at the same moon, a touch melancholy but not sorry to be where I am. In fact, the issue is not distance from home, but alone-ness, the belief that with distance comes separation. I remember years ago someone telling me about how he had always yearned to see Victoria Falls. Finally, on a business trip to southern Africa, he had a chance to go, but he was by himself. "And there I was," he told me, "looking at the falls and thinking, so what? What's the point of being here alone?" Years later, I went to Victoria Falls also. I was on my way back to Paris from a tempo-rary assignment for the *Times* in Mozambique, and a stop at Victoria Falls was easy. I arrived late in the morning and had lunch on the breathtaking balcony of the Victoria Falls Hotel, all colonial elegance and gentility. I noted a family at the next table, parents and children, and they seemed to be having a good time. What I imagined observing them was that they didn't have to think of their native land because they had one another— they were their own native land. Whereas I, drifting alone, having spent two weeks at an old Portuguese hotel in Maputo, eating my meals by myself on a terrace overlooking the Indian Ocean, was stripped to the solitary essentials. I went to Victoria Falls out of a kind of duty, for my geographical education, and as I watched it thunder gloriously before me, my main thought was about coming back sometime with a companion.

I wondered, as I huddled in my sleeping bag at Tash Rabat, about Hsuan Tsang. Did he long for his native land as he made his slow progress through the high valleys of Kyrgyzstan? Or did his Buddhist discipline steel him against useless sentiments? The monk almost never speaks of emotions (we will see the one major exception in India). He was not a poet. In fact, he was an ideologue on a mission to rescue humankind from falsehood and perplexity. My sense is that he was too much of a fanatic to think about the moon and who back home might be looking at it. I sense that he saw his trip as too important for him to allow loneliness to be a factor.

In fact, Hsuan Tsang says very little of his visit to the mountainous regions of the Road of Great Events, the stretch of territory between the Middle Kingdom and the Hindustani cradle of spiritual wisdom. From the Bedel Pass, which crosses the present Chinese-Kyrgyz border at about thirteen thousand feet, he would have had to go over the Borkoldoy Range, then the Yetin-Bel Range to the Barskoon Pass, from which he would have descended to the Issyk Kul—a long and very rough walk. His visit to the Great Khan, which probably took place in or near the current city of Tokmak in the Chuy River Valley, was a drunken revelry. "The Turks worship fire," the monk told Hui Li. In other words, they were

Zoroastrians, like the Parsees of India today, though they converted to Islam not long after the monk's visit. "They do not use wooden seats, because wood contains fire, and so even in worship they never seat themselves, but only spread padded mats on the ground and so go through with it," Hui Li writes, that phrase "and so go through with it" showing a subtle contempt. Hsuan Tsang, it should be remembered, was still traveling with his escort from Gaochang, who presented their letters of introduction and their gifts to the khan. But when the feast began, the pilgrim was impressed. The banquet tent, he says, was so ornamented that the "eye was blinded with its glitter." The khan's officers, dressed in embroidered silk, sat in front on a long mat. The khan's bodyguard was behind them. "Although he was but the ruler of a wandering horde," Hui Li writes, the contempt for the barbarian peeking through the prose, "yet there was a certain dignified arrangement about his surroundings."

In fact, the Great Khan, who is called "Tung" in the Chinese sources, was a powerful monarch whose sway extended between Persia in the west and China in the east. Hsuan Tsang seems unaware of this, but a century before, these western Turks (who centuries later migrated to the land now known as Turkey) had defeated the Huns and engineered a network of commercial alliances that went all the way to Byzantium. "He was magnificent in battle and attack," says the *Tang Shu,* the official Tang Dynasty history. His troops, according to our pilgrim, carried long lances, banners, and bows and they "stretched for so far that the eye could not tell where they ended." Tokmak was the summer residence of the khan, but his capital was at Chash, the modern Tashkent. He wanted good relations with China, and, in the time-honored tradition of paying tribute to the Son of Heaven, he sent Tai Tsung, the Tang Dynasty emperor, a belt of pure gold studded with ten thousand precious stones. He asked in return for that ultimate gift for a barbarian chieftain, a Chinese princess, but there is no evidence that Tai Tsung presented him with one.

René Grousset, helpful as always for an understanding of the political context of Hsuan Tsang's journey, speaks of the time of his visit to Tokmak as a kind of quiet before the storm. Not long afterward, much was to change. In Persia, the Sassanian Empire was about to be forcibly converted to Islam. The Tokharian kingdoms of the Tarim Basin, including Kucha, were to be crushed by Tai Tsung and thereafter left open to the invasion of the Uigurs, still today the majority population between Urumqi and Kashgar. And the great banquet in Tokmak witnessed by Hsuan Tsang "was the final gathering of all the Turks on their native soil before the banners went their separate ways to meet their various destinies and weave their various epics."* The Turks would make their mark on universal history in many other ways, through the Seljuks and the Ottomans, the hordes of Mahmud of Ghazni, who conquered India, and the armies of Tamerlane. Right there on the plain of Tokmak in the year 1207, Temeudjin defeated his rival Gutchluk and became the undisputed leader of the Mongols, later giving himself the name Genghis Khan.† What Hui Li disdained as but a wandering horde was the predecessor for several of the greatest empires in history.

Still, whatever he thought of his hosts, he seems to have had a good time. "They filled their cups and emptied them in succession," Hui Li says of the Turkish legions, "ever more animated, during all of which time, the sounds of all kinds of music resounded in a confused clang. And although the character of the music was the common sort of the barbarians, yet it was nevertheless very diverting to both the ear and the eye, pleasing the thoughts and the mind." The dinner was heaps of boiled mutton and veal, which the monk could not eat, so they specially prepared for him rice cakes and cream, barley sticks and raisins. When it was all over, Hui Li reports, the khan was overjoyed at having been blessed by the teachings of the monk, and he begged him to stay.

"You have no need to go to India; that country is very hot," he told his guest. And not only hot. "The men there," the Great Khan declared, "are naked blacks without any sense of decorum and not fit to look at."

Obviously, the khan did not know his monk.

"Notwithstanding all this," Hsuan Tsang replied, "I desire to go and gaze on the sacred traces and earnestly to search for the Law."

"IN THE FOREST inhabits wild boar and sometimes you can rarely see brown bear and you can see very rarely snow leopard. I have seen one time snow leopard. So wonderful. Also here inhabits ibex, wolf, fox, hare."

We were leaving Tash Rabat, and Sasha was filling me in on the Kyrgyz fauna. We drove over the At-Bashy Range and then down the other side on a switchback road that Andrei took at terrifying speed. Back in the valley, we passed mud-hut settlements surrounded by grazing yaks,

---

* Grousset, *In the Footsteps of the Buddha*, p. 67.

† Ahmed Rashid, *The Resurgence of Central Asia: Islam or Nationalism?* (Karachi: Oxford University Press, 1994), p. 139.

horses, and occasional camels. Ancient railroad cars, with their iron side ladders still attached but their wheels replaced by rubber tires, seemed the most common habitation—even though there wasn't an actual railroad within two hundred miles.

"When was building in Siberia everywhere was such house," Sasha said. I think he was talking of his childhood, which he had told me he spent in northern Siberia, explaining that recycled railway cars were common in the old Soviet Union. "Since on wheels can transportation everywhere. Usually you see in summer pasture. It is more cheaper than yurt."

I asked Sasha how the Kyrgyz nomads got the railway cars over the mountains to their summer pastures, but he didn't understand the question.

"By the way," said Sasha, "white yurt is rich person's yurt; gray yurt is poor person's yurt."

We entered our first large town, on the edge of which was a large Muslim cemetery, a hillside crowded with stone mausoleums, triumphal and ugly. And then we encountered a funeral procession. First there was a truck carrying the coffin and a few men, one of whom held aloft a large black-and-white photograph of the deceased. Then there were perhaps two hundred men on horseback, all of them wearing identical conical hats. The horseback procession was followed by what seemed like every car in the town, mostly Soviet-era standard-model Lada 1800s, straw-yellow Ladas, Ladas of red-flag red, donkey brown, grassland green, high-altitude mountain blue, all of them with exaggeratedly wide grilles, like men pulling their lips apart at the corners of their mouths. We stopped for *kumyz* along the side of the road. "Kyrgyz national drink," Sasha said, and he and Andrei laughed again. *Kumyz* is fermented mare's milk, sour, poured out of cured sheepskins and drunk from Chinese-made porcelain rice bowls, perhaps imported over the Torugart Pass.

On we drove, the Land Rover roaring and vibrating on the lumpy road. We followed one river valley after another. Always, it seemed, there was a man alone riding a horse, a boy or two waving a fish at us from alongside the stream, magpies streaking over the road just ahead of the Land Rover, a single green Lada coming from the other direction and in the middle of the road, and a stout woman in a blue jacket worn over a flowered dress, holding her hand out for a car to stop.

"Lenin," said Sasha, and he pointed to the top of a bluff where I could see a strange sculpture of what Sasha described as "our former leader," a kind of black metal framework, like a photographic negative, through whose open spaces could be seen the sky and the clouds.

"Any of Stalin?" I asked.

"What?"

"Are there any statues of Stalin?"

"It's a pity, but no."

"Why is it a pity?"

"Is joke," Sasha said.

We drove on.

"But old people say life better in Stalin period," said Sasha abruptly. "Also they believe he won Second Great War."

We came over the crest of a hill and a vast panorama of snowcapped mountains lay before us to the north, jagged and iridescent and as though suspended from the sky rather than rising from the earth.

"Tianshan Mountains are divided in such parts," said Sasha. "Eastern part located in western part of China and small part located in Kazakhstan. Northern range divided into Kirghiz Alatol, Kyungey Alatol, mostly in Kazakhstan; Central Tianshan include Terskey Alatol, Borkoldoy Alatol, and many others."

We came to Sary Bulak—Kyrgyz for "Yellow Spring"—where we had very sour yogurt and very good fried local fish in a railroad car converted to a restaurant. From Sary Bulak the road sundered a broad agricultural valley into two equal halves, then went up another gradient. When we emerged over the top at a place called Kok-Moynok Bik, we were in the river valley that would lead us all the way to Bishkek.

"Welcome to Chuy River Valley," Sasha announced, "where once existed Great Silk Road, the wellspring of culture of Central Asia."

"Thank you," I said. "It's good to be here."

We went through rich farmland. Tokmak, where the pilgrim had met the khan, whizzed by, a group of institutional buildings lining the road, and in the late afternoon we arrived in Bishkek, capital of the Kyrgyz Republic. I stayed in the Hotel Bishkek, a gloomy, sullen, Soviet-style place where your presence, which came, in my case, with demands for a towel, some soap, and toilet paper, seemed to be a mighty annoyance to the employees. But there was hot water for a shower. I roamed the streets and found a small market where fresh vegetables, drinks, and ice cream were being sold. I dined on roast chicken and salad at a restaurant called Kafe Altyn Kush on Soviet Street. On the way back to the hotel, I passed the small market again and bought some ice cream on a stick and was eating it when a young blond boy tugged at my shirtsleeve and begged me to give it to him, which I did. He dashed off without a word, as if afraid I would ask for it back, and devoured it under a streetlamp. I wandered the dark, quiet, leafy streets and found an outdoor beer garden where two American lawyers and a retired British civil servant, all of them volunteer legal advisers to the Kyrgyz government, were talking.

"This is the most democratic country in Central Asia," one of the three, named Howard, was saying. "It's the one that has most eagerly adopted the Western way of doing things, and the one where it has failed most completely to work. The economy is in a state of collapse. Corruption is a major problem. There's a Canadian gold-mining company that paid the government eighteen million in permit fees last year, and the money has yet to turn up on the government's books. It went directly into the pockets of officialdom. This is not like the Soviet Union. This is corruption without murder. They haven't had an assassination. These are not mean people. It's just that there's no economy. There's no market here. They don't produce anything. This was always a taker country. The Soviets used to pour billions of rubles into this place. It always ran a deficit. Now they get the money from the IMF and Western donors like us. That's why they're democratic. So the money will keep flowing in."

When I got back to the hotel, which was just a block from the café, a small, sad old woman at the entrance offered to sell me a Russian newspaper. I looked into my wallet and pulled out a five-som bill and gave it to her. I was unused to the currency and I thought that five was a meaningful amount. The old woman took the bill and looked at it as though she could not quite believe her good fortune. I went to my dreary room, for which I was paying seventy-five dollars, and realized that I had very generously given the woman the equivalent of eleven cents.

10

The Bridge Nobody Crosses

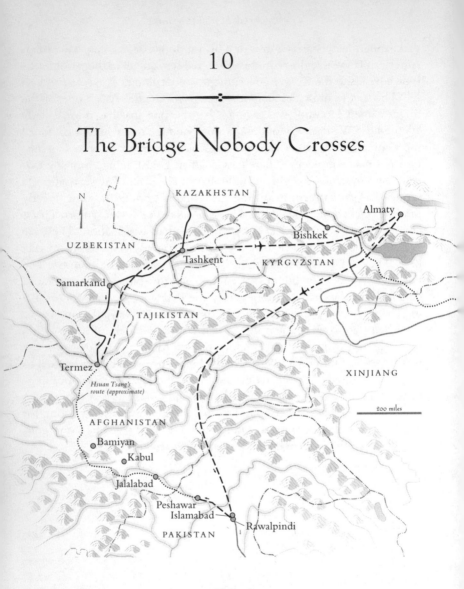

R OADS THAT ALL were once within the same vast country now cross
international borders in the Central Asian republics that have fallen
like fruit from the former tree of the Soviet Union. I had planned to take
the overnight train from Bishkek to Tashkent, the capital of neighboring
Uzbekistan, but the trains were canceled. So said Vika, the beautiful,
unsmiling Russian woman at Dostuck Trekking who handled my dossier
when we arrived from the Chinese border.

I seemed to be the only customer, even though Kyrgyzstan offers fantastic possibilities for trekking, mountain climbing, whitewater rafting, and other outdoor activities. But the country is hapless, out of kilter; it is fumbling, and the reigning business philosophy is to get a lot of money out of a small number of clients (or, in my case, a single client) rather than smaller amounts of money from a large number of clients.

I asked Vika why there were no trains. She looked at me as if I had asked her for intimate details of her personal life (which actually I was curious to know, though I didn't ask) and told me the reason. The Kyrgyzes owed money to the Kazakhs for the use of the railroad tracks that went through Kazakhstan on the way to Tashkent, so in order to pressure the Kyrgyzes into paying, the Kazakhs had blocked the trains. The bus, which also follows a route that goes through Kazakh territory, was the only economical overland alternative. In fact, the bus ticket for the 350-mile, twelve-hour trip was five dollars, cheap for me, though perhaps not a small amount of money in a country where the average retirement pension is fifteen dollars a month.

"Bus is six o'clock," Vika informed me.

"Six a.m.?"

"No, is night bus."

"There's no bus that goes during the day?" I asked.

"No, only night bus." She was silent, gazing at me, an impediment to her happiness. It wasn't that she was unfriendly, I realized. She was nervous. She had large brown eyes and pellucid skin, but no gift for repartee. "We can get ticket for you and take you to bus station."

"Great. Thank you."

"Cost is twenty United States dollars, plus price for ticket."

"Twenty? How far is the bus station?"

"Is far."

"Okay," I agreed.

Dostuck Trekking was in a pleasantly modern office down an unpaved alley that no taxi driver in the Kyrgyz Republic seemed able to find. "Show him card," said Vika. I did show the card she had given me, which had a calendar on it and the Dostuck Trekking address in English and Russian. But still the taxi drivers would search for it in vain and then search for a telephone to call and ask for directions. That is how I got to see the university and the museum and the presidential palace and the parliament building, vast edifices surrounded by even vaster esplanades of cement. Late on my second afternoon in Bishkek, somber Vika and another employee of Dostuck Trekking picked me up at the hotel and took me to the bus station.

"Here is National Library," Vika said as we drove through Bishkek. "Used to be Lenin Library." There was sadness in her voice, but I didn't think it had to do with Lenin. "Here is Frunze Museum." Mikhail Frunze was the Russian general who conquered the Central Asian republics after the Bolshevik Revolution. Bishkek was called Frunze until 1991, when Kyrgyzstan became independent. We drove a bit farther.

"Here is headquarters of KGB," said Vika.

"Still?" I inquired.

"Yes, still we have KGB."

"This is bus," Vika announced as we drove into a kind of industrial yard. The bus was a ramshackle green thing with German (former East German) markings. It was surrounded by a crowd of threadbare Central Asians. "Is luxury bus."

"It looks very luxurious," I said. I was still trying to ingratiate myself with the uncooperative Vika, but sarcasm, of course, was not the way to do it.

"Your seat is 8A."

Vika gave me the ticket which Dostuck Trekking had procured for me, and waited silently for me to get out of the car.

"Well, thanks for everything," I said.

"You're welcome."

"You never smile," I said.

Vika smiled wanly.

"Have a nice trip," she said.

THE BUS WAS crowded and creaky. I sat next to a former soldier in the Soviet army who wore his medal-emblazoned army jacket. He was large, had skin like a raw beet, thinning gray hair, and plastic glasses held together with Scotch tape, and he smelled powerfully of garlic. He smiled at me, shook my hand, and showed me a Russian magazine he was read-ing. Next to him a very large woman in a flowered dress was standing in the aisle and wiping her brow with a handkerchief. Her presence there made me claustrophobic. There wasn't much legroom. A television hung from the ceiling behind the driver, and on it the conductor played violently amplified, Russian-dubbed, long-forgotten violent American movies—*The Big Hit* was first, followed by *The Taking of Pelham One Two Three*. When at about ten o'clock we arrived at the Kazakh border, three scowling policemen got on the bus just as cars were falling off cliffs and exploding in ravines on the screen. Two passengers were taken off for passport inspection while a gang of ruffians in *The Big Hit* grabbed a pretty girl, bound and gagged her, and threw her into the back of a van. By the time the two passengers had returned, the girl had been liberated and the kidnappers killed in a carnage of automatic weapons fire. The bus continued on its halting, repair-plagued journey through the night. I commiserated with the moon, visible through my grimy window galloping beyond the shadow play of trees. Venus streamed just behind it.

We arrived on the outskirts of Tashkent at about 5:30 a.m., and while I was still collecting my bags a young man of about twenty or so wearing an army camouflage jacket asked me if I needed a taxi. I did.

"Tashkent?" he asked.

"Yes, Gostinitsa Tashkent," I replied in my well-oiled Russian—Hotel Tashkent.

"Airport!" the kid said. It was a statement, not a question.

"No," I said. "Hotel. Hotel Tashkent. *Gostinitsa. Nyet* airport."

"Airport! Okay!"

"What's with the airport? I'm not going to the airport. *Nyet* airport. Hotel," I cried.

"Okay, hotel."

"Gostinitsa Tashkent. You understand?"

"You okay?" the boy asked.

"Yes, I'm okay," I said. "Gostinitsa Tashkent, okay?"

"No problem," the boy said.

"How much?" said I.

"Ten dollars."

"Ten?"

"Yes."

"Ten dollars? You're sure?"

"Yes."

"Let's go."

"You okay?"

"Yeah, yeah, I'm okay."

In the fog of unfamiliar places and languages, your seasoned traveler didn't know exactly what border he was crossing, Kazakhstan-Uzbekistan or Kyrgyzstan-Uzbekistan, though it didn't really matter. The border station appeared to be across a dirt courtyard in some official-looking cement buildings where the other passengers were going. But my driver steered me into a bare room on the near side of the courtyard. Sitting behind a desk and on the desk and loitering on broken-down chairs were some rough-looking guys in T-shirts and dungaree jackets and army surplus pants creased around the buttocks. They demanded my passport and currency declaration. They spoke Russian.

"*Deklaratsia,*" they said.

"*Nyet deklaratsia,*" I said.

"Dollars?" they asked.

"Yes, dollars."

"How much dollars?"

I didn't respond. I didn't want to pay a Kazakh tax or a Kyrgyz bribe, whichever it would turn out to be. I also didn't want the camouflage kid to know that I was carrying $2,500 in cash, in a money belt under my shirt. We were at an impasse, in the midst of which the Kazakhs or the Kyrgyzes (I looked at the map later; they were Kazakhs) ordered me out into a corridor and in front of an iron-grilled window at which I was supposed to make some sort of payment. But a loud discussion among the customs crew erupted nearby. Everybody seemed distracted, so the kid and I quickly walked away to the Uzbek border station. We were not pursued.

"You okay?" he asked.

"Yeah."

The Uzbek passport check was quick and easy. Once we were through it, the kid picked up a friend of his, another kid—big, mesomorphic, also about twenty years old. We got to the car, which was small and tinny, and the kid drove it too fast, swerving to avoid potholes and looking over at me to ask if I was okay. I pointed to my eyes and then to the road. "Keep 'em on the road, okay?" I said. The other kid, who was in the backseat with my duffel bag and my computer case, was singing his knowledge of world affairs. "State Michigan!" he exclaimed, apropos perhaps of some football game of which I knew nothing. "Bill Clinton! Monica Lewinsky." He snickered. It was somehow reassuring that my president's fondness for being fellated in the White House was known here in the border regions of Kazakhstan and Uzbekistan.

Finally, after swerving into a gas station and buying a couple of gallons of gas, we pulled up to the Hotel Tashkent, another cavernous Soviet-era dive reminiscent of the Hotel Bishkek. Actually, we didn't pull up to it. The kid parked a discreet distance away and then made a money motion with his fingers, the thumb rubbing two fingers, a universal code. I pulled out a ten and two singles, the agreed-upon amount plus a tip. The kid's face went dark and angry.

"No!" he said.

"You said ten," I said.

"No, no," he said. "I say . . ." and he held up his ten fingers and blinked them several times. "Ten, ten, ten, ten, ten!" I gave him a pen and he wrote "50" and a dollar sign on his palm. He cocked his head and looked at me, as if daring me to resist this extortion. The one in the backseat grinned. I took out another single and handed it to him, but that did not improve the atmosphere. It was six-thirty and nobody was in sight besides the two of them, and one of them, the grinning kid in the back, was in control of my $2,500 Dell Inspiron 3500 portable computer and most of the rest of my luggage. There's never a KGB agent around when you need one. I felt my skin go prickly with fear, which I tried my best not to show. Show fear and they'll take everything you've got, I felt. That has happened to me twice, both times on dark streets, once in Johannesburg, South Africa, the other in supposedly safe and secure Amsterdam, young guys surrounding me, laughing happily while holding knives on me and taking my wallet and my watch; there wasn't anything I could do about it except try to stay calm and show proper submission, which is what I did—or, perhaps, make some suicidal gesture of resistance, which I didn't. I gave the kid another ten. He blinked his ten fingers four more times and cocked his head. I took out another ten and told him that was it. No more. He settled for it, to my relief, and I got out of the car.

"You okay?" the kid asked and grinned and held out his hand in a gesture of camaraderie.

I walked away and into the hotel, schlepping my bags.

The woman at the reception, fat and solicitous, asked me how it was to travel alone.

"I'm used to it."

"It must be dangerous," she said in serviceable English. How did she know?

I told her I tried to be careful.

"Well, be careful in Tashkent," she said. "Don't let anybody talk to you."

"Thanks for the advice," I said.

I HAD TWO related purposes in Tashkent. One was to see if there was some way I could get into Afghanistan, through which the monk had passed on his way to India. The second, as a fallback position, was to get at least to the banks of the Amu-Darya River in Termez on the southern border of Uzbekistan, which the monk had crossed.

The first question was easy. Before I left the United States, I had talked with Barnet Rubin, the Afghanistan expert at the Council on Foreign Relations in New York, and he had convinced me that it was pretty much impossible for an American to follow the monk's route down the middle of the country, from Termez on the Uzbek side over the Hindu Kush to the Khyber Pass and into Pakistan on the other. First, the ongoing fighting between the Muslim fundamentalist Taliban and various other factions inside Afghanistan made travel in the country hazardous. Second, since the Clinton administration bombed supposed terrorist camps in Afghanistan in 1998, Americans have become extremely unpopular. Fall into the wrong hands in Afghanistan and you could be a dead man. I gulped. And third, Barnet said, the border between Termez and Afghanistan has been closed anyway ever since some terror bombings in Tashkent. The Uzbek police believed that Muslim extremists, aided and abetted by counterparts in Afghanistan, were responsible for terrorism in Uzbekistan, so crossing at Termez was a moot point.

In Tashkent, I went to see Sergey Bochko, a Russian who is in charge of the local United Nations Drug Control Program, which, among other things, monitors the Central Asian drug trade. This makes Sergey a student of Afghanistan, since Afghanistan is the source of the drugs that pass through Turkmenistan, Uzbekistan, and Tajikistan on their way to consumers in the West.

"Do you know any foreigners who have gone to Afghanistan lately?" I asked.

"I've met some, but they were all Indians or Pakistanis."

"Really? Some non-Afghans have been able to cross the country from north to south?"

"Well, yes, but they cross the border in Tajikistan and they are usually Ismaili Muslims with close connections to the Aga Khan organization in Dushanbe."

I clearly didn't qualify. I also didn't have a Tajik visa, and, in any case, the route from Tajikistan would be far to the east of the route taken by the monk. And the major Buddhist site in Afghanistan in the seventh century—a site where there remain two giant statues of the Buddha and a cave-temple complex that the monk saw on his trip—is Bamiyan, northwest of Kabul and several hundred miles from the route via Tajikistan. The local news agencies were reporting heavy fighting in Bamiyan, which was being hotly contested between the Taliban and forces loyal to the former president Burhanuddin Rabbani, its chief rival. In China and Kyrgyzstan, though my route had diverged from that of the monk, I had not missed any of the major stops on his itinerary. But to risk my life to go to Afghanistan and not to see Bamiyan made no sense at all.

"What about Termez?" I asked Sergey. "Any problem getting there?"

"That's a sensitive area right now. If you go by car you might make it through, but most likely you'll be stopped at a military checkpoint. If you had a letter from your embassy, that might help."

I went to the embassy and asked Karen Aguilar, the press attaché, if she would write such a letter for me. She called the head of the embassy political section, John Fox, who happens to be her husband, and asked if such a letter could be written. "I doubt it," she said before making the call. "That would be a diplomatic letter and I don't think the United States government wants to write a diplomatic letter so that a journalist on a private trip can see the Friendship Bridge."

Fox was of the same opinion. Moreover, he told his wife, the entire hundred-mile stretch of Uzbek–Afghan border along the river was a heavily patrolled military zone. Maybe I would be able to get through to the river, but it was extremely unlikely, and if I did get stopped, there was no telling what sort of treatment I would receive, given the current paranoia about spies and terrorists. And even if the embassy was willing to help me get official permission, it would have to write a diplomatic note to the foreign ministry, which would pass the request on to the Uzbek military, a process that would take several weeks at a minimum and even then permission would probably not be given.

"Well," I said. "I guess I'll give it a try." I would take the bus to Samarkand the next day. I would hire a car there and try to drive to the Amu-Darya. I called a hotel in Samarkand to see about a room at a hotel that had been recommended to me there.

"Do you speak English?" I asked the person who answered the phone.

"Yes."

"Good. I'd like to make a reservation for tomorrow night."

"No problem."

"Good. Do you want my name?"

"Jelyat."

"No, my name, not your name."

"Jelyat," Jelyat said.

"Well, Jelyat, I'll be arriving rather late. How can I be sure that you'll have a room?"

"Big room, small room."

"Umm . . . well, a small room would be fine."

"Yes, big room, small room."

"I see. Can you tell me the price?"

"Price?"

"How much does a small room cost?"

"Thirty-three Usman Yusufu."

"No, I have the address. I'd like to know the price. How much?"

"Yes," said Jelyat. "Big room, small room."

I FINALLY DID get a reservation in Samarkand at a bed-and-breakfast called the Gostinitsa Furkat. Before leaving for Samarkand, I visited Louise Hidalgo, the BBC correspondent in Tashkent. The BBC is the only news organization from the West that keeps a full-time bureau in Uzbekistan. Her opinion was that going to Termez and to the river would be a cinch. She had done it a few months earlier, taking a car from Samarkand, and nobody had stopped her.

"So you think I can just go, no permissions, no nothing?"

"Yup," she said. "I just wouldn't stand there with a camera snapping away."

Later I spoke to Dmitri, a smart and savvy Russian I had met the day before at the United States Information Agency. It was Dmitri who had helped me with my reservation at the Gostinitsa Forkat, which, by the way, turned out to be clean, charming, and hospitable.

"Louise Hidalgo from the BBC went to Termez and the Friendship Bridge and had no problem," I told him.

"She probably went before the bombings," Dmitri said. He meant the terror bombings in Tashkent, which had followed an assassination attempt against President Islam Karimov. "Since then they've really tightened up. There will be checkpoints. I think it would be difficult even for us."

With these contradictory opinions swimming in my mind, I took a taxi to the bus station and got on an old orange-and-white bus for Samarkand.

This was an event. Samarkand! I love even the name of the place, its initial sibilance, the Coleridgian consonants that follow—SSSammmarKAND! It was a bonus for me that the monk passed through there. Actually, everybody passed through Samarkand during the era of the Road of Great Events. It stood at the center of the road's main branches—south to India over the Amu-Darya River and across the Hindu Kush; through the Kizilkul Desert to the west, or back to China the way I had come.

Samarkand became synonymous with a certain poetic romance many centuries after the monk, of course, when it was built up by Tamerlane as his capital, and then turned into a great seat of Islamic learning by his grandson, Ulegbek. In any case, how utterly exciting to be going to Samarkand, and by bus, through the flat plains of what the monk would have called Sog, its inhabitants, mostly fire-worshippers, what we call Zoroastrians and he called Sogdians.

"Their religion consists of sacrificing to fire," the monk noted. Still, he liked the place: "The precious merchandise of many foreign countries is stored here. The soil is rich and productive, and yields abundant harvests. The forest trees afford a thick vegetation, and flowers and fruits are plentiful. . . . The inhabitants are skillful in the arts and trades beyond those of other countries. . . . The king is full of courage and the neighboring countries obey his commands."

In fact, the monk was treated disdainfully at first by the king, but eventually the monarch listened to his teachings. This is a standard element in Hui Li's narrative—the monk approaching a skeptical, unbelieving barbarian ruler and quickly winning him over by the superiority of Buddhist wisdom. But while the king of Samarkand "rejoiced" and asked to become Hsuan Tsang's disciple, others were jealous. When the monk and his escort went to a temple to take shelter for the night, some local priests pursued them and attempted to burn the place down. This angered the king, who in an assembly at court ordered that the culprits' hands be cut off. The monk refused to allow this barbaric punishment, so the king satisfied himself with beating them severely and banishing them. The people flocked around the monk, who formed a Buddhist priesthood out of them (says Hui Li in one of the more hagiographic portions of his book). "It was thus that [the Master of the Law] transformed their badly disposed hearts, and corrected their evil customs," he says.

The bus was hot—a sauna, a Native American sweat lodge. The ride was five hours. A rotund and sweating conductor had noisy arguments in Russian or Uzbek with half of the passengers when it came to collecting their fares. The bus showed a kind of ethnic geography. In the front were Russians; Uzbeks were in the middle; in the back were several rows of colorfully dressed Tajiks, smaller, finer-boned, more ornamented. One bewitching teenage girl with gleaming black eyes wore a white sequined sheath and gold earrings. The Tajiks got off at a highway intersection and disappeared into the agricultural landscape. I shared a seat with an Uzbek woman who was mightily intrigued by the exotic creature beside her, to whom she offered sunflower seeds and conversation in Russian. Though I speak virtually no Russian and she spoke no English, we managed to exchange a good deal of information. She was Uzbek. She had five children. I was going for the first time to Samarkand. She knew somebody who played the piano in New York. The architecture on the outskirts of Samarkand was not good, but inside, the buildings of Tamerlane were gorgeous.

Along the route I noticed a number of police checkpoints, which made me think that perhaps the diplomatic opinion about my access to Termez might be correct and the journalistic one wrong. This suspicion gained strength when the bus broke down a few miles outside of Samarkand and the passengers were invited to disembark and make their own way to their destinations. I got off, and two policemen approached me. They examined my passport and my Uzbek visa, closely, as if they contained the answer to the riddle of the sphinx. *"Deklaratsia,"* they said, and I told them in sign language that I didn't have anything that would pass for a *deklaratsia*. I was supposed, I supposed, to have gotten a foreign-currency *deklaratsia* at the Kazakh border, but I hadn't. "Problem," said one of the policemen and disappeared with my passport into a nearby soft drink stand to use the telephone. Around us were abandoned factory buildings, abandoned construction sites, the refuse of a failed system. Across the street was a restaurant called HOLLYWOOD. In the distance, under a gauze of haze, was Samarkand. So close. SSSammmmarKAND! The monk, who did not have to deal with Russian cops demanding to see nonexistent papers, traveled this very route, his face turned to the sun, his thoughts on the wisdom of India.

At last the policeman reappeared and gave me back the passport.

"Problem," he said again, shaking his head sadly, as if to tell me that this was hurting him more than me. He told me to get into a taxi.

"Money," he said, and pointed to the taxi driver.

"Okay," I said. "Money."

"Five dollars," the taxi driver said.

I thought I was being made to pay my own fare to the police station for further investigation into my "problem." Maybe it was my black-market currency transactions back at the Gostinitsa Tashkent. I don't usually change money on the black market, but as soon as I settled into my room at the Hotel Tashkent, a cheery chambermaid came into my room offering me a rate nearly five times the bank rate. If the difference is that great, the bank rate is robbery. Or so I justified giving the chambermaid fifty dollars in exchange for which she gave me enough Uzbek som to fill a small briefcase. The wads of cash, wrapped in rubber bands, were in my shoulder bag, making it bulge guiltily. But just as I was figuring out how I would explain away my undocumented money, the taxi driver turned to me expectantly, and I realized he wanted me to tell him where to go.

"Gostinitsa Forkat," I said, and the driver responded, much to my relief, even when I discovered that the hotel he took me to was not the hotel I wanted. Still, the wrong hotel was better than the police station. We visited another two or three wrong bed-and-breakfasts, but I persisted in demanding to be taken to the one where I had a reservation, and eventually we did arrive at the Gostinitsa Forkat on the edge of the Old City. I eagerly drank a cold beer while contemplating the meaning of the police check. Perhaps they were just amusing themselves, self-importantly checking on a foreigner. But if they were doing that on the outskirts of their country's biggest tourist destination, what would they do on the outskirts of a town next to the troubled and militarized Afghan border where tourists did not venture?

"No problem," they said at the Gostinitsa Forkat when I asked their help in hiring a car and driver for the trip to Termez. My plan was to go two days later. First I would have a day to see the sites of Tamerlane's city.

The hotel called a driver and negotiated a deal with him over the phone.

"Ask him if I can go to the bridge on the Amu-Darya," I said.

"Bridge?"

"*Most,*" I said. I had learned the Russian word for "bridge" to use in case of a police check in Termez. "Amu-Darya *most.*"

"Ah! *Most.*"

"Yes, *most.* Can I go to Amu-Darya *most*?"

There was a moment of conversation between the hotel owner and the driver.

"Why not?" said the owner of the Gostinitsa Forkat. "No problem."

IT'S ABOUT 250 miles from Samarkand to Termez. Along the way, my driver, Adim, drove through at least a dozen *militsia* checkpoints. At each one there would be a barrier over half of the road, two or three bored policemen sitting next to a piece of concrete sculpture. There would be a stop sign. We would stop. And then, when no policeman emerged to check our documents, we would proceed.

The land was flat just out of Samarkand, then it rose up into tree-less hills overhung by clouds. The day before I had visited a museum in Afrasayib, an ancient city and archaeological site that was probably the place that Hsuan Tsang called Sa-mo-kien, though it was centuries before the Samarkand built by Tamerlane and Ulegbek. The Afrasayib museum displayed an inscription by a later traveler than the Chinese monk, translated into English: "I go upstairs on the citadel of Samarkand and I saw more beautiful view which some time I charmed: fresh verdure trees, shinning castles, running canals and endlessly cultivated earth." Adim and I rushed by towns and villages with names like Kitab, Shahrisabz (where Tamerlane was born), Qamashi, Karashina, Sayrab, Chilanzer, Sherabad. In between them were roadside stands—a sheep's carcass hung on a hook, a few men in square black skullcaps embroidered in white, smoke rising from a shashlik pit, the whiff of roasting meat. We stopped and bought some fresh rhubarb, and ate it raw, like celery sticks. Adim kept saying, "Tomorrow Tashkent," which sounded like a revolutionary slogan, but he was angling for more business. I had been clear when I arranged for the car—one hundred dollars to be taken to the Amu-Darya River where I could see the border with Afghanistan. Then the driver would return to Samarkand alone, while I would spend the night in Termez and fly to Tashkent the next day.

We reached Termez in five hours, and Adim said, "Hotel?"

"*Nyet* hotel! *Most*," I insisted.

Adim crossed his arms to make an X. He was giving me to understand that the bridge was off-limits, that we were not allowed to go there. He said, "Bomb," pronouncing the second *b*. He was referring to the Tashkent terror bombings of February, since which the Friendship Bridge had been closed down.

I lacked the linguistic resources to remind him that when I had booked his services, it had been on his own assurance that there would be "no problem" about going to the Amu-Darya *most*. Nor could I communicate to him that the *most* was the whole point, that I didn't care to spend a day of my life in Termez out of some strange weakness for seedy towns in south Uzbekistan. Now he was pretending that the deal was to go just to Termez and that the *most* was a surprise.

"Tomorrow Tashkent!" he said smiling.

"Tomorrow Tashkent," I replied, holding out the prospect of further business, if I was happy. "Today *most*, Amu-Darya *most*." I pointed the way ahead. Uselessly I said in English, "Let's give it a try. Let's see how close we can get."

Adim stopped the car next to a few teenage boys to ask them the way to the bridge. They made the same X sign with their arms. It occurred to me that this arm-crossing conveyed the belief that I wanted to cross the bridge, not just see it, so I pointed to my eyes and said, "Only look," and then I made a walking motion with my fingers and said, "*Nyet* cross. Only look, *nyet* cross." I sounded extremely silly to myself.

Adim rose to the occasion. He began driving aggressively. At every intersection he would ask whoever was there how to get to the *most*. Or, at least, I heard the words *most* and "*Amu-Darya*." In this manner we made our way steadily from one street to the next. Likewise, whenever we came to a *militsia* checkpoint, Adim would stick his head out the window and ask for the Amu-Darya *most*. Instead of stopping us and scrutinizing our identity papers, the police would give a friendly wave in the required direction, and we would continue along until the next checkpoint, where we would get another set of directions.

Finally we found ourselves on a road running parallel to the Amu-Darya, which could be seen as a gun-metal-gray glint about half a mile away.

"Afghanistan!" Adim shouted, pointing south at the low-slung terrain on the other side of the river.

"Yes, good," I said, feeling that at least I had seen all the way to the other side. "But keep going. *Most!* Okay?"

"Okay!"

After several minutes, the road turned up an embankment and toward the river. A few hundred yards farther on, we came to a set of black-and-white road barriers, placed to make a vehicle swerve from one side of the road to the other. We pulled up alongside a lowered barrier pole in front of a cinder-block shack. Three very young soldiers stood around in camouflage uniforms, and they were carrying slung over their shoulders very long automatic rifles whose make I didn't recognize. Beyond them, perhaps two football fields away, the Uzbek end of the Friendship Bridge could be seen on the other side of some abandoned buildings, probably the former border post. And beyond the bridge in the dim, cloud-darkened late afternoon was the dusky shore of Afghanistan.

In his *The Road to Oxiana* the English traveler Robert Byron talks about approaching the Amu-Darya, which he called the Oxus, from the Afghan side. It was the mid-1930s, a time when young Englishmen like Byron, Graham Greene, and Peter Fleming set off for unbeaten tracks, and Byron's main aim was ruins. Like his namesake, Lord Byron, he was enraptured by all relics of imperial grandeur. He wanted to see the Persian ruins of Sogdia, but, given Soviet-British hostility, it was impossible for an Englishman to travel north of the Amu-Darya, just as it was not allowed for a Russian to set foot in India. When Byron reached Mazar-i-Sherif, the large town in northern Afghanistan, he began asking for official permission to travel to the river opposite Termez, from which point, he had been told, he would at least be able to see the ruins on the river's far shore. An Oxford-educated Afghani doctor recommended that he write a request to the local governor, a certain Mohammad Gul Khan, in such elaborate language that it would be impossible for the local bureaucracy to translate it.

"Your excellency's capital holds everything to delight the visitor, nevertheless the chief, the unique attraction of the district is denied him, that, in short, he who comes to Mazar-i-Sherif will be treated as a spy, a Bolshevik, a disturber of the people, if he asks to tread the shores where Rustam fought," Byron wrote. This letter is smug, condescending, but funny. "All we desire is a sight of the River, and any point will serve this purpose if Your Excellency cares to suggest another."*

Byron was informed that permission for foreigners to visit the river had to be obtained in Kabul, several days' journey away, and in the end he was unable to go. "I should like to have seen the ruins of Termez," he says wistfully, and then he describes what he has heard of them, especially a minaret drawn by an earlier traveler.

As for me, I would have liked to visit Mazar-i-Sherif and especially Bamiyan, the main destination for Hsuan Tsang on his route south from Termez to Peshawar. Byron went there. It dates from the fifth century, and aside from a number of important cave temples, its most famous monuments are two giant statues of the Buddha—one 174 feet high and the other 115. They did not impress Byron, who wrote: "It is their negation of sense, the lack of any pride in their monstrous flaccid bulk, that sickens." Hsuan Tsang, contemplating the same statues, does not wax rhapsodic either, but he is more favorably impressed. "Its golden hues sparkle on every side, and its precious ornaments dazzle the eyes by their brightness," he writes of the larger stone figure. It must have been in better shape when he was there, a mere two centuries after it was carved. The rumors now are that the statues are in a state of disrepair. They have been vandalized by the ultrafundamentalist Taliban, which is repelled by any graven image. Still, I would have liked to see Bamiyan. And while I knew I would most likely not achieve that goal, at least I wanted to stand by the shores of the Amu-Darya and look across to Afghanistan.

Adim, who now understood my urgency in this matter, conveyed my

---

* Robert Byron, *The Road to Oxiana* (New York: Oxford University Press, 1982), p. 251.

request that I be able to walk up to the bridge. The soldiers firmly said no, and crossed their arms in the X sign. Closed. No closer approach allowed.

I had planned for this eventuality. I got out of the car and shook hands all around. I said, "New York," and swung my body to one side. "Uzbek-istan," I said, and swung my body to the other, striving to impress these soldiers with the great distance I had traveled. Then, still positioned on the Uzbek side of things, I said, *"Most,"* and pasted a look of entreaty on my face. I drew a little diagram in my notebook, showing the river, the bridge, and where we stood. Then I indicated the spot where I wanted to go—to the bridge. I pointed at my eyes. "I only want to see it."

The soldiers were nice boys, a bit shy; they wanted to accommodate me. They showed no surprise that a foreigner should emerge through the concrete barriers late on a Sunday afternoon and begin pleading with them to get closer to a river that held no special allure for them. They looked at each other. I made a sign to one of them that we should go together. I smiled.

Finally they relented. They said something to Adim, who nodded to me and pointed the way to the bridge. One of the soldiers walked with me, his boots tapping loudly on the concrete roadbed. In the distance, from the marshy territory along the river to the left, came the hooting of an owl. We walked past several abandoned brick buildings. As the bridge hove into closer view, I was surprised at how narrow it was, just a simple trestle bridge barely wide enough to permit two lanes of traffic. This was the point at which the former Soviet Union had supplied its forces during its decade-long occupation of Afghanistan. It seemed unequal to the task.

About one hundred feet from the bridge, the young soldier signaled for me to stop. I took out my notebook and referred to my design, show-ing a man walking just a little bit farther. The soldier made an X with his arms. I walked ahead just a few more feet. I figured the kid wasn't going to shoot me. I got to within about fifty feet of the bridge. On the other side, Afghanistan seemed a mirror image of the Uzbek side of the river, marshy lowlands, a couple of long sheds, the road extending out from the bridge and quickly disappearing in some scrubby brush.

The kid shouted something at me in Russian, and I stopped walking. This was as far as I was going to go. Close enough. I could see the gray water coursing westward. But still, like Byron longing to come here, I longed to go there and to follow the monk as he made his way over the Hindu Kush to Bamiyan, the Khyber Pass, and Peshawar. There was no bridge in the seventh century, but it was easy to cross the river. Now there is a bridge, but it is impossible to get to the other side.

11

Self-Annihilating Arguments

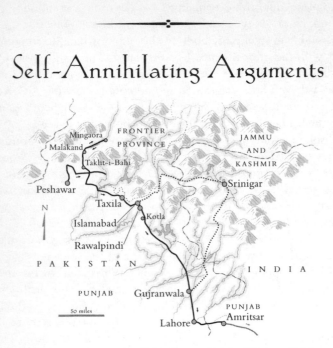

AFTER THE BLEAKNESS of the former Soviet Union, Pakistan comes at you like something detonated, a plenitude of color and mass, weirdness and catastrophe. The day I arrived by air from Tashkent, the newspapers were full of disasters. "Twelve Killed in Bomb Blast" was the banner headline. The *Islamabad News* cited an unidentified police source in Lahore to the effect that the blast, which came from a bomb attached to a parked bicycle, was the work of RAW, the Research and Analysis Wing of the Indian Intelligence Service. The day before, the papers had reported heavy artillery exchanges between Indian and Pakistani troops quartered at 21,000 feet in Kashmir. Meanwhile, Asif Ali Zardari, the imprisoned husband of former prime minister Benazir Bhutto, was "in hospital after being injured during a police interrogation." What a delicately unsuspicious way of putting that. The wounds to the neck and mouth were self-inflicted, the police said, Zardari's way of avoiding interrogation.

China is buttoned-down, self-controlled, repressed, conformist, practical, guided en masse by the principle of postponing gratification. It is becoming a variation on the Western experience. The Islamic former republics of the Soviet Union are tawdry and friendly, pared-down versions of something familiar, something from Russian Communism. Pakistan is different, and Peshawar and the Northwest Frontier Province (of which it is the major city) is especially different. Peshawar, which the monk believed to be the gateway to India, is an eruption, a stained and aromatic profusion.

I checked into my seventeen-dollar-a-night room at Green's Hotel on Saddar Street and went in search of the Saeed Book Bank a few blocks away. Calls of "Change money," "Just come in, have a look," "Buy a knife from Afghanistan" pursued me. The street spilled with antique carpets, plastic buckets, bottles of blue glass, gasoline pumps, copying machines, cans of vinyl emulsion, blackened pots of chickpeas simmering in sauce, Honda generators. On Saddar Street was Decent Stationers, Muslim Insurance, Delight Photostat, and Ever New Confectioners. Aging policemen with mustaches and rifles as old as they were stood guard at banks. They wore blue berets. Motorcycle rickshaws buzzed by, decorated with birds of paradise and nonspinning spinning wheels. From some hellish place down below emanated the stink of sewage, and it mixed with the smell of the simmering chickpeas nearby and the odor of half-burned gasoline.

This is the territory of the Pathans, who are known as tribesmen to the other Pakistanis—the Punjabis, the Sindhis, and the Baluchis. The Pathans are half Afghan, half post-British-colonial. The British fought thirty-two wars against them before finally subduing them (it was in one of those wars, in 1897, that Winston Churchill first made a name for himself as a journalist). The men wear the *shalwar kameez,* a kind of long cotton shirt extending below the knees, beneath which are loose cotton pants of the same color and material. They are tall, strikingly hirsute, fine-boned, handsome. The women, when you see them, which is rare, wear a long headscarf called a *dupatta.* Their large dark eyes gleam like candles from within the shadows of their veils and shawls. The Pathans speak English, supposedly, but try to talk to them and you will find that it is often an English so steeped in another culture that you will have difficulty understanding it, and they you.

That day, early in the morning, I had taken a one-hour flight from Termez to Tashkent. I was almost unable to get on the plane because the Russian woman at the glassed-in ticket counter at the Termez airport was inexplicably unwilling to take my money. I wanted to pay in dollars, which was allowable according to a sign on the window, but the Russian woman intransigently refused to take my fifty-dollar bill. The plane was soon going to leave without me, which evoked in me murderous feelings toward this bureaucrat, and then I understood the reason for her behavior. I picked the word "bazaar" out of the otherwise incomprehensible, urgent speech she kept making. She was trying to tell me that if I changed my dollars at the black market in the bazaar, the ticket would cost me the equivalent of twelve dollars, not fifty. It bothered her to see a nice boy like me paying at the extortionate official rate. I pointed at my watch and shrugged and pushed my money at her under the window. "No time for bazaar," I said. She sighed and sadly took my money. My murderous sentiment turned to affection.

From Tashkent I flew an hour on an old Soviet-era Ilyushin to Alma Ata, the capital of Kazakhstan. We passengers were made to stay on the plane, so, for the second time (the first was on the Bishkek–Tashkent bus), I was on Kazakh soil without actually touching it. Then we flew over Afghanistan, which was covered in clouds. It was the second day in a row that I had seen Afghanistan without being able to go there. After a flight of two hours my Airbus 300 landed in Islamabad, where I spent a night, and the next morning I picked up a domestic flight for the twenty-minute hop to Peshawar. While waiting at the airport, I struck up a conversation with a pleasant, ample Englishman who was watching the England-Zimbabwe World Cup cricket match on the waiting-room television. I had him pegged for a businessman or a diplomat, but it turned out he worked for the Seventh-Day Adventist church in Pakistan and was waiting for a flight to Lahore.

"Pakistan must not be an easy country to be a missionary in," I offered.

"Well," he replied, "it's illegal to convert a Muslim."

"You're a missionary in a country where it is illegal to proselytize?"

"We've been here for a century," he said. "We have one hundred churches. We have schools and hospitals. We have a dental clinic in Peshawar."

"Who are your parishioners?"

"There are Christians here. There have been Christians in India since Saint Thomas went to Madras in the first century."

I asked what happened to a Muslim who decided to become a Seventh-Day Adventist.

"They impose the death penalty," the man said. His tone was flat, matter-of-fact.

"Do they actually kill you?"

"Oh, sure," he said. "Usually a family member. I know one man who spends his entire life moving from one place to another. If somebody in his family caught up with him, he'd be killed. Stabbed to death, most likely."

On the television screen at the airport, an English batsman named Hussain was scoring runs off a Zimbabwe bowler named Olongo. A very large man in a flowing *shalwar kalmiss* sat down in a seat opposite us and smoked a cigarette as he watched the match. We live in a global village, but we are not all the same.

"If somebody kills somebody because he converted to Christianity, would he be prosecuted?" I asked.

"Oh, no," the Seventh-Day Adventist said. "The police would do nothing."

The police also do nothing in Pakistan if a husband kills his wife because she has asked for a divorce. For the woman to ask for a divorce, even if her husband beats her, is a crime in Pakistan. In the few days that I was in the country, there were newspaper articles about what were called "a boy and a girl" who committed suicide because the parents of one of them refused to allow them to get married. There were feeble protests against a government decision made some time before to disband forcibly some 2,500 nongovernmental organizations that existed in Pakistan. In a speech to celebrate Pakistan's nuclear capability, a man named Pir Syed Izhar Hussain Shah Bukhari, described by the *Islamabad News* as a prominent religious scholar and the leader of the Jamiat Ulema-e-Islam, a political party, bemoaned the country's failure to install a true Islamic system. "God has gifted us the boon of a separate homeland with an invincible defense, but we Muslims are ungrateful persons as we have failed to bring in an Islamic rule in the country," he said.

PESHAWAR WAS the capital of Gandhara, and it was Gandhara that gave Buddhism to the world beyond India. When the monk came here, the city was to him already an ancient place, steeped in a glorious history and partially in ruins. He writes of great monuments—the Bodhi Tree under which sat the four Buddhas who existed in the thousands of eons before the Buddha we know. "Its branches are thick and the shade beneath somber and deep," he writes. "Secret spiritual influences guard the precincts of the tree and exert a protecting virtue in its continuance." Near the tree was a giant stupa built by King Ashoka of the third century B.C., the ruler who adopted Buddhism and made it mandatory throughout northern India. The monk describes the stupa, still in existence when he was there (no longer), its statues and paintings, the "brilliant light," the "exquisite perfumes, the musical sounds that can be perceived at times and that were the work of saints and eminent sages."

But for Hsuan Tsang, Peshawar's greatest significance was as the birthplace of Asanga and his younger brother Vasubhandu, the monk's two great progenitors, the fourth-century theorists of his own Yogacaran school of thought. To earthbound, practical minds these two men of Peshawar might appear the creators of a sort of stratospheric nonsense, a high philosophy of nothingness, and, as one of those earthbound and practical people, I am sometimes inclined to that view. They are certainly hard to understand. Yet they also represent a remarkable level of sophisticated speculation on the nature of reality, a sign of how advanced in nuanced reflection the society of Gandhara was.

There are no physical traces of the monuments Hsuan Tsang saw in Peshawar, and anyway, you don't at first feel impelled to think about the higher reaches of Buddhist philosophy in so Muslim a place. But at good old Saeed Book Bank I found English translations of some of the sutras and a couple of histories of Buddhist philosophy, and I read them late at night in my room at Green's Hotel for what I could learn about Peshawar's famous native sons. The average person, even the average worshipper at a Buddhist temple, does not engage in deep speculation about the nature of reality and ultimate truth. For most worshippers, Buddhism is a teaching. It tells them to moderate their desires and to show benevolence and compassion toward others who suffer—thereby, and somewhat contradictorily, to earn merit that can be cashed in for a better sort of reincarnation after death. Life is hard, they know, and it will be even worse in the next rebirth if you are bad. People pray to the Bodhisattvas, who are treated as gods, for a cure for illness, or for healthy children, or, as our pilgrim himself did, for a way out of the desert. But Buddhist philosophy, expressed in the difficult, arcane, abstruse, often enigmatic sutras and sastras, is overwhelmingly concerned with the higher-flown philosophical matters. In particular, its focus is on the true nature of things as a way of escaping the inevitably painful cycle of existence. Ignorance is a defilement of the mind that gives rise to selfish desire, to cravings, to attachments that can only end in old age, grief, sickness, despair, and death—in short, in suffering. Ignorance of the true nature of reality is thus central to Buddhism, and the elucidation of that true nature, the ultimate truth, is what the vast and recondite edifice of Buddhist philosophy attempts to determine.

So where do the sages of Peshawar come into this picture? Asanga and Vasubhandu are famous for having struggled to surmount a tradition in

Buddhist philosophy that traced back to another major figure, a South Indian named Nagarjuna, who developed what is called the Middle Path, which, as he put it, "transcends all points of dispute." The Buddha taught that we must be free of attachments to sensual desire, to the desire for existence, and to ignorance, but we must also be free of our attachment to our opinions, including our attachment to truth. Nagarjuna concentrated on this last, problematic category, the attachment to intellectual conviction, to being right. One of the commentators on Buddhism whose work I pondered, John Snelling, likened Nagarjuna's thinking to that of Ludwig Wittgenstein many centuries later, especially Wittgenstein's contention that his philosophical arguments were self-annihilating.* It is a way of saying that Absolute Truth is a kind of Absolute Freedom from any notion of human-created meaning, even from the meaning that would come if we understood the Truth.

Nagarjuna elaborated the key concept of *sunyata,* which translates as "emptiness." The idea is that everything is empty of any sort of permanent, independent existence. Here we have one of those paradoxes in which Buddhism abounds, one of those contradictions that seems beyond the power of language to resolve. The Buddha is supposed to have said: "One cannot properly express the emptiness of all dharmas in words." But though emptiness may be inexpressible, it is an essential concept. Because everything is dependent on something else, therefore nothing has independent existence. The Buddha said: "Where there is no perception, appellation, conception, or conventional expression, there one speaks of perfect wisdom."

What then of the world that we perceive, the world that we bang into when we fall, that we eat when we are hungry, that blinds us when it takes the form of the sunrise? Nagarjuna hastens to assure us that the concept of *sunyata* does not mean that nothing exists. There is a "conventional truth," as he called it, that we live by day to day, and that conventional truth is that the world exists. It is a bit like the theory of atoms. We see a piece of wood as a dependably solid object that can be nailed to other pieces of wood and made into a house. That is conventional truth. Absolute truth to a physicist would be something different, wood as a collection of atoms and molecules that are themselves made up of protons, neutrons, and electrons, all held together by electromagnetic forces and none apparent from appearances alone. In Buddhism there is

* John Snelling, *The Buddhist Handbook: A Complete Guide to Buddhist Schools, Teaching, Practice, and History,* p. 90.

the world as it is ordinarily perceived (conventional truth) and there is the Ultimate Truth that all things, even the mind that perceives Ultimate Truth, are empty. In *sunyata,* there is eternal impermanence, the hyper-instability of all phenomena. Another, very good explicator of Buddhist philosophy may help—or, then again, maybe he won't—when he puts things this way: "Emptiness is not a 'nothing,' it is not nihilism, but equally it is not a 'something,' it is not some absolute reality; it is the absolute truth about the way things are, but it is not the Absolute."*

For Asanga and Vasubhandu, Nagarjuna's philosophy was a negative portrayal of the world; it tells us what it is not, not what it is. To describe what it is, they developed the idea of a "store consciousness" that gives rise to the illusion that the self is a real entity, separate from every other entity. The store consciousness is a bit like the Freudian unconscious in that it powerfully affects the content of our conscious thoughts without being a part of active consciousness. In this sense it is very modern. Imagine that already in the fourth century in faraway Peshawar philosophers understood that this thing we think of as the mind is actually made up of several parts, sometimes in conflict with one another as each tries to colonize the entirety of the mind. In the Yogacara philosophy, we don't get ideas just from our five senses; we get them also from the seeds and traces that have been deposited in our store consciousness, a sort of natural, pre-existing characteristic of the mind and the one that gives us the illusion that we exist. We are not *tabula rasa,* in other words, blank slates upon which our experience writes a sort of fresh text. We come with a sort of program, and the only way to see through it and beyond it is many years of calm study and meditation—hence the association of the word *yoga* with Yogacara.

As I read about these concepts in Buddhist philosophy by the dim light of my sole lightbulb in Green's Hotel, I felt that I sort of got it and yet didn't get it. I often have that sense with Buddhist theology, whose ultimate idea so often seems almost within reach but then fades away, as if it were a mirage. Reading the sutras and the sastras, one has the impression that something luminous and adamantine shimmers just beneath the page, but then it cannot quite be captured in any noncontradictory way by the logical mind. It always requires a leap beyond verbal formulation, a leap that is expressed in Buddhism by all those paradoxes in which contradictory statements are held to be true. "Suchness," said the Buddha, "does not become, nor does it cease becoming."

* Rupert Gethin, *The Foundations of Buddhism* (New York: Oxford University Press, 1998), p. 240.

The irreverent thought has occurred to me that much of Buddhist philosophy consists of slippery wordplay which enables the philosopher to have things any which way. Or is it that I am simply too grounded in Jewish metaphysical notions to grasp the more elusive Buddhist ones? Judaism is not easy, but its concepts are down-to-earth—do this, don't do that, do justice, love mercy, walk humbly with thy God. My father used to read *The Sayings of the Fathers* with me, a collection of Talmudic aphorisms that makes up an essential part of any Jewish education, and I encountered in that book phrases that have stuck with me ever since: "Truth and the verdict of peace are yours to adjudicate in your gates." " If I am not for myself, who will be for me? If I am only for myself, what am I?" These are aphorisms worth pondering, which I have done over the years, but there is nothing ultimately ungraspable about them. They assume things that Buddhism does not: that, for example, there is a God; that the self is real; that the purpose of life is not to penetrate to some exceedingly unobvious truth but to obey the 613 moral and ethical rules that are enumerated in the Bible.

Perhaps it is my grounding in the this-worldliness of Judaism that makes me wonder sometimes if the mysterious verbiage of Buddhism is not a sign of the brilliance of the Buddhist scheme of things but rather an indication that the premises are untenable. I'm not speaking here of the commonsensical and appealing notion that happiness lies in something other than the pursuit of selfish pleasures. I'm talking about other things—the denial of the existence of the self, for example, or the idea of emptiness, originating with the Buddha but developed by Nagarjuna, Asanga, and Vasubhandu. I couldn't tell, sitting there in the birthplace of the latter two of these men, whether the idea of emptiness was an astonishing, counterintuitive insight or an ersatz profundity. All things are empty of their own existence—including the knowledge that all things are empty of their own existence? Isn't there a logical problem in there someplace? If it is true, as Yogacara doctrine would have it, that everything including the self is a product of mind, what is it that is deluded into thinking that it exists, except the self itself? I didn't know how to answer that question.

Instead, I closed my Buddhist books with the hope that I might achieve a greater understanding when I got to Nalanda, where the monk went to study with the greatest masters. But I also made the assumption that Hsuan Tsang, being, after all, Chinese and thus probably rather reflexively empirical, was actually as troubled by the question of absolute truth as I was—and that was why he traveled.

IN PESHAWAR I called Professor Fidaullah Serhai at the *Frontier Post,*
where he is a political columnist. Before becoming a journalist, he was
the director of the Peshawar Museum and one of Pakistan's leading
archaeologists. I explained that I was tracing the monk's steps in Pakistan
and wanted to learn as much as I could about the history of Buddhism in
Gandhara.

"I'm frightfully busy," he said.

"Well, I know I'm calling on short notice, but I have nothing scheduled for the day, other than to go to the museum, and I could meet you
anytime you are free."

"I'm in a very bad situation," he said. "There's no computer available
here today and I have a very important column to write."

"Perhaps if I called you later."

"You see, we don't have enough computers here, and I have to wait
until one is available, how long I can't tell you."

I left the hotel and got into a motorcycle rickshaw. "The Peshawar
Museum," I said. I knew only roughly where the museum was. The
driver nodded knowingly and took off into pandemonial traffic in what
seemed like the right direction. There is a small mirror in the passenger
compartment of these rickshaws, and in it I watched my skin vibrating as
the vehicle buzzed along, making the sound of a giant bee. We got onto
the Grand Trunk Road heading east, past Pakistani military installations,
past the Pearl Continental Hotel, past the Hissar Bazaar, the old British
fort adorned with nineteenth-century cannon, and into the stream of
long-distance trucks bound for Rawalpindi, Islamabad, and Lahore.

I tapped the driver on the shoulder. "The museum?" I shouted over
the general cacophony. He looked back at me and shook his head knowingly. It had been my assumption that "museum," pronounced slowly and
with a subcontinental lilt, would be one of those words understandable to
all in this part of the world—English speakers, Urdu speakers, speakers of
Pashtoon, of Hizari, of Dari, of Punjabi. "Myew-zee-umm," I shouted,
catching another glimpse of my shuddering chin. But by now we were in
the Peshawar suburbs and it was clear that my driver had no idea where I
wanted to go.

"Turn around," I yelled and signaled a U-turn. We turned. I saw two
policemen standing at a traffic circle and bade my driver stop. "Peshawar
Myew-zee-umm," I said. This caused a long conversation in one of the
many local languages between my driver and the policemen. Trucks,

highly decorated with colorful geometric designs, with ornately carved wooden cabin doors, and with all manner of pendants, reflectors, banners, and bangles, roared by inches away. I had reason to reflect on the cultural determination of distance, the tolerable distance between vehicles and persons being far smaller in Pakistan than it is in America. The conversation ended, the driver pressed onward. But after quite some time, we still had not arrived at the myew-zee-umm. We had crossed Peshawar, going past the area of the Saddar Bazaar, past what is still called the Cantonment (the British-built military encampment), until at last I realized that the driver had taken me to Peshawar University. But I remembered quite distinctly that the museum was near the Pearl Continental Hotel, not far from where we had had our lengthy, arm-gesturing exchange with the police.

"Pearl Continental," I shouted, and we jolted across all of Peshawar again. At the hotel, the doorman translated for me and the driver, understanding where I wanted to go this time, took me quickly to the elegant colonial-era building where the Peshawar Museum is housed. A sign posted there said: "Closed at 3 p.m. for staff meeting." I looked at my watch. It was 3 p.m. I went back to the Pearl Continental and called Serhai.

"This is a very busy day," he shouted. "I have a very important article, but there's no computer!"

I told him where I was staying and hung up, feeling discouraged. But an hour after I had gotten back to Green's Hotel and was reading the Heart Sutra in my room, the telephone rang.

"This is Fidaullah Serhai," a familiar voice said. "I'm in the lobby."

"I'm coming right down," I said.

Serhai was a smallish man, clean-shaven, which in Pashtoon society indicates a liberal, nontheocratic bent. He looked to be about seventy years old and he chain-smoked. We sat down for tea.

"I am a Pathan of the Yusufzai tribe," he said. "The Yusufzais are the most superior of the Pathans, because the language we use is the purest Pashtoon, the literary language."

I asked if the Pathans in Pakistan were the same as the Pathans across the border in Afghanistan.

"We were divided by the British. They created a border where there had been no border. So now in Afghanistan we are Pashtoons and in Pakistan we are Pathans, but we are the same people." He lit another cigarette. "I speak Pashtoon, Urdu, Dari, Hizari, Hinko, Punjabi, and a little English." He said this not boastfully (though with some false modesty about his English) but informatively, to give me an idea of the linguistic variety of the region. " 'Dari' means 'intruder,' " he said, speaking of the major non–Pashtoon ethnic group of Afghanistan. Dari is related to Persian and is spoken mostly in western Afghanistan, Kandahar, and Herat, near the border with Iran. It bears some relationship to Pashtoon and Urdu, because of their common Mogul ancestry and the infusion of many Arabic words into both. That I knew, but as Serhai began a crisp capsule history of Gandhara, I was surprised to learn that the region also had a connection with the ancient Near East and with Aramaic, a Semitic language closely related to Hebrew and using the same alphabet.

"Gandhara extends from the fifth century B.C. to beyond the seventh century A.D.," he began. "The word 'Gandhara' derives from the Sanskrit word for 'Land of Fragrance.' It refers to the Peshawar Valley, including Swat, Malakand, and the entire right bank of the River Indus. The earliest reference to Gandhara is in the Rig Veda, which is the first book of the Aryans. According to this book, the people of Gandhara produced fine-quality wool. The second reference to Gandhara is found in the rock edicts of the Achaemenids, a royal dynasty of Persia. These are from the fifth and sixth centuries B.C. In 326 or 327 B.C., Gandhara was conquered by Alexander the Great. The Greeks ruled for two hundred years. Coins have been found that mention the names of thirty-nine Greek kings and four queens. These are bilingual coins, Greek on one side, Harashti on the other. Harashti is a script written from right to left. It derives from Aramaic.

"The Greeks were conquered by the Scythians. The Scythians were conquered by the Parthians. The Kushan people, from Gansu Province in China, overthrew the Parthians. One of the important rulers of the Kushan Dynasty was Kanishka, and he was a Buddhist who sponsored Buddhism in Gandhara. In the fifth century A.D. this area was invaded by barbarians, the White Huns, and they destroyed all the Buddhist monuments. There was no stability. The Hindu religion revived. Toward the end of the eleventh century, Islam came to this part of the world. It was brought by Mehmud of Afghanistan."

He now shifted from political history to religion.

"King Ashoka was responsible for the introduction of Buddhism into this part of the world. That was in 256 B.C. He brought in the Hinayana form of Buddhism. The Greeks who were here became Buddhist. They are known as Indo-Greeks, or Bactrian Greeks. Their stronghold was in Afghanistan. When the Kushan people overthrew the Parthians, they introduced Mahayana Buddhism to this region. The Jaulian Monastery in

Taxila was the second great Mahayana university. The first was Nalanda, in Bihar state in India."

I touched on the differences between Hinayana and Mahayana Buddhism earlier. Hinayana Buddhism is most commonly described as the Lesser Vehicle, the form of Buddhism that stresses a kind of personal salvation for which only a select few are qualified. Mahayana, or the Greater Vehicle, is a universalist doctrine. It holds that any person can become a Buddha, can achieve enlightenment and escape *samsara,* the cycle of existence with its illusion of the self, its infinite suffering. But Serhai, while not disagreeing with this view, had a different perspective, one that accounted for the enormous output of Indo-Greek art that Mahayana produced.

"In Hinayana the teachings of the Buddha are emphasized. In Mahayana, it is the image of the Buddha. In Hinayana, Buddha is a philosopher. Mahayana is a magical form of Buddhism. Buddha becomes a God. Buddha becomes an object of worship. His image is worshipped. His teachings disappear. In Mahayana they need an image. So the Greeks, who ruled for two hundred years, used the head of Apollo. This is Gandharan art. Some have called it a provincial school of Roman art. The subject matter of Buddhism is the life of the Buddha. Gandhara influenced the entire Buddhist world. The craftsmen of Swat were in great demand. So the paintings you see in the caves in Bamiyan were a branch of Gandharan Buddhism, made by the craftsmen from Swat. Another branch went to China, where the cave temples tell the Jataka tales, the tales of the previous lives of Buddha. Then it goes to Japan. All of the gods of Japanese Buddhism were born in Gandhara, right here in Pakistan."

As he spoke, I felt a kind of enlightenment myself. So that is what I had seen in Turfan and Kucha, and what I would see on my return visit when I went to the greatest cave temple of them all, the Mogao Caves in Dunhuang in western Gansu Province. Of course, having read a fair bit before I embarked on my trip, I knew some of the basics of this history: that the Greeks had become Buddhist, which explains why so much of the art of Central Asia, including that of Xinjiang, showed powerful Greco-Roman influences—the folds of the toga, the largely Caucasian, Apollonian heads of the Buddha, and these themes combined with the graceful *contrapposto* of classic Indian sculpture. The Buddhist images that one sees from Bamiyan to Dunhuang are like the Hindu gods dressed in Greek clothing and given Greek faces. The art spread during the heyday of Buddhism because wealthy merchants, seeking to acquire merit for their next life, sponsored the building of new temples all along the great trade routes that extended from India to Gandhara and Bactria all the way to Chang-an.

The missing ingredient, furnished by Serhai, was the importance of Mahayana Buddhism, and its creation of a kind of Catholic Church of Buddhist belief, filled with illustrated stories, with visual portrayals of a figure who had become an object of worship. The monk who journeyed in Gandhara was already visiting the ruins of a civilization that had never fully recovered from the White Hun depredations of two hundred years earlier. But he visited these ruins in the spirit of a Catholic who today visits Jerusalem to retrace the Stations of the Cross. The monk's great predecessor Fa Xian, who came to Gandhara in the fifth century, on the eve of the Hun assault, described a flourishing Buddhist culture. Fa Xian went to the great Buddhist centers—Takht-i-Bahi just north of Peshawar, Butkara in the Swat Valley to the north, and Taxila to the east—and he visited these places as capitals of his own faith. Hsuan Tsang went to the same places as a kind of antiquarian, carefully chronicling what remained of the olden days—how many stupas were standing, which were in ruins, and what rear guard of Buddhist monks remained in attendance in them. Since his visit, fourteen hundred years have passed, during which Buddhism completely disappeared from Pakistan. The Pakistani government has protected the relics and put the most important pieces in museums. I went to the major sites, feeling as I did so that the monk must have had some of the same feelings as I did: that in looking at the ruined temples, the schools, and the monasteries, one was contemplating a grandeur that, already in the monk's time, belonged to the past.

Both of us, I would think, experienced a certain reverence for ruins as dignified emblems of the eternal human condition. They are humbling, these piles of stone, because they attest at once to the impermanence of things and to the grand temerity involved in the effort to make them permanent. They have a sic-transit-gloria-mundi poignancy to them, the poignancy so poetically exploited by the nineteenth-century romantics surveying the wreckage of Athens or Rome. They show where the paths of glory ultimately lead. Hsuan Tsang rarely spoke of his emotions. He did so only once, as we will see. He was decidedly not a romantic. He reports tonelessly on the wrecked state of the many monuments he visits, his ostensible purpose to compose a sort of guide to the Buddhist world that he encountered, past and present. He doesn't try to draw out of them some deeper reflection on the meaning of history. But he must have felt a great sadness at the depredations of the Huns, the same sadness that the

Romans felt to see the Temple of Apollo turned into a stable by the Goths.

As I set off for the Swat River Valley, I anticipated a sadness as well, a sadness and an amazement at the triumph of Hunnish barbarism, especially knowing that Buddhist culture in particular was never resurrected in Gandhara. To see the ruins of Gandhara is to view one of the lesser-known artifacts of that constant alternation in human history between the builders of civilization and the destroyers of it. Once there was the tinkling of bells in these places, the basso beating of drums; there was some of the best sculpture and painting that humankind has ever produced; there was heated and learned debate on the nature of reality and ultimate truth. Now there are impressive piles of carved and fitted stone presided over by some minor tourism department functionary looking for tips. The past is a great teacher, and I was impressed that in the case of this particular past, the seventh-century monk from China and I would be confronted with the same lessons.

MY DRIVER'S NAME was Mumtaz and he was Pathan, he told me. "I can speak Pashtoon, Urdu, Hinko, Punjabi, some Persian, some English." Mumtaz said this in the same manner as Serhai, not boasting but laying out the linguistic landscape. He adopted the same tone as he pointed out the Peshawar Library, the Grand Trunk Road, the jail. Mumtaz was trim and efficient; he had a neat mustache and eyes that blazed from within deep sockets. We rode a Toyota jeep and we plunged into the early-morning chaos of Peshawar, redolent of truck, bus, and motorcycle rickshaw exhaust. In the center of town, workers were putting the finishing touches on a large papier-mâché mountain. It was in preparation for the following day when the country would celebrate Yaume I Takbeer, Day of Victory. The day in question would mark the first anniversary of the country's initial nuclear bomb explosion. That event, the cause of a government-sponsored frenzy of patriotism, had taken place on a mountain, the "mountain that exploded," the newspapers called it, the mountain that would cow India into fear and respect. I noted that the Urdu word for "day," *yaume,* was almost identical to the Hebrew word, *yom,* as in Yom Kippur, Day of Atonement. (This is because the Urdu term is derived, via the Muslim conquest, from the word for "day" in Hebrew's sister language Arabic.)

"Pakistan very busy and very pollution; America not pollution,"

Mumtaz said, ignoring the fake mountain. He slowed for a donkey ambling across the road indifferent to the onrush of motorized vehicles. "In America no this," Mumtaz said. He was referring to the donkey. "But in Pakistan, everything in between road—donkey, tonga, bicycle, horse. In America, discipline. Pakistan, no."

"We're not so great in America," I said.

"But America no this," Mumtaz repeated.

We edged through the rush to the edge of town, passing an Afghan refugee camp, the sugar refinery, the flour mill, a footbridge over the Landi River—all duly pointed out by Mumtaz. "I am your driver, your guide, your guard, your friend," he said. We headed out into the country, and in an hour or so we stopped for a look at ruins of the old city of Chaksadda, the original capital of Gandhara and a place described by the monk. There wasn't much to see there, but Takht-i-Bahi nearby was extraordinary, the most exquisite ruin I'd seen so far. It is atop a steep rocky promontory overlooking a plain dotted with farming villages, persimmon orchards, and fields of melons, tobacco, and sugarcane. I climbed up and was greeted by a ragged caretaker, happy to see a customer. He pointed out the platforms where sculptures had once been, the monks' cells, the well, the dining hall, the remains of the stupas. Then he brought me to a small collection of Buddha heads that had been found around the place by unauthorized diggers. He asked me how much I was willing to pay for them. I said I wasn't a buyer. He asked me to change money. He asked me to give him some money, which I did. I was then chased back down the hill and to the car by a clutch of young men eager to sell me relics—coins, heads, rings, and shards of ancient pots.

We continued north following the Swat River, which was broad, fast-running, and coffee-colored here, on our partial tour of the monuments in the Swat Valley that Hsuan Tsang also visited. We crossed the Malakand Pass, near which Churchill had observed one of the many wars between the British and the Pathans. At the top of the pass we stopped at a soft-drink stand and sucked down sweetened mango juice in waxed cartons. We drove several hours to Mingora, where it was still humid and hot, but which offered views of snowcapped mountains farther up the Swat Valley. There I visited a sleepy museum with a few interesting Buddhist relics excavated nearby, and I walked through a grove of trees alongside some agricultural fields to clamber over the ruins of the two Butkara monasteries that have been excavated there. At Takht-i-Bahi I resisted the black market offer of the caretaker to sell me some recently excavated Buddha heads. I was chased by boys flogging old coins and reproduction

Buddha rings. In Butkara I was approached by Senaullah, who told me that he wanted to be an English teacher, so he practiced by guiding tourists through the ruins. He was intense, worried, sincere. He had a beaked nose that would have served wonderfully for an anti-Semitic caricature. He was very nice. He invited Mumtaz and me to the rooftop balcony of his house for tea. We talked about the importance of Islamic education in Pakistan and watched as the evening faded over the Swat River and the distant mountains.

THE NEXT morning, the headline in the *Frontier Post* was TWO INTRUDING INDIAN MIGS SHOT DOWN; ONE PILOT KILLED, OTHER CAPTURED; LOC TENSION ESCALATES. The LOC was the Line of Control, the border between the Indian- and Pakistani-controlled parts of Kashmir. In the Swat Valley there were no signs of war, but we were told that the day before, truckloads of Pakistani troops had been on the road past Mingora to reinforce the country's troops in Kashmir. Mumtaz and I headed into the particle-charged chaos of local traffic, heading back the way we had come the day before. The destination was Taxila, where there are important remains of Gandharan cities and Buddhist temples. At Noshwera we joined the Grand Trunk Road, which once went all the way from Kabul to Calcutta. In fact, it still does, though because of the latter-day erection of national barriers nobody can travel it from one end to the other anymore, another example of the way travel is actually more politically difficult now than it was for most of history.

In any case, the Grand Trunk Road was thick with trucks and buses, highly decorated. The buses are shaped like hippopotamuses and driven as though they were charging bulls. They are windowless in the summer. People ride inside and on the roof, hanging on to the luggage railing as the bus swerves and rockets. The Qayun coach bore the inscription "Good-bye and have a noice day," as if the orthography were striving to reproduce a cockney accent. The trucks were decorated with eagles and eyes, kaleidoscopic diamonds, hearts, red reflectors, black banners, blue pendants, and silver bangles, the dominant colors being green and yellow, and the decorations themselves stemming from a tradition wherein all modes of transport, including the horse-drawn tongas of current-day Lahore, are carefully, lovingly adorned. They have cabin doors made out of carved wood like Balinese temples. The cabin windows are small and square and make the drivers almost invisible, a quick, dark frame of swarthy face with mustache.

We went by gypsy encampments, a few tents of patched canvas set up on ragged ground. In the towns, beggars would stand by the car window and look in, waiting. They don't actually say anything or ask for anything; they simply look, like a cashier expecting payment. And when you hand a tired few rupees out the window, they take them and turn away without a word or a gesture. Schoolboys in uniforms, gray shirts and pants, a gray beret with a red patch sewed onto it, trotted along he road. We passed several Pakistani military installations marked by signs—CMH (which means Combined Military Hospital), Artillery Mess, Garrison Engineering Corps, Artillery Depot. We lumbered through Jahangira. At Attock we crossed a bridge where the Kabul and Indus rivers intersect. The monk, as near as I can figure out, crossed the Indus somewhat north of here, presumably by boat. Near the Wah Cantonment, we sped by the border between the Northwest Frontier Province and Punjab, and at three different points the police were pulling over trucks for examination. Mumtaz explained that they were looking for goods smuggled from Afghanistan.

At Taxila, I climbed up to the Jaulian Monastery, originally built in the third century B.C. by Ashoka and already in ruins by the time the monk visited it eight hundred years later. As always, a bearded, leathery, and unavoidable Muslim was at the top waiting to be my guide, but this one turned out to be good. He said his name was Dilshad Jaulian, and I never understood whether he took that name from the monastery of which he was the caretaker or whether it was a sort of determining coincidence. He spoke in sentence fragments, as if he were reading an outline of his presentation rather than the presentation itself. First he explained that the Gandhara stupas, one of which was at Jaulian, were originally built to hold the Buddha's relics, but that over time a very small number of relics were spread over a very large number of monasteries.

"Buddha dies. Ashes, bones, teeth—eight stupas. All in Gandhara. Then fifteen thousand stupas. China, Japan, Thailand, Indonesia."

Dilshad fixed me with a stare, silently inviting me to contemplate these implausible numbers.

"Eight stupas. Fifteen thousand stupas. Ashes, bones, teeth," he repeated, allowing me to draw my own conclusions.

Dilshad waved his finger at me and invited me to take a picture of a beautiful smiling Buddha carved into one of Taxila's remaining on-site friezes. Having noticed the sign prohibiting photography, I hesitated for a minute.

"Government say no pictures. No pictures, nobody come Taxila. Stupid," he said. "You take pictures. You show friends. Friends come."

He continued with history. "First Buddha university, Nalanda." Nalanda was the university in India which was the monk's primary destination. He stayed there to study for seven years. "Ashoka build Nalanda," my guide resumed. "Third century. Ashoka dies. Second Asian center, Jaulian University. Mahayana university." Dilshad lingered so long and so sonorously on the word "Mahayana" that he practically turned it into an aria. "Third university . . . Swat. Northern area. Tantric Buddhism. Last university . . . Kashmir."

"This place Jaulian second to fifth century A.D. Near river north side big city. Two hundred years more later, Buddha Siddhartha with sixty people visit India. This mountain Mergalla. Three-hundred-year banyan tree. Buddha stay there. Now many tourists. Banyan tree E-7 Block, Islamabad. Two hundred years more later, Alexander controls Taxila. Stayed five weeks. Then King Ashoka. Later Saint Thomas. Kushans last to here. This university Roman name, Jaulian. Eighteen subjects—science, art, religion. Taxila city three times earthquake. Third century A.D. special Greek architect came here to make wall earthquake-proof." Dilshad then bent over to show me a piece of wall where large round pieces were surrounded by small pieces.

The monastery looks out over the Punjabi Valley to some high, conical hills to the southwest. We walked along all of its remaining walls, examining the impressive number of carvings that remain. Dilshad explained what he called the "mixed culture" of them: "Indian symbol, Greek art, Greek symbol, Indian art," he said. I asked him if he had heard of the monk, and he exclaimed, "Tang San!" as if we had improbably discovered a common acquaintance. "Professor man! Professor Tang San! Seventh century coming. But first White Huns." He took on a confidential look. "Sir," he said. "Buddhist people, no fighting, no meat. Good people. White Huns very bad. Like Russian. Like in Hungary."

His point was that when the monk came here, the Jaulian Monastery was already in ruins and that the monk looked at them in the way that Edward Gibbon looked at the ruins of Rome, to appreciate the greatness of the past. A bit slow to understand this, I asked him several times why the monk would have bothered to come here if the place had already been wrecked by the White Huns. Patiently, he told me:

"Sir. Jaulian twenty meters underground. British come. Tang San same thing. British like eagles. Tang San big power."

Unlike the caretaker at Takht-i-Bahi, Dilshad did not offer to sell me Buddha heads. He didn't ask me if I wanted to change money, and he didn't even ask to be paid. At the end of my visit, he took me through a gate to a point overlooking the valley below. An irrigation canal, which had once been a river, ran from the foot of the hill and wound through the agricultural fields. Here and there were clusters of buildings surrounded by trees. Dilshad pointed to the conical peak that thrust itself through the hazy hot air.

"Gasan Abdul Mountain," he said, identifying the peak. "Twenty-five miles. Gasan Abdul Muslim holy man." But then he evoked an image of life here on this hilltop monastery, this ruined seat of learning, as he imagined it to have been in the third century. "Students sit down here. Night. Almost dark. Students looking. They see river walking. They see Gasan Abdul Mountain big stupa. They see city, Taxila. Big. The sun press mountain. The mountain area gold, the city black, the river silver." Dilshad waved his hand over the scene below. "I am here thirty-two years," he said. "Thirty-two years. Every day. Every night. Every time night I come here. This view. I look every night."

HSUAN TSANG SPENT a long time in Gandhara, wandering from monastery to monastery, recording their condition and the numbers of their priests and the doctrine they followed. Most important, he catalogued the Buddhist miracles that occurred in each place, sounding, as he did so, very much like the Mahayanist described by Serhai. For the Chinese monk, the Buddha was decidedly a god and miracles were the language he spoke in.

"On the shores of the southern sea," the monk writes while contemplating a ruined stupa in the Swat Valley, "there was an old decayed tree in the hollows of which five hundred bats had taken up their abodes. Once some merchants took their seats beneath this tree, and as a cold wind was blowing, these men, cold and hungry, gathered together a heap of fuel and lit a fire at the foot of the tree. The flames caught hold of the tree and by degrees it was burned down. At this time among the merchant troop there was one who, after the turn of the night, began to recite a portion of the Abhidharma Pitaka. The bats, notwithstanding the flames, because of the beauty of the sound of the law patiently endured the pain, and did not come forth. After this they died, and according to their works, they all received rebirth as men."

These bat-men all "became ascetics," the monk continues approvingly and credulously. "They practiced wisdom, and by the power of the sounds of the law they had heard they grew in wisdom and became Arhats [enlightened ones] as the result of the merit acquired in the world."

Mumtaz took me to Rawalpindi and dropped me off at the Shalimar Hotel, where I would spend the night. From there I took the train to Lahore to visit the museum of which Rudyard Kipling's father was once the director. Outside is the cannon, the Zam-Zammah, that Kipling's Kim was sitting on when we first meet him in the famous novel. The museum's *chef d'oeuvre* is the fasting Siddhartha; it is a Christlike Buddha, a remarkable work showing a man who is starving and yet maintains a pose of philosophical tranquillity, like those bats that would rather hear a recitation of the Law than fly to safety. But the starving Siddhartha is actually symbolic of the nonflagellatory path to enlightenment. In his early years, the Buddha practiced extreme denial, including fasting, but when he failed to achieve enlightenment in that way, he turned to the Middle Path instead, the sensible, commonsensical way between the extremes of self-mortification and self-indulgence. It is one of the most attractive aspects of Buddhism and most appealing to Hsuan Tsang, who, as we will see, was appalled when he reached farther into India, at the extremes of self-punishing Hindu asceticism.

Outside the museum is Kipling's Lahore, the second city, after New Delhi, both of the Moguls and the British. I toured the Mogul Fort, where a guide (it's impossible not to have a guide; they persist until you hire them) warned me, as I began to poke around inside a darkened chamber, about snakes curled up in the recesses of the rooms. I went to the Great Mosque across from the fort. I saw the Mogul emperor Jehangir's tomb and went on a walk at night in search of what were described to me as dancing girls. Mogul cities are all alike. There is the fort, there is the mosque, and then behind the mosque, accessible through a rear gate, is the entertainment quarter, where men of means went to watch the girls dance. But Kipling makes a night ramble through the Mogul city, which he called "the City of Dreadful Night," more interesting in the nineteenth century than it is today. "I would wander till dawn in all manner of odd places—liquor shops, gambling and opium dens, which are not a bit mysterious, wayside entertainments such as puppet-shows, native dances," he wrote. "One would come home, just as the light broke, in some night-hawk of a hired carriage, which stank of hookah-fumes, jasmine-flowers, and sandalwood."* During my brief ramble, there was a bottle of bootleg beer served to me in my hotel, but no hookah fumes and, in fundamentalist-threatened Pakistan, no liquor shops either. I had that feeling once again of having been born too late.

* Harry Rickets, *Rudyard Kipling: A Life* (New York: Carroll & Graf, 2000), p. 69.

The next day I took a car to the border with India. We went down a long tree-lined road alongside a canal to the Pakistani town of Waga. Then there was a strip of barbed wire and a few low buildings beyond which cars were not allowed to go. I got out and showed my passport, while a Pakistani porter carried my bag. At the customs checkpoint, another man, presumably a civilian, maybe the brother or the cousin of the customs inspector, changed my few remaining Pakistani rupees into Indian rupees. He tried to persuade me to change some dollars into Indian rupees as well, promising me a better rate than I would get on the other side. I declined.

The road to the Indian side was about two hundred meters long. I could see the barbed-wire barriers stretching away on either side, beyond which water buffaloes were grazing. There were no soldiers, no visible military presence, though clearly the armies of both sides were close at hand. At the actual border, marked by a chalk line on the pavement, the Indian guard made a point of having the Pakistani porter put my bag down while it was still in Pakistan. I moved it three feet to India, where it and the computer bag that I had carried myself were picked up by two Indian porters. As if to illustrate the phenomenon of India's partition in 1947, everybody on the Pakistani side of the line was Muslim and on the Indian side, Sikh—porters, customs inspectors, immigration police, waiting touts, and taxi drivers. My Indian porters directed me to a customs shed, where they pointed to a list of items I would not be allowed to carry into India:

1. Tallow fat of any animal origin
2. Animal rennet
3. Ivory (unmanufactured)
4. Wild animals, their parts and products.

I assured my bronzed and turbaned companions that I was carrying no contraband, and I proceeded to passport control. Ahead of me was a Pakistani man with two handsome young boys, two enchanting small girls, and a wife wrapped in gauzy gold-brocaded material. I noted in the immigration officer's ledger that at nearly 3 p.m., one hour before the border closed, I was the eighteenth person to cross from Pakistan into India that Monday on the only land border open between the two countries. This produced an elegiac mood in me. This was, after all, the road between Lahore and Amritsar, a road on which thousands and thousands of travelers passed each and every day for perhaps three thousand years, until nationalist politics intervened and a frontier was created where none had existed before.

Among those many travelers was the monk. Though it is not clear where he crossed what is now the border, the scholarship indicates that he probably passed through Lahore to Jalandhar, the Indian city about fifty kilometers southeast of Amritsar. Amritsar itself was founded in the sixteenth century by Ram Das, the fourth guru of Sikhism, so if it existed at all in the monk's time, it was not worthy of note. Its best-known landmark is the Golden Temple, which is the St. Peter's, the Mecca, the Solomon's Temple, of Sikhism. It was the place where the infamous Colonel Dyer opened up on Indian demonstrators in 1919, killing anywhere from 379 to 550 of them depending on what inquest into the event you believe. In 1984 and 1986, Sikh extremists, who wanted to expel non-Sikhs from the Punjab, seized the Golden Temple, which was retaken both times by Indian troops with much loss of life.

But I was not thinking about this turbulent history as I crossed the frontier and headed in a taxi through the flat landscape of the Punjab. I was thinking of the next stage—getting from Amritsar to New Delhi and then to the Buddhist holy places that were the main destinations of the monk's pilgrimage. At this stage of his journey, he no doubt was thinking of Lumbini, where the Buddha was born; of Bodhgaya, where he received enlightenment under the Bodhi Tree; of Nalanda, the great university, where he would study with the masters for seven years. Perhaps he was thinking, inspired by Nagarjuna and Vasubhandu, of the illusoriness of the world of forms. Perhaps he was contemplating some way out of the great contradiction in the Mahayanist doctrine: how to persuade others that the very act of persuasion has no existence; that, indeed, all perception is by definition a phantom, a trick played by the unenlightened consciousness.

I watched ahead of me the Pakistani family with the four children squeeze into a taxi. The monk was interested only in Buddhism, and no doubt as he crossed over into India proper his mind was on the sacred relics that lay ahead of him. I was thinking of getting from the border to Amritsar and of the dark-eyed Pakistani children, desiring to have one just like them.

12

An Orphanage in Amritsar

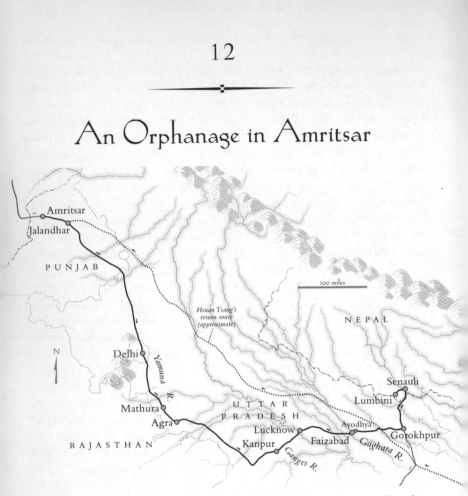

I ARRIVED IN AMRITSAR and found a pleasant place to stay on the edge of town, Mrs. Bandheri's Guesthouse. I got out of the taxi feeling tired. I was shown to my room in a bungalow at the edge of a verdant and well-tended patch of lawn. I noted with pleasure several types of birds—myna birds, seven sisters, sparrows, mourning doves. I asked for afternoon tea and toast with cheese and tomatoes. My room was clean and shabbily genteel, with purple flowered floor tiles, sun-faded curtains over the windows, and a quick gecko peeking out from the nonfunctioning air conditioner. A ceiling fan kept the hot air moving. I lay down to wait for the tea to arrive, my stomach feeling as though it were a hive of bees. I got up to go to the bathroom and almost fainted. I recovered but felt feeble, as if my interior were turning liquid. In the bathroom, dripping water made a bottom-of-the-well sound that echoed luridly in my ears. The toilet flushed with a lot of clanking and wheezing and gurgling, like someone dying of consumption. Back in the room, I unscrewed a water bottle, thinking it would be wise to rehydrate, and the sound of the cap on the threads of the bottle seemed like metal scraping metal.

I lay back on the bed under the fan. The porter's knock on the door, telling me that my tea was ready and set out on the table just outside my room, reverberated like gunfire inside my skull. I struggled to get up, thinking of my toast with tomato and cheese, arranged under a protective cheesecloth tent, and my tea, kept warm by a dun-colored quilted coverlet, on the shaded porch outside. Each time I tried, I gave myself five more minutes to sleep, until I realized that it was the middle of the night, and that I might as well sleep until morning. I did, my rest troubled by dreams of cobras slithering over the tiles of my room, waiting for me to get up and visit the bathroom, which I did several more times, turning on the light ahead of me and looking out for reptiles.

I slept until 9 a.m. The porter looked anxiously at me as I appeared on the porch. I told him he could clear away the sandwiches and tea and bring breakfast. I ate Indian cornflakes with yogurt, two fried eggs, four slices of white toast with butter and orange marmalade. I drank four cups of strong tea with hot milk, and attributed my queasiness of the night before to fatigue, heat, and a transient germ or two. There is nothing more scary then getting sick in some Third World country where you don't know anybody and you don't have a good feeling about the general state of medical treatment, so I was much relieved to be feeling better.

I went off to see the Golden Temple, which turned out to be a rather long bicycle rickshaw ride away. My driver, a Hindu named Gopal, pedaled skillfully through the tapestry of Amritsarian life. Whole families riding in other rickshaws were also going to the Golden Temple. The rickshaws have a movable sort of canopy that, when the sun has gone down, can be folded back like the hood of a baby carriage. I noticed a child sprawled out in the crevices of just such a folded-back canopy, bouncing up when her conveyance hit a bump and settling back down again like a flounce of silk. She was an object of beauty, featuring large black eyes and glowing brown skin. Her grandmother, not much bigger than she, rose and settled like a feathered thing next to her on the canopy while her mother and father and sisters and brothers rode on the seat in front. I lost sight of them when my driver turned into some profuse streets overhung with signs in Hindi and English and leading to the temple.

There you stand in line to deposit your shoes. You are told to put something on to cover your head and, if you have no covering of your own, you go to a cardboard box filled with squares of cloth and you choose a bandanna, red with lacy gold thread in my case, and wind it around your head. There were thousands of people at the temple, whose main component is a golden-roofed pavilion set in the middle of a vast rectangular pool. Pilgrims come there and prostrate themselves on the broad walkway that surrounds the pool. On the other end is a complex of bright white domes that look as if they were made out of Reddi Wip. Drifting from the golden pavilion itself is the chanting of the Sikh holy book, the Adi Granth.

I stayed only a short time, feeling like an intruder into somebody else's ceremony, and self-conscious of my silly headgear, though nobody made me feel odd or unwelcome. I stood on the edge of the walkway for fifteen minutes to watch the pilgrims come and go, hoping that I would feel moved, but what I felt mostly was a philistine stirring in my bowels, a reminder of the sloshy ailment that had afflicted me the night before. Gopal pedaled back through the maze of small streets, eventually regaining the main road, which is the Grand Trunk Road on its course from Lahore to New Delhi. On the right I noticed a large gate with a sign reading "Central Khalsa Orphanage," and I asked Gopal to stop there.

"Do you think I can go inside?" I asked him.

"You are welcome," he said, wagging his head in that Indian way.

Inside the gate, I went to a suite of rooms labeled "Office" and asked if I could have a tour. The orphanage director, who later gave his name as Harinder Singh, seemed unsurprised by my sudden appearance and request. He showed me around, telling me that the orphanage was the largest in Punjab, with about 260 children, about thirty-four of whom were blind. All creeds, denominations, and races were accepted, though there was a glistening *gurdwara* on the premises, a Sikh temple. "Here we give them comprehensive study of all religions—Hindu, Muslim, Christianity, and Sikhism," Singh told me. The orphanage was founded in 1904. It is supported largely by private donations. The children either have no parents or have only one parent who is unable to support them. I asked whether any of the children would be adopted, and Singh told me that since the youngest was already six years old, they were deemed too old for adoption. The orphanage was a clean and peaceful place. Singh showed me a large, airy octagonal room still under construction and designed to be a place for meditation. "It will have soft music," he said, "to have a soothing effect."

It was almost lunchtime, and as I talked with him the children—all boys—emerged from classrooms to go to the dining hall. They wore white shirts loose over khaki pants, and their uncut hair was tied up in the half-turban known as a patka, not the fully wound turban of Sikh men but a single wrap of cloth—yellow for the blind boys, blue for the others. As we stood there, the boys in blue patkas came up to us, reaching down briefly, deftly, to touch our feet. Some of them then stood for a brief hug or a pat on the back. They sat in four straight rows on the masonry floor of the dining hall, and after a lengthy responsive chant, the boys' voices echoing in a pleasant sort of choir, they were served their lunch on metal plates, eating with their fingers in northern Indian style. They did not talk as they ate. I watched one blind boy, about eight years old, feeling his food with his fingers for a long time before slowly and deliberately scooping it up with pieces of chapati. Earlier I had photographed some of the sighted boys, who were eager and happy to pose before the camera, and I wanted to take this boy's picture too. There was melancholy in his aspect, a kind of resignation. He was the last one to start eating and the last one to finish, after which he stood up, stepped over his plate, and walked unaided into the bright square of light outside the door and down the walkway toward the classrooms. I left my camera in the bag where it belonged. To photograph him would be to announce that I could see what he couldn't—himself.

I made a modest donation, for which I was ceremoniously given a receipt. "You won't find such an institution elsewhere in all of India," Singh told me—except, he added, the orphanage for girls in Jalandhar. I believed him. I thought about visiting the girls' counterpart, since I would be passing through Jalandhar on the train to Delhi later that afternoon, and I could, with some inconvenience, stop for a while and then pick up a later train. I longed to make that stop. The fantasy was that I would find a little girl just like the dark-eyed one I had seen earlier in the rickshaw, that I would adopt her and take her home with me and give her a loving home and a rich American life.

I didn't stop in Jalandhar, though later, when the train stood in the station there, I felt a sense of incompleteness, as you do when something you have been collecting, say the complete works of a favorite writer, is missing one piece. I had wanted to gather not just one but both of the Sikh orphanages of the Punjab into the wicker basket of my experience. But I also knew that the real missing piece for me would not be found in Jalandhar, the Punjab, India. The visit to Amritsar had helped me to understand where the missing piece was.

One Buddhist teaching is that one's fate is determined from within, not imposed by circumstance from without, that wisdom comes not from studying the exterior world but from cultivating the power of mind for self-reflection. I have always yearned for children of my own, but the yearning, given my inability to marry, has always remained abstract, un-realized. But at the orphanage in Amritsar I felt the same sort of shift in the direction of moral equilibrium that I felt when I watched Zhongmei walk down the platform at the Kucha train station. The missing piece lay within me, but maybe, when I got home, I could summon up the wisdom so that it wouldn't be missing anymore.

"HURRY AND AVAIL the golden opportunity." So said the advertising placard on the road from Agra to Mathura, a flat road through dry territory already far from Amritsar. The opportunity was to buy a Zenith television. I had taken the Sabhathi Express train from Delhi at 6:15 a.m., arriving in Agra three hours later, and hired a car immediately to go to Mathura, about two hours' drive north. Mathura is not a Buddhist center today, and it has no ruins; but the Buddha taught there once, according to legend, so the monk went to pay homage on his way to the Buddhist holy places farther east. He describes the size and disposition of the stupas and temples that flourished then, the number of priests and their ideological orientations. His account here is not interesting, but Mathura is. It's one of the holy cities of Hinduism now, the supposed birthplace of Krishna, one of the most beloved of the incarnations of Vishnu, who is in turn one of the three manifestations of Brahman, the one, ineffable, and formless god. When I was there, it teemed (the only word for it) with Indian pilgrims. It's a scene.

I had taken a night train from Amritsar to Delhi, and I spent a couple of days ambling around Connaught Place, looking up a couple of the American correspondents based in South Asia. We talked about the looming conflict along the LOC where Pakistan and India seemed to be gearing up for war. The conventional wisdom was that Pakistan had infiltrated guerrilla fighters, pretending that they were local Kashmiri "freedom fighters" over whom they exercised no control. There was much speculation as to the identity of these fighters, who had established redoubts high in the Dardistan Pangi Range of the Karakorum Mountains, almost daring India to send high-altitude troops to dislodge them. Some believed that they were Afghans, sent to fight in Kashmir in gratitude for Pakistan's support of the Taliban, which had taken control of most of Afghanistan. Others believed that they were homegrown fighters from Pakistani-controlled Kashmir, led clandestinely by Pakistani officers, who had been indoctrinated into the great cause of Kashmiri liberation and the glory of Islamic martyrdom. The reasons attributed to Pakistan for this venture, which was eventually defeated by Indian air power, were obscure. The most common explanation was that the Pakistani government of Prime Minister Nawaz Sharif was, as with the Yaume I Takbeer celebration of the Pakistani atomic bomb, drawing attention away from domestic failures by stirring up anti-Indian hatreds. (Sharif was arrested in a military coup not long after my trip and was sentenced to life imprisonment on a dubious charge of airplane hijacking.) So what if Pakistan is a place where power outages occur ten times every day; what could be more important than the liberation of those parts of Kashmir that still suffered under the Hindu yoke?

All of this seemed relevant to me because the monk went to Kashmir and I didn't. He seems to have followed pretty closely the same route that I took from Peshawar to Mingora and then back across the Indus River to Taxila. Then he went north again, crossing the mountains to Kashmir, where he was received in splendid fashion by the king, who had him ride on an elephant and surrounded him with acolytes. The monk spent two years in Srinigar before resuming his travels, coming south again to Lahore, to Jalandhar, past New Delhi, and then south to Mathura.

His stay in Srinigar must have been a rich time for the monk. One of the great Buddhist centers of learning was there, and Hsuan Tsang spent his time preparing for the more serious study that would come in Nalanda. He studied Sanskrit and Sanskrit grammar, about which he later wrote a detailed treatise. He read the strict rules of logic that governed not only Buddhist debate in India at that time but religious debate in general.

Arthur Waley, the great English translator of Chinese and Japanese literature, tells of the dramatic, portentous, nearly life-and-death nature of these religious debates, which played a role almost like that sports events play in the West today. Great tournaments were held—near the end of his Indian sojourn, Hsuan Tsang was to prevail in one against the Hindus and the Hinayanists sponsored by the great king of northern India himself—during which great scholars demonstrated their mastery of the texts and their ability to demolish their opponents. When one was defeated, one made a formally abject admission of failure—"My argument is defeated;

yours is established"—and, sometimes, Waley says, was then thrown into prison.* There were various systems of logic, especially the so-called "old logic," which was developed by our esteemed friends Asanga and Vasu-bhandu, and the later, more streamlined "new logic," the product of a later scholar named Dignana. Both established axioms of debate and taught how to recognize the different kinds of arguments that ought not to be accepted—known as the Thirty-three Fallacies. Unfortunately, nei-ther Hsuan Tsang himself nor Hui Li gives any details about the nature of this logical training, other than that it was strict and rigorous, and I have searched in vain for some historical record that might, for example, iden-tify even one of the aforementioned fallacies. But Hsuan Tsang does pro-vide in *Chronicles* a pithy corroboration of Waley's sense that the stakes were high.

There were, he writes, eighteen schools of thought in India, and they were "constantly at variance, and their contending utterances rise like the angry waves of the sea." Knowledge was rewarded in a systematic way, according to the amount of it a member of a monastery could show. "He who can entirely explain one class of books is exempted from the control of the *karmadanya* [the monastery's steward]." Mastery of two classes of books entitled the priest to what our monk calls an "upper seat"; three classes of books got him "servants to attend to him and to obey him"; five classes brought an "elephant carriage"; six a "surrounding escort." When "one of the assembly distinguishes himself by refined language, subtle investigations, deep penetration, and severe logic, then he is mounted on an elephant covered with precious ornaments, and conducted by a numer-ous retinue to the gates of the convent." By contrast, if one "breaks down in his argument, or uses poor and inelegant phrasing, or if he violates a rule in logic and adapts his words accordingly, they proceed to disfigure his face with red and white, and cover his body with dirt and dust, and then carry him off to some deserted spot or leave him in a ditch." Such an action would not seem to reflect the Buddhist injunction to be compassionate, but the Chinese Master of the Law does not seem dismayed by this. In such a manner, he writes approvingly, "do they distinguish between the meritorious and the worthless, between the wise and the foolish."

IN MATHURA, my driver, whose name was Munna, wanted fifty dollars for the trip from Agra to Mathura and back. He had a long, spreading

* Arthur Waley, *The Real Tripitaka* (London: George Allen and Unwin, 1952), p. 32.

198

mustache and an ingratiating manner. We went to the Hindu temple where Krishna was born. "Watch out for pickpocketers and beggars," Munna warned. I stepped out of the car into a human swirl, child beggars and postcard hawkers and would-be guides and Hindu holy men, the so-called sadhus, with long gray beards and glittering eyes of the sort that Coleridge could only have imagined.

The temple, which is called Shri Krishna Janmbhoomi, is garish and tasteless. Before I entered, I passed through a meticulous search by Indian police guarding against terrorism. Indian security forces have been on the alert since Muslim-Hindu clashes over temples and mosques in the city of Ayodhya in 1992. The Shri Krishna Janmbhoomi is on the site of a former mosque, which (according to the Hindus) was built during the Mogul time on the site of Krishna's birthplace. A guide approached me.

"I am temple Brahman," he said.

"What's a temple Brahman?" I asked.

The man either did not understand or felt the question to be so ignorant that it warranted no answer. He produced an identity card complete with his photograph and thrust it in front of my nose.

"I see, but what's a temple Brahman?"

"Yes," said the man.

"A temple Brahman is a priest," said another man who approached me and pushed the first man gently away. "My name is Mathurish," he said. "Means 'man from Mathura.' I am very good English speaking."

"Good, show me around," I said.

In 1912, the Italian poet Guido Gozzano wrote of a philosophical disillusionment that he experienced during a trip to India. The Hinduism of the Upanishads had been among the loftiest and most refined religious expressions of mankind, he felt, but Hinduism had deteriorated into the vulgar worship of a panoply of tinsel gods. "What has the rabble done to the divine treasure of the Vedas?" he asked. "To what filthy idolatry has the sublime heritage of the Upanishads, essence of the Ineffable, the One, the Absolute, been reduced?" The question is a good one. The Krishna Temple is full of gaudy dolls with people praying to them or chanting shrilly and repetitively to the accompaniment of bells and drums. A visit makes abundantly clear where that monotonous anodyne chant of the Hare Krishnas in America comes from—indeed, the world center of the International Krishna Consciousness Movement, founded by Swami Prabhupada, is near Mathura in Vrindavan. At one point, while recounting a story of the ten reincarnations of Vishnu (Krishna being the eighth of them), Mathurish used the word "mythology," and that gave me an opening.

"Do you really believe these stories of gods and reincarnations? Are they true or is it just mythology?" I asked. It was an impertinent question. I would not be so bold as to pose such a question to a priest in a Catholic church. But Mathurish was indulgent with me, even if his answer was not crystal-clear.

"I believe three things," he said. "History is true. India happened. Muslims happened. British happened. Is true. Mythology is true. Just like heredity. Your father, your mother, they are true. Lord Krishna, Lord Rama, Lord Buddha, they stayed here on the earth. That is also true."

I hired a boat and was poled along the Yamuna River to watch as the pilgrims bathed. The river did not seem clean, yet there were herons stalking fish along its shores and entire flotillas of large, menacing-looking turtles. The water was a dark brown. The men wore only loincloths and stood shoulder-deep in the water immersing themselves, rubbing their faces and hair, or making circular motions with their hands while quietly chanting. The women remained fully dressed in their saris. Children cavorted around them, diving and splashing as children do in brown and dubious rivers all over Asia. To a Westerner, bathing in this river would be close to inconceivable: even if fish and turtles apparently survive in it, the water does not meet our standards of hygiene. And yet it was a grand scene, the row of ghats, thousands of people washing away their sins. It is very impressive, shocking and inspiring at the same time, this Indian conviction that purity of soul can be achieved by bathing in some rank and immemorial river. If your goal is to escape existence rather than to exult in it, then what do a few bad smells matter?

Later I went to the Mathura Museum to see the few remnants of Buddhism in the town. The museum is in a hot and sleepy institution with high ceilings in the Victorian-Mogul style. Among its many statues are some red sandstone Buddhas of the first century B.C. While I was wandering through the exhibits, a few men in saffron robes came through the entryway. They were monks from a monastery in Mandalay. Like the monk from China, they had paid homage to the Buddha relics and the holy places of the Buddha's life. They looked with intense interest at the Buddha statues, ignoring those of Shiva and Vishnu and the other Hindu deities. I spoke with one of them and told him of my own mission to follow Hsuan Tsang's route, but the mention of the monk from China didn't seem to ring a bell. Or maybe I had stumbled on some burning doctrinal question. I vaguely remembered reading that in Burma, Hinayana Buddhism, the Buddhism that Hsuan Tsang treated contemptuously and dismissively as heretical, is predominant. Maybe the monk from Burma felt that I was riding the wrong vehicle, but he didn't see any point in trying to correct my mistake.

The monk from Mandalay and the monk from China, whatever their sectarian differences might have been, were similar in their devotion and their willingness to travel. The monk from Burma was smiling, round, soft-spoken, shy. He was a bit uncomfortable with this inquiring foreigner but patiently stood there as I plied him with questions about what he and his companions had seen and where they had been. It was difficult, because the monk's English was rudimentary and I speak no Burmese. I told him that I'd been to Butkara, Takht-i-Bahi, and Taxila, and he said that I was very lucky. The members of his group had been unable to get visas to Pakistan.

"In Taxila, Buddha cut off head," the monk said.

"Yes," I said. I remembered that in his account of the visit to Taxila, Hsuan Tsang repeated the stories of the Buddha's previous lives.

"This is the spot where Tathagata formerly dwelt when he was practicing the discipline of a Bodhisattva; he was then the king of a great country and was called Chandraprabha; he cut off his head, earnestly seeking the acquirement of Bodhi, and this he did during a thousand successive births," the monk wrote. The *Chronicles* are full of tales of bodily mutilation. The most famous of them, the one where the Buddha cuts off his arm to feed a hungry tiger, took place in Mankiala, between Islamabad and Lahore. For one thousand of his almost infinite number of previous births, the Buddha, who was the king of a country north of Peshawar, plucked out his eyes and gave them in charity. The monk says that in a temple in Afghanistan he saw an eye of the Buddha that is "so bright that its rays dart forth from the box to some distance outside."

"Why did you come to Mathura?" I asked the monk from Mandalay.

"Yes," the monk replied.

"Mathura," I repeated. "Why . . . you . . . come . . . here?"

"Oh," said the monk, understanding. "Not much Buddhism here."

"There's nothing at all," I said. "Only Hindu and Muslim."

"Just a few statues," the monk said sadly, looking about.

"So why did you come here?"

The monk fixed me with his serene vision.

"Buddha come here," he said. "Here he teach disciples."

"I guess that's why the monk from China came here too," I said.

The monk smiled in nonreply. I wanted to tell him of the glorious sight that the monk saw in Mathura. He describes assemblies of priests making offerings and visiting the sacred objects, so many of them that "the smoke of incense rises in clouds and flowers are scattered in every direction like rain." But I wasn't sure he would understand me.

"It's important for you to go everywhere Buddha went?" I asked instead.

"Yes," said the monk. His tone was solemn, liturgical. "Pakistan no give visa." He smiled.

"That's very bad," I said, but the monk did not seem to endorse my annoyance. To be annoyed is to attach oneself to the illusion of a self, to be fettered by excitability and by the desire not to be annoyed. If only I could attain such wisdom.

I said goodbye. He bowed and clasped his hands together in the Buddhist salutation, so I hastily and awkwardly did the same thing. He was easy to like, this monk in his wrinkled robe and bowed shoulders and sandals. I thought but didn't say that it had become important for me also to go everyplace—or, at least, most of the places—the Buddha had been, though I couldn't claim a spiritual purpose. It was the traveler's acquisitiveness, the yearning for a complete set of destinations, for the full accomplishment of the task.

I TOOK THE TRAIN from Agra overnight to Lucknow. My companions were two elderly women in saris who brought dinner with them, spooned out of aluminum-foil packages and eaten with chapatis. They offered me a sweet, which I accepted, already lying down in my upper berth. I slept better than I usually do on trains. The compartment was air-conditioned, and I had to wrap myself tightly in the blanket to keep warm. In Lucknow I got a porter to take me to a train connecting to Faizabad, which, as it turned out, was leaving right away. Then came three hot hours in the company of what appeared to be five Indian brothers. Near the end, I stood between cars and leaned out the open door while rural India passed slowly before me.

I went to the bus station and took the local bus to Ayodhya to see the temple of Hanuman and the Rama Temple, which was the scene of the worst of the Hindu-Muslim fighting in 1992. A self-described guide picked me up after I had seen the Hanuman temple, and since I didn't know the way to the Ram Janam Bhumi, the Rama Temple, and since there didn't seem to be anybody who could speak English, I hired him, promising fifty rupees, about $1.25. He took me to what he called the temple office, where an overly cordial man who described himself as a doctor had me write down my name and address, my occupation, and, when it turned out that my occupation was writer, the names of the books I had written. Then he carefully copied the information into a notebook, telling me that he hoped I would send him my books.

"I will send you so many material," he promised.

The Rama Temple was an armed camp. It is the counterpart to the Krishna Temple in Mathura. One is the birthplace of Krishna, the other the birthplace of Rama, whose followers are even more numerous and, it would seem from recent history, more prone to assaulting the infidels. Both are old Hindu temples that were converted to mosques during the Mogul period, and both have been the scenes of Hindu-Muslim violence. In Mathura the mosque still stands, but the mosque in Ayodhya was torn down by Hindu mobs in 1992, and ever since it has been a zone of high security. Soldiers are everywhere. One submits to three body searches in order to get inside. Pilgrims are required to keep to a cement walkway enclosed by a high wire fence surmounted by barbed wire that weaves through the site of the ruined mosque, while outside the bars the soldiers stand guard. Finally, you end up with a brief view of a kind of makeshift Rama shrine inside a tent. A man pours a spoonful of holy water into your palm and you drink it, thinking of bacteria. He gives you some small round sugary things and you eat them. You make obeisance to the gaudy Rama in the tent, and then you move on, single-file.

Then it was back to the good doctor, who angled for a donation by giving me a Rama painting I didn't want, offering me a soft drink that I also didn't want, and engaging in conversation of a forced cordiality that neither of us could understand. I reluctantly made a donation of one hundred rupees, for which I was given an official receipt, in Hindi. Two more temples were on the tour, where my guide made it clear he would be insulted if I didn't perform the rituals myself—and then leave some baksheesh on the chintzy altar. I did so. Then he asked again for one hundred rupees for himself, but I stuck to our agreement and paid him fifty, feeling principled and, as always in these situations, cheap. You can't win in India. You are too rich compared to them to win morally. I went back to the bus station, squeezed into a crowded motorcycle rickshaw, and went back to Faizabad, an hour away, for the night.

Afterward I read a brochure the doctor had given me, and regretted even more my donation. The doctor had talked to me about his hopes for Hindu-Muslim peace, but the brochure was a straightforward justification for the actions of the Hindu mob that tore down the Mogul mosque.

Religion aside, imagine at the end of the twentieth century an ancient piece of Mogul architecture torn down to make room for a shlocky Hindu temple with its shiny idols. It is worse than an atrocity. It is bad taste.

IT WAS A long ride to the Buddha's birthplace. I arrived fifteen minutes early for the 5 a.m. bus at the Faizabad station, but every seat was already taken, or claimed by those who shouted at me from outside the bus when they saw me get near the place they had reserved for themselves. I got off, figuring I'd have to wait for the next bus. But then room was made for me in the middle of the back seat, and on that bed of nails I sat for seven hours to the Indian town of Senauli on the Nepalese border. At one point we backtracked a considerable distance when the driver apparently took a wrong turn. But there was nobody on this bus who spoke English, and I therefore remained ignorant of some of the interesting details—such as why we stopped so often and simply sat there, the driver at the wheel, the passengers in their places, no visible obstruction ahead of us. There was a repair performed about ten feet short of a railroad crossing that was crossed by two racketing trains as we stood there. I was closely observed by a motorcycle cart full of Indian women, and I observed them in return— they were beautiful women, but there was something savage about them too, tigerlike. It was in their large eyes and brilliant teeth speckled with crimson betel juice and in the hardness of their stare.

It was dust and pandemonium on arrival in Senauli, orchestrated by a fat policeman with an orange whistle and a bamboo baton for discipline, but there was no discipline. At least a hundred buses, maybe more, lined the narrow road waiting for customs inspection. The rickshaw drivers brawled for the right to carry me to the immigration checkpoint, a kilometer away. A fat Indian policeman banged an exit stamp into my passport, and a few hundred yards farther down the traffic-clogged road I filled out two long tissue-paper forms and, in exchange for twenty-five dollars, got a Nepalese entry visa. A few minutes later, I crossed by rickshaw to the Nepalese side and found a car to take me to a hotel in Lumbini about ten miles west.

Lumbini is the birthplace of the Buddha. Buddhists from many nations have erected temples there, each in a different national style. The Chinese have built one that resembles a miniature Forbidden City. The Thais are there, and the Japanese in force, and the Burmese, the Sri Lankans, and the Tibetans. I dragged myself wearily through a tour of the temples.

My taxi driver, furnished by the hotel, told me the temperature was 45 degrees centigrade. That's 112 degrees Fahrenheit. The Buddha's actual birthplace is marked by an uninteresting stone shrine surrounded by fields buzzing with locusts. Nearby is a fetid pond where the baby was washed by his mother. Nobody was there except for a volunteer guide who tried hard but didn't speak English. I was feeling the onset of an intestinal pestilence. I asked the driver to take me back to my hotel, which was in the Japanese style. I had a tatami room and a Japanese-style bath. There, despite the heat, I shivered feverishly all night, worried again that I would be too sick to recover by myself, and wondering, if that should be the case, how and where I would get some medical help. I wrapped myself in my futon and dreamed of a prince who cut off his arm and gouged out his eyes and cut off his head, slicing and hacking away at the flesh for a thousand generations until, finally, he was permitted to stop.

13

The Maharaja of Ruin

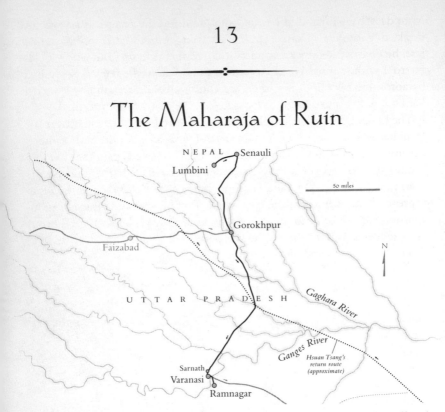

I WOKE UP FEELING weak but better, believing that I hadn't suffered from something bacterial but just been laid low by the heat. I went back across the Indian border and the baked plain to the city of Gorokhpur by taxi. In Gorokhpur I got the overnight train to Varanasi, the city of the dead, the holiest of Hindu cities. I checked into a modest guesthouse, had some breakfast, and went right out to find a rickshaw to take me to the famous ghats, or bathing places, on the Ganges River. It was his reaction to the scene of Indian religious life along the river that most revealed the monk's Chineseness. He had come down the river from Allahabad, which is at the confluence of the Jumna and Ganges rivers. Near there he had his famous encounter with robbers. Having survived that, he expresses an awed distaste for the extreme asceticism of Hinduism that he began to observe as he traveled the Gangetic Plain. Our pilgrim was unconvinced by the arguments of the Brahmans that it was an asceticism practiced for the sake of spiritual truth, though he marveled at it. As I have related, the Buddha attempted extreme asceticism for six years and, after almost starving to death, repudiated it in favor of the Middle Way. In the world of our monk, devotion to spiritual quest was taken for granted, but, as a Chinese, he would not have endorsed the mutilation of his body, which was a gift to him from his honored parents. He describes one of the most extraordinary of the Hindu practices:

> The heretics who practice asceticism have raised a high column in the middle of the river; when the sun is about to rise, they immediately climb up the pillar; then, clinging on to the pillar with one hand and one foot, they wonderfully hold themselves out with one foot and one arm; and so they keep themselves stretched out in the air with their eyes fixed on the sun, and their heads turning with it to the right until it sets. When the evening has darkened, then they come down. There are many dozens of ascetics who practice this rite. They hope by these means to escape from birth and death.

They still do, and they create one of the great spectacles of human life, the throngs who perform ablutions by the banks of the Ganges, the millions who are cremated here, their ashes allowed to wash into the sacred waters. What makes Varanasi so special? I asked an old man. Why do people come here to die? He was toothless and dressed in a flimsy purplish dhoti. He walked painfully with a staff. He had been introduced to me by the Maharaja of Varanasi as a scholarly expert on the city. His name was Vaikunth Nath Upadhyay. He squinted at me schoolmarmishly, surprised by such a naive question.

"If you die in Varanasi," he said, having found a formulation primitive enough for this ignorant foreigner, "you won't be born again."

Upadhyay was the fruit of what had become my own small obsession in Varanasi. I wanted to interview the aforementioned Maharaja to ask him about a controversy that had begun to appear in the Indian newspapers. I met a woman journalist in New Delhi, Tavleen Singh, who had written a column in the weekly *Indian Express* about the appalling pollution of the Ganges, her point being that the very river where people seek to purify their souls poisons their bodies. "Those who live with the filth every day say that the secret of enjoying Benares is to rise above it," she wrote. "You have to exist at a spiritual plane, they say." But there are dead rats in the river, and dead human bodies, and millions of gallons of sewage pouring into it every day, and the religious leaders, the political leaders, even the environmentalists, make no outcry. "Where are the Shankaracharyas?" she asked. The Shankaracharyas are the five major

Hindu leaders of India, each living in a different holy city. "Why is not one of them able to stand up and announce that any good Hindu guilty of using the banks of the Ganges as a toilet is making seriously bad karma for himself?"

Hence, in part, my interest in the Maharaja of Varanasi, a man who had been Maharaja for some fifty years. He was reputed to own half of the bathing and burning ghats on the Ganges. He disposed of enormous prestige. When he went out, he drew large crowds of Hindus straining to catch a glimpse of him. This was the case even though the Indian government abolished what remained of aristocratic privilege in 1971. The maharajas saw much of their land and property confiscated, in return for which they received inadequate stipends and police protection. Since then, maharajas have been a kind of classic impoverished nobility, too proud to work even as they watch their fortunes dwindle and their palaces collapse. But the Maharaja of Varanasi was a kind of *primus inter pares* of Indian royalty. He owned ghats along the holy river. He was different. And, moreover, he was old. He had been a maharaja since the days of the British. He would have stories to tell.

"Is he rich?" I asked my rickshaw driver, who had mentioned him with reverence.

The rickshaw driver just smiled at me, showing a betel-stained semi-toothlessness. It was a stupid question. Rich compared to a rickshaw driver?

My first thought was to go to the tourist office and ask advice there about meeting the Maharaja. But when my rickshaw driver, who displayed a certain savoir faire, began pointing out to me the Maharaja's various properties, I asked him where the great man lived. He took out a map and pointed to a town called Ramnagar, on the opposite shore of the Ganges from Varanasi and a few miles upstream.

"Is it possible to see him?"

"Yes sir." The rickshaw driver's head swiveled like a marionette's.

"Not just see him with my eyes, but meet him, talk to him."

"No problem. You take boat."

The rickshaw driver had a friend, Choonoolal, who was a boatman. Choonoolal had taken others to see the Maharaja. He told me the standard procedure: "You are going to Maharaja's house. There will be policeman. You are giving policeman card. Policeman is going to Maharaja. He is giving card. Maharaja is saying yes, no."

"Let's go," I said.

The boat was a long, paint-flecked shallow-draft rowboat. With Choonoolal at the oars we progressed upstream, past the red brick Niranjani Ghat ("Only live the holy man," Choonoolal informed me). We went past small herds of water buffalo taking their late afternoon dip, then past the Prabhu Ghat (another exclusive preserve for holy men) and the Join Ghat, which has twin burnt-yellow towers. When we got to the middle of the river, the boatman began to sing. He stopped rowing to take a few sips of water from the Ganges. "Here clean," he said, putting great singsong stress on "clean." "Someplace dir-TEE; here cle-EEN." He was small and wiry and very brown. He wore an orange loincloth that just barely covered his private parts. From time to time he took a small dose of tobacco into his palm and kneaded it with a white substance he called "calcium," then popped it into his mouth.

After a few minutes we had left the city behind. The river was a greenish brown here, not exactly pure and fresh, but compared to the conspicuously fouled shoreline it did seem clean. A broad sandy flat ran from the far shore to a row of trees perhaps a half mile away, and Choonoolal told me that the river would cover all of it when the monsoon comes. But now it was before the monsoon and very hot. Kites wheeled over the sandy flat. Down well-worn paths came women in colorful saris carrying babies on their hips.

"Burning ghat," the boatman said, pointing out a great pile of logs on the far bank, a cremation point. "I will tell you dead body story," he said, and he began with the portentous phrase "God is the Shiva." But when I began reflexively to scribble in the notebook I always carried with me, he told me that I had to pay money for his dead man story. Knowledge is wealth. If I was going to convert the boatman's knowledge into a salable literary commodity, he reasonably wanted his cut.

"Well, don't tell me any dead body stories then," I said and put the notebook away.

"You pay mo-NEE!" Choonoolal said, his voice becoming shrill.

"I pay for boat," I said, getting a little shrill myself. "Not for talk."

"Never mind," the boatman said. "I telling story. You writing in book."

"Okay," I said.

Choonoolal then gave a pretty good concise description of Hindu funerary practices, the way the deceased are carried on stretchers down to the river, and how, when a man has lost a close relative, he shaves his head and beard (and his mustache, too, but only if the deceased is his father).

Various rituals are followed and then the body is burned, a process that, the boatman said, takes about three hours. Most interesting are the five categories of dead people who cannot be cremated.

"Small baby, leprosy, cobra, smallpox, and holy man," Choonoolal said. "That body big stone wrapping, putting in river. Only one body no stone—cobra snake. That body put in river swimming." Translation: Small babies who die, or dead holy men, or people who fail because of leprosy or smallpox are not cremated but weighted with a stone and sunk into the river. Those who have died after being bitten by a cobra are floated stoneless on the water. "People see body swimming say, 'Ah, cobra dead.' They praying God."

Why the different treatment of the victim of snakebite? I asked.

"Small baby same as the god," Choonoolal said. "Cobra is god Shiva. Leprosy no good man. Smallpox god is the mother. Holy man god is Brahma."

As Choonoolal spoke, a dead cow floated down the river, its body covered with avid crows. The stench of rotting flesh crept over the river.

"I am alone," Choonoolal suddenly declaimed. "Six years wife go. She go live with father. Take children. Father rich man. Two trucks, one Ambassador car, one Maruti car. I am boatman. I no house, no home, no truck, no car, no wife, no children. I sleep river. I eat river. I am alone." There was no tone of self-pity or complaint in this. Choonoolal seemed to be speaking informationally, not piteously. After a few minutes went by, he asked: "You have job in America? You have job for Indian boatman? I want to go America. You have job you give me?"

The Maharaja's palace, otherwise known as Fort Ramnagar, loomed up on the far bank just beyond a pontoon bridge that crossed the Ganges. From a distance it was imposing, with large rounded towers and robust ramparts surmounted by a network of buildings with colonnades, porticoes, arches, and cupolas, all of it a delicate blend of ocher, yellow, and red. We pulled the boat up to the shore and walked into a nest of soft drink and food stalls outside the palace. Inside the gate it became clear that the Maharaja of Varanasi was the Maharaja of a crumbling past. It would be hard to imagine a palace in worse shape. Stucco peeled off interior brick, cornerstones and foundation walls were corroded, plastic bottles and scrap paper accumulated in numerous courtyards. I had no business cards with me (a result of the China part of the trip, when I was keeping my journalistic identity a secret), so I wrote my name and affiliation and my purpose in coming to India on a page torn out of my spiral notebook. It was not elegant, but I hoped it would do the trick. Then, carrying my little written application for an interview, I followed Choonoolal from one person to another in an effort to find somebody who would take it to the Maharaja.

In such a way did I observe an entire large cast of royal retainers, each of whom spoke only to Choonoolal and took no notice of me. There was a round man in a white dhoti walking on the parched grass of the palace courtyard and vigorously brushing his teeth with a willow twig. There was the guardian with a yellow piece of cloth draped over his head who waved a bony finger in a gesture of refusal. There was a skinny man in a stained and smudged T-shirt and purple loincloth. After some time wandering through what had once been exquisite courtyards, I espied a sign saying "Office," but I saw no office. I saw only a few closed and battered doors, rooms with broken furniture, rooms with broken windowpanes, one room with a dusty bench on which were lined up four brass tubas, relics of some long-ago brass band. The policeman at the gate foretold by Choonoolal didn't exist. At one point, the man with the yellow cloth on his head did take notice of me. He mimed sleep and pointed to the Maharaja's quarters.

"He is sick," Choonoolal explained. "Sleeping."

"Maybe we need to pay some baksheesh," I said.

"Not yet," Choonoolal said, and he signaled to me to be patient, to wait for him, as he dashed off, his loincloth flapping, his shrill voice echoing in the palace's tawdry chambers.

At last a man in Western-style shirt and trousers accepted my petition and went off with it to the Maharaja. He returned a few minutes later.

"You come back at ten-thirty p.m. The Maharaja will see you."

"Ten-thirty tonight?" I asked.

"No, tomorrow morning," the man said. "Ten-thirty p.m."

"You must mean ten-thirty a.m.," I said. India was bewildering.

"No," the man said impatiently while a crowd gathered around to listen. "Morning, morning. P.m! P.m!"

I took a deep breath.

"I'm sorry, sir, but p.m. means nighttime. A.m. means morning."

"Well, come in morning," the man said.

"Morning. You're sure?"

"Come in morning, no nighttime."

"Okay," I said. "See you tomorrow, ten-thirty, um, a.m."

We rowed back past the burning ghat, and Choonoolal pointed out a body swathed in red brocaded fabric that had been placed on the ground at the edge of the water while a group of men carried logs down the bank to prepare a funeral pyre. We put the boat on shore nearby and watched, with Choonoolal gesturing at me to take pictures. When you visit the burning ghats in the main part of Varanasi, you are reminded repeatedly that photography there is strictly prohibited and that a tourist can find himself being hotly pursued by a crowd of offended mourners if he is caught violating that prohibition. So it took some persuading that here on the far shore, where there were only the sandy flats and the riverbank and the kites and plovers, where Varanasi was only a hazy downriver skyline, it was all right to take pictures.

And so I did, snapping away as the pyre was built, stakes driven into the ground to keep the logs in place. Eventually the shrouded body—it was a woman; a man would have been shrouded in white—was placed on the logs. The shroud was loosened but not removed, and I could see that the woman's head was wrapped tightly in cloth.

When the pyre was ready, the bereaved husband appeared, wearing only a white cloth wrapped around his waist and loins. His head and beard were shaven, but not his mustache. He faced the Ganges and said some prayers. Then, holding a sheaf of smoking straw, he walked around the pyre five times. I continued to watch and to photograph, my own bare feet marinating in the Ganges holy waters. The husband used the burning straw to set the pyre alight. And at that point, I was asked by the funerary participants to take a picture of the bereaved man next to the burning pyre, and to send it to him. It would be the last picture of him next to his wife, I was told. The man posed stiffly, formally, and with great dignity as close to the pyre as he could without cremating himself. I took some pictures and carefully wrote down the name and address of Shova Yado. Milkman. Village Goraphur near Mapi. PS Jamalpur. District Merjaphur. Uttar Pradesh. India.

I sent a photograph. I hope he got it.

THE NEXT MORNING I was back on the boat and heading again for Ramnagar and my appointment with the Maharaja. There was a light cloud cover and a breeze that kept the heat at bay, but it made the boating more difficult. Choonoolal struggled silently to keep the boat headed upriver, but the wind pushed it around toward the south shore. Finally he got out of the boat altogether and pulled it over his shoulder with a line tied to the bow, splashing through waist-deep waters while I sat and watched him labor.

"Let's tie the boat up here and walk to the palace," I said, seeing the fort looming up a few hundred yards ahead. A difference between Americans and other people: We are uncomfortable seeing others labor physically while we are at ease. It is for that reason that we don't like rickshaws, especially the original rickshaw, the conveyance pulled by a trotting coolie while the passenger sits on a seat behind him. We have legs; we should use them for our own locomotion. Others, especially people with a long history of class difference, like the Indians or the English or the Chinese, are untroubled by this. In Hong Kong, an Englishman told me: "The difference between us and you is that you don't know how to treat servants." And so I offered to walk to the Maharaja's palace while my boatman took it as a matter of pride (or perhaps of the amount of money I would give him later) to convey me to my destination with the least effort on my part.

"Sit down," he growled.

We got to the palace with a half hour to spare before my ten-thirty appointment. I used the time to visit the museum set up on two floors that showed the decrepit relics of the maharajan life. There were "bullock-drawn vehicles" and various other carriages, broughams, tongas, and landaus. A collection of antique cars followed, including what looked like a Rolls-Royce (there was no label or plate identifying it, but it had that elongated, grandiloquent quality of a Rolls or a Bentley). An old Buick rusted nearby, and so did a few other internal-combustion buggies that would be worth something if only the Maharaja would see to some minimum maintenance. Next was a remarkable collection of nineteenth-century palanquins of various shapes and sizes. There was one called Chaubanshi, another called Shivika, a third called Kamlashan; there was Nalaki, Tondar, Airy Tam-Jam, and just plain Tam-Jam, the variety alone suggesting the many ways in which a Maharaja could have others do his walking for him. An ornate and enormous elephant chair sat dustily near the palanquins. Next were weapons: braces of dueling pistols, Burmese swords, matchlock rifles, and blunderbusses. In another room, portraits of maharajas were displayed—the maharajas of Kashmir, Hyderabad, Indori, Potiala, Bhopal, Baroda, and other places.

The British did not eliminate the maharajas; the colonial government formed alliances with them and allowed them to remain as figureheads while the real power was in London. At independence, when India was partitioned, there were still some seven hundred recognized maharajas. Our own Maharaja of Varanasi was shown in one photograph entertaining the visiting king of Nepal. Along the tops of the walls among the cobwebs and the flecks of peeling paint were many antlers, cheaply mounted.

I began to conjure up alliterative epithets for this former potentate: the sultan of spiderwebs, the doge of dust, the raja of ruin, the liege of litter, the panjandrum of pollution, the sire of staring into space. Why didn't he at least have some of his many minions tidy the place up? I wondered. The answer, I think, has to do with the remains of the caste system. The Maharaja's retainers do not sweep or mop or engage in routine maintenance. Like him, they preside over the process of decay while laboring not.

"The Maharaja is praying," said one of these minions when at precisely ten-thirty I presented myself at the entryway to the private quarters. "Come back at eleven o'clock."

We stood in a kind of courtyard foyer. A set of marble stairs led upward. Next to us was a policeman armed with a rifle that seemed to have come from the Maharaja's museum collection.

Choonoolal led me out to a portico that hung over the Ganges, and I sat there surveying the mournful view. From below, the vehicles on the pontoon bridge made a sound like canvas flapping in a stiff wind. On the other side of the river, boys were leading water buffalo into the water. On this side, beyond the pontoon bridge, children were playing in the river. Boats were pulled up on the shore for repair, getting coats of shiny black pitch on their hulls. Behind us, the Maharaja's private quarters rose up ornate and corroding, like a beautiful dowager whose skin is drying, cracking, falling off. Doves roosted in the cornices. Kites glided overhead. In the downriver distance the skyline of Varanasi was almost swallowed up by haze.

We presented ourselves at the new appointed time but again were refused entry, this time in Hindi, so I couldn't ascertain the reason. Choonoolal began stalking through the compound as he had the day before, his shrill voice ringing through the antique premises, while I waited next to the policeman. Several of the men from the day before came and went. They spoke to Choonoolal, and I was impressed by the cordial respect they showed the boatman, but none of them acknowledged me. Choonoolal, who had put a blue plaid shirt on over his loincloth for his appearance at the palace, scurried back and forth, disappearing into one courtyard, reappearing from another, his voice seeming to come from several places at once. Finally, after much perseverance on his part, a servant appeared dressed in a flowing tunic cinched at the waist. He led me upstairs into a reception room and told me to sit and wait.

Time passed. It was hot. I was thirsty, but there was no offer of tea or a cold drink. When I asked for some water, the servant said, "No English,

Hindi, Hindustan." This is India, he was telling me, Hindustan; don't expect to get along here if you don't bother to learn my language. I appreciated the anticolonialist sentiment, and yet I also wondered if he had been instructed to be patriotically inhospitable. I examined the room: the marble floor, the French doors leading to a columned portico overlooking the courtyard, curving tree trunks wedged between bricks below and beams above to shore up the roof. There were more antlers on the walls and more cobwebs; there was half of a stuffed leopard, or perhaps it was a panther or even a small lion—the deterioration was too advanced to tell. There were carved marble lintels, bulbless light fixtures, dangling electrical wires, fluted columns, a pile of rolled-up tapestries.

"Come here." The servant now led me back out the way we had come, down the stairs, through the courtyard, past the museum, and upstairs to a second-floor office where a man of about forty sat behind a desk. He looked at me and waited for me to speak. I told him my story briefly, my trip from China, the monk, my visit the day before, my note on spiral notebook paper, the promise of an interview at ten-thirty.

"He never receives in the afternoon," the man said.

"That must be why he granted me an appointment this morning," I said. I looked at my watch. It was noon.

"He's had some work to do this morning."

"They told me he was praying."

"That too."

"Is there a telephone number I could call in the future?"

The man wrote one down on a piece of paper.

"You can speak to his secretary, but his secretary isn't here just now."

"I assumed you were his secretary."

"I am his son."

"Oh," I said enthusiastically. "So you're the next Maharaja."

"I don't know."

During this exchange, which was not unfriendly, the Maharaja's son had sent off the servant, who now returned. The two spoke briefly in Hindi.

"He will see you, but you might have to wait," the son said, gesturing for me to follow the servant.

"You mean you're not the only son?" I asked.

"Yes, I'm the only son."

"Then why don't you know if you'll be the next Maharaja, or is it impolite to ask?"

"I can't reply," he said, but he smiled.

I followed the servant back to the reception room with the antlers and the French doors and the tree trunks holding up the ceiling. After five minutes I was ushered to another set of stairs leading to the roof. On a charpoy was the elderly man I would later know as Vaikunth Nath Upadhyay. In a corner, reclining on a wicker chair under a canopy, was a handsome gray-haired man of perhaps seventy or more.

"Yes?" he said. The tone was not welcoming. "What do you want?"

"You are the Maharaja of Varanasi?" I asked.

"Yes."

I explained my mission as briefly as I could—China, the monk, the book, my wish to have a brief interview.

"No," said the Maharaja.

"Why not?" I asked.

"I don't like to be misquoted."

"I don't misquote people."

"You should have written a letter."

"Are you aware that I was told yesterday that you were giving me an appointment for today at ten-thirty?"

"Yes."

"So you knew that I had an appointment at ten-thirty?"

"Yes."

"Then why have I been kept waiting for two hours?"

The Maharaja gave a shrug.

"I've spent the better part of two days trying to see you and you have nothing to say about this?"

"Why do you want to see me?" he asked.

"Because I thought it would be interesting. Because you've been a maharaja for a long time. Because we don't have maharajas in America."

"I know."

"So, let's just converse for a few minutes."

"No."

Silence.

"You should have written me a letter."

"You should have kept your ten-thirty appointment with me."

"I didn't know what you wanted."

"I put on my note to you that I was a journalist at the *New York Times* and that I was writing a book about India."

"A little piece of paper is not courteous."

"I'm sorry, sir. I didn't mean to be discourteous, but given the time available, it was the best I was able to do."

"If you wanted to see Bill Clinton, would you simply show up at his door demanding an appointment?"

I did not point out the many obvious flaws in this analogy between a has-been maharaja and the president of the United States.

"If Bill Clinton gave me an appointment of his own free will, he would have had the courtesy to keep it."

It was at this point that the Maharaja offered me Upadhyay, who could tell me everything I needed to know about Benares, he said. I thanked him, wished him good health and a long life, and walked out. I understood that he hadn't wanted to be bothered by an importuning outsider, and I figured that he had promised me an appointment since it had bothered him to send me away empty-handed. Probably he thought that I wouldn't return the next morning anyway. The Maharaja might be an anachronism, but he was an anachronism with attachments. He belonged to a society, a network of friends and associates. It was through them that a stranger should make his appearance, or, at least, through a letter requesting an interview—not through the intermediary of a half-naked boatman and a note scrawled on a piece of wrinkled paper torn out of a spiral notebook. What had resulted was this unsatisfactory halfway measure, an appointment granted but avoided, a meeting that was not a meeting.

Still, I drew a conclusion from my abortive encounter with the Maharaja of Varanasi. In its dilapidation and its state of disrepair, the castle seemed to mirror the river that flowed beside it. The Shivali Ghat, which was owned by the Maharaja, was where I picked up my boatman and boat, and when I did so, I couldn't help but notice a roaring, fetid, sewage-smelling stream that rushed by it to empty into the Ganges. The stream ran through a neighborhood of open drainage ditches that also smelled of sewage, all of which eventually made its way into the very river where thousands washed away their impurities every day. I thought of Tavleen Singh's call for the religious and political leaders of Varanasi to begin some action to clean up the river. But there is a tremendous passivity in Varanasi, and the Maharaja embodied it, a pious kind of lassitude. Things don't change. The river flows; people empty their refuse into it; other people, or maybe the same people, bathe in it, die in it, are dumped into it after they have been burned. The river remains holy. The dead are not born again.

"Half of India is illiterate," Tavleen told me in New Delhi. "The simple people who bathe in the river want to make themselves holy, and they don't know about bacteria."

I thought of Choonoolal leaning over the gunwales of his boat, scooping up river water and drinking it from his cupped palm and telling me that in some places it was dirty but there it was clean. Did he have any choice? Is he going to spend half his daily income buying bottled water at forty cents a quart, this man who probably makes on average two or three dollars a day? Probably his waste goes into the river too, either directly or indirectly. Where else can it go?

"Why doesn't he fix the place up?" I asked Upadhyay. I was speaking of the Maharaja's palace, but I could have been speaking of the River Ganges. "The place is a mess. There's litter and garbage everywhere, and all these people sitting around and doing nothing."

We had left the Maharaja's rooftop and had made a very slow course across the grassy courtyard, Upadhyay walking with a cane and literally gasping for breath. We now sat in a kind of library, an archive, a room of dusty books and ledgers like a nineteenth-century British bank. When I tried to move my chair closer to his so that I could hear him better, I saw that one of its legs was broken and that the chair was propped up by bricks. I knew how impertinent my question was. Who was I, this ignoramus of a foreigner, this post-imperialist unschooled in Hindu philosophy, to be pointing the finger of hygienic accusation? But I pointed it nonetheless, angry at having been kept waiting in the heat while the Maharaja lounged on his roof and the palace crumbled beneath his slippered feet.

"Because he has no businesses," Upadhyay said, "only properties. Because he's a very religious man. He's not a political man. Because there's no money."

14

A Detour to Hong Kong

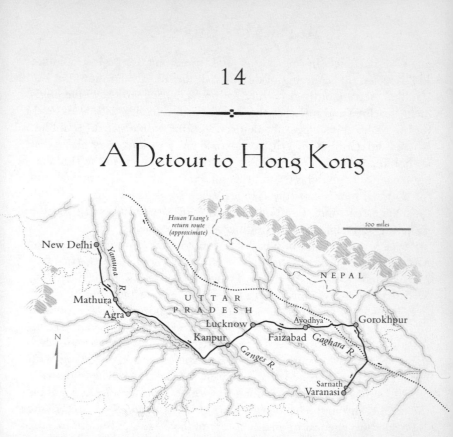

S ARNATH, ONLY a few miles from Varanasi, is where the Buddha delivered his first sermon. The monk went there, and so did I, by motorcycle rickshaw, on my last day in Varanasi. I thought I would stop there just
before Bodhgaya, which is where the Buddha received Enlightenment,
but as we will see in a moment, my plans were foiled by a combination of
Indian trains and a seizure of caution on my part. Still, I did go to the
Deer Park, where the Buddha, having achieved enlightenment, passed on
his discoveries to a group of disciples, and there it seemed natural to think
some more about what might be the ultimate question, not of my journey but of Hsuan Tsang's, about the nature of the Ultimate Truth.

Sarnath represents a kind of culminating point as well as a beginning.
The beginning was the teaching of Buddhism, which, obviously, is
important, but Sarnath is also where the Buddha's long search—which
required a thousand previous incarnations—reached its conclusion. A
logical way to visit the Buddhist holy places would be to follow the main
events of the Buddha's life itself, the sacred narrative whose elements are,
like the main events of the life of Jesus, what give believers their spiritual

points of reference. In the case of Jesus, the events are birth, teachings, and miracles, the gathering of disciples, death, and resurrection. For the Buddha, they are birth, departure for home, ascetic struggle, enlightenment, teaching and miracles, the gathering of disciples, and death, and, for the Mahayanists especially, deification. One would start in Lumbini, where I did start, but then the path would go to various other places that do not line up well geographically. To follow the events in the Buddha's life sequentially up to his death in Kusinagara would be to roam back and forth several times across the Ganges Valley, so Hsuan Tsang and I both took the easier route, Lumbini first but then Sarnath (teaching and the gathering of disciples) before Bodhgaya (enlightenment).

Sarnath is to Buddhism what the Mount of Olives is to Christians or Mount Sinai to Jews. It is the place where the Central Tenet was first formulated and received. As Hsuan Tsang traveled backward in time from Sarnath to Bodhgaya, one senses a tone of portent creeping into his narrative. It thickens, becomes dense with its accretion of legend, prophecy, and event. Every mountain, river, forest, and glade makes our pilgrim recall the life of the Buddha, or the edifying previous lives that are illustrated in the cave paintings, faded and ruined and yet glowing with minutely depicted scenes, that I saw in Turfan and Kucha and that I would see in Ajanta and Dunhuang. As the pilgrim travels, he recounts the main events in the hallowed drama of Wisdom and Salvation, giving as he does so a poetically concise history of the origins of Buddhism, and, along the way, outlining the elements of his own search for the Truth.

The story begins when the young prince known as Gautama leaves his wife, his son, and the home of his father, who was a king, in order, as his father put it, perhaps ironically, "to practice wisdom." Our pilgrim recounts his father's distress at his prodigal son's departure but also his desire to take care of him. "Alone he wanders through mountains and plains and lives apart in the forests," the king tells five men whom he will send to look for his son. The men (if this differs from other accounts, remember that I am summarizing our pilgrim's recitation of the sacred story) are three members of his household and two of the Buddha's maternal uncles. As they journey, the five, who are to become the first five disciples, debate the proper means of attaining Supreme Wisdom. The two uncles believe it to be "by rest and by pleasant discipline." The other three advocate "painful discipline," which is the conventional Hindu method—fasting, meditation, what Christians would later call the mortification of the flesh.

Hsuan Tsang notes that without hearing this debate, the prince who was to become the Buddha had already adopted painful discipline, most importantly fasting. "Considering this to be the true way to overcome sorrow," Hsuan Tsang writes, "he took only a few grains of rice and millet to support his body." When the two maternal uncles found their nephew and saw his choice, his emaciated condition, his physical anguish, they departed in disappointment. It wasn't their way. The three members of the king's household were pleased, and they stayed to provide moral encouragement to their charge. But after six long years the prince had not achieved *Bodhi,* Enlightenment, and he therefore decided to abandon his fast—to the distress and disillusionment of the three advocates of painful discipline. They "sighed and said, 'His merit was just ripening and now it is all dissipated! For six years he endured penance, and now in a day he has lost all his merit!' " The three also decamped and found the prince's two uncles who had left earlier. Together they arrived at the consensus that the prince's quest for "the deep mysterious law and its perfect fruit" would come to nothing because the prince himself was a madman. "What need we think about him more? The mention of his name but adds sorrow to sorrow," they told one another. For reasons that are not made clear, the five did not return to the king's household but went to the Deer Park in Sarnath.

Gautama, though abandoned by his disciples, was not alone. The rice and milk that he agreed to eat came from a farm girl named Sujata who had taken pity on him in his emaciated state. Still, he was skin and bones—as the statue of the emaciated Buddha in the Lahore Museum shows him to be—and even as he accepted Sujata's daily food offering, he fell into deep despair, uncertain where to go, doubting seriously for the first time that supreme wisdom would ever be his. One day he dropped his eating bowl in the flowing Nairanjana River. He followed the bowl to the other side of the river, and in a garden in the city now called Bodhgaya, he sat under a pipal tree and there fell into a deep trance, a state of perfect calm and equilibrium. A satanic figure named Mara, who rode on a great elephant, arrived in an effort to snare the Buddha's mind, to tempt him with his own ravishing daughter (this part of the story is a favorite theme of the cave temple painters), or to weaken his resolve with hunger, storms, and sleepiness. But the Buddha, having practiced the perfections over a thousand eons, was easily able to resist Mara's threats and blandishments. The Buddha reached down with his right hand and touched the earth, calling upon it to serve as his witness—thereby giving future sculptors one of their favorite pieces of iconography. Mara fell off his elephant while the Buddha remained in his state of utter calm, gaining deeper and deeper knowledge until, after seven days, he conceived the Four Noble Truths: the truth of the nature of suffering, of the origin of suffering, of the cessation of suffering, and of the way leading to the cessation of suffering. Hsuan Tsang himself traces this spiritual and philosophical journey with elegant concision:

The Bodhisattva, having triumphed over temptation, still sitting motionless at the foot of the tree, bent his thoughts upon the universality of suffering and upon the means of abolishing it. His gaze took in the whole universe. He saw the endless cycle of rebirth unfolding to infinity, from the infernal world and the world of the animals right up to the gods themselves, through all eternity. And every birth, every life, every death was suffering.

Then the Bodhisattva, his mind thus in contemplation and completely pure, during the last watch of the night, just as dawn was breaking, at the hour of the beating of the drum, achieved Enlightenment. Tracing back the chain of causality, he discovered that the cause of universal suffering was the thirst for existence, and that the thirst for existence was based upon our false conceptions of mind, the self and the material world. Thus to abolish the thirst for existence by doing away with its intellectual causes was to abolish suffering. . . . Such was the inner Enlightenment, the revelation of perfect wisdom by which the Bodhisattva finally became a Supreme Being.

Having achieved Enlightenment himself, the Buddha cast about for someone worthy of receiving his teaching, and he thought of the five disciples who had left him to go to Sarnath. "Then Tathagata, rising from the Bodhi Tree, went forward with measured step and dignified mien to the Deer Park; shining with glory, the circle of his hair reflecting its brilliant colors, his body like gold." Seeing him approach, the five disciples vowed not to rise or speak to him, but Tathagata's sacred appearance, which affected all creatures, led them quickly to forget this vow. "Tathagata gradually instructed them in the excellent principles, and when the season of rain was finished, they had obtained the fruit."

The joy that Hsuan Tsang experienced in being in Sarnath comes across in his recollection of the stages of the Buddha's life, and yet he was at the same time in a somber, valedictory mood. He was now very close to his most important geographical goals, Bodhgaya itself and then the Buddhist university of Nalanda where he would study with the great Indian masters. The great Truth that had inspired his monumental journey in the first place was within sight, and yet, as he travels from Sarnath to Bodhgaya, he seems at once excited and gloomy, filled with stories and with a sort of evil premonition, as if, like the Buddha before him, he is not sure that perfect wisdom will be his.

Not far from Sarnath, he visited a forest which he believed was the site of one of the more beautiful of the Jataka tales. The hunters of the king of Benares (the old name for Varanasi) were killing deer indiscriminately. The king of the deer—the Buddha in an earlier incarnation—sought to mitigate the carnage by making a controlled act of submission to the human king. "Pray," the king of the deer said, "let us each day offer you one deer for food, which the king will then have fresh and good, and we shall prolong our life a little day by day." The king of Benares agreed, and the pact was carried out until one day it became the turn of a pregnant doe to be sacrificed. The doe pleaded with the king on behalf of her unborn offspring, asking for her death to be postponed until her fawn was born. Seeing her distress, the king of the deer went to the palace of the king of Benares. "Why have you come here?" asked the human ruler. "There is a female in the herd big with young whose turn it is to die," the king of the deer said, "but my heart could not bear to think that her young, not yet born, should perish, and I have therefore come in her place." The king of Benares, hearing this explanation, replied: "I have indeed the body of a man but am as a deer; you have the body of a deer but are as a man." Filled with pity, the king renounced the daily sacrifice and vowed to leave the forest for the exclusive use of the deer. It became the world's first game preserve.

Hsuan Tsang pressed on and eventually reached the Bodhi Tree in what we now call Bodhgaya. There he describes in minute detail almost every stone and every patch of ground. But again he seems overwhelmed, and he offers a plaintive and rare personal note, an expression of doubt over his worthiness to be following in the footsteps of Tathagata. "At the time when Buddha perfected himself in wisdom, I know not in what condition I was in the troublous whirl of birth and death," he says in the middle of his copious description of the temples and sites of Bodhgaya. "But now, in this latter time of image worship, having come to this spot and reflecting on the depth and weight of the body of my evil deeds, I am grieved at heart, and my eyes are filled with tears."

The year of this lamentation is 636, seven years and more than six thousand miles after Hsuan Tsang's departure from Chang-an. Surely, given his mood, he must have thought about the purposes of his long mission, about the many miles he had come so far, and about the imminence of his arrival at Nalanda, where he would study. For Hsuan Tsang and for the Buddha, the solution to suffering was a problem of the intellect, of proper understanding. It is in its way an epistemological question, a puzzle about the nature of reality and how we can know it. The Yogacara tradition of Asanga and Vasubhandu to which Hsuan Tsang was dedicated was an outgrowth of the Buddha's own great revelation: that suffering was based on a false conception of mind, self, and the material world. In the Yogacara view of things, the falseness of the conception consisted of the illusion that those things—mind, self, the material world—were real when, in truth, they were illusory.

But from there came the Great Question—indeed it was the Great Question the answer to which led Hsuan Tsang to forsake his comfortable life in China, to cross mountains and deserts, and to come to India. If all is illusion, then isn't the very belief that all is illusion an illusion as well? This can be put in terms that the Frenchman René Descartes would have understood a thousand years later when Western philosophy finally began dealing with these ultimate epistemological issues: If all is illusion, what is the nature of the entity that is experiencing this illusion? Descartes's famous solution to that problem was to postulate the existence of the self. I doubt, therefore I am. But Buddhism denied the reality of the self. What did it put in its place? How did it get around the viselike grip of the central paradox: that if all is illusion, then nothing can be known?

There is a passage in *The Defense,* a novel by Vladimir Nabokov, in which the main character, Luzhin, a chess prodigy, is mesmerized by a celestial paradox. He remembers an illustration of the mysteries of parallelism in which he saw two infinitely long intersecting lines, one laid over the other and moving apart. The point of intersection of the two lines "glided upwards along an endless path" as the lines were pulled apart toward a parallel position, but even when they were parallel, the point of intersection "was doomed to eternal motion, for it was impossible for it to slip off." What inflames the mind is the existence of two statements that are true and contradictory at the same time. The lines are parallel and the lines intersect. The self exists and it is an illusion. The material world is a product only of mind and mind is material.

At times in his account of his travels, Hsuan Tsang conveys something that seems distasteful to our sensibility today. There is a Goody Two-shoes didacticism to him, a pedantic quality, an insistence not on saving humanity from suffering but on proving himself right in his interpretation of an arcane dogma. But, in my view at least, he redeems himself when he worries about the troublous whirl of birth and death. There is poetry in that unease and there is a mind on fire as it contemplates the awesome paradoxes that a lifetime of thinking and studying had so far been unable to resolve. And so I see him as he arrives at the gates of Nalanda weary and full of self-doubt, and afflicted with a sense of his own past sinfulness and present inadequacy. I see him as a slightly pompous, nearly fanatical figure, overstuffed with learning, an idiot savant. And I see him as a hero, a saint, the man who risked his life in order to acquire not power or wealth but understanding of the deepest mysteries of life on the planet.

THE CHIEF RELIC in Sarnath is an imposing rounded brick tower atop a stone pedestal, one of the oldest Buddhist relics in existence. It was built in the third century by King Ashoka to memorialize the great event that took place in the Deer Park, and it is still in pretty reasonable shape, a powerful brick tower rising into the Indian sky. The pilgrim from China gazed at it, and so did I. Then I made the rounds of the various temples, built, as in Lumbini, by schools of monks from various Buddhist countries, hoping to find someone with whom I could share a sense of the importance of the place. I visited the Chinese Temple, but there were no Chinese there. A fat smiling monk sat on a charpoy in a side room and greeted me with great cordiality, telling me he was from Tibet. I asked him if there were any Chinese monks present, and he said, "No, only Thai monk." I found one of the Thai monks, who said there were no Chinese monks.

"Why?" I asked.

"I don't know," he replied.

Two monks were chanting at the Japanese Temple. One of them handed me candies wrapped in cellophane. Outside the Tibetan Temple was a poster enumerating Chinese atrocities against Tibetans. Inside, along with frescoes of one thousand Buddhas, was an imposing Buddha statue and small models of orange-robed monks in display cases on either side of it—45,056 of them, all identical. In back was an enormous prayer wheel, perhaps ten feet tall, the turning of which rang two large bells, one higher-pitched than the other, the two creating a mystical, discordant harmony. And there was a martyrs' stupa, dedicated to the 1.2 million Tibetans who, according to the placard, were killed under the Chinese occupation.

I returned to Varanasi in the late afternoon to get the train to Gaya, the closest point to Bodhgaya reachable by train, and as I waited on the platform I was struck by the amazing world that is an Indian railway station. This was the Indian dystopia in a kind of distilled form, horrible and fascinating: the many people on the unclean floors, grimy and ragged, sleeping, waiting, staring; the women with that wild look, and with their gold earrings, their bangles, their nose pieces, their bracelets, the gold thread in their saris, the lustrous red of their silks and cottons; the sadhus covered in ash with those Biblical beards and that demonic glint in their eyes; the Muslim women in black; the soldiers walking around with ancient wooden-stocked rifles; the porters in red shirts and white turbans, the children, the hawkers, the beggars, the limbless, the mangled; those who sat in silence and those who pled for help, or who chanted the products they had for sale.

Then there was a shoeshine boy with a look of suffering and contempt in his eyes asking if he could shine my sandals. I gave him two rupees to go away. A while later he came back in his smudged shirt and his bare feet and his disturbing smallness, and when I motioned with my arms for him to move along, he performed a perfect imitation of that motion, an imitation full of mockery and controlled fury. He was precocious in his mastery of the ironic gesture. The motion I had made was not the correct Indian motion of dismissal.

When the Indians motion for somebody to get lost (a child beggar or a skinny old man with an ingratiating smile or a woman with dry skin taut around her cheekbones holding a child on her raised hip and pointing to its mouth), they wave the wrist imperiously in a counterclockwise corkscrewing motion, fingers splayed and describing an ascending arc. But I had motioned underarm as though throwing a ball to a child, making not so much a get-out-of-here gesture as a move-along gesture. The boy parodied it and then picked up his wooden shoeshine box and moved down the platform. I noticed that the next person he approached smiled at him and engaged him in a brief conversation full of complicity, but then the boy moved on from that person without shining his shoes. The boy appeared several more times moving up and down the platform, meandering among the supine and seated bodies, the piles of luggage, the hawkers' carts and stands. I never saw him shine a single shoe or a sandal. He couldn't have been more than seven or eight.

I had not made a train reservation, so before going to the platform I had gone to the foreigners' booking office in the Varanasi train station to see if there was a seat available on the night train to Gaya. The Indian railroads set aside quotas for travelers with foreign passports, seats that can be sold at short notice. This would seem to discriminate unfairly against Indians, but train tickets in India sell out weeks, even months, in advance, so without the emergency quotas, foreign visitors would basically not be able to travel by train in India at all.

"I have no more tourist-quota berths," the clerk had told me. But he saw that I had a railway pass that gave me the right to unlimited train travel in India for a month.

"Go to the sleeper cars, where there will be a conductor," he told me. "Show your pass to him and he *will* find you a berth."

"What time is the train to Gaya?"

"It's four p.m.," he said. It was then around three. "It will reach Gaya at ten. Go to track seven. The Gaya train will come there."

I thanked him and went to the platform to wait. Four o'clock came and went but the train did not. There were no announcements; there was no arrivals-and-departures board. A vendor of soft drinks told me that the Gaya train was late. "You wait," he said. I was tired and hot and I wanted a shower and I was feeling some unease about my safety. The guidebooks warn that it is best not to arrive in Gaya at night and that, given reports of banditry (or, as the Indian newspapers call it, "dacoity") in Bihar, India's most poverty-stricken state, it was especially dangerous to travel after dark between Gaya and Bodhgaya. Robberies and murders were supposed to take place along that road, where the dacoits had a good chance of finding well-off foreigners and pilgrims. An on-time arrival in Gaya would have been fine; there would, I assumed, still have been plenty of travelers on the road at ten o'clock. But now the train was at least two hours late, which meant that I wouldn't arrive in Gaya before midnight, and would have to find a hotel in Gaya for the night rather than go to Bodhgaya right away. Meanwhile, I noticed that some people who had been sitting on their bags on platform seven since I had arrived there suddenly and inexplicably got up and left, taking their luggage with them. I asked one man why they were leaving.

"Yes," he said.

"But why? Is there some news about the train?"

"Yes," he repeated and went away.

Another man who had been seated on a wooden bench in the middle of the platform got up, and I took his place, pulling my bags near me. It started to rain, and a stream of water began to fall off a tattered yellow canopy above, splattering the middle of the bench. This led a wiry young man to slide toward me. He was ostensibly getting out of the rain, but he sat much closer to me than he needed to for that purpose, his elbow resting in my side. He stared at me, and when I scowled at him, he simply looked back. I got up and moved back to the edge of the platform, taking my bags with me. After a short time, the young man left.

The atmosphere smoldered after the brief rain. It had been 42 degrees centigrade in Varanasi that day, about 110 degrees Fahrenheit, and the heat and humidity seemed to concentrate under the long corrugated metal shelter over the platform. To pass the time, I enumerated the component parts of the station edifice that together gave it its character: the ocher walls trimmed with Mogul red; the green wagons so unsleek, so worn-out with overuse; the tumult on the trains that pulled in and out of the station as I waited, the third-class carriages tumbling with people. These trains are iron rickshaws, underpowered and overburdened, their dark interiors glowing with patient faces. The platform overpasses (quaintly called "foot over bridges") clattered with pedestrian traffic. The afternoon wore on; the light dimmed. Here and there fluorescent bulbs were switched on while naked bulbs dangling from loose wires remained unlit. A few minutes after six o'clock a train lumbered onto track seven and stopped. I asked a descending passenger who seemed from his middle-class appearance likely to speak English if it was the train to Gaya.

"Hopefully," he said and piled his luggage onto a porter—two suitcases and a cardboard box atop his head, shoulder bags draped on each shoulder.

I gathered my bags and looked for a sleeper car where I thought I might find the conductor, but there were no sleeper cars. I searched in vain for a conductor, any figure of authority.

"Gaya?" I said to a passing porter. The porters always know which train is going where.

This porter made a vague gesture with his arm toward the opposite platform.

"Gaya here," said the helpful soft-drink vendor. He too pointed to the opposite platform, alongside track six, not seven. I had almost gotten on a train going someplace else.

"But I thought the Gaya train was on track seven," I said.

"There's been a change," the vendor told me.

At about eight o'clock the train to Gaya pulled in. I found a sleeping car and got on. There was a conductor, and I showed him my rail pass.

"No vacancy," he said.

"Well, where can I get a seat?" I asked.

The conductor waved me down the platform.

"What the hell does this mean?" I asked, waving my arm in imitation of his gesture, imitating the shoeshine boy who had imitated me.

"Go there," said the porter, repeating his gesture.

I walked down the platform to the next car, another sleeping car. Trundling my luggage through the narrow passageway, I looked into the compartments. Each of them was already crammed full. I lugged my bags to the second-class car, and it was standing room only. I got my bags into the purgatory between two of the cars and found most of the floor space occupied by other travelers. I stood there, surrounded by supine or seated figures, and contemplated my situation. I would have to stand for six hours and I would arrive in Gaya between two and three in the morning. Earlier I had thought of something else. At some point or another I was going to have to get a visa for the return trip to China. I had planned to do that when I arrived back in Delhi after my tour of the Buddhist holy places and the south of India was finished. I began to think that rather than go to Bodhgaya right away I should see my present discomfort as an omen. Maybe I should go back to Delhi and take care of the visa and go to Bodhgaya on some more auspicious occasion.

The train began to move. Should I stay on or jump off? I didn't want to go to Gaya at that hour. I needed more time, better preparation. I dragged my bags off the moving train and stood on the platform watching it slowly pick up speed and disappear into the murky distance. I took the foot over bridge to the foreigners' booking office, which was being shut down by the clerk who had given me advice earlier.

"You told me I could just show my rail pass and I'd be able to get a seat on the train to Gaya," I reminded the ticket-seller.

"Yes," he said.

"Well, it didn't work."

"The train has left?"

"Yes."

The man looked at me.

"Is there a train to Delhi tonight?" I asked him.

"There's a train at eleven tonight," the ticket agent said.

"You can get me a sleeping berth?"

The man looked into his computer.

"I have one seat in second class, three-tier sleeper, no two-tiers left."

"Good," I said. "I'll take it."

The Delhi train, originating in Calcutta, pulled into the Varanasi station at two in the morning, three hours late. I arrived in Delhi the next afternoon. I called the Chinese embassy just to gauge the reception I might get if I applied for a Chinese visa there.

"You can come in and make out an application and we will investigate your case," the man who came to the phone said.

"What do you mean, 'investigate my case'?" I asked.

"We will check your Indian visa and your Pakistani visa," he said, "and we will make a decision."

"How long will it take?"

"Four business days," he said.

That sounded bad to me. First, it was likely that the application would be forwarded to the foreign ministry in Beijing for approval, and if that happened I had no chance. In the meantime, there was another problem. When I had arrived in Amritsar, or maybe it was Mathura, a hotel clerk pointed out that I had been issued a "J" visa by the Indian consulate in New York. "J" means journalist. I had not noticed that before and I was glad that no Chinese immigration official had noticed it either, but now, suddenly, that telltale letter seemed likely to do me in. If the Chinese consulate intended to study my visas, surely they would notice it, and then my application would just as surely be rejected. My best chance, I felt, was to return to Hong Kong, which was a seven-hour flight from Delhi, and get another of those no-questions-asked visas from my travel agent there.

I bought a round-trip ticket to Hong Kong and left the next evening on the overnight flight.

FOR SOMEONE arriving from New Delhi, Hong Kong is like an orbiting space station. The new airport thrums with the sound of its manmade atmosphere. A train whooshes its way to the center of Hong Kong in twenty-two minutes. Each car has a delicately curving electronic chart telling you where you are during the course of the trajectory. At the stations, a voice announces in Cantonese, English, and Mandarin on which side of the car the doors will open. Uniformed service personnel wait with luggage carts for you to use when you disembark. They do not ask for, or expect, tips. The downtown station and airport terminal is a glass chamber with glass elevators. Outside, translucent towers seem to dissolve in the metallic sky. The air-conditioning sweeps into the streets from the open shopping arcades. Elevated pedestrian flyovers soar over the streets. The signage is trim and sleek. The shop windows glitter with luxury. I looked at the faces of the Hong Kong pedestrians as they went complacently about their business. It was hard to realize that the day before I had been in the New Delhi railroad station buying my ticket to Gaya, the booking office a scene from some sinister netherworld where thousands of ambulatory people climbed around thousands of recumbent ones and lines of interminable length stretched before every ticket window.

I stayed three days in Hong Kong with an old friend of mine who lives in one of the many Hong Kong apartment buildings overlooking the South China Sea. From my bedroom window I watched freighters and ferries making their way through the channel between Lamma and Hong Kong islands. The sea sparkled under my window and the outlying islands beckoned romantically like Chinese Bali Hais. India seemed very far away, and so did the monk and his travels. And when, provided with a new visa for China, I returned to the airport to fly back to India, I went with mixed feelings. I was eager to resume my pilgrimage even as a part of me clung to Hong Kong.

15

The Holy Places

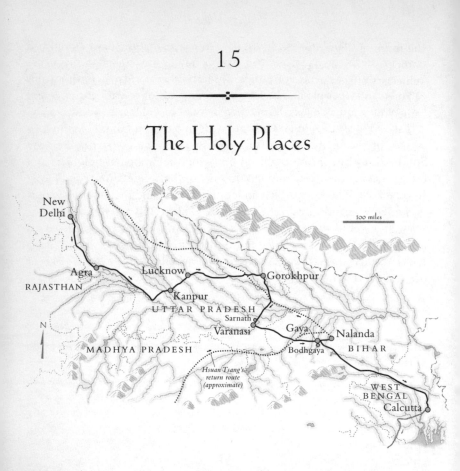

I TOOK the Doon Express to Gaya. I would, given a choice, always want to take a train named so poetically. Doon Express. Actually it meant that I traveled in a second-class sleeper with all its windows broken, so that the night air of northern India rushed typhoonlike through the compartment for the entire journey, and the other passengers, fearful of thieves, chained their baggage to the metal bars of the sleeping bunks.

I had no metal chain or lock, so I pulled my bags up onto my bunk, my computer underneath my duffel bag, my shoulder bag wedged next to the wall, and I passed a watchful, sleepless, windblown night. The train pulled into Gaya at 5 a.m. Heedful of the guidebook's warning about dacoity on the road to Bodhgaya at night, I thought I'd stay in the station until daybreak. But small events sort of sweep you along. There was no place to stay in the station, which was as gloomy as a Transylvanian castle. The porter carried my bags through the station exit and I found myself in

The Holy Places

the murky Indian night in a parking esplanade where several taxi drivers competed for my business. One driver pointed to a Land Rover–like vehicle—actually it was an Indian-made Tata jeep—that seemed capable of busting through any dacoit roadblocks. (Actually, anybody who is determined to do so can stop a car on the road—a few boulders or a log or two will do the trick.) We set off through winding lanes near the train station, swerving to avoid the bicycle rickshaws that suddenly materialized out of the darkness. As we left the station, a young man with a scarf over his head, giving him a cobralike appearance, jumped into the car, and for a few minutes I meditated on the possibility that the famous dacoits were actually taxi drivers. But the two young men talked more casually than most people would if they were contemplating murder and robbery, and I gradually relaxed. As we approached the site of the Buddha's Enlightenment, a faint line of pinkish purple appeared on the eastern horizon. After half an hour, just as the magenta flow at the edge of the sky dissipated into an ash-colored dawn, we pulled up to the Mahayana Guesthouse.

I slept for a couple of hours, then went to the Mahabodhi Temple, where Hsuan Tsang came fourteen hundred years before. It occupied a large rectangle on the edge of the ramshackle, sacred-cow-infested Hindu village and was marked by a huge gray stone carved stupa. It made an impression. The walkways were lined with thousands of colored banners, illustrated Tibetan passages of the sutras. I was standing at the top of a stone stairway leading down to the temple grounds looking for the famous pipal tree under which the Buddha received Enlightenment when I heard a voice behind me recounting a story of King Ashoka and his wife. Ashoka was the monarch of the third century B.C. who converted to Buddhism and made it the state religion of northern India. His wife was against it.

"Wife of Ashoka very jealous woman," the voice said. "King Ashoka turn to Buddhist believer and she no happy."

I turned and saw a small man wearing a green padded vest and glasses. He spoke in a kind of singsong, like a traditional storyteller, and, as I was about to discover, he had many stories, all available in books but somehow more appealing in his semigrammatical retelling of them.

"Ashoka's wife was thinking, 'He's come to follow the way of the Buddha, so maybe he leave the house.' This is because Buddha left the house, left the wife, left the father, left the everything. So she is thinking, 'Maybe Ashoka leave the everything too and don't take care of the royal place.' So she was thinking to cut the main point. The main point means Bodhi Tree. 'Maybe if I cut the tree, then Ashoka return to home.'"

The Bodhi Tree, of course, is what everybody comes to see in Bodh-gaya, and the day I was there, several thousand Tibetan monks, all in identical maroon robes, were at the temple, seated in long rows on the ground and chanting a sutra, turning long narrow pages of Tibetan text as they did so. Around the temple was a profusion of Tibetan flags, and there were thousands of small bronze cups burning oil.

"You want guide?" said my storyteller.

"How much?" I asked.

"I am Buddhist, no doing business," he said. "You make donation what you want."

"Okay," I said.

"I show you seven important places in Mahabodhi Temple."

"You mean you're not going to finish the story of Ashoka and his wife first?"

But my guide, who turned out to be named Ashok Kuman, after the great king, did tell the story, which is the story of the Bodhi Tree itself, and that story is in turn the archaeological history of the Mahabodhi Temple. I listened to it against the background of Tibetan chanting that filled the air with a mystical, throaty sort of drone and gave the place an agreeable measure of timelessness.

According to the story, Ashoka's worried wife, whose name was Trixila, sent men to cut the tree down. In response, the distressed King Ashoka ordered milk and water to be poured on the roots and in so doing produced two new saplings. One of the saplings he entrusted to his son and daughter, Mahendra and Sanghamitta, who took it to Sri Lanka, where it exists to this day. The other he kept in its place, protecting it from animals by a high stone fence, known as Ashoka's Railing, parts of which, 2,300 years old, are still in their original places. To protect the tree from any future acts of vandalism by his wife, Ashoka began to build a kind of fortress temple with thick walls around it, but, said Ashok Kuman, Buddhist pilgrims coming to pay homage to the tree told him that the Buddha himself had not authorized the construction of temples, and so Ashoka desisted.

Several hundred years later the sapling had grown into a great tree and the Kushan King Kanishka was in power. It was he who completed the first temple.

"Kanishka," said Ashok Kuman. "Kushan Dynasty. Second century. Come from Afghanistan. Say why no temple? So he start temple. After Kanishka, Palas Dynasty come. Palas from Bengal. He feel this place no nice. Nobody make Buddha statue. He find good face, make big Buddha. Buddha statue still here."

"Really. The original statue?"

"Yes, original statue. But after Palas come Muslims and no Buddha followers after that. At that time, river run here and fill temple with mud. One thousand years mud. Then British man Cunningham come.★ Eighteen-eighty. Cunningham find statue. But when he dig, statue head fall off. Cunningham does not want to chop off head. Accident. Head put back on with cement but leaves marks on neck. Dalai Lama come here. He say statue no nice. Puts gold on old Buddha image. After that archaeology man come here. He say, 'Why you paint statue gold?' After that many people discuss. This temple under trust. So trust talk to archaeology man, say, 'Because break I paint gold. If not break, I no paint.' "

My guide took me on a tour of the temple and its environs, and as he did so I imagined Hsuan Tsang being taken on a similar tour. I saw the Buddha image covered in gold paint. I paced the ground that the Buddha paced and looked at the Bodhi Tree from the hill from which the Buddha stared at it for seven days, without blinking. Ashok took me across the fabled Nairanjana River—it's now called the River Falgu, which you can cross via the Sujata Bridge—and we walked along the ridges between agricultural fields, past herds of water buffalo, goats, and skinny cows, and up a small hill where Sujata's house was. In the distance over the straw-colored plain rose a mountain within which is the Mahakala Cave, where the Buddha practiced severe austerities for six years before discovering the Middle Way. Below us, colorfully dressed women were threshing sheaves of rice. Two small boys came up the hill asking us for money. One of them was upright, the other crippled, moving with ferretlike speed on his knees and hands, his feet dangling above him in the air like a scorpion's tail. The fields were planted with potatoes, eggplants, cauliflower, and onions. We walked along a path of beaten earth to the spot under a banyan tree where Sujata gave the Buddha milk and rice. Then we walked across the riverbed, which was dry in the summer season, back to Bodhgaya.

Hsuan Tsang says nothing about sitting under the Bodhi Tree itself, and I didn't do that either. The monk reveals a certain disappointment at its size. "Whilst Buddha was in the world the height of the tree was several hundred feet," he wrote, "but as wicked kings have continually cut it

★ The reference is to Alexander Cunningham, considered the father of Indian archaeology.

down and destroyed it, the tree is now only about fifty feet high." It isn't much taller than that now, though it is thick and has a luxuriant growth of shiny pointed leaves. The tree that one sees in Bodhgaya now was brought as a cutting from the tree that still grows in Sri Lanka. Despite its relative smallness, one looks at it with reverence, knowing that at this very spot 2,500 or so years ago one of those human revelations occurred that was to influence the rest of history. And yet, as I stood there listening to the gravelly chant of the Tibetans and watching a young Western woman sitting cross-legged and meditating next to the stone balustrade that forms an enclosure around the famous tree, I was also aware of a lack of something in my spirit.

I have been to the Western Wall in Jerusalem, to the Church of the Holy Sepulcher, and to the birthplace of Confucius, and I must say that I am more inspired by the idea of those places than by their actual physical embodiment. For Hsuan Tsang, I have to believe, Bodhgaya was a kind of return, a coming full circle to the place where Truth was born. For me the various holy places seem to be saying that I don't really belong anyplace at all. At the Western Wall, which one might say is "my" place, I felt vaguely intimidated by the black-coated, bearded Hasidim who seem to occupy the space. I didn't feel that I knew enough of the liturgy to be comfortable in their presence. I didn't know exactly what to do except stand there and try to squeeze some meaning out of the actual site of Solomon's Temple. Now, at the place where the Buddha achieved Enlightenment, thoroughly pleasant, satisfying, as I glanced at the Western woman with eyes shut and body perfectly still I realized that in spite of my fascination with Buddhism and my desire to follow the monk's trail, this wasn't mine either. I knew it from the absence of shivers up my spine and from my feeling that the person sitting there played the role for me of the Hasidim at the Western Wall. This is unfair to her, perhaps, but her presence and her posture seemed forced to me, contrived; there wasn't so much spiritual wisdom in it as a desperate attempt to submerge oneself into something, someplace.

I WENT to Nalanda, too, hiring a car and driving with Ashok Kuman over what may be the worst road in India, a thoroughfare whose buckling surface and knee-deep craters testify to the corruption of Bihar Province. "Contractor very bad man," Ashok reported. "He take money, use poor material, road no good." Nalanda is a magnificent ruin, a sprawling complex of brick residential compounds and stupas where for half a millennium the greatest Buddhist scholars in the world studied. Hsuan Tsang, whose reputation preceded him, was accorded an elaborate welcome. "Two hundred priests and several thousand lay patrons surrounded him as he went," Hui Li tells us. "They recounted his praises and carried standards, umbrellas, flowers and perfumes." Then twenty men who were "skillful in explaining the religious books and were of dignified carriage" conducted the Chinese Master of the Law into the presence of the monastery's revered leader, known to the Indians as the Treasure of the Good Law, a historic Buddhist philosopher named Silabhadra.

This was a great moment for Hsuan Tsang, the moment he had traveled for. He approached the Treasure of the Good Law on his knees, his head bowed to the ground. He kissed his feet. Silabhadra was the latest in a line of disciples that went back to Asanga and Vasubhandu, the creators of Yogacara philosophy, and thus to Hsuan Tsang he had kingly status. "Would that your reverence, of his great compassion, receive me for the purposes of instruction," Hsuan Tsang begged, his head still bowed.

He was readily accepted. Silabhadra called on his chief disciple to tell how three years earlier he, Silabhadra, had suffered a terrible illness, punishment for misdeeds committed in a previous life. His suffering, in which his hands and feet cramped painfully and his belly felt as though pierced with a knife, was so great that he hated his life and wished to starve himself to death. But three heavenly figures, one the color of gold, another of silver, a third of bright crystal, appeared before him and instructed him not to cast his body away. Instead, they told him, "you must widely disseminate the true law." Moreover, they made an astonishing prophecy: "There is a priest of the country of China who delights in examining the Law and is desirous of studying with you; you ought to instruct him carefully."

Hsuan Tsang, of course, was deemed to be that priest, and he was treated with the respect given to one whose appearance has been prophesied. He took up his abode in a four-story residence. Every day he received twenty betel nuts and twenty nutmegs, an ounce of camphor, and a peck of a large-grained aromatic rice known as Mahasali. He received monthly allotments of oil and butter "and other things according to his need," and, as always, he made shrewd observations. There were many thousands of students at Nalanda, which was a kind of Harvard of its time, the place where people claimed they went, even if they didn't, in order to gain social advantage. "The priests . . . are men of the highest ability and talent," the pilgrim says. "There are many hundreds whose fame has rapidly spread through distant regions." In order to weed out those who "usurp the name of Nalanda and in going to and fro receive honor in consequence," the "keeper of the gate proposes some hard questions; many are unable to answer and retire." It was hard work being at Nalanda, where, the monk tells us, "the rules are severe and all the priests are bound to observe them." Hsuan Tsang engaged in celebrated debates, demolishing his opponents, especially the Hinayanists among them, and, more often than not, converting them to the Great Vehicle.

What truth did Hsuan Tsang acquire? In Nalanda, according to Hui Li, he studied the Yoga Sastra, the Hetuvidya Sastra, the Sabdavidya Sastra, the Shatpadabhidharma Sastra, and many others, their names alone ringing a message of inaccessibility to the uninitiated. But it is possible nonetheless to speculate on the fundamental question that confronted the monk and, indeed, all followers of the Yogacara doctrine.

On the trip to Nalanda and since then I have read as much as I could about the subtleties of Buddhist thought, translations of the sutras themselves as well as secondary works—Waley's very useful *Real Tripitaka,* the invaluable *Foundations of Buddhism* by Rupert Gethin, and Grousset's *On the Trail of the Buddha.* But since I was in the very place where the Buddha lived and where Hsuan Tsang paid homage, I tried also to sit at the feet of the masters there and to learn what I could of the Truth from them.

I asked at the Mahayana Hotel where the best scholars in Bodhgaya could be found, and I was directed to a place called the Root Institute on the outskirts of town. I took a bicycle rickshaw past rice and vegetable fields and small hotels to a dirt track that plunged into the flat farmland. Tibetan visitors in maroon robes strolled alongside the road. In the various distances were the gleaming roofs of the temples built by Buddhists of many countries in their national styles. A scaffolding surrounded an immense image of the seated Buddha, just being installed.

The Root Institute is a place mostly for foreigners who come for courses in Buddhist philosophy and meditation. Buddhism in India having slowly died out as of the ninth century or so, India itself is a strange kind of holy land, one that provides the authentic soil for Buddhist learning and practice but few native masters. In the morning I had gone to a rooftop near the hotel where a gracious and sympathetic young man from Cambridge, England, held meditation classes for novices. I sat cross-legged on the roof, cushions protecting against the hard surfaces, and listened while the man, who gave his name as Ladi Tavajra, told a group of six of us to concentrate on our breathing.

I counted my exhalations, then my inhalations. I focused on the tip of my nose, the air going in, the air going out. I tried to follow a single molecule of oxygen as it entered through my right nostril and made its way down my windpipe past the various valves to my lungs, where it mixed with blood and circulated to my extremities before it turned into a molecule of carbon dioxide and took a return trip, exiting, just to be different, by my left nostril. I listened intently to the sounds of Bodhgaya, the birdsong, the scraping of a pot, the putt-putt of a motorcycle, the water-over-rocks sound of female voices below where on my way to the class I had noticed a large banner inscribed with the words COCA-COLA WELCOMES HIS HOLINESS THE DALAI LAMA.

I was fidgety. I couldn't stop myself from scratching an itch, then scratching it again. I heard a dog barking and thought of the scene, common in Bodhgaya, of scraggly animals picking at piles of garbage. I wondered, as I tried to empty my mind, why the many monks who ambled through the town examining the peddlers' offerings of prayer wheels and stone carvings of the Buddha didn't get together to clean the place up. Bodhgaya is a place of many beggars, especially small children with crippled legs like the boy I saw at Sujata's house, who lie in wait near the entrance to the Mahabodhi Temple and scamper across the flagstone ground at the feet of any Westerner they see. I kept pocketfuls of change to drop into their hands. Later I visited an Indian monk who ran a school for orphans and crippled children. He told me that the child beggars were dropped off in the morning by their parents and picked up in the evening. Some of the families, he said, refused to put their children in school because they lived on their earnings. "They are happy if they have a crippled child," he said. "They make more money than they would if they worked as farmers." I went to two rooftop meditation classes, and I liked the idea of achieving a certain mental repose, which is a precondition for Enlightenment, but Bodhgaya made my mind too busy to meditate.

At the Root Institute I met two monks, Feydor from Germany and Neal from Australia. They wore Tibetan robes. They invited me to an excellent vegetarian lunch at the institute's outdoor cafeteria, and while we ate they tried their best to answer my urgent questions about Hsuan Tsang and Yogacara and the mind-only school of thought. If the purpose of Enlightenment is to end suffering, I asked, what difference does it make whether the external world is real or not?

Neal took a deep meditative breath and bestowed on me what I thought was a slightly pitying look, as if he felt sorry for one who understood so little.

"Very simply," he began, "the Buddha taught that there is suffering and it has a very specific cause. All suffering is due to a disturbance in our mind. Our minds are afflicted, and the fundamental affliction is not knowing the nature of things. So, in order to eliminate all suffering, we have to experience the way things are. We have to understand the nature of the wrong view and then to understand what is right."

This much I understood, though I appreciated Neal's succinct description. Most people who practice Buddhism do so through chants and meditation in an effort to cleanse their minds of everyday static and to achieve thereby a higher state of awareness. The high points of philosophy do not matter very much to them. But to the Buddha and to priests and to wandering Chinese pilgrims, the Buddha's basic idea, that we have a false grasp of reality, has engendered a two-thousand-year exploration of the true nature of reality. It makes Buddhism susceptible to a certain intellectualism, which can be seen anytime you witness two saffron-robed Tibetans locked in theological disputation. They argue with great animation, scoring points with excited hand movements and loud cries that sound like "Chut!" The mind-only school that was to Hsuan Tsang the Ultimate Truth was one of several longstanding efforts by Buddhist philosophy to grasp the all-important underlying nature of reality. But all of the schools share one common precept. It is that the entity that most of us identify as the self, the I, the unchanging constant that undergoes the experiences of life, does not actually exist.

"According to Yogacara," Feydor put in, "we have a subconscious grasping of a substantially existing, self-supporting self. In other words, in an emotional situation, a very strong sense of self emerges, and it seems very real. That leads to an attachment to the happiness of that self. This is related to another kind of ignorance, which is that phenomena exist separately from consciousness. The false idea is that reality and the consciousness that grasps it are two different things."

My reading had taught me that fundamental to this elimination of the self is none other than Nagarjuna's concept of *sunyata,* emptiness or voidness. As we have seen, it is a fabulously mystical concept whose main premise is that one must be free not only of attachments to things in the world, but also of attachment to the things of the mind. One must understand that the self, for example, is an illusion, and one must also be free of an attachment to that understanding. We become attached to the Truth, in other words, that one should not be attached to the Truth. Gethin cites some marvelously elusive and poetic lines from the sutras about this, using the term "dharma" to refer to a teaching, to a mental act: "Dharmas are like dreams, magical illusions, echoes, reflected images, mirages, space; like the moon reflected in water, a fairy castle, a shadow, or a magical creation; like the stars, dewdrops, a bubble, a flash of lightning, or a cloud—they are there, but they are not there, and if we reach out for them, we find nothing to hold on to."★

There are many problems here, and it is with them that the greatest Buddhist minds have been occupied ever since. If all is empty, one could ask, then what difference does anything make? And, after all, the Buddhists do believe in responsibility, in right actions; otherwise why would some people be reincarnated as lizards and others as kings? And, as we have seen already, it is difficult to answer the question: If there is nothing, then what is it that apprehends that nothingness? Is it mind? And if the mind exists, then there is something, isn't there? I asked Neal and Feydor how they dealt with those questions.

Feydor provided a description of what I had read in Gethin on Vasubhandu's distinction between conventional truth and ultimate truth, which was an essential element of the commentary on the mind-only school that Hsuan Tsang wrote when he got back to China. Even if there is nothing, we are forced to live as if there were something, and that there is that something becomes the conventional truth. "When it is wrongly grasped," Nagarjuna said, "emptiness destroys the dull-witted, like a snake that is wrongly grasped." Even the Buddha himself went around referring to himself as a self, an I, an independent entity different from other people.

"If you have a car," said Feydor, explaining the notion of conventional truth, "it can serve the function of a car even if it is a product of mind. This is the Middle Way. You don't negate existence. With conventional wisdom, we can exist."

I brought up my suspicions that this is nothing but verbal pyrotechnics, mystical stuff with no real meaning, or perhaps an escape from the impossible logical implications of theory. Buddhism is full of antinomies: "There is no ignorance and no cessation of ignorance," for example. Wasn't the fundamental notion of Yogacara, that everything is mind but we don't have to live that way, a kind of higher nonsense? I knew that I was being impolite, but I wanted to know.

"No," said Feydor, who remained calm and sweet-natured even as his voice took on a certain intensity, like one of those Tibetans leading up to the cry of *Chut!*

"There is a valid reason why a Yogacaran would say that everything exists in the mind," he said. "Your monk Hsuan Tsang was not concerned

★ Rupert Gethin, *The Foundations of Buddhism*, p. 237.

just with existing. What he was looking for was the very root of suffering. And the belief that phenomena exist outside of mind is the basis for the belief in the existence of the self, and a belief in a substantially existing, self-supporting self is the root for negative emotions like desire and anger. It is what causes us to create negative karma, which causes us to have a new rebirth and to have suffering in the new rebirth. It's like a chain reaction. To understand that phenomena are in the nature of mind is at the beginning of another chain reaction that leads to ultimate wisdom."

Is that it? We talked some more, and then I got up from the lunch table and shook hands with Neal and Feydor and found a rickshaw for the ride back to the hotel, my mind whirling with half-assimilated concepts. Was there an answer in there someplace? I wasn't sure, though I was sure that all of this was very interesting. The Yogacarans wanted to avoid complete emptiness even as they agreed that two entirely contradictory statements—the self does not exist and the nonself does not exist—are both true. Grousset cites as the equivalent of Descartes's famous formula, Vasubhandu's refutation of universal emptiness: "The existence of pure idea is established by our very awareness of the unreality of idea." Or as Grousset puts this: "Pure idea is an illusion; therefore pure idea exists."*

I have a mystical understanding of that notion, but I couldn't put an explanation into words. The same is true of the ultimate truth that Hsuan Tsang learned while he was at Nalanda. That truth is this: All is appearance, a product of mind. This includes the physical world, but it also includes the mental world that perceives it. Later, when he got back to China, our pilgrim, using the words echoed centuries later by Gethin, wrote that the world was "like an optical illusion, like a dream, like a mirage, a shadow, an echo, like the moon reflected in the water." But so too is the knowledge that all is appearance, a product of mind. Once we understand that, and once we have achieved the higher mental state of having no attachment to that understanding, we are able to penetrate to what Hsuan Tsang and the other Yogacarans call "suchness," or the absolute nature of things.

What is suchness? When Hsuan Tsang went back to China, he wrote a vast commentary on the philosophy of Vasubhandu in which he described suchness as a long series of opposites—being and nonbeing, self and nonself, ideality and reality. But it was Feydor, dressed in his maroon Tibetan robes and speaking in his German accent, who gave me the crux of the

* René Grousset, *In the Footsteps of the Buddha*, p. 292.

matter. What do you suppose Hsuan Tsang was trying to find out? I asked him. What difference did all this philosophy make?

The answer is that he was striving for the fullest possible triumph over the cravings of the self, which, in turn, required the fullest possible philosophical elaboration on the nonexistence of the self. And the reason he wanted to enter into a complete state of nonselfhood is that only in that way could he achieve the purpose of Mahayana Buddhism, which is to help others escape the ties that bind them to the otherwise inevitable agony of existence.

"The ultimate antidote is selflessness," Feydor said. "And when you realize that the object of your self-attachment is an illusion, you can achieve the selflessness that is the beginning of Buddhahood."

What Hsuan Tsang hoped to achieve at Nalanda was a cultivation of the mind that would enable him to bridge what, to us less enlightened folk, seems an unbridgeable contradiction. He wanted, by meditation, by the calm, intense concentration that the Buddhists call mindfulness, to arrive at the sort of rapture strong enough to make the body defy the laws of gravity and levitate. Hsuan Tsang, who believed in miracles, probably believed that levitation was possible. His goal, though he declared his own unworthiness for it, was to become a Bodhisattva, an Enlightened Being, but to do so, he had, somehow, not to be attached to his own Bodhisattva-hood. The Diamond Sutra, which our pilgrim knew by heart long before he set off on his journey, teaches that attachment to emptiness is the same as attachment to the self. The Buddhist philosophers use the metaphor of a raft, or of a medicine. The raft brings you safely across the river, and in that sense it was necessary, but having gotten to the other side of the river, it now has to be abandoned, otherwise it will be a burden. But of course a mental state is not a bunch of logs tied together. To want to become a Bodhisattva but not be attached to the desire to become a Bodhisattva is a little like that old joke that you can walk on water as long as you don't think of a hippopotamus. It is a sort of spiritual Heisenberg uncertainty principle: To know a thing you must observe it, but the process of observing it changes its nature.

So it is with emptiness and the nonexistence of self. For Hsuan Tsang, Ultimate Truth would be the truth beyond truth, the truth that can be known but cannot be expressed in words. "No one can attain any of the fruits of the holy life and keep them . . . unless he patiently accepts this elusiveness of the dharma," says one commentary.* A century after Hsuan

---

* Cited in Edward Conze, *Buddhist Texts Through the Ages* (Oxford: Bruno Cassirer, 1954), p. 281.

Tsang, the great Chinese poet Po Chu-i expressed this idea in a tone of respectful bemusement:

> *What I must learn is that all substances lack true substance,*
> *To linger on the extinction that leaves no trace is to make fresh traces.*
> *Forget the word even while it is spoken and there will be*
> *Nothing you do not understand.**

In other words, this is what must be learned, but it is impossible to say what it is. We can be skeptical that a truth that is beyond language, or, if not beyond language, can only be expressed in self-annihilating contradictions, is not truth at all. It is mysticism. "It cannot be grasped, it cannot be talked about," the Diamond Sutra says of the true way. "Gone beyond the power of words like a candle blown out by the wind." Hsuan Tsang himself, who set off hoping to "unravel the tangle of error and destroy the misleading influences of false teaching," does not give details of the doctrine that he studied at Nalanda. His goal in this sense was simply to make better translations than existed in Chinese already, and when he went home, he devoted the rest of his life to that project. But my sense is that over and above the specific doctrinal points he wished to resolve, his immersion in the mind-only school of Yogacara Buddhism would have led him to want to achieve a kind of ecstatic understanding. He wanted to reach a level of consciousness so high that it transcended the normal categories of human understanding—and at the same time, having achieved it, no longer to experience the desire that propelled him on his long and arduous journey in the first place.

Is it possible? Did he do it? I doubt it. But then again, since I didn't attempt to replicate that part of Hsuan Tsang's journey—the part involving disciplined meditation and study—how could I know? Maybe he did realize his purpose and detach himself from it at the same time. As for me, I continue to read here and there in the Buddhist texts looking for the Truth that cannot be expressed in words. And while I remain skeptical about the Buddhist antinomies, I also remain reverential toward the Buddhist civilization of the seventh century. So unlike the European ecclesiastical tyranny that existed at the same time, the kinder, gentler Buddhist church proclaimed in essence that spiritual power, for it to be pure, had to be renounced at the instant it was acquired. While Christianity was enforced by miracle, mystery, and authority, the Buddhists—who were

* Conze, *Buddhist Texts*, p. 281.

far more numerous and widespread than the Christians at that time—strove, at least in theory, to achieve authority without being attached to it. Ideally, they practiced what they called the Six Perfections, including the perfection of wisdom:

> In that even when his body is dismembered, he looks upon the phantom and image of his body as upon so much straw, a log, a wall, and arrives at the conviction that his body has the nature of an illusion and contemplates his body as in reality being impermanent, fraught with suffering, not his own and at peace. That for him is the perfection of wisdom.*

Nobody ever said that it would be easy to become a Bodhisattva, a celestial Enlightened One like our pilgrim's hero Avalokitesvara, to whom he turned for solace years before his stay in Nalanda when he almost died in the desert. But it is clear that Hsuan Tsang sought to know the nature of the internal state of mind that he would have to attain were he to become one. That is what he called the sweet dew, the rain of the Law. He wanted to know how he could be heavy and levitate too; how he could walk on water by not thinking of a hippopotamus; how the lines could be perfectly parallel and intersect forever in the heavens.

---

* Conze, *Buddhist Texts,* p. 123.

16

The Synagogue of Calcutta

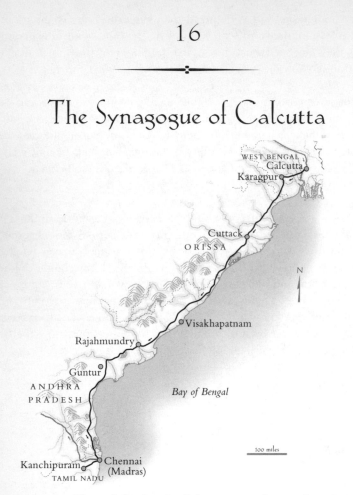

I ARRIVED AT Howrah Station in Calcutta—on the continuation of the Doon Express from Gaya—thinking of the synagogue. I had spotted its location in a fold-out map acquired at an Indian Government Tourist Office. It was shown to be on Synagogue Street, which made sense, but I wondered if there were any Jews left in Calcutta and, if there were, how many there would be. It was late Friday afternoon, almost time for the Sabbath to begin. At such times as these I often long for a dose of ceremony. Having heard the monks from Tibet chant the Law in Bodh-gaya, having meditated on a rooftop with Ladi Tavajra and discussed *sunyata* with Neal and Feydor, I felt an urge to reestablish my tribal connection.

This is a constant with me, the tribal connection. I don't know what else to call my attachment to Judaism, which is not based on religious observance so much as it is on a kind of moral aesthetic, an unwillingness to be disloyal. Years have gone by in my life during which I failed to set foot in a synagogue; I may feel strangely alienated from the Hasidim at the Western Wall; but my tribal attachment has never faded. On one of my early trips to China in 1979, I spent a week in Shanghai, passing a good deal of my time in an unsuccessful effort to meet an elderly woman named Annie Isaacs who, I had been told, was the last Jew left in the city. I never found her (or, more accurately, she declined, through an intermediary, her Chinese doctor, my requests to visit her). But I spent hours wandering the streets of the Hongkou District, where the Jews of Shanghai had been interned by the Japanese occupiers during World War II, using an old guidebook to locate the buildings that once housed the Jewish community center, the Jewish school, and the synagogue.

Once, trying to explain to Zhongmei the nature of my feelings, I showed her a photograph in a book called *The Children of Izieu,* which was published by Serge and Beate Klarsfeld, the famous French Nazi-hunters. The book collected all the information that was available about forty-four Jewish children who had been taken from a farmhouse refuge near Lyons in the South of France and sent to Auschwitz, where all of them were murdered. There is one photograph that especially moves me, of a pretty blond girl and her father. They are sitting on grass in a park someplace. The girl, wearing a threadbare brown sweater, is leaning up against her father, who smiles at the camera from behind her. "They killed her," I told Zhongmei, "because she was Jewish," and, suddenly and unexpectedly, that photograph of a girl I never knew who had been dead for half a century sent me into something close to a paroxysm of weeping. "I don't know if you can understand this," I said to Zhongmei, "but I want to be Jewish because of her and her father." Zhongmei, whose family has its own history of persecution at the hands of the Japanese in Manchuria, and who needs no lessons from me about suffering, understood perfectly well. That girl, whose name was Sarah Szulklaper, is not the only reason for my attachment. I love the music too, and I admire the long accumulation of deep thought about ethics and law contained in the Talmud and the commentaries. But my fundamental loyalty is to Sarah and to the others like her. My feeling is that it would somehow be unbearably light, insouciant, spiritually shallow, to give up on my Judaism just at the moment when being a Jew entails no danger, not even any important exclusion, no decisive inconvenience. And so I wanted to explore Buddhism and the answers that it gives to the serious questions about life and its meaning, but, having done so, I wanted, upon arriving in Calcutta, to find the local Jews.

I followed my red-turbaned porter to the Howrah Station esplanade, past the sign that said "Grievance Redress Bureau," past Higginbotham's News Stand and neat pyramids of bananas and rumple-skinned tangerines. My black-and-yellow Ambassador taxi forced its way onto the suspension bridge over the Hooghly River, and as we descended into the density of Calcutta's traffic, I was reintroduced to the fume-choked, klaxonating, potholed, rubble-strewn, overpopulated semichaos of the Indian urban landscape.

A haze of gray pollution lay over the river. Pedestrians hurled themselves in front of passing cars and then hurled themselves further onto nonstopping buses. At the bottom of the bridge a policeman in a blue sweater stood with his arms folded, benignly watching the vehicular fury. I saw the Tarpaulin Shop, a Catholic church, the Punjab National Bank, the broad expanse of Chowringhee Road (now called Jawaharlal Nehru Road) going past the Maidan, the long rectangular park where the British used to have their fort and their racetrack.

Steamy, corroding, poverty-wracked Calcutta does not enjoy a good reputation. The city's most famous image is a black hole and its most famous person is Mother Teresa, who created the Hospital for the Destitute, the Home for the Dying, the Hospice for Lepers. Calcutta summons up images of medieval plagues and suffering. It is the only major city I have seen that still has old-style rickshaws, the kind where indifferently overweight passengers are pulled by ragged men on foot who are happy for the business. What is striking about rickshaws is the elevation of the passenger seat, held aloft by the rickshaw's large spoked wheels, and how low by contrast the driver seems to be. Calcutta is a city deeply resigned to the afflicted human condition. And yet there is a grandeur to Calcutta. It reeks of the human drama. It was wonderful to arrive there.

The taxi took me to the Fairlawn Hotel on Sudder Street, where women wrapped in flimsy cottons sat with children on their laps and pleaded for money from the passing members of the international backpack brigade. Sudder Street is the place to stay in Calcutta, unless you can afford to stay at the plush Oberoi Grand on Jawaharlal Nehru Road or the marvelously named Tollygunge, which is the golf club. Years ago on my first trip to India I went to Sudder Street hoping to stay at the Fairlawn Hotel, the street's ramshackle finest. It was too expensive for me, and a street urchin led me instead to a Parsi widow named Mrs. Sidhwa who maintained a small guesthouse on the second floor of a large home with balconies. I had a large room to myself with mosquito netting and a ceiling fan. She cooked and provided formal and enjoyable company.

There was one other guest at Mrs. Sidhwa's, a graduate student in political science at Harvard, where I was also a graduate student. He took me to a political discussion group, and there I met a young man of my age named Amitabh Roy who invited me to stay at his family's large home elsewhere in the city. In such a way—from the street urchin to Mrs. Sidhwa's to the cordial embrace of the large Roy family—was I absorbed into the world of Bengali intellectuals, writers, journalists and young, foolish, idealistic, entirely likable Marxist political activists. Amitabh introduced me to the editor of one of the city's newspapers, who told me he was a Jew. We went to the border of what was then East Pakistan—about to become Bangladesh in an Indian-supported revolt against West Pakistan—and I met for the first time in my career a flood of refugees. I had told the Roys of my dream of becoming a journalist, a dream they took to be my actual condition, so that on the border where the refugees streamed into camps, weeping people beseeched me to tell the world of their plight. After two weeks, I left the Roy household, over the protests of Amitabh and his beautiful fiancée, his mother, his father, his uncles, his friends. We stayed in touch for a few years, but then our correspondence petered out as these things often do, and I lost all trace of the family that had received me so warmly in Calcutta. Until my arrival on the Doon Express from Gaya, I had never been back.

This time I stayed at the Fairlawn, a small sign that my material condition had improved in the intervening twenty-nine years. I was greeted by Violet Smith, who owns the place with her husband, and she assigned me a room off an outdoor corridor in the back, past a room crowded with memorabilia. On my long-ago other trip to Calcutta I had viewed the Fairlawn as the epitome of colonial-style luxury. Imagine my surprise to discover that it is actually a tatty old dowager with ancient plumbing and stained whitewashed walls and plain boot-camp beds. Never mind. Mrs. Smith, an Armenian whose parents fled to Calcutta to avoid being slaughtered by the Turks in World War I, gave me an affectionate and motherly greeting that went right to my heart. After all that time on the road, I felt a tug of sentiment upon being called "darling" with a British accent.

"Tell me," I said. "Years ago when I couldn't afford the Fairlawn, I stayed at Mrs. Sidhwa's Guesthouse. Is she . . . ?"

"Oh yes, number ten," said Mrs. Smith. "Of course, everybody knew her, poor woman. She's dead now."

"Ah. Well, I guess I'm not surprised. She was not young even then."

"Yes," said Mrs. Smith, showing sympathy, "it must be ten years ago already."

There was a moment of silence.

"Another question," I resumed. "There's a man I'd like to find in Calcutta named Amitabh Roy."

"Do you have his address?"

Before my departure I had gone through my disorganized collection of papers, especially my old address books and my boxes of ancient correspondence, but it was a hurried search performed when China was more on my mind than India, and it turned up no record of Amitabh.

I shook my head.

"No telephone number either?"

"No."

"Poor darling. That's a terribly common Bengali name. There will be thousands of Amitabh Roys in Calcutta."

"Mm. Well, I suspected as much." There was another moment of silence.

Finally, I asked Mrs. Smith about the synagogue, but as I asked, I was feeling that I had waited too long for this return trip to Calcutta, that things had changed and the traces of my previous life here were too faded to be recovered.

Mrs. Smith told me to go quickly to see David Nahoum at the sweet shop in the Hogg Market nearby.

"He's the last Jew in Calcutta," she said. "He can tell you what you want to know."

"The sweet shop," I said, thinking of the portent of the phrase "last Jew in Calcutta." "How do I find it?"

"Everybody knows it," said the good Mrs. Smith. "Go quickly, darling, before it closes."

I ran to the Hogg Market down a narrow street crowded with peddlers' stands and rickshaws. A movie theater glowed in a perpendicular alley. Fried *puri* cakes and nicely browned, crispy-looking *dhosa* pancakes on outdoor charcoal grills filled the air with a spicy odor. Merchants cried out invitations to visit their shops. Shoppers shopped. Beggars begged. Rickshaw wallahs pulled on the enameled handles of their vehicles looking for fares. The Hogg Market (now called New Market) was in an oxblood Raj-era building ahead of me. Somebody took me into a maze of indoor alleys and directly to the sweet shop where Indian women young and old were buying *gulab jamun* pastries, moist and round and in sugary syrup, and vanilla cakes with icing. The cashier received me cordially and told me that Nahoum was gone. There were no Friday-night services, but the Jewish men would be gathering at the synagogue at six o'clock the next morning for the regular Sabbath prayers, and I was welcome to go.

And so the next morning I bestirred myself early and appeared at the imposing portal of the synagogue, which was inside its own small courtyard off, not Synagogue Street, but Canning Street.

"Are you a Jew?" a man asked me at the entrance.

"Yes," I said.

"You're not a *cohen,* by any chance?" A *cohen* is a person descended from the priests of the Temple in Jerusalem, who trace their ancestry, according to the traditional account, from Aaron, the brother of Moses. They are the first to be called to the Torah during the Sabbath service.

"No."

Where are you from?"

"New York."

"Come in."

There were nine men sitting on heavy cane-back benches arranged in a square beneath the high balcony overhang, and since I made the tenth person needed for a minyan, or quorum, without which the Sabbath service cannot begin, they were happy to see me. The synagogue had a high central nave, stained-glass windows, wrought-iron balustrades. There was a large central bima from which the prayers would be led. I met Nahoum, who looked vaguely like Sydney Greenstreet in *The Maltese Falcon,* and the other members of the community, all of them getting on in years but solid, respectable, imposing. The synagogue, Nahoum told me, had been founded in the nineteenth century by Jews who had come to India as traders from Baghdad. There had once been three synagogues and several hundred Jews in Calcutta, but there were now only these men who came to the synagogue, their wives, and a few others. All the children had emigrated to the United States, Israel, Canada, or Australia. The synagogue still ran two schools—one for girls, one for boys—where there were Muslims and Hindus but no Jews as students.

Nahoum helped me find my place in the Hebrew prayer book, and I followed the unfamiliar Sephardic service. I was accorded the honor often given to a guest from far away of being called to the Torah during the reading of the weekly portion (which was the episode of the parting of the Red Sea), and I managed the required Hebrew blessings, self-conscious of my Ashkenazic pronunciation. I descended the bima noting the paradox that back home I had not been called to the Torah practically since my Bar Mitzvah, and yet here in Calcutta . . . You have to go far sometimes to find out who you are.

While the service continued, one of the assembly introduced himself to me as Mordecai Cohen. He was a swarthy, substantial-looking man in a suit and tie and said he came originally from Dacca, the capital of Bangladesh.

Cohen recited for me the names of some of the prominent Jews of India, with particular emphasis on Jackie Jacobs, the governor of the Punjab and a cousin of Cohen's wife. He also spoke of a General Mordecai who, he said, had arranged the secession of Bangladesh from Pakistan in 1972. Cohen also had that stout, proper, vaguely exotic but hard-to-place look of Sydney Greenstreet in *The Maltese Falcon*. He told me that one of his parents was from Persia, the other from Aleppo, Syria. He said in his perfect English that he spoke nine languages, including Nepalese, which he learned from the family's household servants in Dacca.

"I left Dacca in 1968," he said.

"Why?" I asked.

"There was nobody left," he said. A note of melancholy crept into his voice, and as the story of the parting of the Red Sea was intoned from the Torah, I thought about all of the disappeared worlds of Asian Jewry: the aforementioned Aleppo, Baghdad, Isfahan, Teheran, Cochin, Bombay, Calcutta itself, Tashkent, Bokhara, Harbin, and Shanghai, all former outposts of the Diaspora where once there were impressive synagogues and schools, Torah scrolls, and the chants of the Sabbath, shrunken to a residue like this one in the Maghen David Synagogue. Calcutta induced a valedictory mood in me, a sense of the irrevocable lostness of the past.

Calcutta is one of several places in Asia, most of them run by the British, that for a hundred, two hundred, a thousand years were cosmopolitan agglomerations, cities where Jews, Parsis, Muslims, Arabs, Persians, Nestorians, and others came from afar to trade or to settle. Beirut was another such place, and so were Aleppo, Istanbul, and Baghdad, though the great South and East Asian cities of this genre were Bombay, Calcutta, Shanghai, and Hong Kong. I had a historical vision of the Jews especially, who arrived in Baghdad with the Babylonian captivity and remained there for 2,500 years. Then nineteenth-century British colonialism combined with the extortionate and tyrannical rule of Daud Pasha of Baghdad induced some of the Baghdad contingent to try commercial opportunities elsewhere. Starting in 1828 with David Sassoon, they moved from the Ottoman Empire to the British, thereby beginning one of the more important commercial migrations of history, a great event on a subroute of the Road of Great Events.

The Jews took ships across the Arabian Sea to Bombay, where they set up trading companies. The great names here are Sassoon and Kadoorie. The Parsis, coming down from Persia, paralleled the Jewish movement, the great name in that group being Tata, which is still the name of one of the titanic industrial conglomerates of India. The Parsis stayed, the Jews branched outward, going to Calcutta and then beyond to Shanghai, where they built most of the grand buildings of the famous Bund along the Whampoa River and near the Suzhou Creek. They went to Hong Kong, where their role was less conspicuous than in Shanghai but where the Kadoories nonetheless owned the Peninsula Hotel and the Peak Tram and built a still-functioning synagogue on Robinson Road. I used to go there during my Hong Kong years to have Sunday brunch, meet with my fellow members of the Far Eastern Diaspora, and enjoy the view of the harbor. The Jews in the British Empire replicated the age-old history of the Jews of Egypt during Roman times. They were not natives; they were more like the colonizers than the colonized, and they were tolerated by the foreign rulers for their commercial and intellectual skills, and for the fact that no nationalist, anticolonialist sentiment could coalesce around them. They were like the Jews of Moorish Spain, until their Most Catholic Majesties Ferdinand and Isabella expelled both them and the Muslims in 1492. They were like the Jews of the Ottoman Empire, from Alexandria to Baghdad. The Jews did not threaten the established colonialist order, but because they were friendly to the ruling people, they were seen as vaguely treasonous, fifth-column-ish, by the native peoples. In his magisterial *The Origins of the Spanish Inquisition,* the historian B. Netanyahu argues that anti-Semitism was born in Egypt during the Roman occupation.

There was no anti-Semitism in tolerant India, already accustomed to a profusion of peoples and beliefs. The strange thing is that the British, with whom the Jews identified, disliked the Jews far more than the Indians ever did. But that is another of the many paradoxes of Diaspora history. The important thing for me being there during the last few minutes of Jewry in Calcutta was that this Diaspora history also belonged to the Road of Great Events. Under the benign dictatorship of the British Empire, the mingling of peoples and goods across Eurasia produced a workable cosmopolitanism. Then came World War II, the violent end of colonialism, and the creation of new nations, including, not least, the nation of Israel. With those developments came the ethnically exclusive nation–state. And now the great cosmopolitan commercial cities of Afro-Eurasia, from Alexandria to Shanghai, are no more, and the Jews are an aging residue, an exhibit in the museum of soon-to-be-forgotten history.

"I didn't want to be alone," Cohen was saying. "I didn't want to be the only one left, so I came here. In Dacca I worked in the radio and the TV as an administrator and a censor under the military government. I was trusted to make right decisions. Now I work for a company that makes razor wire. Yes, I went from making right decisions to making razor wire." He smiled.

Cohen said he had two brothers and three children, all of them else-where, and I imagined his world to consist of his wife and the other stoutly aging Indian Jews in the synagogue that early Saturday morning.

AFTER HSUAN TSANG had studied for two years in Nalanda, he took a trip east to Bengal and then south as far as the holy Hindu city of Kanchipuram. He wanted to pay continued homage to the important sites of Buddhist history, and he especially wanted to go to Ceylon, now Sri Lanka, where, as we have seen, a sapling from the original Bodhi tree had been transplanted. He doesn't tell us much about his southern jour-ney. He highlights a few places here and there, mostly enumerating the temples and stupas that were in existence, along with a few more legends from the Buddhist store of morality tales.

When he got to Kanchipuram, he met some Singalese monks who told him that civil war and famine raged in Ceylon, making it impossible for him to go there. Instead, he crossed the southern Indian peninsula to the area where Bombay is today. He then zigzagged across India again, making his way back to Nalanda, where he studied with his teacher Sila-bhadra for one more year. During that year, he was received in the ancient capital of Kanauj, on the Ganges River, by the great king of India, a devout Buddhist named Harsha. The king organized his participation in two great theological debates that, according to Hui Li, Hsuan Tsang glo-riously won. And then, finally, his mission accomplished, the pilgrim begged permission to return to China. Reluctantly, the king gave it. He loaded Hsuan Tsang's many books and Buddha statues onto elephants, gave him letters of introduction, and sent him on his way.

For me, therefore, it remained to follow the monk's progress to the south, then to Bombay, then to the great Buddhist and Hindu cave tem-ples at Ellora and Ajanta. I would not go on to Nalanda again but would make instead for New Delhi, from which, provided with my Hong Kong travel agency visa, I would take the overland trail through Pakistan and back to China.

As I thought about what lay ahead, the idea formed in my mind that Zhongmei might join me for this final leg of the journey. She had performed in the United States while I traveled, but now she was free for the time being. To take the Karakorum Highway to China was a dream I had nurtured for a long time, and it was the sort of thing I would have done alone in the past, remaining lonely but unencumbered, so that whatever might happen could happen. But I had thought a lot about Zhongmei since seeing her walk away on the platform of the Kucha train station, and I missed her. I had carried on an imaginary conversation with her in my mind, in Tash Rabat and on the bus to Tashkent and in the heat of Lumbini and on the way to visit the Maharaja of Varanasi. Now here I was traveling alone again, feeling, again, like that friend who went by himself to Victoria Falls. Why not, for a change, travel as part of a team? In the past, my travels had been a kind of subterfuge, a way of ending my love affairs in a passive, cowardly way. If I stayed away long enough, the girl of the moment would finally lose patience and leave me of her own volition. But suddenly, this time, I was gripped by a fear that I might lose Zhongmei if I stayed away from her for too long. Let me not ruin this one, I said to myself, and I went to an Internet café on Sudder Street in Calcutta and e-mailed her, asking if she would join me in New Delhi. The next day I went back to the café on Sudder Street and typed my way into my e-mail program. The message came through with suspense-building slowness, but the reply was in the affirmative. I had told Zhongmei just, please, get any old ticket and I would pay for it, but she found an inexpensive fare on Singapore Airlines. She was going to have to fly eight hours to Amsterdam from New York, ten hours to Singapore, and, after spending most of the day in Singapore, another seven hours to India, and she was willing to do it. We fixed a precise date and time two weeks hence when I would pick her up at the airport.

I walked with a jauntier step on my last day in Calcutta, during which I arranged my train tickets for the remainder of my Indian circuit. Late in the afternoon of the day after that, I went back to Howrah Station to board the Cormandel Express to Madras, the large city in the south now officially called Chennai. I got a berth in what is called air-conditioned second class, which was a big improvement on the non-air-conditioned-second-class berths I'd had on the Doon Express. The carriage was calm and orderly and relatively clean. My compartment was closed in by brocaded curtains. It had a little plastic-topped table beneath the window, two cupholders, and reading lamps above each berth. We pulled out of Howrah exactly on time, rumbled past the bridge over the Hooghly River, and passed through the battered suburbs. We went through a flat landscape of rice paddies, banana plantations, and groves of bamboo. Shortly after nightfall we stopped in Balasore, and a fellow passenger joined me in the compartment and began talking about Calcutta.

"Its problems date from partition," he said, speaking of the 1947 separation of British India into India and Pakistan, the former mostly Hindu, the latter Muslim. "So many people from East Bengal came then, and the city didn't have the infrastructure or the economy for them. It still doesn't."

My interlocutor wore a plaid shirt over white trousers, and he spoke so softly that I had to lean forward to hear him over the rattle and rumble of the train. I offered him a mint, and he gave me a cheese-and-vegetable sandwich that his wife had packed for him. We talked about Calcutta's Marxist Party, which has run the city for many years. "It's Marxist only in name," he said. "They've built an impressive political organization, and they're less corrupt than most of the state governments." The man said he worked for a bank and was heading for a training conference in Bangalore. To get there he would be a day and a half on the train to Madras and then go overnight on the Bangalore Mail to Bangalore, a lot of time for a trip that could have been made in less than two hours by air.

"Flying was not within the budget prescribed," he explained. He was very serious.

With that we fell silent, and we never spoke again for the entire night and next day. From a passing vendor I bought a vegetable cutlet, served with a dollop of spicy ketchup. I watched as the man in the bunk above and opposite me, a short Muslim with a large square beard and white skullcap, said his prayers, heavily bowing down in the general direction of Mecca. Later I ran into the Muslim outside the lavatory, and he asked me where I was from.

"The United States," I said.

"I spent eleven years in South Africa," he said, looking at me for approval.

"Really?" I said, but neither of us proved very good at small talk beyond this exchange and we spoke no further.

Service people in burgundy jackets went by offering more cutlets, chicken and vegetable, sugary tea with milk, bottles of mineral water, boiled eggs. There was no dining car on the Cormandel Express. An outside vendor passed through selling chains and locks. I read and went to sleep and woke in the morning to a well-watered tropical terrain with thick vegetation and darker-skinned people than I had seen before. Thatched villages clotted with palm groves and banyans were overhung by heavy clouds. When the sun finally broke through, it illuminated a layer of dew on the marsh grass and the banana leaves; then it rose to reflect a burning yellow in the flooded rice fields. The train stopped in Vijayawada, the site of an important Hindu temple, outside of which men could be seen squatting in the dry grass relieving themselves. Nearby herds of goats grazed. White birds, egrets I think, flew ghostlike away from the train. A boy in a green shirt with black short pants walked toward it on a dusty red road.

I arrived late in the afternoon in Madras, which was hot, noisy, and polluted, found the Pandian Hotel, which my Lonely Planet guide suggested for good value, had a dinner of chicken *tikka,* freshly baked *nan,* and a cold Singha beer, and went to sleep early.

As long as I was journeying to the south I felt I ought to try to meet the Shankaracharya of Kanchipuram, whom my friend Tavleen Singh had spoken about in her article about the pollution of the Ganges. My idea was that Hsuan Tsang would have sought out the notables of Indian spiritual life wherever he went, Hindu as well as Buddhist, and that, while I was not optimistic that so exalted a figure as the Shankaracharya would receive me, I would try to do the same. The Shankaracharya of Kanchipuram is especially exalted, being higher in rank than the other four.

The bus for Kanchipuram wasn't crowded when I got on, which was rare in my experience of Indian buses. The welcome from other passengers was warm. "Are you going to Kanchi?" a man already installed on a green plastic seat asked me.

"Yes."

"Then you are on the right bus. Take any seat."

I sat next to an open window. A parade of peddlers moved through the bus—sellers of fresh grapes, plastic pouches of spring water like transparent bean bags, pens and combs, gold chains with costume jewelry lockets, green bananas, garlands of jasmine, spiced roasted chickpeas served in cones made of newspaper. An aged and bent-over woman carried a zinc bucket of raw potatoes. Outside were shops: the Sri Baba Travel Agency, M. Ramakrishna Glass, the M. A. Jacobs Furniture Department Store, Visanthakawari Medicals. We passed the Southern Railroad office, a building in the best Mogul-British style with graceful towers surmounted by corroding masonry cupolas. The train station was red brick with an arcade in white trim. I noticed an advertising slogan for the Indian Bank: "Deadly Woods Are Removed; Fogs Cleared; March Ahead into the Third Millennium; 91 Years of Trust."

The bus picked up passengers along the route, and soon every seat was taken and the aisles were crowded. I had a hard time not staring at a Tamil woman who boarded holding an almost naked baby. A woman with a seat took the baby for her, but she herself had to stand, holding on to the back of a seat for support. She wore a purple cotton sari and a gold nose piece and bracelets of string around her wrists. She was finely carved and sinewy, with long upswept eyelashes, dark skin, ebony hair, and finger-nails smudged with red, perhaps from the powder she used to create her *bindi,* the circle of color she painted between her black eyes. She took her fare of twelve rupees out of a colored cotton purse. She looked tough, as if she could thrash twice her weight in male troublemakers, but she was also very feminine, with a long neck that showed its ligatures when she turned her head to check on her infant in the other woman's lap. She wore earrings too, a circle of diamonds around a smaller circle of rubies around a final diamond in the center.

In two hours we arrived in Kanchipuram, and I was happy to get out of the bus and stretch my legs. A rickshaw driver asked me where I wanted to go, and when I told him the name of my hotel, he said, "Give me ten rupees and I'll take you there." I recognized the rareness of a rick-shaw driver who gave an uninflated price to a foreigner, and he became my chauffeur for the next two days. In Calcutta, I had called Tavleen to obtain her advice about the best way to get an interview with the Shankaracharya. She had told me she would call ahead to introduce me to the great man's chief of staff, one Raja Ram. In any event, she said, I should just ask for the *mutt*—temple—when I arrived in Kanchi. "Ask for Raja Ram when you get there."

"Do you know the *mutt*?" I asked my rickshaw driver. He was a thin man with a mustache and a black-and-gray checked shirt.

He gave me that Indian nod which looks like no but means yes.

"You know it?" I asked. I was incredulous. Things didn't usually go so smoothly in India.

"Yes, I know it," he said, and we bounced away on Kanchipuram's potholed streets, past what seemed like a thousand small silk stores and silk-weaving workshops, further demonstrations of the euphonious poly-syllabicism of Tamil life: D. K. Dasarathah & Bros. Silk, Sri Seethalakshmi Silks, Mahavishnu Silks, ABM Subramanisah Silks. There were small hotels, fruit stands, small Hindu temples marked by carved gray towers and stone gates.

As the spiritual headquarters for a religion of some 800 million people, the Kanchi Mutt is singularly unimposing. This is no Vatican, no St. Peter's. Then again, Hinduism is a religion of worldly renunciation. There is no association in it between material wealth and the state of grace that, in Max Weber's famous view, was at the core of capitalism. I was bidden to take off my shoes outside a masonry gateway. This led to a large, ramshackle interior space, on the other side of which was an airy open courtyard. In the main office was a bank of metal storage cabinets with a mysterious sign: "For the preservation of valuable palm leaf and other essential manuscripts." An iron grille marked off an inside corner of the room in which several men with bare torsos and horizontal stripes of ash across their foreheads sat cross-legged behind low tables. One of them beckoned to me to sit down, which I did on the smooth, swept tile floor. I asked if Raja Ram was in.

"He is not here," the man said.

I realized that since I had spoken to Tavleen, she had had no way of contacting me to let me know if she learned that my trip to Kanchipuram would be in vain.

"Oh," I said.

The man looked at me sympathetically. On the wall above him was a calendar with a gaudy picture of Shiva, who is one of the three main expressions of the one Hindu God, and the legend "Satellite Messaging for the First Time in India." A plastic tray overflowing with rubber stamps and an inkpad was on the floor. I noticed a photograph of an elderly, almost naked man sitting on the floor and wondered if that was the Shankaracharya himself.

"Do you expect him back?" I asked.

"No."

"Oh, dear," I said.

"What is the purpose of your visit?" the man asked. He was brusque, but there was a kindness in him. He wanted to help.

I told the man that I was an American writer traveling Hsuan Tsang's route. I mentioned Tavleen Singh and my hope of meeting the Shankaracharya.

"You wish to meet His Holiness?" the man asked.

"Yes."

The man showed no surprise that an American visitor would walk in unannounced and without an appointment and ask to see the chief spiritual leader of all of Hinduism. Still, he had bad news. "His Holiness is traveling now, but he will be back in three months' time and you can see him then if you want."

"Three months?"

"Yes."

"That's a bit longer than I'm planning to stay."

"I see."

"Where did His Holiness go?" I wondered.

"In one week he is reaching Bombay."

"He's going to Bombay?"

"Yes, it is the entire entourage going there."

I told the man that I would be in Bombay in a couple of days. He took out a scrap of paper and wrote down an address in Bombay: Sri Sankara Mutt; Patunga (C.R.) Bombay.

"It's the place where the Tamils are living in Bombay," he told me. "You can meet the Shankaracharya there." Then he gave me the telephone number of the Shankaracharya's host in Bombay.

The next day I went back to the Kanchi Mutt and got a tour, along with a brief history of the Shankaracharya. I learned that about 2,400 years ago, Lord Shiva, one of the manifestations of the Supreme Being, took the form of a human being who was to be a universal guru. Thus, the Shankaracharya is actually a reincarnation of Shiva. "Shankar" means "Shiva"; *acharya* means "teacher." The Shankaracharya is the Shiva-teacher, the guru, and a guru is a god in human form who shows his disciples the right path to salvation. I saw a large chart that listed every one of these incarnations of Shiva, seventy of them, beginning with Sri Adi Shankara in 477 B.C.

"It is an unbroken line," my guide told me. "The sixty-ninth and seventieth Shankaracharyas are still here. The seventieth is a young man of less than thirty.

"There are always two Shankaracharyas," he continued, "a senior and a junior. This is the case even though the two of them together are counted as one of the five Shankaracharyas of India. The older guru chooses a thirteen-year-old boy to be his successor. The boy is given extensive training, and at the appropriate time, when the preceptor is too old to perform his functions or when he decides to spend the rest of his time in meditation, the younger one becomes the Shankaracharya. Both live the life of the renounced man. They only possess the simple implements of daily life, wooden sandals, a wooden spoon, a wooden bowl, a clay pot. The sixty-eighth Shankaracharya was over one hundred when he died.

He didn't use electricity, but he had a flashlight if he needed it and a magnifying glass. As long as he was alive, he never traveled by car or by plane. He walked the length and breadth of the country, and only when it was absolutely essential did he travel on a bicycle-drawn cart sitting on a basket filled with straw."

While we talked, schoolboys sitting in several rows on a marble platform were chanting the Vedas for the benefit of a television crew from England. All around were pictures of the current senior Shankaracharya, Jagadguru Sri Jayendra Saraswati Swami, and the younger one, Jagadguru Sri Sankara Vijayendra Saraswati Swami. They were pictured sitting crosslegged on the ground dressed in orange robes that leave one side of the torso bare and were pulled up under the thighs. I remembered a passage from the Bhagavad Gita:

I am the taste in the water. I am the radiance in the sun and the moon. I am the sacred OM in all the Vedas. I am sound in space. I am virility in men. I am the sweet fragrance of the earth and the heat in the fire, the life in all beings, the austerity in ascetics. Know Me as the seed primeval of all beings. I am the strength of the strong when it is untainted by desire and passion. I am Love that moves all beings.

Nice.

17

The Shankaracharya of Kanchipuram

A ND SO IT WAS across India to Bombay aboard the Mumbai Mail,
air-conditioned second class—Mumbai being the official name now
for Bombay. A sign on the train warned of something called the "Biscuit
Gang" whose members, "posing as passengers," gave adulterated biscuits
to their unsuspecting victims. The biscuits put those who ate them to
sleep and their bags were stolen. I had plenty of time to reflect on this
during the thirty-hour trip. I thought about the vegetable sandwich I had
unhesitatingly accepted from my fellow passenger on the Cormandel
Express to Madras. Fortunately, there seemed to be no Vegetable Sandwich Gang.

I arrived in Bombay in the middle of the afternoon, checked into my
hotel, and went straight to the Taj Mahal Hotel for high tea. There I sat in

the restaurant in the old part of the hotel and looked at the view. The basalt triumphal arch known as the Gateway of India, built for the visit of King George V in 1924, stood alongside the harbor. Down below was a milling crowd of tourists and local strollers. There was a snake charmer sitting on the ground in front of a straw basket; he would knock the top of the basket off whenever a foreigner came close and a sleepy-looking cobra would rise up out of it. Peddlers wandered about selling small glass boxes of saffron. Pleasure boats were anchored south of the Gateway. Inside I sipped Earl Grey tea served in a fine china cup and filtered with a heavy sterling silver strainer, and gorged myself on little cakes, little waffles, creampuffs, some *rasmalai,* and a *gulab jamun* (both sweet Indian desserts), and a round lacquered biscuit or two that did not render me unconscious. I struck up a conversation with a middle-aged American couple—they gave their names as Neeraj and Sumati—at the next table who told me they were spiritual seekers in Bombay come to study with a guru. They looked more like Rotarians or tennis players than the acolytes of somebody in an orange robe, but they both said they worked for a few months each year so they could earn enough money to spend the next few months in India.

According to my friends in Kanchipuram, the Shankaracharya was due to arrive in the city the next day, so the next morning I called the Bombay number I had been given for his local host. There was no answer. I took the commuter train to the Sri Sankara Mutt in Patunga in the northern suburbs of Bombay. The train left from Victoria Station, possibly the most beautiful railroad station in the East, a gray stone edifice with cathedrallike towers and archways. I took a wooden seat in the sparsely populated second-class section beneath a profusion of hanging straps that swung in unison back and forth as we rolled through a stained and tarnished urban landscape. There was Masjid Station, Sandhurst Road, Byculla, and Chinchpokli, outside of which were a series of signs warning about AIDS—"One Life, One Wife"; "To Avoid AIDS Don't Change Beds." Then came Currey Road, Parel, Dadar, and Patunga.

I got out and walked into a bustling market street where people directed me to a yellow temple with huge black enamel elephant statues outside, but the gate was closed. Signs announced various special prayers to be said "during the visit of their holinesses Pujya Sri Jayendra Saraswati Swamigal and Pujya Sri Sankara Vijayendra Saraswati Swamigal," but clearly neither of these two spiritual leaders was on hand on the day I was there. I poked around to the back of the temple and found an elderly woman who, when asked about the Shankaracharya, replied, *"Nehru,*

Nehru." I didn't know if she was for some mysterious reason invoking the name of Jawaharlal Nehru, India's first post-independence prime minister, or if she was naming a district of Bombay where the Shankaracharya was to be found. I made my way back to the market street near the train station, where I had seen signs for public phones. I walked past a collection of flower shops where huge garlands of roses and honeysuckle hung from hooks. A cashier sat cross-legged on the floor of a kind of elevated hut while underneath, looking like figures in some medieval representation of Purgatory, other men sat hunched over stringing roses and honeysuckle into strands.

I found the public phone across the street, but there was still no answer at the host's number. I went back to the temple and this time encountered a uniformed guard, who told me that the Shankaracharya would not be back until the next day. I had a reservation on the train for Aurangabad the next day, and, wanting to stick to my schedule, which I had to do in order to be on time for my rendezvous with Zhongmei in New Delhi, and not feeling a meeting with the Shankaracharya to be essential to my project, I decided to bag the whole thing.

I rode the train back to Bombay, had a fish tandoori for lunch at Leopold's, and then walked to 18 Madame Cama Road, a significant address in my personal history. The YWCA International Guesthouse, an imposing, grayish, corroded building with a columned portico and stolid masonry gateposts, was at that address. It was where I had stayed for a week or so on my only previous trip to Bombay, twenty-nine years before, when I was desperately looking for a subject for a newspaper article.

Bombay in a sense was my moment of truth, a critical moment in my life after I ended my brief Paris period and left for Asia desperate to turn the trip to practical advantage. Paris was an interlude. But I had been studying Chinese and the history of China for five years, and it was in Asia that I wanted to give some direction to my until then directionless life. I didn't know exactly what direction I wanted to go in, but I knew vaguely that I should travel overland from Paris to India, then to Southeast Asia, and finally to Hong Kong and Taiwan, and that something would happen en route. My idea, as I've said, was that I would become a journalist, and before leaving Paris, I had written some letters to American newspaper editors telling them of my impending trip and asking if I could send articles along the way. Only the editor of the *Christian Science Monitor* in Boston replied, saying that he would read what I sent him, and on that basis I appointed myself that fine newspaper's roving foreign correspondent. I had never published a word of anything in my life, despite a few earlier efforts to do so. Still, I had confided to a friend the plan that was forming in my mind by which I would eventually get a real job on a newspaper. I would write articles as I traveled and send them to the *Monitor*. I would thereby create an impressive portfolio of published works, and eventually, after I returned to the United States, I would show that portfolio to get a full-time, proper job.

"Yeah, right," said my friend, "and I'm going to be in my school play and become Cary Grant."

"You'll see," I said confidently, but I wasn't confident. I was worried. I certainly didn't know what I was doing. As I journeyed across southern Europe and the Middle East, from Italy to Greece to Turkey, Iran, Afghanistan, Pakistan, and India, I failed to provide the editor of the *Monitor* with a single piece. Not that there were no opportunities. On the train across Turkey from Istanbul to Erzerum, I experienced grizzled Turks in skullcaps laying their prayer carpets down on the floor of our second-class compartment and bowing to Mecca. I got stopped at the Iranian border because I had traveled under the mistaken impression that I didn't need a visa to Iran. The Turks kept me and an Afghani businessman—traveling from Berlin in a similarly undocumented situation—in the border station for two nights and a day, letting us sleep on waiting-room chairs. On our second morning, the Iranian border guards issued five-day transit visas for both of us. On the way to Teheran, the bus broke down and we spent another night, our third in a row, on pulled-together chairs, this time in a roadside pilaf-and-tea house in the middle of the Iranian desert.

I roamed Teheran talking to merchants in the bazaar about life under the shah, and I wrote nothing about that either. I went by bus to Herat with an Afghan friend, and when he went on to Kabul I stayed in Herat, where I hung out with expatriate hippies, smoked hashish, and met an English girl named Melissa who within hours had left me for another traveler, a blond guy from Sweden. I took the bus to Quetta in Pakistan, the train to Karachi, and (because I didn't find out until I got there that the Pakistan-India overland border crossing was near Lahore) the plane to Bombay, all the while scribbling in a notebook, trying to come up with an idea that could be realized in eight hundred words. Finally, walking out of the "Y" on Madame Cama Road, I was approached by a young man who asked me if I wanted to change money, sell my camera, maybe buy some marijuana.

"No," I said, "but I'd like to talk to you."

"You want to talk to me?" He seemed flattered.

"You know about the black market, right?"

"Right."

"I'd like to write an article about the black market in Bombay."

"Right."

"Can I ask you some questions about what you do when you change money, for example? Who do you sell it to? How does the system work?"

"You are writer, isn't it?"

"Yes," I proclaimed boldly.

"You wait for me here tonight," the young man said. "I'll show you things in Bombay that no tourist ever sees."

He took me by taxi to a crowded area and into a huge house with dark corridors and a small room where three other young men seemed to be waiting for me. For a minute I thought I was about to be robbed and murdered. In fact, all they wanted was to sell me some hashish, and I bought some, grateful that they had spared my life. When I wrote my article, I gave my guide the name Ganga, which, I suppose, was a variation on Gunga, as in Kipling's "Gunga Din," or maybe it was a variation on *ganja,* which is "marijuana" in Hindi. Ganga took me to a wide, chaotic avenue where, he promised, I would see "the cages," which were barred windows behind which prostitutes struck seductive poses. We went into a whorehouse and looked at the whores close-up. Not feeling that my life would be in danger if I didn't buy the proffered service, I declined to avail myself of one of them despite Ganga's urging to "have a little pleasure, man." Back on the street we drank a heavenly concoction of honeydew melon, sugar, milk, and crushed ice, and then we went to a harbor area where Ganga showed me the ships that smuggled things to India across the Arabian Sea. "Tax high," he explained. "Smuggler no pay tax." And then, after a few hours and much talk, he brought me and my small cellophane packet of hashish back to the YWCA International Guesthouse. There I sat down to write, finishing my article in the early morning and bringing it to the post office to send to the *Monitor.* Later that morning, looking in my shoulder bag, I discovered that my traveler's checks were missing, which required me to go to the police and make a report and apply to American Express to replace them (which it did, but not for a couple of weeks). I talked to the officer on duty at the police station while a cellful of locked-up Indians looked on sullenly.

Months later I arrived in Hong Kong and got some mail, including two envelopes from the *Christian Science Monitor* with checks inside. One was for an article I sent later; the other was for my piece on Ganga—with the more interesting parts, the hashish and the whores, excised. Ganga had probably stolen my traveler's checks but had also given me the subject of my first published story.

Standing in front of the YWCA many years later, I had to resist the urge to flag down passersby and tell them that this is where it all began for me, right here on Madame Cama Road in Bombay, and that my plan had worked after all, more or less, even if now I did not exactly feel that all my life's ambitions had been realized, that, indeed, I was experiencing a desire to escape, at least for a time, the comfortable cage that my earlier adventure in Bombay had led to. I suppressed this ancient-mariner impulse and instead strolled slowly back to my hotel, trying to make out the meaning of this visit.

Of course, I had known all along that my trip would take me to Bombay and that I would stand outside the Y on Madame Cama Road and, as it were, turn the clock back to an earlier self. I wanted, I suppose, to close the gap created by the intervening years, to create a unity out of my life, to recapture, not my youth, because that is not given to us, but at least the feeling that I had when I was young, nervously ambitious, and ready for anything. The truth is that I did not feel strong emotions; there was no symphonic swell. Certainly I did not stand there with the feeling that all my youthful undirected eagerness had become a mature, wise sense of fulfillment now. If anything, the feeling I had was how little I had changed from the avid postadolescent I was then, desperate for any experience that I could write down and desperate to make something of myself. The middle-aged me was not desperate anymore and some of the avidity had faded, but I was still avid enough to feel that I wasn't finished yet. I could perceive the qualities that had driven me to venture far away in the first place, to feel that success for me, worldly success, would lie on some distant shore. What lingered was my sense of nonbelonging, of being, as it were, no good at basketball. It was a sense of nonbelonging that translated all those many years ago into an impulse to find something that the folks back home didn't know enough to look for, and to make my mark with it. The black market in Bombay then; a route of spiritual adventure traveled by a seventh-century Buddhist monk from China now.

"Different now and yet the same," Stephen Dedalus says in James Joyce's *Ulysses,* as he examines his features in a cracked looking glass and thinks of his younger years. The boy who was myself and stayed at the Y is gone, but a great deal of him endures in the middle-aged man who came to Madame Cama Road nearly one-third of a century later looking for him, and for himself.

PERHAPS THE MEMORY of my former eagerness led me to be eager again, and to try again the telephone number I had for the Shankaracharya's host in Bombay. This time a woman answered.

"I am trying to reach the party of the Shankaracharya of Kanchipuram," I announced.

"Yes," was the answer.

"Do I have the correct number?"

"Yes."

"Is Raja Ram there by any chance?"

"He is doing *pooja*." That meant that he was praying.

"Can you tell me how I can reach him?"

"He is in *Nehru*," I heard the woman say.

So Nehru was a place. The woman gave me a phone number there. I called it and a man answered.

"Is that the entourage of the Shankaracharya of Kanchipuram?"

"Yes."

"Ah, great. Listen, I'm a writer from New York, and I'd, uh, well, if it would be possible at short notice, I'd . . ."

"You want to see the Shankaracharya?"

"Yes."

"You can come."

"Well, the problem is that I have to leave Bombay in the morning, so I was wondering . . ."

"Yes, you can come," the man said.

"Now?"

"Yes."

"Oh, that's great. Where are you?"

"Nehru," the man seemed to say.

"Could you spell that?"

"N-E-R-U-L."

"Oh, so it's Nerul." I was soon to learn that not having heard of Nerul in Bombay was a bit like not having heard of the Bronx in New York. It would not occur to a local person to explain that it was a place-name.

"Where in Nerul?"

"Lowdown Peerloons," I heard the man say. "You just come to the Eshighyayess School of Management."

"Lowdown Peerloons?"

The man sounded impatient.

"I am not understanding the American accent well," he complained.

"I am having some trouble with the Indian accent," I said.

"Just come to Eshighyayess School of Management near Lowdown Peerloons, Nerul," he said and hung up.

I was staying at the Harbor View Hotel, whose staff I enlisted to speak Indian English to the man on the phone, whom I called again. In this way I learned that Lowdown Peerloons was a brewery called London Pilsner, a well-known landmark in Nerul, and that Eshighyayess was the S.I.E.S. (for South Indian Education Society) School of Management. It was not clear why a Hindu papal figure would be hanging out at a business school. The hotel found me a taxi driver who knew the way. Nerul was across the Thana Creek in New Bombay. The taxi driver said it would take about two hours.

"Oh, boy," I said.

"It is far," the driver said. "And now it is rush hour."

"Let's go," said I, and we were off through the foul dust of the Bombay streets. The words "God Is Love" were stenciled on the dashboard of my tiny Hindustan Motors Company Premier sedan, whose low roof forced me into an uncomfortable crouch. At the edge of Bombay proper we went past the biggest shantytown I had ever seen, an enormous stretch of slum built on marshy ground just before the bridge over the creek. The bridge was a gaseous snarl of truck traffic in which my little car seemed like a mouse among elephants. Going over it, the Premier coughed and sputtered so much I was afraid we wouldn't make it. But finally at about nine o'clock, well after dark, we pulled up to a collection of large modern buildings festooned with colored banners and out of which could be heard the sound of Vedas being chanted.

"Who are you looking for?" a young man asked me very politely as I got out of my taxi.

"The Shankaracharya of Kanchipuram," I said.

"Yes. He is here. Follow me."

The young man took me into the S.I.E.S. School of Management. I took off my shoes at the entrance. The sound of chanting grew louder. We passed through an immense open space where three hundred priests in white loincloths sat on the floor around square tables festooned with flowers and small stupas. Their foreheads bore the three horizontal ash marks that are the sign of Lord Shiva. They sat cross-legged and with rhythmic arm motions tossed jasmine blossoms into brass pots of water. I stood for a while transfixed by the scene. On the walls were large black-and-white signs indicating corporate sponsorship of the event taking place before me. I wondered if the Shankaracharya was someplace in the room. Perhaps that was his voice being amplified on loudspeakers and filling the room with throaty, minor-key Sanskritic chants. The young man led me away from the prayer hall to a corridor where several men in white dhotis were sitting on chairs. I introduced myself to one of them. He rose smiling and shook my hand and said his name was V. Shankar. It was he who had spoken to me on the phone earlier.

"I'm sorry we had difficulty communicating," I said. "Also the line wasn't very good."

Soon I was embraced in a friendly and informative welcome. The men there seemed pleased by my presence and my interest in the Shankaracharya. Shankar explained that the S.I.E.S. School of Management was about to inaugurate a thirty-foot-high statue of Hanuman, the Hindu monkey god, which was the reason for the Shankaracharya's presence there. The priests in the other room had brought water from all of the sacred rivers of India. The Vedic chanting and the tossing of flowers would purify it. It would be poured over the statue, which would also be showered with 1,008 gold coins during the official consecration ceremony a few days later. The coins would then be given to the poor. Shankar introduced me to the director of the school, who explained that the S.I.E.S. School of Management was affiliated with the London School of Economics, but it added into the curriculum courses on religious values and ethics, not just Hindu ones but those of all religions. Then Shankar took me back to the large prayer room and to another part of the school complex. We walked down a wide corridor where several dozen people were sitting on the floor waiting. We stopped outside a glass door decorated with sheaves of dry yellow flowers. He handed me off to a man with a streaked gray beard who looked, despite his loincloth and bare chest and ash marks, a bit like Sean Connery in *The Name of the Rose*. This was Mr. Ramayanam, who described himself as a sort of aide-de-camp to the Shankaracharya.

"I am with him twenty-four hours a day," he said. "You're going to meet the junior Shankar."

A few minutes later, the said junior appeared, swathed in a simple maroon robe and holding a long bamboo staff. He had a round face, a closely cropped head, and a few days' growth of very dark beard. He was not tall but there was a physical density about him and the kind of unselfconscious ease that I supposed must come from being the incarnation of a god. He had a twinkle in his eye and a bronchial cough. Perhaps it was the pollution. He gave me a friendly smile and wiggled his head in that Indian way that says, "I am well disposed to you." I liked him.

Ramayanam explained who I was. The young Shankaracharya coughed for a good long minute and took a seat on a low wooden stool, resting his staff over his left shoulder, holding the low end of it between his toes. Ramayanam gestured at me to sit on the floor opposite him.

"Not too close," he said.

I pointed to a spot on the floor.

"Is this an appropriate distance?"

"Yes."

I plopped down, crossed my legs, and took out my notebook. Local men, women, and children waiting for their turn with the Shankaracharya, but butted in on by me, sat alongside and watched.

"Ask anything," Ramayanam said. "You can speak to him in English, but he'll answer in Hindi and I'll translate."

I had thought in the taxi about the questions I should ask. I wanted something that would provoke an epigrammatic rather than a lengthy answer. I knew I wouldn't have the time, and didn't possess the knowledge, to engage in a real discussion of Hindu philosophy. My real purpose was not so much to learn as to have the experience of meeting an official incarnation of Shiva, a pope-guru, a living god. So I had decided that I would tell the story of Rabbi Hillel being asked if he could teach all of Judaism standing on one foot. I made it clear that I was not asking the Shankaracharya to do a balancing act, but that the question required a very short answer, a phrase or two of spiritual essentials.

"Hinduism is a way of life," the Shankaracharya said, answering my question. The answer certainly was brief. But it did not state a principle.

"What is the most important principle of that way of life?"

"Simple living and high thinking," he said.

I asked the Shankaracharya about Indian poverty, which he said was not as bad as the foreign and local press made it out to be. What consolation do you give to the poor? I wanted to know. His answer was that some who have no place to live may be philosophically higher than some who are wealthy. I asked him what advice he had for a visiting journalist. He replied: "By your writings do good for others." It seemed like good advice to me.

I had thought about asking other questions: What about the pollution of the Ganges? Is there a connection between Hinduism and Indian poverty? Is the world real or is it merely consciousness? But I didn't feel, as a visitor who had been so cordially received, that such questions would be appropriate. Anyway, the Shankaracharya soon began asking me questions—about China, about American-Indian relations, about Indian-Chinese relations—and as he did so, the people who had come to see him began approaching, slipping themselves in between our sentences as it were. One woman told him that her husband was sick. A man said he was starting a new job and wished for His Holiness's blessing. With each person, the young Shankaracharya gave that friendly head wiggle; he murmured a brief phrase; he reached behind him for a pinch of large-granule sugar in a bowl held within reach by a hovering aide; and he dropped the granules into the grateful palm of his petitioner. That person would then prostrate himself or herself at full length on the ground before getting up to leave. The Shankaracharya was, by my standards, perfunctory as he performed these ceremonies, but there was a gentleness to his practiced and confident gestures. He was unaffected, devoid of any trace of imperiousness. There were smiles and head wiggles and eye movements as he made his brief gestures of blessing and consolation, and the people who had come to him for comfort left content.

As I got up to leave, Sri Sankara Vijayendra Saraswati Swami reached into his bowl of sugar and deposited a handful of it into a square of newspaper and put it on the floor in front of him. I picked it up and folded it over and put it in my pocket. Ramayanam led me away, telling me that the senior would be passing from his meeting room to his sleeping quarters and perhaps he would give me a few minutes.

And so I got two Shankaracharyas for the price of one trip to Nerul. The senior emerged into a corridor. He was smaller than the junior but had some of the same physical solidity to him, and he was similarly lacking in pomp and circumstance. He was just there, stopping to joke with a group of schoolboys who stood shyly by. Ramayanam told him who I was, and together the three of us walked up a flight of stairs toward the senior Shankaracharya's quarters. On the way, Ramayanam asked me if I was a Catholic or a Protestant.

"I'm a Jew," I said.

We entered a sparely furnished office room with a standing electric fan, a carpet, a canvas duffel bag, a sleeping mat on the floor, and a basket of fruits and vegetables. The Shankaracharya sat on a cushion; Ramayanam and I sat on the rug in front of him.

"So you are a writer," Jagadguru Sri Jayendra Saraswati Swami began. He was friendly, avuncular. He had a deep husky laugh and crooked teeth.

I told him about my travels from China to India and about Hsuan Tsang, whose route I had followed to Kanchipuram. The Shankaracharya wanted to know about the state of religious practice in China and what the monk wrote about Kanchipuram. I answered as best I could.

"Can you explain Hinduism to me while standing on one foot?" I asked.

The Shankaracharya smiled.

"The goal of a man is to know the truth," he replied.

Touché, I thought. A wonderful answer, in the league with Hillel's, which was "What is hateful unto thee, do not do unto others," and one that was full of the difference between East and West. In the Judeo-Christian tradition, the operative concept is faith, faith in an all-powerful Supreme Being even when the evidence does not indicate His existence. The issue for a Christian or a Jew is only secondarily: Is it true? Primarily it is: What does God demand of me? In Hinduism and in Buddhism, the issue is less belief in the Supreme Being, though there is a Supreme Being, one with many manifestations, including the Shankaracharya in front of me, than it is the true nature of reality, the reality that lies behind appearances and whose apprehension will enable the devotee to escape the grip of earthly attachment and experience a higher happiness.

I asked the Shankaracharya whether to a man who knew the truth the self was an illusion or whether it was real.

"The 'I' is an illusion," the Shankaracharya said, "but that illusion needs to be experienced, and it is only by experiencing it that it can be known as illusion. The point is total surrender to the Almighty. There you will not experience the pettiness of the self. The self will not arise. If it does arise, then you have not surrendered."

We talked about Hindu temples, and the Shankaracharya said that temples were a relatively recent development in Hinduism, only about three thousand years old. Before that there were no temples and no idols.

"The body is the temple and God is inside. That is our concept. At a later stage the temple was built and the God was installed inside of it."

Does that mean that the idol is the God?

"God is omnipresent, omnipotent, and omniscient," the Shankaracharya replied. "Installing Him in the temple is symbolic. God is everywhere, not in a particular place. But men cannot conceive without a symbol, so the symbol is put into the temple. It is not the end. It is only the beginning."

The Shankaracharya invited me to continue talking, but my train was leaving at 6 a.m. the next morning for Aurangabad, and I told him it was time for me to go. He placed a pomegranate in front of him. I picked it up, put it in my bag, and went out to find my taxi.

18

To the Kunjerab Pass

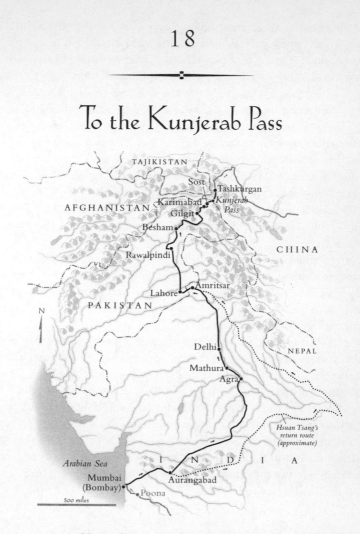

THEY BEGGED Hsuan Tsang to stay, not to go home. After he completed his circumnavigation of India and returned to Nalanda, he was prevailed upon by none other than the great King Harsha, the last native ruler of all of northern India, to engage his adversaries in an eighteen-day public debate. This took place in 643 in Kanauj, then the royal capital but now an unnoticed town on the Ganges. According to Hui Li, the kings of eighteen Indian states and several thousand Buddhist monks were present. The issue was the Little Vehicle heresy that took the world of phenomena to be real, which didn't stand a chance against the devastating logic of Hsuan Tsang, who, having prepared himself in Kashmir and Nalanda, effectively defended Mahayana idealism. The Chinese pilgrim was brought to Kanauj in a procession of twenty thousand elephants (or so says Hui Li, who would have gotten this information from the Master of the Law himself), preceded by the beating of one hundred metal drums. Also according to Hui Li, the anti-Yogacarans plotted to murder the Chinese debater, but when King Harsha got wind of the plot, he threatened to cut off the hands and rip out the tongue of anyone who harmed him, a threat that may have helped Hsuan Tsang prevail in the theological contest. His fame now at a peak, the monk decided that he had accomplished what he had come to India to do.

"China is a country of men of no importance, and shallow as to religion, which is why the Buddhas are never born there," the priests of Nalanda said.

"No," replied the monk. "In that country of China the superior magistrates are clothed with dignity, and the laws are everywhere respected. The prince is regarded as sacred, the ministers are faithful, parents are loving, children are obedient, virtue and justice are highly esteemed, age and uprightness preferred in honor."

Hsuan Tsang, who had left China illegally fifteen years earlier, was no doubt worried about the reception he would get back home. His patriotic speech, given to Hui Li after he had been received back into the good graces of the emperor, may have been designed for its public relations effect. In any case, when King Harsha himself pleaded with him to stay longer in India, Hsuan Tsang warned him that those who prevented the dissemination of the True Law would be born blind in their next incarnation. And so the monk went back to Nalanda to collect his books and statues. He was provided with elephants and an escort of men, and he set off for the long journey home.

I WENT FROM Bombay to Aurangabad, a seven-hour train ride away, where I made quick trips to the caves at Ellora and Ajanta. These are the westernmost of the fabulous string of Buddhist cave temples (Ellora's space actually is shared with Hindus and Jains) that stretches all the way to Dunhuang in China's Gansu Province, about six thousand overland miles away. The monk's India pilgrimage took him to the vicinity of Ellora and Ajanta, but he makes no mention of the caves, so it is not clear that he visited them. Ajanta, which was lost in the forest for a thousand years before being rediscovered by a British hunter in 1819, is one of the great treasures of world art. If the monk didn't go there, he should have.

I hired a car, a white Ambassador sedan, and set off early in the morning from Aurangabad through a terrain of straw-colored, treeless hills and farmland planted with sugarcane and cotton. My driver was an aging Muslim with a white beard, a white skullcap, and an impeccable white shirt with cotton epaulettes. Alongside the road, men with scarves over their heads walked with their hands clasped behind them. There was a sign that said CHAT BEGINS, and the road began a steep switchback descent alongside a valley of scorched orange-and-yellow fields speckled with trees. A few kilometers later, the sign read CHAT ENDS. We crossed a dry riverbed and pulled into a parking area crowded with postcard and trinket sellers.

The cave complex itself is an enormous horseshoe-shaped rock formation suspended over a valley of thick vegetation. You can imagine the British hunter, whose name was John Smith, coming across it from the side where the parking lot is now and glimpsing through the jungle undergrowth the opening of a cave. Inside, if he went inside, he would have seen that very special glow of the Indian cave paintings, a candlelight color with streaks and daubs of emerald and rust, ebony, cerulean blue, and singed gold. The paintings especially show a refined sensualism, the luminous, eloquently crowded quality of the paintings and sculptures in which the Buddha and the Bodhisattvas take on the athletic refinement of the Hindu gods. Ajanta gives substance to the Hinayana complaint that Mahayana converted the austere original Buddhism into a kind of riotous polytheism dominated by a pantheon of highly sentient divinities.

As at the Kizil Caves in Xinjiang, the Jataka stories provide the main themes of the paintings at Ajanta, but the art there does for Buddhist legend what the late Renaissance did for Italian Catholicism, which is to subvert it for human purposes by exalting the ideal human form. If there is a more sensuous female figure in existence than the portrait of Queen Maya in Cave Number 2 at Ajanta, I don't know where it is. She is dark-skinned—one of the interesting things about all the Buddhist paintings from Ajanta to Dunhuang is the varied skin color of the portraits. Her bare full breasts have been depicted with erotic precision. She leans against a carved column of a palace, one leg—adorned with an ankle bracelet—on the floor, the other bent at the knee so the foot rests on the column behind her. She wears gold bangles in her hair, bracelets on her wrists, and necklaces of gold and precious stone, and she gazes with a soft smile and gleaming eyes on a man holding worry beads in his hands who looks admiringly up at her. To see these paintings and sculptures in the chiaroscuro of the caves where they were made so long ago is a thrill, a vastly more powerful and moving experience than it is possible to have in any museum. It is fortunate that after Smith informed the Nizam of Hyderabad, the local ruler, about them, no eager British archaeologist removed them to London.

From Aurangabad I went to New Delhi, arriving the day before Zhongmei. I stayed at a modest guesthouse away from the center of town, had dinner at the very luxurious home of the very cordial parents of an Indian friend who lives in New York, and the next evening picked up Zhongmei at the airport. There was a moment of great anxiety, of disorientation, when I stood at the entrance to the arrivals hall (the guards threatened to shoot me with their blunderbusses if I crossed the threshold). I saw Zhongmei looking uncertainly around her, and I waved my arms vigorously to attract her attention. She seemed to look right at me and then looked elsewhere as if searching for somebody else. I waved some more, and the guards warned me sternly to stay where I was. At last, Zhongmei came toward me, still with a disturbingly blank look on her face. Then recognition dawned.

"I was waving my arms like a madman trying to get your attention," I said.

"I didn't recognize you," she said.

I had stopped shaving after crossing the border into Kyrgyzstan and by now had a fairly good growth of beard.

"Do I look that different?" I asked.

"Well, if I didn't recognize you, you must look different," Zhongmei said. "I saw you waving at me and I thought you were a taxi driver trying to get my business."

Zhongmei's hand, which I held in the Ambassador taxi we took through the hot New Delhi night, felt cool and soft in mine. I gratefully smelled the familiar aroma of her hair, and I teased her with the bad news that we would be staying at a very simple little place, a little shabby and without reliable hot water, but, after all, we Buddhists traveled simply. "It's okay," she said seriously, "I don't care," and then I took her to the newly renovated Imperial Hotel, which is spacious, gleaming, marbled, and gilded opulence itself—air-conditioned comfort, strikingly costumed service personnel, silky linens, all-night room service, and a lush tropical garden and swimming pool. We ordered some tea, served in a heavy silver teapot with a heavy silver tea-leaf strainer and delicate porcelain cups, and

Zhongmei told me her performances, which were in Colorado, had gone well, and I told her about the Maharaja of Varanasi, the synagogue in Calcutta, and the Shankaracharya of Kanchipuram. And then I slept deeply and soundly in the way you can only sleep when you are persuaded that, despite your worries, all is well.

We spent one day seeing the sights in Delhi, including the Red Fort, the sprawling ruin with its oxblood-red and marble-inlaid palaces where the Moguls once ruled all of India; the Great Mosque, built by the Moguls, as always, within walking distance of the fort; and Chandni Chowk, the nearby warren of shopping streets. We saw a performance of Indian dance early in the evening before going to my friend's parents' home for a dinner of many spices and simmering things and fresh fruit for dessert, and then the next day we took the air-conditioned express train to Amritsar, the same train I had taken in the other direction a few weeks before.

We stayed at Mrs. Bandheri's Guesthouse, watching the myna birds hunting for insects on the lawn as we had our breakfast. The border crossing to Pakistan was the same as the one in the opposite direction. It produced an idea about a correlation: The more trouble a country gives you at customs, the poorer that country is. On the Indian side, not only were our bags thoroughly searched, but I was made to change my one thousand remaining Indian rupees, about twenty-five dollars' worth, lest I violate the foreign exchange controls by carrying them out of the country.

Pakistan, which is in more desperate shape, politically and economically, than India, was easier but more corrupt. A tall, striking soldier who looked like Omar Sharif checked our passports and bid us an eloquent "You are most welcome to Pakistan." The customs agent told me if I changed some money with him, he would "help" me. A few minutes before, someone else standing around the immigration counter had offered to change money and I had declined—having just changed my Indian rupees on the Indian side. But the customs agent's offer made me think quickly about the opposite of "help," which was hinder, obstruct, or charge an exorbitant import duty on my computer or camera, and I decided to change fifty dollars. The man at immigration was irate. "I am immigration," he said, walking after me as I searched for a taxi. "I ask you change money, you say no. Why you change at customs?"

"Because I wanted to avoid trouble," I replied, but he wasn't listening.

"I am immigration," he said again, the point being, it would seem, that any traveler of taste and discernment would change his money at immigration, a higher class of squeeze.

I had to give the taxi driver a destination in Lahore, even though our purpose there was to have lunch and find the bus to Islamabad. I told him Faletti's Hotel, which I had heard of. Faletti's is old and therefore summoned up images of faded Raj splendor, like Raffles in Singapore, the Eastern and Oriental in Penang, the Oberoi Grand in Calcutta, the Taj in Bombay. But it turned out to be a seedy, dingy mansion, once great but no longer. I inquired about the bus to Islamabad and was told at reception that it left the next morning at nine. I was sent to an office—room number four.

"When do you want to go?" a man there asked me.

"Now. This afternoon. Right after lunch."

"There's no bus anymore today. The bus is every morning at nine."

"That's it?" I asked.

"Yes."

"Only one bus a day to Islamabad?"

The porter who had directed me to room number four came to my rescue.

"PTDC bus at nine; TDCP bus at one," he said.

"Where's the TD . . . whatever-it-is bus?"

"Lawrence Road," he said.

That would be T. E. Lawrence (of Arabia) Road. It was noon by my watch, time for a quick lunch in Faletti's dismal restaurant. Dismal and slow. Had I learned nothing, I asked myself, about the impossibility of quick in South Asia? We had been there fifty minutes and the food had not yet come. I went to the reception to ask if there was a later bus, and the clock on the wall reminded me that Pakistan is half an hour earlier than India. I felt like Phineas Fogg in *Around the World in Eighty Days* being saved by the International Date Line. I was impatient to get started on the Karakorum Highway trip and did not want to spend a night in Lahore, especially not at Faletti's. I ran back to the restaurant. The food arrived. We ate quickly and got a taxi. We made the bus by about one minute.

IT ZOOMED UP the superhighway called the M2, which rivals the Autobahn. Curtains were tightly drawn against the pounding sun, so we couldn't look out the window, and despite the efforts of an air-conditioning system, it was hot and airless, smelling of yesterday's dinner. Zhongmei, who, after all, had hardly had time to rest up after her trip from New York, hardly spoke during the trip, which made me uneasy. I thought she might be regretting having come. At one point, television monitors lit up and a ridiculous and exceedingly overamplified Indian movie came on.

I was beginning to get the hang of Indian movies, or at least the Indian movies that are produced in staggering abundance in Bombay, all displaying the same ingredients. There's the male lead, handsome in a brawny sort of way, and the female lead, beautiful and, in her curvilinear way, brawny too. They do a lot of singing and dancing, the dancing very energetic, with a lot of rhythmic hip thrusts as if the performers were hammering nails with their bones. Even middle-aged women in saris form chorus lines and brutally seesaw their bosoms. The hero uses the martial arts when he gets into trouble, and this comes with the exaggerated sound effects pioneered by the Hong Kong kung fu film industry.

All of that is standard. Then come the variations. The female lead, who is in show business, gets angry at the male, who seems to fail her in some mysterious way. There are two rival businessmen, a Sikh with a purple turban and a braided beard, and an immensely fat Hindu, also bearded. He looks like Luciano Pavarotti. The girl calls him Daddy-Ji, and he is the bad guy. The movie is in Hindi, which can be understood by Urdu-speaking Pakistanis, but certain phrases are said in English, conspicuous among them being "Shut up!" "Come again?" "Have a nice day," and "I was born to love you, baby." The lovers do their song-and-dance numbers, which are lavishly produced, in glamorous places—on a helicopter flying over a meadow, on the top of a double-decker bus, in a park in London with Big Ben in the background, in some Xanadu of a hotel back in India with swirling lights, fountains, and terraces. Eventually, the boy saves the girl from the fat Hindu. Or, in another variation, the boy who has left the girl for a foreign floozy realizes his mistake and comes crawling back. Or the family, which has refused to allow the girl to marry the boy, relents and gives its consent. But then the girl gets sick and dies, though not before the couple do some synchronized gyrations to celebrate their happiness. They look lovingly at each other. They sing to break your eardrums. They do not kiss, though they do give each other brief hugs and look at each other with oxen eyes.

There is no nudity, though a kind of pious pornography invests the entire production. The girl has sizable breasts. She wears a short skirt which stretches over ample hips. She looks like a Hindu stone sculpture, sensuous and round, Lakshmi or Parvati, the wife of Shiva. The boy looks like the eleventh reincarnation of Vishnu, though his good looks are too standardized to be interesting. And always, no matter what else might be happening, there is the sudden flowering of shrill song and gyroscopic dance. I read a summing up of the Indian movie industry in *India Today* magazine, and the article cited one of the better-known directors to the effect that it's impossible to develop drama when the studios require that the screen erupt in Busby Berkeley–type dance numbers every fifteen minutes.

We arrived in Islamabad at around 6 p.m. and checked into the Munfarid Guesthouse, which I would recommend to anyone going to the Pakistani capital. Zhongmei sprawled out on the bed and went to sleep right away while I watched CNN just in time for the world weather report. The day's highs for twenty or thirty cities across the globe were scrolled. Islamabad was the hottest, 104 degrees. No wonder the air-conditioning on the bus had seemed ineffectual.

That night we met our guide and our driver, and the next morning they picked us up in an open-air jeep that had seen better days (I was worried by its treadless tires, which looked as if they had been sanded down) and we set off on the first leg of our trip on the Karakorum Highway back to China, seven hours to Besham. The guide was Ferman, a slight, shy man with a small backpack and a small mustache. The driver was an ex-soldier named Ali. We followed the Grand Trunk Road to Taxila, which, some archaeologists believe, was the starting-off point for the missionaries of the first century A.D. who first brought Buddhism to China, traveling the same route we would take. We went through the Wah Cantonment up to Abbottabad, where the terrain turned rugged and hilly. Terraced rice paddies reflected the afternoon sun. For a long time we followed a stream flowing at the bottom of a steep valley until finally it emptied into the Indus, broad, colored like a peach, and swift. The guesthouse in Besham was right alongside the river. Each room had a little terrace. In the dining room I asked the waiter if there was any fresh fruit for dessert, and when he said there wasn't, I asked him: "Why not? The market is full of fresh fruit. Why don't you have any here?"

The waiter walked away, and Zhongmei told me I was becoming rude and short-tempered. "You've been traveling too long," she said.

"What do you mean?" I said. "They ought to have some goddam fruit. They should make an effort."

She just looked at me.

"Sorry. It must be the heat," I said. It wasn't just the heat. It wasn't just the accumulation of small deprivations that makes itself felt on a long trip, the prolonged absence of the breakfast food you like, the unavailability of anything but curry, the slowness of things, the absence of cold drinks, the infuriating illogic by which the state guesthouse has no fresh fruit just at the moment when some fresh fruit would be enormously soothing. It was that Zhongmei still seemed a bit listless and I thought that if I could provide her with some fresh fruit, she would feel better. I left an extravagant tip and resolved to regain my sense of perspective.

In the morning, we were up at five-thirty to walk by the Indus in the cool morning air. We looked at the spot where the river narrows between two cliffs, which is where Fa Xien, according to Aurel Stein, crossed the river in 403. We bought a watermelon in the market and were off for a long, very hot drive to Gilgit. We drove in silence, each of us smothered in the rush of hot air. The Indus, which we followed for almost the entire trip, cut between crumbly mountains and changed from peach to mud. Mountain streams emptied ribbons of icy blue into it. We stopped at a gully to dip our hands into clear, cold water. Some trucks were parked at the same spot, and a man in a rust-red beard and black Pathan costume came over to shake my hand and, just being friendly, invited us to partake of their lunch, which we politely declined. Later we took pictures of ourselves standing in front of Mount Rakaposhi, which is 25,551 feet high, right there next to the road, a stream descending from it and running under a bridge. It is one of the most impressive sights I have ever beheld. We ate our watermelon at another scenic lookout where you can see the junction of the Himalayan, Karakorum, and Hindu Kush ranges, jagged ice-covered peaks in the far distance. We walked to a lookout off the road, and when we got back, an odd encounter took place, something out of a Monty Python movie

A red car coming from the direction of Gilgit screeched to a stop next to us, and a Pakistani woman jumped out and made straight for Zhongmei.

"How do you do," she said extending her hand. "You're Chinese, aren't you?"

"Yes," Zhongmei replied.

"So glad to meet you," the woman said. She was slim in diaphanous pastels, with dark eyes that batted in the sunlight. Her accent indicated that her amiable greeting had about exhausted her English.

She took Zhongmei tightly by the hand and led her into the middle of the road, instructing a man who had also gotten out of the car to take a picture.

"Nice to meet you," she said once the photography session was over, and she ran back to the car, which peeled off southward, leaving us in its mysterious dust. I wondered what had provoked this little episode. Maybe the woman simply wanted to affirm the good relations between Pakistan and its giant neighbor, which had given it the technology it needed to explode its atom bomb.

When we were back on the road, it was so hot my nostrils seemed scorched and I couldn't find a place to get leverage against the bucking of the jeep, since everything I touched scorched my hand. Zhongmei wilted under her straw-brimmed hat. I had unillusioned thoughts about the horrors of travel. This is not fun, I thought. This is not even interesting. Our heads lolled on our backrests as the jeep groaned on. I became indifferent even to the narrow misses that occurred each and every time a truck or bus came from the other direction. I lost interest in the edge-of-the-cliff position of our jeep suspended as it was with its too-smooth tires over the Indus down below. I let my heat-stoked imagination roam. What would our chances of survival be if the jeep slid on some gravel and went over the cliff? If it reached the water on its fall, we would have a small chance, especially since we were an open vehicle and there was room to climb through the roll bars even as the swiftly flowing river took the jeep with it. Then again, the river was shallow and the jeep might hit the water on its side and plunge to the riverbed smashing its occupants against it, after which the passengers would become entangled in the submerged car to drown if they had not already been killed by the impact. Would it be possible, I wondered, to hold on to the roll bar above and a side bar in such a way as to cushion the impact, to manage to stay within the confines of the jeep and not be hurled into the riverbed below? Even if that was possible, it was more likely the jeep would hit the rocks before the water and then instant death would be pretty much certain, though again I felt that if one used near-superhuman strength to brace oneself against the fall, perhaps survival was possible. I imagined us speeding past the face of the cliff. Would I, like that character in Thomas Mann's story, say to myself: "So this is what it's like to be falling over the edge of a cliff. Is that all there is to it? Is there nothing more?"

I once wrote a review in the *New York Times* of a collection of American sermons, and there was one from the nineteenth century delivered by a black preacher in Kansas named Brother Carper that had as powerful a description of desolation as I had ever read. Brother Carper spoke of "a scene of unrelieved waste, an ocean made of powder into which the curse of angered heaven had ground a portion of earth," and where "huge great rocks like shattered shafts and fallen monuments in a neglected graveyard would lift their mossless sides above the accumulating sand." He could have been talking about the Karakorum Highway, which Raj-era explorers and pundits had followed on their way to the Pamirs, where George Hayward met his nasty end at the hands of Mir Wali's cutthroats.

Hayward's story and the overheated monotony of the road led me to imagine an adventure of my own. I was a secret agent who had parachuted into enemy-occupied territory in order to help organize the resistance, but my cover was blown and Pakistani partisans were speeding ahead of the enemy to smuggle me to safety. I was wounded, of course, and would spend the night being cared for in some safe refuge while the woman who had sprung out of the red car near the mountain lookout applied compresses to my forehead to keep me from burning up. I would sleep feverishly and in the dead of night I would wake up and see her eyes gleaming in the dark. Days would go by like that. I was a man who had risked all to come to the aid of this afflicted country, so the partisans were determined in their gratitude to save me. The jeep would buck along narrow mountain trails unknown to the enemy. The sun would beat on its back. We would climb high into the river valley and I would be spirited into tree-shaded villages where the ripening apricot trees hung over winding stone walls. We would drive down narrow, rutted, and rocky paths past walled compounds, one of which we would enter through a green-painted wrought-iron gate, and there, in a small stone room hung with carpets, I would sleep on a rope bed watched over by my large-eyed nurse.

There would be trouble. The nurse would have an inamorato, a melancholy, aggressively hirsute Muslim who had been promised her in marriage and who would betray me to the enemy when he saw her state of infatuated devotion. We would have to leave in the middle of the night and drive over rough roads under a full moon. We would come to the village of Karimabad, where fourteen hundred years ago a Chinese monk named Hsuan Tsang came for refuge from the night and where I would be told it was extremely unsafe for me. The nurse's intended had family there and the blood-feud tradition of Pakistani villages would require that they kill me. But someone would know of a steep track to the east of the village that led to a cousin's farmhouse high up in the pasture. The jeep would climb up paths steeper than I thought it was possible for a jeep to climb. In places, the road would be so narrow that we would knock stones off the enclosing dry walls. The turns would be so abrupt that we would have to make them in two passes. I would hear rushing mountain water all around us as we climbed ever higher. Outside the car would be schoolgirls in red scarves looking at me with bright, surprised eyes as I passed. The houses would be stone and set in the midst of terraced potato fields. Here and there a bearded farmer would crouch near an irrigation canal. They knew who I was but would not betray me, I would be told.

"You will be safe here," said Ferman, who insinuated himself into my fantasy. Ferman had found the driver, who was a good one, not like some of the others I'd had. He would coax the jeep upward for nearly an hour over stone paths and loose gravel, the wheels never more than inches from the edge of the cliff. At last we would arrive at the edge of a meadow. The Hunze River Valley would stretch below us, a broad belt of green and faded yellow, and beyond the valley would be Rakaposhi, a spectral immensity in the day's fading light. From here, once my wounds were healed, we would start to walk toward the Hindu Kush and over the border to Afghanistan, and when the war was over, I would return here on this same heated highway to say thanks to the men who had saved me, and to glimpse one more time the glowing eyes of . . .

Right.

Later when we arrived in Gilgit, the hotel manager told me that all those years of British occupation had taught the people of the northern territories how to take care of the foreigners who came into their midst. "We would know anyway," he hastened to add, "because we feel it natural to honor those who have come so far to see our country."

Opposite the hotel was a playing field where boys were playing soccer. Suddenly the sky clouded over and the wind kicked up. The electricity went out in the hotel, and I lit a candle, sensibly provided, even though toilet paper and hot water were missing. I realized that it was Friday night, the Sabbath. I sat in a wicker chair on the terrace outside the room and watched the storm. Dust from the playing field blew like a curtain across the road, but on our side in the hotel garden the air seemed clean, filtered by the swaying willows. A sign suspended from hinges like in a Western saloon banged against the bungalow wall and eventually crashed to the ground. Doors and window shutters made loud noises someplace in the dark. I hoped for rain, but there was none. So this was what it was like to be in a dust storm in Gilgit on the hot, high road from India to China. We went into the candle-lit dining room, where we had a skinny chicken curry. Suddenly I was enjoying myself again. It was the sudden storm, the candlelight, the sign banging on the clapboard, the sound of the water splashing as I poured it over myself with a plastic ladle, the exoticism of it all. Zhongmei too seemed to come to life after a hot bath. Yes, this is what it's like to be traveling from Pakistan to China, and ain't it grand.

WE RUMBLED UP the Karakorum Highway for two more days, following the Indus, then the Gilgit River, then the Hunza River to Sost, where one goes through Pakistani immigration. The scenery inspired wonderment at the tenacity and durability of the travelers along the Road of Great Events. A couple of hours after Chilas the great mountains were all visible, first Nanga Parbat (26,660 feet), then Rakaposhi, then Disteghil Sar (25,869 feet). Years ago a friend of mine took an early-morning plane from Calcutta to New Delhi. Out the window of the airplane in the distance she could see the Great Himalayan Range, ragged and snowy and shaded pink by the early sun. "It was important," she remarked later, meaning that to see the great mountains of the earth carries with it something mystical. It's what Freud called the oceanic feeling, though it is inspired by vast upthrustings of earth and rock rather than limitless bodies of water. It is strange in its way that the monk never mentions mountains as objects of beauty or reverence. To him they were obstacles, no more moving it seems than deserts or forests or darkness or cold weather or highwaymen or other things or conditions that impeded his progress. I am different in this respect. When we passed directly below Rakaposhi, we had been at an elevation of about 6,000 feet. Under our feet was the bridge that went over a roaring torrent of glacial melt. And to the west rising in front of us with nothing in between us was 25,551 feet of mountain, a colossus. It was important to see it.

We continued on our way.

I liked Gilgit, set in its rugged scenery and exotic with its narrow streets and interesting bazaars. We walked in the market looking at woven woolen shawls and fur hats, but we didn't stay long. We pressed on to Karimabad, where we spent the night at a place called the Eagle's Nest, on the edge of high pastureland overlooking the Gilgit River Valley. The jeep took us there past ornate terraced potato patches and poplar trees. There were beautifully wrought, very high dry stone walls and masonry farmhouses. The road was so narrow, steep, sandy, stony, and full of sharply angled switchbacks that I vowed not to be in the jeep when it made its downward trip the next morning.

We stayed at a hotel that was built on a ledge above the valley. We sat at a table on a patch of grass in front of our room and drank tea as we gazed at the Karakorum Mountains spread out like a tapestry before us. Dinner was served on the roof, the usual stringy chicken curry but served with a glass of sweet grape wine—contraband in this country. Pakistani moonshine. It went with the view of the mountains in the distance, the winding Hunza River Valley below, the clumps of trees, the stone cottages, the cool air, the terracing, the brilliance of Mars and Venus, which made their appearance low on the horizon before the sky glowed densely with the brightest stars I had ever seen. We got up at four-thirty to see the sun rise. We walked up a hill to a vantage point where both Rakaposhi and Disteghil Sar were visible. About twenty middle-aged Japanese tourists were there ahead of us, occupying the best vantage points and scowling in the dim dawn light. They had come up from Karimabad by jeep and were disappointed when the first rays of the sun hit the mountains. The truth is that the event was anticlimactic. There was no sudden illumination of the black mountain by a mystical line of dawn red, no sense of the earth tilting crazily in the void of space. It was more an unspectacularly gradual whitening of the atmosphere. Within minutes, cries of *Ikimasho,* "Let's go," arose from the Japanese visitors, who turned and trotted back down the hill.

Avoiding the jeep ride down, Zhongmei and I walked the road later in the morning, my knees and calves turning pulpy and weak after about half an hour. Travel is exhausting, but it is not exercise. I was out of shape. We took pictures of some boys cavorting happily in a shallow brown pond. Zhongmei posed for pictures with every local kerchief-wearing girl she saw. The air was cool but the sun intensely strong at nine thousand feet. The Gilgit Valley stretched below us on both sides of the silt-gray river, bounded by the surrounding mountains. When we reached the bottom we were thirsty and hot. We found our friends Ferman and Ali sitting at a table under a grape trestle at a hotel called the Kisar Inn, a favorite of what the Lonely Planet guide calls bottom-end travelers. Sure enough, as we sat there and took refreshment, three robust, sweating young men from Scandinavia arrived on bicycles and sat down, too. One of them told me they were part of a group of five that had set out from Gilgit the day before, bound eventually for Kashgar. The other two were still on the road.

At another table a young, pleasing woman from New Zealand with an antipodean accent was settling her bill with the hotel owner. She wore round, schoolmarmish glasses and a long blue skirt and spoke in subdued, dulcet tones. Her money handed over, she put on her backpack, which rose heavily over the back of her head. She also swept into her arms a second, smaller backpack that she wore in front of her. She had a brief conversation with the hotel owner about where to find the bus for Gilgit.

The owner, seeing how burdened she was, offered to send a boy with her to help her get to the bus stop, which was more than a mile away. But she calmly and politely declined and was soon on her way, descending carefully to the dusty roadway and heading off slowly under her burden in the direction of Karimabad center.

In *Moby-Dick*, Ishmael, Melville's narrator, includes a brief chapter that he calls "a six inch epitaph to one Bulkington." Ishmael saw this Bulkington getting off a ship in New Bedford. Two days later he saw him shipping out again on the *Pequod*, Ishmael's ship. His rapid return to the sea made him a kind of existential hero for Ishmael. Here was a man who stayed on terra firma for only two days before shipping out again for two more years. "The land scorched his feet," Ishmael says. Hearth and home repelled him. He unburdened himself, in other words, of comforting illusions and accepted the formlessness of the sea.

I felt the same way about this young woman from New Zealand. She was traveling alone. She did not seek out our company, or that of the strapping bicyclists who arrived before she left. She was alone and intrepid and about as far away from home as it was possible for her to be. And all the guidebooks warn that women traveling alone in Muslim Pakistan are in danger of harassment or worse. After she left, I regretted not having spoken to her. I wanted to know where she was going and where she had come from and why she had undertaken her journey in the first place. I wanted to know what she expected to find here on the Karakorum Highway, and why it was important enough for her to endure a long, solitary journey away from hearth and home.

It was like that for Hsuan Tsang too in some places. Not here, because here he was accompanied by King Harsha's escort of men, horses, and elephants, but elsewhere he had crossed deserts and mountains by himself under his heavy wood-framed pack. I realize that I had a certain image of him during his Lone Ranger times, walking slowly on, holding a staff in one hand, a fan in the other. I had romanticized him, turned him into a figure in a Chinese landscape painting, melancholy, dwarfed by boundless nature, but heroic, indomitable. The young woman trekking toward the bus made me see this journey to the West in grittier terms, as a grimmer task, as an endless slog through boring and barren landscapes. Let this be a tribute to her, a young and nameless woman imbued with the spirit of Bulkington. I hope she finds what she's looking for and then goes home, gets married, has kids, and never travels by herself again.

•　　　•　　　•

WE GOT TO Sost at four-thirty in the afternoon and bought tickets for the next day's bus to China. There is nothing in Sost except, fortunately, a clean and comfortable PTDC (Pakistan Tourism Development Corporation) motel, to which I repaired bedraggled and sweaty from the final three hours in the jeep. Sost is strictly a customs and immigration post, a single stretch of asphalt lined on either side by low-slung administrative sheds and pounded by hundreds of Pakistani trucks. The rock-strewn, treeless brown hills were splotched with still unmelted snow. The hotel manager accompanied me to buy our bus tickets, and I asked him if there were a lot of travelers crossing the border these days.

"Very few," he said. "The season won't start for another few days, when the Pakistanis go on vacation. Lots of them will go to China."

"Oh, Pakistanis go to China for vacation?"

"Yes, a lot of them."

We were walking past a row of sheds that served as shops, and some roadside motels and money changers with signs in Chinese.

"Do you see many Chinese?" I asked.

"There's very little traffic coming from the other side," he said.

I thought about the monk in this connection, his unusualness as a Chinese, one of those stay-at-home people who, with some exceptions, like Brave King and Zhongmei, don't go in for foreign adventure travel. The Karakorum Highway is not for them.

I WOKE UP early and anxious, thinking about my next and last Chinese border crossing. The night before, preparing for the worst case, I had attached passwords to all of my computer files, so that in the unlikely event the Chinese customs police investigated my hard drive, they would be unable to read anything there—unless they tortured the password out of me; hardly likely. Zhongmei and I had a conversation.

I told her I was worried about two things. One was that my Hong Kong visa would arouse suspicion. The Chinese, of course, know what the foreigners know: that people who have trouble getting visas the normal way, at a Chinese consulate or embassy, get them through travel agents in Hong Kong. My second concern was the "J" on my Indian visa. It had gone unnoticed during my earlier China border crossings, and there was no reason for it to be noticed now. I hadn't seen it myself. But now that I knew it was there, it grew larger and larger the more I thought about it, until it blazed from the page like a neon sign. My colleague

Patrick Tyler, formerly the *New York Times* Beijing bureau chief, had told me a few months earlier that he had tried to enter Xinjiang and a customs inspector had noticed a journalist visa in his passport.

"They got very excited and started shouting, *'Ji-zhe! Ji-zhe!'* " Tyler said. Journalist! Journalist! They held him in a hotel until he managed to escape past his guards and hitch a ride on a truck back to Beijing. Since then he had been unable to get a new visa to enter China. If some border guard noticed the "J" stamped on my Indian visa, I would surely be stopped and expelled and, having gotten this far, I would be unable to finish the journey.

Zhongmei and I got our story straight. We would tell the truth, namely that I was a book critic for the *New York Times* and that we were traveling in China together. We would provide no other information. We would certainly say nothing about any plans for me to write a book about my journey along Hsuan Tsang's ancient route.

"There is no book," Zhongmei wisely observed, "so there's nothing to talk about." Then we left for the Pakistani frontier formalities.

We traveled by small bus from Sost to the Chinese border in the company of eleven lively and friendly Pakistani university students and two dour Dutch backpackers. As the bus pulled out of the customs shed I felt a longing to remain in Pakistan, especially in mountainous Pakistan, in the Hunza Valley where the glacial melt poured crystal and cold down the face of the rock and the apricot trees blossomed and the grape juice fermented illicitly in un-Muslim tankards. This wish was a product not only of my nervousness about the impending border crossing but of the friendliness of the local people. We had been accorded hospitality here and not simply treated as customers.

The bus rumbled up the Karakorum Highway following the Hunza River, which was a kind of khaki brown. We were about sixty miles south of the Oxus River Valley in Afghanistan, which the monk had followed on his return home, and I assumed that the scenery was similar. The terrain was rough, more so even than on the earlier legs of our journey, the hills higher, the road more pressed in by overhanging cliffs. Vast glacial moraines stretched both above and below, huge fields of boulders that looked as if some god had scattered them from on high. At one point we were all asked to get out of the bus so it could detour around some snowdrifts in which two Chinese trucks were impacted. The landscape was not so much magisterial as magisterially ugly. I had expected sweeping snowy vistas, alpine meadows spreading high above green river valleys, but we were too high for meadows or trees and everywhere the views were hemmed in by the surrounding rock-littered earthen mounds.

I watched as the Pakistani signs ticked off the kilometers still to go to the Kunjerab Pass and the border. The spot itself is marked by two signs: One says "Point Zero" and the other "Goodbye." There was a simple metal-bar barrier that was raised for us without passport inspection. We were in China. The road leveled out. After a few kilometers we came to a slight downward grade. We were over the hump at fourteen thousand feet. New Delhi was 1,050 or so miles behind us. Ahead a red Toyota Land Cruiser that I had seen leaving the customs yard at Sost a few minutes ahead of us was parked alongside the road. A few men in the familiar green uniforms of the Chinese People's Liberation Army had emptied it of baggage, which was spread out on the ground in front of a modest shed. Just beyond were two flags of the People's Republic of China snapping briskly in the wind. A soldier came over to the front window where Zhongmei was sitting. She had her video camera out.

"No filming," the guard told her, speaking in Mandarin.

"Okay," Zhongmei said, and she put her camera away.

"You're Chinese?" the soldier asked her.

"Yes," she said.

"Why were you taking pictures?"

"Because I'm returning to China and I wanted to take a picture of the national flag," she replied.

It was the perfect thing to say, not least because it was true. The guard's expression softened.

"Are you a tour guide?" he asked, motioning to the other passengers in the bus.

"No, I'm just traveling with my fiancé." Zhongmei motioned to me sitting behind her. Meanwhile another soldier came into the bus and looked briefly at all the passports. We were then told to get out with all of our hand baggage. I was not unmindful of having been promoted, even if only for political reasons, to the status of fiancé.

"Line up!" shouted one of the soldiers in English, and we lined up— the two Dutch backpackers to the left, Zhongmei and I, the eleven cheerful Pakistanis, all our bags on the floor in front of us.

The soldier paced back and forth as if he were our sergeant and we were a company of new recruits assembled for inspection. Then our bags were emptied one by one. Books were leafed through, even address books. Every item no matter how small was inspected as if the soldiers were antiquarians looking for fakes. Beside us one of the Dutch back-packers was having his turn. Out came a pocket knife and a guidebook and a camera and then a small pack of condoms decorated with a blond naked girl.

"What's this?" the soldier said, staring suspiciously at the picture.

"Condoms," said the Dutchman.

The soldier looked at Zhongmei, who translated.

"Oh," he said and dropped the packet back into the Dutchman's bag. He was smiling. I had the feeling that this border crossing was going to turn out all right, and it did, thanks largely to Zhongmei and the Paki-stani students. After the customs inspection was over, we piled back onto the bus accompanied by a round-faced Chinese border guard armed with a service revolver and a serious mien. He sat in a fold-down seat next to me and made me nervous. Zhongmei was in front.

"What was that all about?" she asked the guard, speaking of the careful inspection of bags.

"Drugs," the soldier replied curtly.

"Really?" said Zhongmei. "There are drug smugglers here?"

"Oh, yes," said the soldier.

Meanwhile, the Pakistanis were overjoyed, delirious about being in China.

"Tell him," one of them said to Zhongmei, referring to the soldier, "that this is the first time for all of us to travel outside of Pakistan, and we all wanted this first trip to be to China."

Zhongmei translated. The guard sat rock-still and stared straight ahead.

The Pakistanis took no notice and began to sing songs. Then they asked Zhongmei to sing a song.

"I can't sing but I can dance," she said, and while the Pakistanis sang, she did a little Indian number, rocking her head back and forth and mak-ing graceful arm movements from side to side.

The Pakistanis erupted in applause. Then it was my turn.

"What is a youth?" I crooned.

> *Impetuous fire.*
> *What is a maid?*
> *Ice and desire.*
> *The time wags on,*
> *A rose may bloom,*
> *A rose may fade,*

So does the youth,
So does the fairest maid.

There were more cheers from the Pakistanis.

"Ask the soldier to sing one for us," one of them shouted to Zhongmei.

She translated.

"No," he said, maintaining his military, protect-the-motherland expression.

"They're so happy to be in China," Zhongmei told him. "If you don't sing, they'll think you don't like them."

"Really?" said the soldier. He couldn't have been more than twenty years old.

"Yes. They have such friendly feelings toward China."

The soldier suddenly took off his cap and threw back his head. His face turned red. I thought he was going to have a stroke. To my astonishment, he blasted out a military song.

We are soldiers and sons of China,
Carrying rifles on our shoulders,
The safety of the people depends on us.

The Pakistani cheers were deafening.

"That was a song by Yu Junjian," said Zhongmei.

"Yes," the soldier said. "Do you know it?"

"He's a friend of mine," said Zhongmei. Later she told me she and Yu had traveled together in the same performing delegation to South America.

"You know him?" The soldier was incredulous. "He's my hero!"

By now the Pakistanis were singing again and the soldier was laughing so uproariously I thought the red tabs on his uniform would pop. The soldier, really in the spirit of things now, became our guide. He pointed to a rough track that wandered up to our left, and I was glad to learn that it led to the Wakhan corridor and the Afghan border about fifty miles away, the route that Hsuan Tsang took. This was confirmed a while later when the soldier drew his passengers' attention to a tomb outlined against a distant hill. "It's called the Princess's Tomb," he said, and he told us that it belonged to a Chinese girl sent as a gift to a Persian chieftain to purchase his loyalty. None other than Hsuan Tsang repeats this legend, an indication that he must have passed very close to here on his descent from the Wakhan Pass. Before she could arrive in Persia, war broke out and the princess had to stay here in the mountains, where her escort built her a palace. Then, when the war was over, it was discovered that the supposedly well-guarded young woman was pregnant—by whom nobody knew. The legend was that each day a handsome boy descended from the sun to be with her, though obviously a more likely candidate for biological father was the very person charged with guarding her. In any case, her escort, having failed to preserve her purity, was afraid to deliver her to the Persian ruler, and so they stayed here in the high Pamirs, and she served the local people as queen until, many years later, she died.

"This is the first time I've ever enjoyed one of these trips," the soldier gushed to Zhongmei after receiving warm appreciation from the Pakistanis for his recitation of the princess's legend. "Usually they're so hard. You have to sit here and stare straight ahead and make sure nothing goes wrong. I go back and forth five, six times a day. There's nothing to do out here. Life is tough."

19

The Nightmare Bus to Khotan

TWO HOURS OF gradual descent later we arrived at Tashkurgan, Tajik for "Castle Rock," the territory from the border to here being the traditional home of the Tajiks, whose language is a dialect of Persian. Passport control was in Tashkurgan, even though we had already passed through customs. Zhongmei went ahead of me, and the clerks were curious about her American passport.

"Do Chinese get the same passports as Americans?" one of them asked.

Zhongmei assured him that they did, whereupon practically the entire office came out to scrutinize this miraculous document, passing it from one hand to another. It disappeared into a back room before reappearing again. My passport was rapidly checked by two incurious immigration agents and, my Indian "J" happily unobserved, I was waved through.

The car and driver we had arranged in Islamabad were waiting for us. We drove for a couple of hours through a spacious countryside to the Karakul Lake, just beside Mount Murztagata, whose 24,000-foot summit was covered in clouds. The camp where we were to stay was a combination frontier outpost and tourist trap. A large, ugly, square building held a large, ugly, square restaurant serving lamb and vegetables fried in red oil. Four yurts were lined up side by side just outside the ugly building and adjacent to a gravel access road.

In the morning a rather large collection of camels and horses were put at our disposal by men wearing the same felt hats I had seen when I crossed the border from China into Kyrgyzstan. I rode a complaining camel for an hour alongside the lake while Zhongmei took her first ever horseback ride. We had breakfast—boiled eggs, preserved cabbage, and rice porridge served in enamel basins. And then we lurched off, three hours to Kashgar on the wavy Chinese part of the Karakorum Highway, through a landscape that was grander, more open, more welcoming, more grasslandish than that on the Pakistani side.

Kashgar looked good. It was sunny and dry, pleasantly hot. The broad avenues that had replaced the narrow Uigur lanes seemed urbane and orderly. The rows of tall poplar trees were elegant. The Seman Hotel had finished renovating its second floor and we got a room there, with a fresh blue-gray carpet and an electric fan and hot water in the shower. When I had lived in Beijing years before, I had looked forward to the season of a melon that comes from Xinjiang called *hami-gua*—half muskmelon, half honeydew, it gave our materially curtailed lives a dose of culinary voluptuousness. The *hami-gua* were ripe in Kashgar, being sold by roadside vendors who cut out long, slender slices on payment of about a dime. For dinner, we went to the night market, where the air hung heavy with the smoke of roasting lamb. We had noodle hot pots and what the Chinese call *lao-jao* for dessert, moist syrupy dumplings with sweet sesame-and-peanut paste inside them.

That night, however, I slept badly, worried about the trip ahead of us. The monk came to Kashgar and then went on to Khotan, four hundred miles across the Takla Makan to the southwest. There he tarried for seven months waiting for permission from the emperor to return to China, and once that was received, trekked along the southern edge of the desert from one oasis to another. The Uigur or Mongol names of the places alone had an exciting exotic-historic ring to them—Yarkand, Karghalik,

Kara Kash, Niya, Cherchen, Charkhlik. They summoned up images of jade bracelets and silk tassels, camel markets and desert brigands. The route would range just north of the Kunlun Mountains, which separate modern Xinjiang from Tibet.

But if Buddhist kingdoms had once flourished on this southern strand of the Tarim Basin, there's nothing much there now. A long-distance bus went from Kashgar to Khotan, but after that, public transportation was going to be ratty and sporadic. Moreover, I was feeling the pressure of a time limit. My leave of absence from the *Times* was soon coming to an end. I would have to be back in Xian within ten days or so, and Xian was about 2,500 rough overland miles away.

That day we had gone to the China International Travel Service for advice. Luyik, who had helped me get to the Torugart Pass on my earlier visit to Kashgar, was there. We asked how much it would cost to hire a jeep for the trip to Dunhuang, where we could get back to the railroad line. Luyik told me to wait while he found out. He was gone for a long time, and when he came back, he simply shook his head.

"That expensive?" I said.

"Yes."

"Well. How expensive exactly?"

"Twenty-five thousand yuan," he said. Over three thousand dollars.

"The bus from Kashgar to Khotan is pretty good," Luyik said. "After that, I don't know. There are probably local buses as far as Ruoqiang, but there's no bus from Ruoqiang. You'd have to find a car." Luyik used the Chinese name for Charkhlik.

"Could we get a car in Ruoqiang?" I asked.

"I doubt it."

And so I lay awake, exhausted in advance by what appeared to be an endurance test ahead. Zhongmei had never complained, but she had nonetheless suffered on the long hot bus rides we had taken earlier in our journey together, and I hadn't exactly loved them either. And what if we took the bus to Charkhlik and there was no bus or car to take us farther east? We would have to double back sixteen hours to Minfeng and take the bus, another fourteen hours, to Korla on the northern edge of the Takla Makan. That would not only be exhausting and time-consuming but, more important, it would take us away from Hsuan Tsang's path. After so many weeks of travel, I was no longer seeing the trip ahead as an adventure but as an ordeal. I was feeling middle-aged, averse to discomfort, cranky.

"Listen," I told her. "It's going to be a hard trip. If you'd rather just fly to Beijing, I'll go by myself and meet you there."

She looked at me with something beyond chagrin in her eyes.

"I want you to go, of course," I said. "I'm just saying if you don't want to you don't have to."

"Don't worry," Zhongmei said. "It's only a few days. We'll make it."

HSUAN TSANG CAME down from the Wakhan Pass more or less the same way we came down from the Kunjerab Pass, descending to Tashkurgan, skirting the Murztagata, following the Qizil Darya River to Kashgar. It was a long and fabulously arduous trek, but it brought our monk back to the western desert after a fifteen-year absence during which everything had changed. Indeed, since he had crossed the Bedel Pass on his way to the Great Khan of the western Turks, China under the emperor Tai Tsung had embarked on the greatest military campaigns since the campaigns of Ban Chao in the Han Dynasty eight hundred years before. By the time the monk reached Khotan in 644, the reconquest of the Western Kingdoms was almost complete. Most of the Turkish or Tokharian princes who had given refuge to the monk, asked him to teach, and provided him with silver and horses and letters of introduction to the next principality had been destroyed in the Chinese juggernaut. The delicate and sophisticated Indo-Persian civilization that had flourished along the Road of Great Events for hundreds of years had disappeared.

The monk, having left the realm of King Harsha, proceeded to Peshawar and then into Afghanistan. In his account of his journey to Hui Li, he tells about the mountains of the Hindu Kush, which were so high that the birds couldn't fly over them. He turned east and climbed the Oxus River Valley to Badakhshan, describing the craggy peaks that lay on either side of the Oxus River Valley—"where the snow falls in summer and springtime" and "night and day the wind rages violently." He spent a month with a Turkish prince, a vassal of the western Turks, who gave him an escort to cross the Pamirs, which he did about one hundred miles north of where we crossed them at the Kunjerab Pass. "The whole landscape was one vast wilderness with no trace of human life," Hui Li says. On the eastern side of the Pamirs in the direction of Tashkurgan, the monk visited Turkic-Buddhist settlements, counting the stupas and monasteries, absorbing a local legend or two, and then passing on, though not before forming a rapid and generally unfavorable impression of the local people. "They are naturally uncouth and impetuous, but yet they are bold and courageous," he says of the inhabitants of Tashkurgan. "Their appearance is common and revolting." Even so, "they know how to express themselves sincerely, and they greatly revere the law of Buddha."

Someplace on the way—most scholars of his journey place the spot between Tashkurgan and Kashgar—he and his party ran into a horde of bandits, and in the panic, his elephants were, as Hui Li puts it, "engulfed in the water and perished." Hui Li does not say if the precious books or the Buddha statues that the monk was carrying from India were swept into the current. "The robbers having passed by," he writes, the monk's party "proceeded slowly to the eastward, over crags and across mountain gorges, descending the heights and patiently enduring the cold." Eventually they reached Och, where the local legend had to do with the time the king was brought before an Arhat sitting in a trance on a mountaintop.

The Arhat was large, with hair over his shoulders and face. The king was told that this was a man who many years before had left his family and entered a condition of great ecstasy. The king, who was devout, asked if the Arhat could be awakened from his trance. A priest told him: "In the case of one who has long gone without food, when he awakes from his ecstasy his body would decay, so that first you must anoint him with cream, which being rubbed into his body will lubricate and soften his muscles." The king himself performed this task, and, that being done, the Arhat was awakened. He asked: "Has Sakyamuni yet attained the unequaled condition of perfect enlightenment?" The question not only demonstrated the Arhat's conviction but the great length of time that he had been entranced. Told that Sakyamuni, which is to say the Buddha, had passed into Nirvana several hundred years before, the Arhat lowered his eyelids, placed his hand on his hair, elevated himself, and caused his body to be consumed by fire, leaving behind his bones as his bequeathed relics. The king had a stupa built on that spot to house the bones. Hsuan Tsang visited it.

Hsuan Tsang turned south at Kashgar to Yarkand and then on to what he called the country of Kustana, which we know by its Uigur name, Khotan. He found it "a great flat covered with sand and stones," which it is. He says that it is famous for its white and dark jade, which it is today as well—jewelers from Hong Kong coming from time to time to buy it. "The climate is temperate, and the common people understand politeness and right principles," and it was a great Buddhist center, with one hundred monasteries and five thousand priests, a vast establishment in the desert.

In three more years, a Chinese army would arrive in Kustana-Khotan and force it to pay allegiance and tribute to China. Indeed, Khotan when the monk arrived there was one of the few places (Kucha was the other) not yet conquered as Tai Tsung established Chinese domination. It will be remembered, for example, that Hsuan Tsang was almost prevented from leaving Turfan by the king there, Qu Wencai, who, as a condition for allowing the monk to continue on his way, extracted a promise: that Hsuan Tsang would return to Turfan and teach there for three years on his way back to China from India. But in 640, four years before the monk's arrival in Khotan, Qu had committed a fatal mistake: He entered into an alliance with the Turks to control the caravan routes between India and China. It was a strange thing to do, given the Chinese resurgence under the Tang. Ten years earlier, the great cycle of Central Asian history began one of its tectonic shifts, and China, weak for centuries, became powerful again. The Tang defeated and slaughtered a horde of eastern Turks, driving them back to the Mongolian Plain. Tai Tsung sent his generals and armies throughout the vast western territory with the intention of subjugating it to his will, by diplomacy if possible, by massacre if not. Kashgar became a tributary of China in 632, Yarkand in 635.

In 640, after Qu Wencai's ill-advised alliance with the western Turks, a Chinese cavalry force appeared without warning at the gates of Turfan, having ridden undetected through the desert. Qu was so terrified by the sudden appearance of this Chinese army that he died of a seizure. The army laid siege to Turfan. When Qu's successor, a young and inexperienced man, came to the Chinese camp to ask for terms, an adviser to Tai Tsung's commander asked, "What's the point of discussing matters with this child? Give us the signal and let's march to the attack." The Turfan leader was taken prisoner and marched to Chang-an, where he was offered to Tai Tsung at the imperial palace. Wine was distributed for three days in what the official history calls "the ritual libation of return." A Turkish chieftain with the Chinese name A-she-na Sho-eul presented the emperor with the jeweled sword of the fallen House of Qu, which had treated Hsuan Tsang with such effusions of admiration. The monk, relieved of his obligation to return to Turfan as Qu's guest, says nothing about this turn of historical events.

A few years later, when the monk was back at Chang-an and dutifully expressing his loyalty to the emperor, Tai Tsung finished wiping out the Tokharian rulers who had provided Hsuan Tsang with hospitality when he was an illegal traveler in 629 and 630. In 647, the Turkish mercenary A-she-na Sho-eul, at the head of a mixed force of Chinese rebels and Tatar soldiers of fortune, carried out a campaign against Turkish tribes in the vicinity of what is now Urumqi. After that, he attacked Kucha, the final holdout against Chinese control in the Tarim Basin.

"It was the combined Crécy and Agincourt of those handsome lords of the Qizil frescoes," writes René Grousset.★ A-she-na Sho-eul beheaded eleven thousand Kuchan regulars. He destroyed five cities in the Kuchan oasis and, according to the official Tang history, slaughtered tens of thousands of women and children. It was a terrible and conclusive event. For centuries, the offshoots of an Indo-European culture had flourished in the north-central Tarim Basin, the chief monuments of which were the paintings of the caves of Qizil, which the monk had visited and where the Chinese now collect exorbitant entry fees from Western and Japanese tourists. Hsuan Tsang was the last Chinese visitor to these enchanted realms before the heavy fist of Tai Tsung pounded them into rubble, forever. Grousset, full of antiquarian tristesse, remarks: "It was the end of the Tokharian world, the end of a world of charm and refinement, belated survivor of the races of old. The brilliant civilization of Qizil was never to recover from this catastrophe."

But the Kuchans were not the last of the people known personally to Hsuan Tsang who fell before China resurgent. In 641, while the monk was in India, the western Turks, whose long braided hair and embroidered robes and ranks that stretched as far as one could see had deeply impressed him in Tokmak, were defeated by a Chinese force near present-day Urumqi. The formerly mighty Turkish tribes fell into disarray, with one of them, the Uigurs of Barkol, forging an alliance with China that was to last for the rest of the Tang Dynasty. When, a few years after the great battle of Urumqi, Tai Tsung annihilated Kucha, Chinese imperial power reached its apex. "Even the states of the Indo-Persian borderlands had bowed to the rising might of the great emperor," Grousset writes. "The Turko-Iranian princes of Bukhara, Samarkand and Kapisa henceforth sent their tribute to the court of Chang-an." The very kingdoms that had received Hsuan Tsang on his way to the west, showing themselves to be powerful and independent, had by the time of his return reoriented themselves toward China, which had in a few years become the greatest power on the globe.

OUR OVERNIGHT bus ride to Khotan was not a pleasure. We got seats near the front. Then just as the bus was scheduled to leave, two local

★ Grousset, *op. cit.,* pp. 236–37.

floozies got on and occupied the seats across the narrow aisle from ours. The seats had been saved for them by the bus's crew, which seemed about as numerous as a crew on a 747. They were all male, they all smoked, and they all bantered ceaselessly and noisily with the floozies, these jezebels with powdered faces and miniskirts and heavy thighs who seemed all the more out of place in this region of threadbare Islamic conservatism. There was a cruelty in their vulgarity, a kind of tyranny in their clinging sweaters and puffy cheeks and fawning male entourage. They shrilled and cackled all night in an otherwise quiet bus, their shrilling and cackling carrying with it the subtext: This bus is ours and we will do whatever we want in it.

I fell asleep at about one in the morning but was quickly awakened when the closer of the two floozies began banging the seats of the bus and the head of the other floozy with a plastic water bottle half filled with ice. Behind us sat row after row of quiet, well-behaved passengers. They were so well behaved that nobody complained even as the clock struck (as it were) 2 a.m.

"Why don't you shut the fuck up," I said to the nearby floozy.

"Heh?" she said. She was Uigur and the banter was in Uigur, so I wasn't sure I had a language in common with her.

"Be quiet," I said in Chinese. Then I tried to think of some appeal that might make moral or practical sense to her. "You're disturbing every passenger on the bus."

"Heh?" she said, and rattled her bottle. The Uigur "heh?" is, I was learning, an attenuated phoneme, uttered in an abruptly rising tone— *"Heeeehhhh?"*—like the first half of a long sneeze.

"Heeeehhhh?" I said in imitation of my fellow passenger. "Why don't you tell her to shut the fuck up?" I said to one of the attendants on the bus, who was suddenly trapped between a demanding foreigner whom he probably didn't understand and the bulging strumpet with whom he was striving to ingratiate himself. He wasn't about to give her any lessons out of Amy Vanderbilt, and I knew that there was nothing much I could do.

A half hour later the bus pulled into a weird sort of town, a vast esplanade of asphalt on the edges of which were a dozen or so outdoor food stalls and restaurants. Most of the passengers simply got out and crouched near the bus, but some, including the floozies, went in search of their favorite delicacies. Loudspeakers screeched the local pop music. The maîtres d'hôtel of the various open-air restaurants clamored for passengers to patronize their joints. There were a dozen or so other buses pulled up onto the esplanade. The smoke from a score or so of identical lamb kebab barbecues hung in the heavy air. People sat on wooden benches or on the edges of outdoor beds and pulled the lamb off skewers with their teeth and drank bottles of warm Xinjiang beer. Their lips gleamed greasily in the light of naked bulbs.

At last we left, and the raucous laughter in the front of the bus continued. When the floozies finally went to sleep, slumped against each other, snoring contentedly, their mouths open to silvered teeth, our driver and his companions of the road sang and whistled for the rest of the night. We arrived in Khotan at about eight that morning, exhausted and irritable. We carried our bags to a taxi.

"The Khotan Guesthouse," Zhongmei said. She spoke in Chinese, giving the name of the hostelry recommended by our guidebook.

"Heeeehhhh?" said the taxi driver.

She repeated her request, tentatively.

"You want a hotel?" A policeman came along, being helpful.

"Yes. What's the best hotel in Khotan?" she asked.

"There's a hotel right here," he replied. "Come with me."

Overlooking the bus station was a local guesthouse. It didn't look like the place we wanted to stay after our sleepless night.

"We want the Hotian Binguan," Zhongmei said. "Hotian" is the Chinese for Khotan. *Binguan* means "guesthouse." Still the taxi driver and the policeman understood us to be asking for a guesthouse in Khotan, any guesthouse, rather than the Khotan Guesthouse.

We set off, and the driver took us to a couple of other places that were not the Hotian Binguan and where we did not want to stay. We stopped to get directions, but nobody seemed to be able to distinguish between the Khotan Guesthouse and a guesthouse in Khotan, so we drove to yet another flophouse. At last, the driver took us, via a process of elimination, to the Khotan Guesthouse, which was set back from the road in its own compound and had an unexpected stateliness to it. It was 10 a.m.

We had a breakfast of rice porridge, peanuts, and pickled cabbage in the enormous dining room filled with large round tables. We went back to the bus station to inquire about further bookings, though neither of us was looking forward to any more bus rides in southern Xinjiang. We learned that there was a daily bus to Minfeng, seven hours to the east. From Minfeng to Qiemo there was another bus, the woman at the ticket office told us. She was drinking tea and reading the newspaper.

"You don't know how often it runs?" Zhongmei asked.

"Once or twice a week," she said.

"Is there any way you could check that for us?" Zhongmei asked hopefully.

"Mei-you," the woman replied.

"What about Qiemo to Ruoqiang?" Zhongmei asked. The woman shrugged and took another sip of tea.

At the hotel we asked for the local branch of the China Travel Service, which we found on the third floor of an unmarked building a mile away.

Four friendly Uigur men, all Chinese speakers, and one Chinese man who spoke Uigur sat there as if waiting for us.

We asked them how we could take the southern route from Khotan to Dunhuang, following as closely as possible the route the monk had taken.

"Nobody takes that route," said a man named Yarimuhammat, who turned out to be the general manager of the Xinjiang Khotan International Travel Service. "People get to Dunhuang by flying from here to Aksu; then you can take the train. Or you could take the bus from here to Korla. There's a very good double-decker sleeper bus. It takes about thirty hours to Korla. From there you could take a train to Liuyuan and from Liuyuan it's just a taxi ride to Dunhuang."

"Is there a bus from here to Minfeng?"

"Yes."

"And from Minfeng to Qiemo?"

"Yes, there's a bus."

"And from Qiemo to Ruoqiang?"

"It's an ordinary bus, a small one. It runs twice a week."

"And from Ruoqiang to Dunhuang?"

"No."

"There's no bus from Ruoqiang to Dunhuang?"

"No."

"But there's a road. How do local people travel on that road?"

"The road is very bad. Nobody goes on that road," was the reply. We were later to learn that Yarimuhammat was telling the truth. Nobody does take that road, though we did. "People from Ruoqiang take the bus to Korla," he said. "And from Korla you can go by train to Dunhuang. Or you could just take the train to Urumchi. From Urumchi there's a direct flight to Dunhuang."

"No, we don't want to take any airplanes. And we want to take the southern Silk Route to Dunhuang."

"Very difficult," said Yarimuhammat. There was silence in the room. "But it's worth it," he said.

"What about taking the bus to Ruoqiang and hiring a car at Ruoqiang?"

"You won't find a car in Ruoqiang. It's just a little country town. There are no cars for hire there. Anyway, the road is very bad. You need a jeep."

I took a deep breath. "Could we get a jeep from here to take us all the way to Dunhuang?"

"Yes."

"How much would it cost?"

"It's by the kilometer."

There was a lengthy discussion in Uigur, with note takings, map consultations and arithmetical calculations on the backs of Xinjiang Khotan International Travel Service envelopes.

"Twelve thousand five hundred Chinese yuan."

I divided by eight. It was a bit more than fifteen hundred dollars.

The four nice Uigurs looked at me sympathetically.

It wasn't the money that made me hesitate; it was my perhaps unfounded sense that public transportation would be more authentic, more in the spirit of the monk's own journey. In fact, this wasn't really true. From Khotan to Xian (via Dunhuang), the monk had traveled with an imperial escort, which provided him with horses and armed guards for the transport of his Indian treasures. The monk had taken a long, lonely, and usually modest road, but he did not spurn making his journey easier when the opportunity was there.

"You're sure there's no car for hire in Ruoqiang? You're not just telling me that?"

"Well, you can go there if you want to, and then you'll see," said Yarimuhammat.

"How many days to Dunhuang?"

"You could do it in three if you drive twelve or fourteen hours a day. You can take as many as six days for this price. It includes the driver's hotel and food."

I took another deep breath. I knew that, really, I had no choice.

"Okay," I said. "For twelve thousand five hundred yuan we'll take your jeep."

KHOTAN TO ME was the very emblem of remote, the place on the edge of beyond, and that gives it several meanings. For those for whom the prosody of ordinary life is unbearable and who therefore yearn to be away, to expel themselves from their own time, Khotan is the platonic away. Look at a map and see it, a small dot surrounded by the vastness of the desert and the jagged heights of the uncrossable mountains to the south and west. This is a place where you can experience all of the gratification and dislocation of a life spent avoiding attachment. But for a Buddhist monk like Hsuan Tsang whose heart thrilled at the site of Buddhist monuments, Khotan was a refuge. There are no Buddhist monuments there anymore, only the already excavated ruins of the temples and stupas that the monk saw. But Khotan was the first place in modern China to be reached by the Law, by the Good News from India. That was because it was one of the first places to become important on the Silk Road. It was in that sense astonishing—a vast commercial and religious emporium in a place of desolation that had no intrinsic or organic existence of its own. It was the seventh-century equivalent of a twenty-first-century space station, a place that lived vibrantly and brilliantly because it connected points that did not mesh organically, those points being nothing less than the east and the west, China and Rome, the Celestial Empire and India.

The impression that Khotan gives now is of a town waking up after a long sleep, a garden being newly watered after a drought. It seems new, and that is disappointing. It has none of the old features—an ancient mosque, antique neighborhoods—that still exist, even if hemmed in by Chineseness, in Kashgar. It has ruins, some of which you can visit by jeep or camel, though this is often only upon payment of staggering entrance fees. Niya, for example, costs thirty thousand yuan, just under four thousand dollars, per visit, which is why a few Japanese archaeologists, backed by Japanese Buddhist tycoons, have gone there but why I didn't. Khotan has state-run jade shops and lots of small private jade shops and a new teeming market where all the cheap goods manufactured in China can be found. The surrounding, heavily irrigated desert blooms; the farms sell their produce to populated regions farther east, and that gives Khotan a clean sort of prosperity. But it has no charm, no Central Asian flavor. It has immensely wide, straight avenues and tile-front buildings lining broad sidewalks. It is the kind of city that seems frozen in the heat of summer, where everyone and every animal move slowly, where even prosperity seems indolent and heavy. Or perhaps it was just the fatigue of the long bus ride that made me see everything as if viewed with a slow-motion camera.

Khotan was not only the first Buddhist place in what is now western China; it was also the first place excavated by Aurel Stein, who, before he did anything else, identified all of the ruins mentioned by the monk in

Chronicles. Stein made two expeditions to Khotan, one in 1900, the other in 1906. He determined that the modern village was not the village that Hsuan Tsang visited. That village was now in a place called Yotkan, seven miles west. Stein met a local treasure-seeker named Turki who showed him some fragments of a stucco bas-relief that seemed to be Buddhist in character. They had been found at a place called Dandan Ulik, where Stein and his crew then went, eleven days by horse and camel.

It was December and very cold. Stein reports that his mustache froze in his sleep and he covered his face with his coat, breathing through the sleeve. The going was through soft sand marked by conical hillocks of tamarisk reed scrub, behind which Stein dug for pools of bitter brackish water. At Dandan Ulik he found the remains of a collection of modest buildings, which he spent three weeks digging out of the millennial sand. He uncovered wattle-and-plaster walls decorated with tempura paintings of Buddhas and Bodhisattvas.

The exciting thing about them, as Stein put it, was that their "style unmistakably derived from Greco-Buddhist art." The paintings were of the same sort as those found in faraway Peshawar and in Afghanistan, proof of the spread of Gandharan craftsmanship over the Pamirs. Alexander the Great had brought Greek art to India, which had become infused with Buddhist themes and transported along with Parthian textiles to what was to become China. Stein also found documents at Dandan Ulik, eighth-century records in a non-Chinese and non-Indian language, the most interesting of which was a petition for the recovery of a donkey that the petitioner had leased to two men who disappeared. The language was a form of Persian.

One striking Buddhist image was of "a powerful ruler" with "a long ruddy face, surrounded by a heavy black beard, a large curling mustache and bushy black eyebrows." The ruler's body was "narrow-waisted in keeping with the Persian type of manly beauty." He wore a brocaded coat, a short curving sword, and high black boots. He had four arms. Across from him was a three-headed demon with dark blue skin, nude but for a tiger-skin skirt below the waist.

Stein was mystified by this strange apparition, the likes of which he had never seen before, and by its strange juxtaposition with the blue-skinned demon. Fifteen years after his expedition to Khotan, he was working in Persia and he realized that the kingly Buddha of Dandan Ulik was a variation on Rustam, the hero of the national Persian epic who overcame demonic adversaries and forced them into loyal submission.

The cave painting in Dandan Ulik, which showed a Rustam-like figure juxtaposed with a subdued demon, was a direct artistic borrowing.

Later, at Niya, Stein uncovered documents in the Kharoshthi script, an early Indian language from the northwest Punjab. Stein knew that no such documents had survived in India itself. But they lent substance to the legend, repeated by Hsuan Tsang, that the founders of Khotan had come from Taxila in the second century B.C. Hsuan Tsang was merely repeating legend without benefit of archaeological evidence when he said that the ancestor of the king of Kustana "was the eldest son of Ashoka-raja who dwelt in Taxila." Banished for unknown reasons, he went north of the Kunlun Mountains in search of water for his herds, and when he came to this place, he built his residence here.

All of this evidence points to the Indian and Persian origins of Khotan. It was conquered and controlled first by the great Ban Chao in the first century A.D., in the unending Chinese effort to control the barbarian domains beyond the Jade Gate and to keep open the routes of commerce to the West. Ban Chao's conquest of the city is one of the legends known to all Chinese schoolchildren. The king of Khotan was under the influence of a Hunnish shaman, a sort of Mongol-Turkic Rasputin. The king and the shaman demanded that the Chinese general sacrifice his prize warhorse. Ban Chao accepted, on condition that the shaman himself lead the horse away. When he did, Ban Chao had him decapitated and sent the head in a box to the king, who, duly terrified, surrendered to the Chinese forces.

HSUAN TSANG'S ARRIVAL in Khotan marked a delicate moment in his expedition. Having decided to return home, he now faced the possible wrath of the emperor, Tai Tsung, whose prohibition against leaving China he had so flagrantly violated seventeen years before. In setting out on his pilgrimage, Hsuan Tsang had practiced a kind of civil disobedience, one of the earliest instances on record. He had in effect proclaimed that there were higher laws than those of the ruler, and those higher laws justified his felonious act of departure. From Khotan, to try to smooth his way with the now well-established emperor, Hsuan Tsang dispatched a visiting merchant of Gaochang with a letter. The merchant traveled with a caravan. It is not clear if he went all the way to Xian himself or stopped in Gaochang and passed the letter on to another messenger who carried it to Xian. In any case, Hsuan Tsang settled down in Khotan and waited for a reply. The full text of the letter was preserved by Hui Li, who, presumably, got it from Hsuan Tsang. It began with references to former sages and "teachers of public morals" who were "illustrious for their eminent talent." It continued:

If we admire these ancient masters for their support of learning, how much more those who search into the secret traces of the profit-bringing religions of the Buddhas, and the marvelous words of the three Pitakas, able to liberate from the snares of the world? How can we dare to undervalue such labors, or not regard them with ardor? Now I, Hsuan Tsang, long since versed in the doctrine of Buddha, bequeathed by him in the Western world, the rules and precepts of which had reached the East in an imperfect form, always pondered on a plan for searching out the true learning, without any thought for personal safety. Accordingly, in the fourth month of the third year of the period of Cheng Kwan, braving dangers and obstacles, I secretly found my way to India. I traversed over vast plains of shifting sand; I scaled precipitous mountain-crags clad with snow; I found my way through the scarped passes of the iron gates, passed along by the tumultuous waves of the hot sea. Beginning at the sacred city of Chang-an, I reached the city of Rajagriha.

Thus I accomplished a journey of more than fifty thousand li. Yet, notwithstanding the thousand differences of customs and manners I have witnessed, the myriads of dangers I have encountered, by the goodness of Heaven I have returned without accident, and now offer my homage with a body unimpaired, and a mind satisfied with the accomplishment of my vows. I have beheld the Ghridrakuta Mountain, worshipped at the Bodhi Tree. I have seen traces not seen before; heard sacred words not heard before; witnessed spiritual prodigies exceeding all the wonders of Nature, have borne testimony to the highest qualities of our august Emperor and won for him the high esteem and praise of the people.

And now, because the great elephant that I had perished in the waters, I have not yet succeeded in obtaining transport for the numerous books which I have brought back. On that account I have remained here a little while, but not having obtained the necessary mode of conveyance, I purpose at once to go forward and visit your majesty. With this view I have sent forward a layman belonging to Gaochang, whose name is Ma Huan-chi, in the company of certain merchants respectfully to present this letter and to announce my purpose.

Seven or eight months later, an imperial messenger arrived with a letter from the emperor:

> When I heard that the Master who had gone to far-off countries to search for religious books had now come back, I was filled with boundless joy. I pray you come quickly that we may see each other. The priests of this kingdom who understand the Fan [the languages of India] and the explanation of the sacred books I have also commanded to come and pay you greetings. I have ordered the bureaus of Khotan and other places to send with you the best guides they can procure, and conveyances as many as you require. I have commanded the magistrates of Dunhuang to conduct you through the desert of shifting sands and I have desired the government to send to meet you.

So Hsuan Tsang left Khotan in 645 or 646 in the company of a large escort. Like him, and with an escort of our own, Zhongmei and I arose early the morning after our meeting with the Xinjiang Khotan International Travel Service. Our jeep was a venerable Toyota. Our driver was named Zhang. He was the Uigur-speaking Chinese who had been in the office when we first showed up. He wore a dude's jeans and a man-of-the-world mustache. He was overly friendly, as if he was putting on an act. He knew everything, the road, the car, the sites along the way, the archaeological history of the Tarim Basin from Khotan to Loulan, and I wondered what trouble we were going to run into with him later. We stopped on the edge of town for a breakfast of lamb pilaf and tea. And then we were off into the Tai Tsung emperor's desert of shifting sands.

20

The Southern Oases to Dunhuang

W E DROVE THROUGH the modern part of Khotan and into the countryside, where the trucks jostled with tractors and donkey carts and farmers sold watermelons and *hami-gua* by the roadside. We crossed the White Jade River and passed under a canopy of poplars. A banner stretched across the road said: "Try hard for the country; Love the country; Strengthen national unity." For half an hour we passed wheat-fields and mulberry trees, grown to feed the silkworms, and then for five hours after that it was the monotony of gravel desert. I asked Zhang if we could make a quick stop somewhere to see the silkworms. We were, after all, on the Silk Road. Zhang waved his hand urgently as if he were swatting flies away from a picnic table.

"No, no, no. Nobody can go inside the silkworm sheds."

"Why not? Are they still trying to keep it secret?"

"Disease," said Zhang. "They're afraid you'll give them some disease."

As we drove on I looked to the south, hoping for a glimpse of the Kunlun Mountains, and I was disappointed not to be able to see them, though they were there, behind a wall of haze. The road was rough but the signage was beautiful—little masonry steles every kilometer bearing a red number representing the number of kilometers to Xining, in Qinghai Province—2,410 from the outskirts of Khotan. A single line of telephone poles, twenty per kilometer (I counted), ran alongside us, bare sticks with

a few wires attached that intensified the feeling of desolation, the emptiness on this lonely road.

We stopped for lunch in a sandblown village on the highway called
Yutian, eating spicy noodles in a dank, earthen-floored restaurant. A
Uigur-language melodrama about airline hostesses was playing on television. After lunch, Zhongmei and I took a little walk and found a *hami-gua*
peddler, who sold us a few slices. We set off again and arrived in Minfeng
(the ancient Niya) about 3 p.m. It was too early to stop for the day, but
our next destination, Qiemo (Cherchen), was eight hours away, so we
had no choice but to stay in Minfeng. It consisted of a few straight streets
running parallel to the main drag; it was quiet; tall poplars swayed in the
hot breeze. Our hotel was filthy and inexpensive and run by two women
who seemed most of the time to be taking naps on cots in the office. We
met two Chinese men in their twenties who seemed just as foreign in the
Uigur town as I did. They said they were traveling by bus but the bus
didn't go farther east for two more days. Would we give them a ride to
Qiemo? They seemed like bright, nice-boy types. I looked at the driver.

"It's your car," he said with his usual aggressive joviality. "It's not my
car anymore."

"Okay, we'll give you a ride," I said.

Later Zhongmei told me that Brave King had warned us never to give
anybody a ride. Never, she repeated. I had not heard this warning. I told
her that it would be fine, but she was worried. I wondered what they
could do. There were the driver and I, plus Zhongmei, three against two,
and they didn't have the look of highwaymen.

Actually, they turned out to be delightful company as we ground
down the gravel track to Qiemo. We talked about archaeology. One of
our passengers was a reader of the Chinese version of *National Geographic*.
He knew of Hsuan Tsang, and we talked of his itinerary, which paralleled
our route on a line about fifty kilometers to the north. In the monk's time
the rivers carrying glacial melt from the Kunluns penetrated fifty kilometers or so farther into the desert than they do now. Over the centuries
as the glacial waters have diminished, the Tarim Basin has expanded so
the settled areas now are closer to the mountains and to the source of
water.

One day in Khotan, Zhongmei and I had accepted an invitation from
the travel service to go to Rawak, a spot in the desert where there were
the remains of a Tang Dynasty stupa. We hired a guide from the Bureau of
Cultural Relics. A jeep took us north into the desert, which was a maze of
under-construction irrigation canals. When we could go no farther in the

jeep, we hiked about two miles through sand dunes to the stupa. It wasn't much—a mud pedestal of baked mud brick atop a broader circular mound in which you could still see the indentations of former doorways. All of it was within a square arena surrounded by a squat retaining wall, while all around the dunes undulated under the wind. The style is Gandharan, similar to Takht-i-Bahi in Pakistan, testimony to Professor Serhai's claim that Gandharan craftsmen built the Buddhist monuments all the way to China. *Rawak* means "pavilion" in Uigur. The temple could be the stupa mentioned by the monk where, according to legend, an Arhat persuaded the king of Khotan to build a monastery and extol the doctrine of Buddha.

Stein, who excavated Rawak in 1901, found ninety-one large statues of Buddhas and Bodhisattvas there. As I stood on the crumbling, empty mound that remains of the temple, I thought how absolutely thrilling it must have been for Stein to have trekked for days into the desert in winter and to find, neglected for more than a thousand years, so many pieces of buried treasure. But for Stein the thrill turned to dismay. He had no time to pack up the statues and take them with him, so he reburied them. One year later, he returned to Rawak and learned that treasure-hunters had unearthed the statues and smashed every one of them, convinced that jewels and gold were hidden inside. The fate of the statues makes one think about Stein, a foreigner who felt free to dig out and cart away the important relics of another civilization. His doing so, like Elgin's taking away portions of the Parthenon frieze in Athens, was an act of imperial arrogance inconceivable today. Indeed, Stein was far worse than Elgin, who at least paid something to the Turkish rulers of Greece, whereas Stein paid nothing to the government of China, which had a presumed sovereignty in this part of Turkestan. But Stein's removals were also acts of imperial appreciation, a recognition of the greatness of what was but is no longer. And one sign of that was the very desecration of the statues. How many of the sculptures and frescoes that Stein and the others, like Sven Hedin, the Baron Le Coq, and the Frenchman Paul Pelliot, shipped to Europe would have survived if they had not done so?

From atop the tower, you could see niches where some of the statues must have been, and you could imagine some Sogdian merchant, his camels burdened and grunting among the tamarisk reeds, making obeisance to the large Buddha on the top. Marco Polo came to China via the route of the southern oases and probably passed by there. The adventurer Yakub Beg laid siege to Khotan and made it part of his short-lived empire. When Peter Fleming came to this point in 1935, Khotan, which he described as full of rebel Uigur soldiers, was so autonomous from the Chinese central government that it printed its own money on paper made from mulberry leaves. But the greatest story of this place, its greatest event after the arrival of Buddhism, was recounted by none other than Hsuan Tsang in *Chronicles*. It has to do with silk, the diaphanous product that had been traded to the Greeks and Romans from as early as the fourth century B.C. There are many legends of how the secret of the manufacture of silk, carefully guarded by all Chinese governments, made its way to the West. What is interesting is that the monk's version of the story corresponds with the story told by historians today.

"In the olden days," he begins, "this country knew nothing about mulberry trees or silkworms." By "this country" he means Khotan. The king of Khotan, unlike the rulers of Rome, was aware of the astonishing fact that this most luxurious of materials consisted of the unraveled and woven threads of the cocoon of a gray-white worm, and he also knew that the "Eastern Kingdom," meaning China, possessed this worm. He knew too that the ruler of the Eastern Kingdom "kept guard over his territory and would not permit either the seeds of the mulberry or the eggs of the silkworm to be carried off." To overcome this obstacle, the monk continues, the Khotanese king applied to the emperor of the Eastern Kingdom to give him a Chinese bride.

When the Chinese king agreed to this, the Khotanese ruler dispatched a messenger to escort the Chinese princess to Khotan. Said messenger, in an appeal to the princess's vanity, informed her that unless she smuggled both seeds and eggs on the journey with her, she would have no material with which to make the robes she was used to wearing. The princess agreed. It was an act of commercial treason against her native country, but people have always given their own economic well-being priority over the national interest. Trade boycotts, like boycotts of books, are made to be broken. And so the princess hid the precious seeds and eggs in her headdress, which no customs inspector at the Jade Gate would dare to inspect. After her arrival in Khotan, the worms were hatched and fed on other leaves, Hsuan Tsang says, until the mulberry seeds could be planted and the leaves had ripened. The princess, now the queen, built a temple where the first silkworms were bred, a place that Hsuan Tsang calls Lu Shi, about one mile from the ancient site of Khotan. "There are about here many old mulberry tree trunks which they say are the remains of the old trees first planted," the monk writes.

There were no such old tree trunks when I was in Khotan. My friends at the Khotan Xinjiang International Travel Service had never heard of any and they did not know where Lu Shi was. But Hsuan Tsang's story accords well with other accounts of the Western discovery of silk. In the fifth century A.D., two Nestorian monks who traveled to Khotan ferreted out the astonishing secret that silk came from a worm that had to be fed on a certain leaf. The Nestorians brought seeds and eggs to Byzantium, where state workshops were set up to weave the opulent cloth and to attempt, for a while, to keep the secret from their counterparts farther west. But the long-held secret was out by then, the extraordinary secret that silk comes from a worm.

QIEMO WAS SURPRISINGLY modern and gleaming, with white-tiled institutional buildings and, arranged on a sun-blinding grid, several broad streets where small sand drifts piled up on the curbs. It was a planned city, a new place, desert-clean and uninteresting. We stayed at a new hotel called the Muzitage that was inside a large asphalt esplanade and featured a spacious lobby with a fountain. After we checked in, Zhang made a call to the local archaeological bureau and arranged a guide to take us, for a fee, to see the ancient relics. The local archaeologists have created a little museum in the former home of the third wife of the richest Uigur in town. The Uigur himself was taken to Urumqi in 1936 by a pre-Communist warlord named Shen Shicai, and he never came back. "Nobody knows what happened to him," our guide told us. The house consisted of many earthen-floored rooms with high, wood-paneled ceilings and knee-high doorsills. The museum's prize possession was a wooden harp dated 770–476 B.C. There are many references to such harps in the literature, but this is the only actual instrument ever found. "We found it the year before last," the guide said. He was a stocky man with a broad face and a crewcut. "We haven't told the authorities in Beijing about it yet because we don't want to lose it." He meant that the authorities would recognize its value and take it away so it could be put in a museum more on the beaten track. I asked him how many visitors had seen the harp before me, and he answered a dozen or so.

Then we were taken to an absolutely flat sand platform in the desert on the edge of town. We drove up to a squat concrete building that stood alone in the middle of nothing, looking like an oddly placed country eating place, like one of those we stopped in on the road from Minfeng. We were invited inside and found ourselves peering into an uncovered tomb with fourteen bodies, half of them skeletons, half of them mummies, lined up in two straight rows inside. As always I was transfixed by the grimaces of these weirdly dead people whose privacy was now being so rudely violated. The theory is that they were an entire family, buried with the implements of their lives, including the precious harp, now in the museum. Probably the tomb was created in two shifts, which would account for the skeletonized state of half of its inhabitants and the mummified condition of the other half. At some point the tomb was opened and air let in, which led the earlier bodies to decay. The later bodies were then deposited and covered up, and they remained undisturbed until archaeologists did their nasty work.

Near the tomb were two cases containing the mummified remains of two more people, presumably a couple. The man was a giant, over six feet tall even in his shrunken 2,600-year-old state. Sand was embedded in his skin. His hands were a gruesome half-skin, half-bone, as if they had been partially stripped for a lesson in anatomy. They were placed over his chest and around a short horsewhip, so he was probably a nomad. A sheep's skin had been draped over his shoulders, and a blue-and-red woven cloth was wrapped around his thighs. He had all of his teeth, most of which could be seen through his death sneer.

His woman was covered in remnants of a red dress—a woven wool bordered with two bands of blue, one dark, one light. She was very young, perhaps a teenager, while the man was assumed to have been in his forties. Was she buried alive with him when he died? She bore no signs of violence, and so it is possible that she was alive when she was put into the ground next to her husband and then died from the lack of oxygen. Of course it is also possible that she died of disease at the same time as her husband, or that she was made to take poison first and was only interred later. In any case, the archaeologists are certain that the two of them were put in their tomb at the same time, and, barring the unlikely possibility that they died simultaneously, this fact alone suggests a painful conclusion regarding the woman.

RUOQIANG WAS EIGHT more hours on the gravel track, an endless and monotonous trip through a flat brown landscape of pebble and scrub. During the entire trip we passed only one vehicle going in the opposite direction, the twice-weekly bus. This, I thought, must be the longest and least-traveled gravel road in the world. We stopped for lunch at a roadside canteen sitting perpendicular to the road, a stucco farmhouse with a dark, earthen-floored interior and a single wooden table outside. It was run by a Uigur woman in a red dress and a blue kerchief. She told us that on a good day she would get maybe eight or ten cars, but two or three was the norm. There were days when she stood in readiness with her slaughtered sheep, her tomatoes, her green onions, and her prepared flour and not a single car came down the road in either direction. Her husband worked on a road repair crew and the two of them lived in a compound surrounded by a battered masonry wall farther back from the road in the desert.

While we were waiting for lunch, the mail truck from Qiemo pulled in across the road, where there was a second food stand almost identical to ours, except for a banner in revolutionary red with white characters saying *qing-zhen shi-tang,* "vegetarian canteen." It stood with a dilapidated vividness against the backdrop of the empty desert and made the word "nowhere" echo in my brain. The doors of the truck opened and about four full-sized men piled out of the cab. Then the back door was opened and another ten or so men spilled out onto the pebbly ground and flocked into the food stall. The mail truck comes every other day. Strangely, it had a large sign, "China Post," in English, not Chinese, and an abstract design in blue and white that looked like an airline insignia. Our driver had no opinion about the invasion of English into Central Asia, but in his usual didactic tone he told us that the mail truck driver made extra money carrying passengers. "There are so many ways that the drivers make money," he said, shaking his head mournfully because, presumably, he was stuck with foreign travelers and therefore had only his travel service fee. I realized that he was angling for a tip or for a commission. He wanted something; his affability was too rehearsed and calculated for it to be otherwise. Sooner or later, I felt, we were going to be in for a showdown.

Lunch came, noodles in a bowl with a sauce of vegetables and lamb poured over them. We were lucky to have such fare in the middle of the desert, this broken-down noplace on what had become the road of no events, but I had very little appetite. A kind of listlessness had infiltrated my spirit, made up of monotony and tummy unease. Our driver slurped his *la-tiao-zi* with gusto while I pulled at mine, one noodle at a time. I wondered where in this dusty and disconsolate flatness the *cesuo* would be, and, surveying a faraway shed or two across a field of spongy earth, I decided to wait. Zhongmei ate quietly. From across the road two men carried slatted boxes of groceries to the woman in the blue kerchief, who carried them inside. We sat for a while picking our teeth and then we were back on the travel track counting telephone poles silhouetted against an immense and silty sky.

. . .

RUOQIANG WAS A few government buildings and some general stores, the old-fashioned sort where there is a counter and behind it rows of Phoenix Garden canned goods and Snow Flake soap powder, cellophane bags of dry noodles, glass tumblers, terry-cloth washrags, and white porcelain rice bowls and a woman in an untucked white blouse who fetches things for you with an extension tool. Zhang was eager for us to go to the ruins at Mi-lan, which are relatively insignificant, and when we declined, he was visibly disappointed. From the hotel reception desk, he made a phone call and canceled some arrangement he had made before. I realized that we were depriving him of a commission. It was paralyzingly hot, and the town seemed strangely oversized. The buildings, which were cement and governmental, were far apart. There are cities and towns that discourage ambulation, and Ruoqiang was one of them. I had expected something interesting, an old mosque maybe with a minaret of latticed brick, narrow, sinuous, Turkish streets, a teahouse where grizzled Uigurs sat on wooden stools and played checkers while camels peering down from on high insolently chewed their cud. But Ruoqiang was just a sand-blown administrative outpost occupied by Chinese functionaries who wore plastic sandals and rode bicycles. We hung around the hotel and I caught up on my notes, and after the sun went down and it cooled down a bit we went to the night market set up on the sidewalk outside the government office. We ate hot pot and cold beer and a *hami-gua* that we carved up ourselves for dessert. The driver was there being very friendly, filling up the air with false cheer, urging me to eat and drink more.

THE NEXT MORNING we left early for the fourteen-hour trip to Aksay. We drove over some rough terrain, tiptoeing across boulder-strewn streams that had washed out the road and dry riverbeds and over the Altun Mountains on a narrow switchback that left our wheels sometimes not more than a foot or two from the edge. To the north we looked over the Tarim Basin, which seemed to disappear into a shimmering indistinctness where all was mirage and nothing was what it appeared to be. The landscape was one of complete featurelessness, of an entire absence of distinctions of horizon and sky, earth and air. The visible things neither existed nor didn't exist; they were there and they weren't there; they were form and formlessness sparkling under a sun whose existence was hard to deny even as the rest seemed to exemplify the Yogacaran conundrum: If nothing but mind exists, what is it that is nonexistence? The landscape was a natural metaphor for the riddle, suggesting something vast and solid as it stretched to the horizon, but actually it was only a manifestation of light, a desert mirage, an amphitheater of glitter and flash glimpsed by a wandering and impermanent eye. The idea cast a spell. I remembered what I had read in Rupert Gethin about dharmas being "like dreams, magical illusions, echoes, reflected images, mirages, space." To understand this is to understand the emptiness of understanding. This is *prajna-paramita,* the perfection of wisdom.

I came out of my trance as we leveled out onto a plateau and then descended into yet another pebbly flatland where at some unmarked point we crossed into Qinghai Province. We drove for a couple of hours and then stopped to eat a watermelon that we had bought before leaving Ruoqiang, spitting seeds onto the dry earth and looking out over the flatness of the land. After a few more hours, we began to encounter signs of settlement: a new row of telephone poles, more substantial, less spindly, more burdened with wires than those that lined the road earlier, a widening of the gravel track, a few road workers with flat-bladed spades tending to the embankment. Then the landscape turned from arid-desolate to arid-industrial, industrial in the ersatz, state-planned Marxist, nineteenth-century way that China is still industrial. There were soot-darkened brick sheds and chimneys spewing plumes of black smoke into the sky, and near these dark satanic mills were brick dormitories with long dark corridors and wooden doors outside of which were brick cooking stands smeared thickly with grease. For so many undifferentiated miles, the landscape had been boring but clean, undisturbed by anything except for the road itself and the faithful telephone poles. Now we had reached the edge of industrial civilization and could smell its fetid breath. We drove past what seemed to be a coal mine and then some oil derricks slowly rotating their large steel arms. Until that point we had seen only one other vehicle since leaving Ruoqiang, a jeep that we passed early on the day's journey. And at the divide point of the Altun Mountains, when we had gotten out of the jeep to survey the Tarim plain below, we could see another car laboriously climbing the switchbacks in our direction, but it never reached us and we never saw it again. Now there was heavy traffic, trucks, road-building equipment, crews with shovels filling motorized carts with desert gravel.

At around three in the afternoon, we stopped for lunch at Mangnai, which we spotted on the horizon about five miles away. It was a set of warehouses and brick dormitories silhouetted against the horizon and some outdoor pool tables. We ate a watery *sha-guo,* a kind of noodle stew boiled in a clay pot, and talked about staying in Mangnai or pushing on to Lenghu, the next town on the map, two hundred miles away.

"Whatever you want," said Zhang.

"Are you tired?" I asked. We wouldn't arrive in Lenghu until after dark, and I didn't want him falling asleep at the wheel. I also didn't want to spend the night in Mangnai, an industrial purgatory where the food was bad and there was nothing to do.

"No problem. If you want to go on, we'll go on."

"Let's go on then."

THE COUNTRYSIDE OPENED up into a rolling plain, with the Kunlun Mountains barely visible through a hazy atmosphere in the south. We went past some swampy ground and a lake. On one side, hills extended to the mountains. After a couple of hours, we turned north, and what the map identified as the Ye-ma Nan-shan, the "South Wild Horse Mountains," loomed up in the far distance. They were the main barrier between ancient China proper and the barbarian kingdoms to the south and west. The Jade Gate was over there someplace, a flat plateau between those mountains and another chain parallel to them and to the north. That was where Hsuan Tsang reentered the Middle Kingdom after his seventeen years on the road, and I asked myself how he must have felt.

Did he experience the mixture of longing and anxiety that I was experiencing as our destination approached? Suddenly I felt a mild unease, a familiar unease. The prospect of arriving at a destination that once seemed impossibly distant brings with it a pleasurable anticipation, but it also carries the hollow sensation of endings. At some unmarked point just ahead, our road would bump over the administrative border between Qinghai and Gansu provinces, Gansu being China proper, no longer the Inner Asian frontier but the Middle Kingdom itself. Our eventual destination, just an overnight and a wake-up away, was Dunhuang, the great intersection of the northern and southern passes of the Silk Road and thus the place where the most fabulous cave temple east of Ajanta was built. Before I set off on this journey, Dunhuang had seemed to me remote and exotic, and it would have seemed that way still had I approached it from the east, leaving Xian and passing through the ever smaller towns in the mountain corridors that lead to it. I had always dreamed of seeing Dunhuang. But coming from the west, and having passed through places like Khotan, Cherchen, and Charkhlik, I perceived Dunhuang as a kind of

Chinese landfall, the last major destination before Xian and the end point of the journey. It would be just on the home side of the border between home and away, and as such it evoked in me the unease I have always felt at the idea of home.

It accounts for a lot in my life, including my chronic ambivalence, my sense of unbelonging. It accounts for why I spent years as a foreign correspondent and why, when I returned to the United States, the country I love, I always, but especially at the beginning, was afflicted by a low-grade melancholia. I remember in 1987 returning to New York after my tour of duty for the *Times* in Paris and going right away to a supermarket to pick up some breakfast food for the next morning. I fell into a depression at the spectacle of all those fluorescently lighted cereal boxes with their gaudy, multicolored cheerfulness stamped all over them. Cereal boxes were the antithesis of adventure. I associated the oversized supermarket with its fifty brands of crackers and its shrink-wrapped packages and its low-fat foods and its temperature-controlled hum and its Muzak and its rubber-wheeled carts with a tedious sort of safety. I associated it with overheated apartments and television game shows and the routine of going to work, getting a salary, paying bills, competing with others (younger all the time) for recognition and promotion. Home is necessary. Home is good. Home is horrible. My dread of it explains why I managed to reach my fifties without having married or had children, even though at the same time I have been lacerated by the Talmudic judgment that an unmarried and childless man is only half a man.

Now, riding on the edge of Gansu where I could see, figuratively, the end point of this trip, I understood what the dread has been all about. Home may be a castle, but it is the castle where you are going to grow old, decay, and die. The time passes at home, and with time comes corruption. When you are on the road, time stands still, or at least it seems to, because you are too busy moving to feel it. The Buddha understood this, and that is why, once he saw life as unavoidable suffering, he left home, abandoning his wife and his children, and undertook a life of wandering, as do the sadhus, the ragged and slightly demented Hindu holy men of today. Home is the ultimate attachment, and to achieve Enlightenment is to sunder attachment. After the Buddha died and his disciples gathered on Vulture Peak to hold the first Buddhist assembly, their leader, Kasyapa, would not allow Ananda, the Buddha's cousin and his favorite disciple, to sit among them. Ananda returned the next morning and declared that all the ties that bound him to the world had been broken, and he was allowed to pass through the door. Home is the primordial tie. I undertook this trip, this last trip, because I was getting too old to keep on moving, because I wanted to have one great final adventure. I wanted to get away to the strangest and most faraway place I could imagine. And now, as I watched the road point at the hazy blue mountains on the other side of which was China, I began to feel that the strangeness and the adventure were already behind me. I wanted to get back to Xian on time and to return to work at the *Times*. And at the same time I felt a kind of negative Proustian remembrance of real life. I felt it like a familiar taste in my mouth that made me want to brush my teeth.

There was nothing on this barren road. It was ugly here. And yet as the jeep groaned on into the descending twilight, I felt a strange affection for the unattractiveness, the scorched emptiness, of it all.

I remember years ago when I was first traveling in Asia, I would be on a train or, in some instances, a plane, and I would experience the opposite of impatience to arrive at my destination. I would want somehow for the rocking monotonous clickety-clack of the train or the roar of the airplane to be prolonged indefinitely. There was something powerfully reassuring about the moment of transit, a suspension of concerns. You were taken care of on the train or the plane. You didn't have to think about any of the vexing details of existence—finding a place to stay, getting your underwear washed, obtaining a map, dealing with taxi drivers and street touts, and knowing whether and how much to tip. I had the same feeling on the barren frontier between Qinghai and Gansu. I was tired of the bumpy ride and of the sight of Zhang's aggressive little mustache suspended over the steering wheel. I wanted to be someplace where I could get my e-mail and have a cappuccino. I wanted to see my mother and my sister and her family, especially her three great kids, who are my only nephews. And at the same time, as I looked out the windshield of our speeding jeep, I took reassurance from the illusion that the mountains ahead seemed to recede even as we drove toward them. On the other side of the mountains was the home that I missed and where I didn't want to go.

21

Last Words

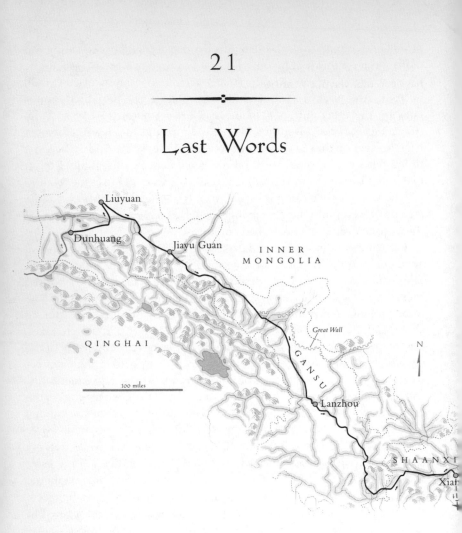

WE REACHED THE GAP in the mountains after nightfall and descended a curved and narrow road on the other side in the gathering dark. Around nine o'clock we arrived at a town whose name I have forgotten. It was a new place, a stucco confection in the desert designed, it would seem, to draw a larger Chinese population to the area. The region on the north of the Wild Horse Mountains was officially called the Aksai Kazak Autonomous County. We saw nary a Kazak, though no doubt they were tending flocks in the surrounding hills. Just to the east was the North Gansu Mongol Autonomous County. This arid region, like what the Chinese today call Xinjiang, collected many peoples—some in the mountains, others on the oasis-strewn plain, room for everybody. It has been that way for centuries.

There was a restaurant open in the town whose name I cannot remember either, and we had bowls of noodles and warm beer served by shy Chinese girls. We stayed in a new hotel with a communal bathroom and a communal toilet down the hall. We washed up out of enamel basins. The next morning, we were up early and went off to find the Yang Guan, another of the historic passes between China and the western territories and the one that Hsuan Tsang had passed through on his return trip. Zhang had told us earlier that he had been there and knew where it was, but he couldn't find it. We drove back and forth on the main north–south road that ran between the Qinghai border and Dunhuang until we came entirely by chance to a sign at a turnoff that said Yumen Guan, Jade Gate.

"Let's go there, since we can't find the Yang Guan," I shouted.

"There's nothing to see," Zhang said.

"Why is there a sign there if there's nothing to see?"

"We should go to the Yang Guan," he insisted. "It has great historical importance."

"I want to go to the Yang Guan, but let's see the Yumen Guan since we're here," I said.

"It's one hundred kilometers. That's two hundred kilometers for the round trip. You didn't pay for that many kilometers."

"We paid for whatever we want to do and wherever we want to go between Khotan and Dunhuang," Zhongmei said. It was good to have her in this negotiation. I felt protected.

The driver gave a knowing laugh, establishing himself as the connoisseur of local custom, especially as compared to us outsiders. He gave us to understand that these side trips, which were lengthy, were going to cost additional money. Zhongmei gave him to understand that this was not the case and if it came to a dispute she was prepared right then to call the Xinjiang Khotan International Travel Service and talk to his boss.

"Never mind, never mind," he said, assuming the attitude of one who makes generous concessions. We were off on the road to Yumen Guan.

In the end we saw both Yumen Guan and Yang Guan, our driver, stoically, tight-lippedly hunched over the steering wheel, taking us over many miles of rumpled desert. The Yumen Guan we saw was not the Yumen Guan that Hsuan Tsang had skirted around on his trip to Hami. That one was the Tang-era gate and was in Anxi to the east of us. This one was a good hour or more to the northwest across the desert from the intersection where we had seen the sign, the jeep slewing in the sand like a sailboat in choppy water. We sent aloft a thick plume of dust to choke anybody who might be riding behind us. I felt a resurgence of the spirit of adventure. The trip wasn't over yet.

We came to a small village thick with grape trellises. We drove over a stream that ran among bamboo groves and then steeply up onto a kind of earthen knoll on the top of which was what remains of the Han Dynasty Jade Gate, complete with Mongol women renting horses to the tourists. I took one and, flopping around like a rag doll, rode it to the top of the knoll, from where I looked over a vista of spectacularly unbounded desolation. In the very far distance the Altun Mountains glistened white, and in between there was a sort of void, a vast emptiness, a molten glitter in which any lone horseman making his slow way toward China would have formed a flickering silhouette to a watchful frontier guard.

Early in the century, Aurel Stein discovered some bamboo slips that identified this spot as the Jade Gate, a finding confirmed by Chinese archaeologists in the 1940s. Here began, or here ended, the Road of Great Events. Zhang Qian, who first brought back word of glorious civilizations to the west of China, would have passed through this way, once on his way west and once on his return. Ban Chao, who subdued the barbarians for the Han Dynasty, would also have ridden his horse through this gate, more than thirty feet high, leading his thousands of men to their distant rendezvous. The soldiers would have looked like the terra-cotta figures buried with the first emperor in Chang-an. They would have marched to the clamor of drums. There would have been a large number of them, carrying pikes, shields, and swords and forming a moving rectangle of military might advancing slowly to the east, where they would slaughter and be slaughtered in the great tradition of Central Asia. I sat on my small Mongol horse, which yearned to return to its stable, and bid farewell to the Great Western Desert stretching back to Khotan, whence we had come. I doubt if I will ever see it again.

Then we went to the Yang Guan, Zhang having gotten directions from some men playing chess at the Yumen Guan entrance. While the Yumen Guan still stands tall on its knoll, with four gates penetrating its thirty-foot-high walls, Yang Guan is a rubble, a spongy mound that was a watchtower two millennia before. Nearby were the remains of a casern of indeterminate date with high walls and battered apertures offering views of the gate and the desert beyond. While we were there a minibus full of Chinese students, chattering and taking pictures of one another, roamed through the site. We repaired to a covered refreshment stand and tourist shop, where we sat at a rickety table and drank porcelain bowls of green tea. A man sitting at the table began talking about the history of the gates. He was jowly and wore plastic glasses, a white shirt with rolled-up sleeves, and the standard-issue gray trousers, and he knew what he was talking about.

"They don't get the sadness of it," he said, nodding toward the noisy band of students. "This is a place of sadness."

"Tell us," Zhongmei said.

"The poems tell the story," the man said. "The Tang poems. They are always about loneliness and solitude and exile. They are about the longing for home."

"Can you tell us one?" Zhongmei said.

The man looked at us with mournful eyes. I wondered who he was and whether he was angling for a tip. Why else would someone pass his days in the little shop of the Yang Guan surrounded by the usual tourist shlock, the jade figurines, the mass-produced paintings of tigers, the porcelain pandas, and talk to ignorant visitors? Was he an exile himself, a victim of some earlier revolutionary excess in China, a man who had reason to talk about solitude and the longing for home?

"Liangzhou Lines," he announced, like a schoolboy about to recite something in class, "by Wang Han." Liangzhou is the ancient name for Wuwei, where, on his way west, Hsuan Tsang was summoned for an interview by the local magistrate, and then began to travel incognito.

> *They are about to drink*
> *The finest wine from jade cups*
> *When the sudden sound of mandolins urges them forth.*
>
> *Don't scorn them*
> *They who drunken fall upon the field.*
> *In ancient days or now,*
> *How many return who go to war?*

"The jade cups were called Evening Radiance," the man said. "The soldiers marched out at the Yumen Guan, and those who returned came back here, at the Yang Guan, but there weren't many of them. Their bones are still out there. No graves. No names. Just the bones. China has the bloodiest history of all the nations."

The man fell silent. He didn't mention the bones of the multitudes slaughtered there by those soldiers.

"Are you a teacher?" Zhongmei asked him.

The man ignored her question.

"Beyond the Jade Gate, spring winds will never blow," he said, reciting another poetic line, and sipping some pale green tea.

I HAD ALWAYS imagined Dunhuang to be a windblown Central Asian oasis, a dusty town surrounded by an earthen wall behind which the camels took shelter. It was perhaps something like that when Stein came here in 1907. Since then it has become a destination resort for Silk Road tourists who go to the fabulous Mogao Caves, the best-preserved Buddhist cave temple site in China, the best east of Ajanta. We arrived from the south and drove down the main street, past numerous glass-fronted hotels, restaurants, and streetside markets. There were large posters and festive banners with flying angels emblazoned upon them. At the town's main intersection, we had to go around a large statue of a Buddhist deity playing the mandolin-like four-stringed instrument known as the pipa, the instrument that, according to the poem recited by our friend at the Yang Gate, summoned soldiers to battle. Probably there had been a statue of Chairman Mao on that spot. The pipa player was better.

"You're not the first white man to come to Dunhuang," Zhongmei said, smiling.

"Coming here I feel like it's really over," I said, speaking of the trip. "Until now it was so . . . barren, and now we're back on the beaten track."

"I know what you mean, but wait until you see the caves. They're incredible."

We checked into a hotel, our first hostelry of more or less international standing since the luxurious Imperial Hotel in New Delhi. We went to the night market for dinner, and, true to the valedictory mood stealing over me, I thought about it as my last night market in Central Asia. It wasn't a good one. It was housed in a large square off the main street of Dunhuang, itself crowded with tchotchke shops, under a bluish translucent ceiling that kept the dankness within. It smelled of washed cement, congealed pigs' blood, and frying garlic. We had noodles in an anemic broth at one stand and red bean soup at another. We walked back to the hotel, and Zhongmei wanted to buy a watermelon. I objected, thinking about watermelon rind in our hotel room. She looked at me strangely, as if not recognizing me. This part of the journey, the neither-here-nor-there-ness of this point of transit, was not appealing to me.

"Sorry," I said.

"Are they sweet?" Zhongmei asked the watermelon seller.

"Sweet," he said.

"Let's see. If it's not sweet, we're not going to buy it."

The man cut out a little wedge of watermelon.

"Now, we have to buy it," I grumbled.

"No we don't," Zhongmei said. "He can just put the piece of rind back in and sell it to somebody else. That's what they do here."

It wasn't very sweet.

"We'll take it," I said, and we carried it back through the warm streets of Dunhuang to the hotel.

Six days before when we had agreed to take our car, Zhongmei had insisted on withholding a couple of thousand yuan of the payment, to be given to Zhang when he delivered us in Dunhuang. We called him in his room and asked him to come down to collect the total due. Before he arrived, I counted it out, worrying about my diminished wad of hundred-yuan notes, which had once been a reassuring inch-thick lump in my money belt.

"Should we give him a tip?" I asked.

"Not more than a hundred yuan."

Zhang knocked on the door and came into the room crackling with false cheer. Zhongmei handed him the wad of hundreds, and when he got to the door to leave I held out our modest *pourboire,* worth maybe ten meals for him on the long road back to Khotan.

"This is for you," I said. "Thank you very much."

"Oh, no no no no no!" he cried. "You keep your money. Use it next time you want to have a tea." And he was out the door and down the corridor, leaving me feeling outdone, outclassed, embarrassed, and relieved, as if somebody had slowly turned down the volume on a scratchy radio.

WE SPENT ALL of the next day at the caves. I fought an afflictive drowsiness the whole time. My back ached. Zhongmei, who had been to Dunhuang before, was happy. She gazed with fiery eyes at the wall paintings, which, though I recognized them to be amazing, full of exquisite color and sinuous form, failed to summon up the proper and appropriate sense of awe. And they *are* astonishing, even when viewed with the pale light of a flashlight. The caves are cut at three levels of a sheer, immensely long sandstone cliff that curves alongside a stream and is partly blocked by poplar trees. As the guidebooks like to put it, Dunhuang's Mogao Caves hold the most important and richest collection of Buddhist art in the world. I wanted to experience it symphonically, to be moved. I was moved at Ajanta, where I peered at ancient images that seemed to glow from some light behind them, awed by their beauty and their antiquity, by the delicate sensibility of the anonymous men who lived out their lives creating them. But I was feeling emotionally and aesthetically flat in Dunhuang, hot and sleepy. I am only moved by Dunhuang now in retrospect, even as I am regretful that I didn't enjoy it more when I was there.

There are about five hundred caves in all, full of the paintings and sculptures that make Dunhuang perhaps not better but certainly much vaster than the caves at Ajanta, which were created at roughly the same time. Dunhuang has the fifth-largest Buddha statue in the world, a stone Buddha of the future, built by the empress Wu Zuotian early in the eighth century. There are entire large walls of small images of the Buddha, in white, green, and black robes. Many of the paintings have a modern, almost abstract look, as if they were models for those dancing figures by Matisse, such as the pair of flying angels in Cave 249. One is all floating sleeves with only a suggestion of arched female torso; the other, below it, is more solid, in black, devilish and male, facing front and foreshortened so the arms and head are large and conceal the body behind. The colors are amazing, and amazingly well preserved, turquoise, emerald, a kind of lavender, a luxuriant red. While there are the customary Jataka stories at Dunhuang, many of the paintings are devoted to scenes of daily life and of court life. Cave 420 shows a merchant procession from Tibet and looks like something from the Museum of Modern Art in New York, a large abstract painting in shades of gray, aquamarine, and black. There are many scenes of dancing girls surrounded by musicians, doing movements that I have seen Zhongmei do when she has performed in New York. Perhaps the most remarkable effect comes from their utter absence of naturalistic spatial logic. The figures, many of them extraordinarily intricate, are arranged both horizontally and vertically on the walls, giving a fantastic, phantasmagoric impression of movement and color.

The first cave paintings date to the fourth century, so when Hsuan Tsang came here, they were already ancient. I assume that the monk did come to Dunhuang, because he would have had to and he would have wanted to, but he didn't say anything about it in his book, probably because Dunhuang, being within the Jade Gate, did not belong to the Western world about which the emperor was interested. The last paintings date from the time of the Muslim conquest of Turkestan in the eleventh century, at which point the caves and their treasures were sealed and hidden by the local Buddhist devotees, thereby saving them from the vandalism that spoiled so many of the paintings in Turfan and Kucha.

The treasure lay hidden for centuries, like the sweet dew of Buddhism itself, until in about 1900 a certain Abbot Wang, a Taoist antiquarian, rediscovered a cache of documents and paintings in what is now called Cave 17. After the abbot came the indefatigable Stein, who bought documents, statues, and paintings from the abbot, including a copy of the Diamond Sutra (now in the British Museum) that was produced in 868 A.D., making it the oldest printed book in the world. The documents were in Chinese, Uigur, Sogdian, Tibetan, and Sanskrit. Later the Frenchman Paul Pelliot arrived and the good abbot sold him some relics as well, these now being housed in the Musée Guimet in Paris. In 1923, Langdon Warner of the Fogg Art Museum at Harvard appeared and, saying he wanted to save the best paintings from tourist spoliation, cut out some frescoes, now at the Fogg. Still, the collection *in situ* is thrilling, if you are in a mood to be thrilled.

VERY EARLY THE next morning we got a car to take us the two hours to Liuyuan—Willow Garden, where there are no willows and where we had been on the way west—to take the overnight train to Xian. We found a barnlike cafeteria and breakfasted on sesame buns, cold fried eggs, and Eight Treasures Porridge (rice, green beans, red beans, millet, and other things in watery broth). We were a day and a half on the train returning to our starting point, rewinding the tape, going backward in time, being pulled inexorably toward ordinary life. In the dining car the waitress recognized us from months before when we had taken this same train in the opposite direction. I was due back at work pretty soon, so I read a book that I was scheduled to review for the *Times* about the savage competition among egomaniacal cyber-magnates—most notably Microsoft's Bill Gates—and it seemed as far as it was possible to get from the Gansu corridor, the muddy Wei River, the closely tended terraced wheat fields rolling past our window. We lumbered through sooty tunnels that smelled like dirty laundry and that amplified the racket of wheels and tracks. I wrote a generally favorable review of the book on my portable computer, feeling that I was probably the only person ever to write a book review for an American newspaper on the Urumqi–Xian express. It's the sort of thing you end up doing when you want your life to consist of incompatible components. I would send the review via e-mail from the hotel in Xian.

We reached the far outskirts of Xian the next afternoon, and I watched out the window as the ancient farmland gave way to industrial sheds and freight yards. I saw a lone bicyclist on a straight road bordered by trees pedaling slowly into the gloaming. Inside the train, a pretty little girl from the neighboring compartment stood at our doorway and stared in at us. I smiled at her, and she sat in the seat next to me and watched me form strange English letters on my computer screen. The service people in their two-tone blue shirts began to sweep the floors of the compartments with short brooms. They gathered up the large red thermoses that we had used to make tea on the trip.

I wondered if this would be my last long train trip in China. I remembered how I had felt on the train going in the opposite direction a few months before, excited to be on the road but worried that I would be caught and expelled and that my dream of following the route of Hsuan Tsang would come to naught. I didn't know if my travels were taking place without the knowledge of the Chinese security police or if they had known about my presence all along and elected to do nothing about it. Probably I will never know, but now I found myself basking in a sense of indifference. It didn't matter anymore whether I was discovered or not. At the same time, I felt a kind of cycle coming to a close.

Nearly three decades before, in 1972, I had made my first trip to China. I was a graduate student and uneasily tempted by the Maoist method of total mobilization, or perhaps more accurately, uneasily going along with the conventional leftist views of those years. I crossed over the trestle bridge from Lowu in Hong Kong to Shenchen in Guangdong Province and within a day or two I had become a lifelong anti-Maoist, a militant opponent of all forms of utopian social engineering. My five-week trip, in the company of fourteen anti–Vietnam War activists, one or two of whom shared my almost instant disillusionment, was a journey from one petty commissar to the next. China was like an immense boot camp with a blue uniform and a single secular religion, the adoration of Chairman Mao.

I remember one train ride in particular, taken in the company of the guides that the China Travel Service had provided for us, from Zhengzhou in Henan Province in north-central China to Shenyang, the former Mukden. We lumbered through an early-spring landscape of sodden fallow fields and low mud-brick villages. In the train I objected to a comment made by a smooth-faced functionary at a people's commune we had been taken to see near Zhengzhou. One of us, collecting information on the workings of Chinese socialism, asked a grizzled old peasant there what was the most important single element in increasing agricultural production. The old man, who wore a rough-cut black jacket and a towel wrapped over his scalp, scratched his stubble as he thought over his answer. But before he could speak, the young functionary, who had arrived in a chauffeured car, put out his hand to silence the peasant. The most important single ingredient in increasing agricultural output, he reverentially declared, was studying the works of Chairman Mao.

What was astonishing to me was that my fellow travelers, except for my one or two comrades in revolutionary disillusionment, failed to be sickened by that comment. Well, we were all young and foolish then, and we have probably all gotten a bit wiser in the meantime. During that first trip to China, however, I was full of angry passion. I felt that I had fallen into a delegation of fools, what Lenin called useful idiots, those who went to the Soviet Union in the 1920s and 1930s and proclaimed its wonders to people back home. When I voiced my disgust with the smooth-faced functionary and with our absence of outrage and with China itself, which was poverty-stricken, regimented, bombastic, and boring, one of the women in our group, our own La Pasionaria, applied a previously unused ideological label to me. I had a *Darkness at Noon* mentality, she said, meaning that I suffered unduly under the influence of Arthur Koestler's book of that name. I didn't have the wit to admit the truth of the accusation and to urge all of us to recognize that China under Communism was a kind of darkness at noon, but I didn't think to say that at the time. I sat in contemptuous silence and waited for the silly pilgrimage to be over.

Physically, the trains actually haven't changed much since then. They are the same army-green color and they have the same poor dining cars and the same slimy toilets, the same three-class hierarchy of soft sleeper, hard sleeper, and hard seat, the same general austerity. In the old days the speakers would come alive at precisely six in the morning with shrill propaganda exhortations and inspirational Communist-choral music. The long-suffering Chinese people willed themselves into a kind of collective auditory numbness to cope with the constant barrage of sound that pursued them into the fields, the factories, the classrooms, the asphyxiating toilets, the hard-sleeper cars that lurched over the North China Plain and that you couldn't ride without a permission slip from your commissar. For several hours on that long train ride from Zhengzhou to Shenyang, several of the men in my group had engaged one of our guides in a conversation about love and marriage. For hours we tried to get him to acknowledge that a woman's appearance, her beauty, was at least one of the elements that would attract him to her, but, sweating with anxiety over this interrogation, he refused to admit that he noticed when a woman was pretty. The sole element in romantic attraction, he maintained, was her devotion to Marxism–Leninism–Mao Zedong–Thought. He said it with a straight face, in all earnestness. I believe that he believed it because he would have been too terrified not to believe it. China was like that.

Now the train's loudspeakers issued forth with syrupy musical sounds and with brief lessons on personal hygiene. The mother of the little girl who sat beside me and watched me type stood at the entry to our compartment. She wore blue spandex pants and raised plastic sandals, and her hair was permed into frizziness. Outside the afternoon sky hung low and gray over the semirural dishevelment. The train stopped at Jinxing, just to the west of Xian, and then began grinding forward again. I tried to reflect on the trip about to come to an end. I had made it, I felt, just in the nick of time, when there was still something different from home somewhere in the world. I remembered that group of retired folk from Florida encountered in the passport line at the Torugart Pass, on their way to a yurt motel, and I understood that the world is already too discovered, and difference is disappearing. I felt glad that I had done this journey, but I suspected as I sat in the train that I wouldn't be traveling like this again. I was going home to marry Zhongmei and to start a family, and none too soon. Finally, at the age of fifty-five, I was going to bring my stubborn extension of adolescence to an end.

When he was on the road from Jumna to Thanesuar in India, in the torrid territory where the Mahabharata took place, Hsuan Tsang reflected on one of the central episodes of that story, Krishna's urging Arjuna into battle. Hsuan Tsang turned it into a statement of Buddhist belief. "Life and death are like an ocean without shores, and they flow in an endless alternation; intelligent beings cannot escape from the eddy in which they are swept away." Riding on the train, I thought I understood what he meant. I took Hsuan Tsang's journey knowing I could not escape the eddy in which I am caught. My feeling, heretical to the monk, is that I will exist only once on this planet, that life and death do not, for the ineffable individual, flow in an endless alternation. And I also believe (closer to the monk but still different from him) that there is a limit to the extent to which you can mold the specifics of your life, that there is no escape, not into the manufacture of Shaker furniture nor into the excitement of travel. The Truth, the Enlightenment, that Hsuan Tsang searched for in his seventeen years on the road was a philosophical one. I had pondered it, and though the Truth that I arrived at in my journey of several months was more pedestrian than his, yet to me it was just as valuable. It was that you do have to go home, home in all senses of that word—to a job, to the dross of routine, to time-consuming responsibilities and obligations, to aches and pains, to the hell that other people make for you sometimes. The truth is the existential one that therein, confronting the mortal realities, is where meaning and wisdom lie. I was going back to write book reviews for a great American daily newspaper, an honest and interesting labor if not exactly an exalting one. So, yes, we wish to find things that can fill up our hearts and provide us with permanent ecstasy. It doesn't happen to very many of us. But it doesn't matter, because there is nothing we can do about the inevitabilities, except to take a bit of time and to think, to make sure the time doesn't go by so swiftly that life becomes humdrum and unexamined. That was the value of my months on the road. I felt good to have broken away from my usual routine at least for a while, to have overcome all those hesitancies of middle age and to have ventured forth as I did when I was young and eager. It's not a major victory, perhaps, but I did see the air glitter above the timeless sands and mountains along the Road of Great Events, when I might have been having another cappuccino at Starbucks. And I was coming back more certain than I had ever been that I would be able to choose love with one woman and all of its obligations, rather than the loneliness that I had felt earlier, without obligations.

Suddenly there were apartment buildings pushing against the edges of the farm fields and long brick walls painted with faded propaganda signs and dusty free markets sprawled out on the edges of vacant earthen lots and factories with broken casement windows and makeshift basketball courts and yellow construction cranes. We crossed a trestle bridge and came into a neighborhood of low-slung houses, their tile roofs weighted with loose bricks. Young men, bare to the waist and wearing gray pleated trousers, hung around and talked on the narrow embankments alongside the tracks. And then suddenly there was Xian's crenellated Ming Dynasty Wall and the North Gate. We had arrived. The journey was over.

THERE WAS ONE last thing to do. The next morning, Zhongmei and I took a taxi into the countryside southwest of Xian to visit the Xing Jiao Si, the Temple Where Teaching Flourishes, built in 669, five years after the pilgrim's death, and dedicated to him. It was the very temple that, several months before, the supposed director of the Lanzhou Art Museum, the one who had written a poem out for us on a flimsy sheet of letterhead stationery, had commanded us to visit. We found a taxi and raced through the Xian sprawl, down a broad highway, under overpasses, past factories, and into wheat and soybean fields. The driver took wrong turns; he muttered irritably about the absence of road markers. Finally he got us there, halfway up a long green hill on a narrow rural lane. Two stone lions marked the entrance, and there were Chinese yellow characters on an oxblood wall: *a-mi-tuo-fo,* the Buddhist mantra. Inside the gates was a gleaming black Mercedes-Benz 500 SEL, perhaps the car of one of China's newly wealthy entrepreneurs, a budding capitalist and, apparently, a latter-day Buddhist patron, a descendant of the Silk Road travelers who earned merit by paying for work at the Kizil Caves and Dunhuang. We bought incense sticks at a little temple shop, walked past the main temple with a large bronze Buddha statue inside, and headed to a five-story pagoda in a separate quiet garden on the far side of it.

During his last years, Hsuan Tsang lived under the patronage of the emperor and worked steadily supervising a team that translated the texts he had brought back with him from India. He was close to Tai Tsung, who became a fervent Buddhist and summoned the famous monk frequently to his side. Hsuan Tsang was with the emperor when he died in 649. In 652, the new emperor gave the monk funds with which he built the Big Wild Goose Pagoda to house his collections. The money came from what were called "missing people," which Arthur Waley speculates probably meant those in the royal household who had been banished or killed in the inevitable power struggle that followed Tai Tsung's death. Hsuan Tsang worked for twelve more years, living at the Xi Ming Si, or West Bright Monastery, which seems no longer to exist. One night in 664, seventeen years after the completion of his seventeen-year journey to India, he tripped and cut his leg. Four days after his accident, he felt unwell and was forced to lie down. He told his acolytes that he dreamed of a host of giants in brocade dress who came carrying flowers, jewels, and embroidered cloth with which they decorated the monastery. "These things," Hsuan Tsang is said to have said, "are the embodiments of such holy works as I have done in my time." Near the end, he told his gathered disciples that his work was finished and there was no sense in his staying longer. His last words are recorded: "Unreality is unreal." He was sixty-one years old.

Zhongmei and I stood in front of the pagoda. It is a graceful structure of yellow brick inside a flower garden surrounded by trees. Hsuan Tsang is buried within. Above the main archway on the first level are four Chinese characters: *Tang-san-tsang-ta,* "Tang San Tsang's Tower." We pushed our incense sticks into the ash of a stone urn and lit them. I stood for a while listening to the breeze whisper the monk's name in the leaves above. I stole a glance at Zhongmei standing beside me and felt that she looked especially radiant. The garden was a peaceful place. I didn't want to leave it. I clung to this last tranquil remnant of my journey on the Road of Great Events. But we had reservations on the plane for Beijing that afternoon. Finally I turned away. Three days later I was in New York, home.

ACKNOWLEDGMENTS

I wish to thank Jon Segal, my editor at Alfred A. Knopf, who stayed with this project during the long years of delay and procrastination and, once the delays were over, helped immeasurably to guide it to completion. Kathy Robbins, my agent, was similarly, invaluably supportive. Others who helped in various ways are Bill McCahill, Ed Gargan, Heather Won Tesorioro, Tavleen Singh, Gayatri Patnaik, Prem and Christine Patnaik, Sheila Sharma, Arjun Mahey, P. J. Anthony, Ahmed and Angela Rashid, Fidaullah Serhai, Andrew Nathan, John Darnton, Joe Lelyveld, Liu Heung Shing, and the person I call Brave King. I am grateful for the cordial receptions I was accorded in India, both at the Root Institute in Bodhgaya and at the S.I.E.S. School of Management in Nerul by the Shankaracharya of Kanchipuram and the members of his entourage. My special thanks to Zhongmei Li, whose love and courage have been indispensable in more ways than I could enumerate.

INDEX

Abbottabad, 282
Achaemenids, 180
Aciman, Andre, 102
Adi Shankara, Sri, 260
Afghanistan, 10, 60, 89, 91, 118, 134,
    159–61, 165, 167–9, 172, 179–80,
    186, 196–7, 265, 291, 294, 308;
    Buddhism in, 160–1, 168, 201;
    Hsuan Tsang in, 159–60, 169, 291,
    299–300; Soviet occupation, 169
Afrasayib, 165–6
Africa, 38, 39, 148, 159
Aga Khan, 160
Agra, 196, 198
Aguilar, Karen, 161
Ajanta, 6, 85, 220, 254, 276–8, 321,
    328, 330
Aksai Kazak Autonomous County, 324
Aksay, 319
Aksu, 42, 108, 114, 120–2, 123, 125,
    138
Aleppo, 252
Alexander the Great, 91, 112, 180, 308
Alexandria, 253, 254
Allahabad, 206
Alma Ata, 172
Altun Mountains, 319, 320, 326
Amritsar, 190, 191, 192–6, 230, 279;
    orphanage in, 194–6
Amsterdam, 159
Amu-Darya River, 160, 161, 162, 165,
    166–9
Ananda, 322
anti-Semitism, 253

Anxi, 72, 73, 74
Arabian Sea, 253, 266
Aramaic, 180
archaeology, 19–20, 58, 178–82, 235
    and n., 278, 282, 307–9, 314–17;
    Chinese monuments vandalized,
    71–2, 85, 314, 331; see also specific
    sites
Asanga, 95, 174–7, 198, 224, 237
A-she-na Sho-eul, 301–2
Ashoka, King, 91–2, 173, 180, 186,
    187, 225, 233–4
Ashoka Pillars, 91
Aurangabad, 274, 276–8
Ayodhya, 199, 202–3

Babur, 144
Bactria, 59, 91, 92, 94, 112, 182
Bactrian Greeks, 180–1
Badakhshan, 299
Baghdad, 251, 252, 253
Bai-dun-zi, 72, 73, 74, 75
Baluchis, 171
Bamiyan, 160–1, 168, 169, 181
Ban Chao, 60, 299, 309, 326
Bandhu, 66–8, 75, 82
Bangalore, 256
Bangkok, 119
Bangladesh, 249, 252
Baoyuan, 127
Barber, Elizabeth Wayland, *The
    Mummies of Urumchi,* 57
Barkol, 302

Index

Index

Shri Krishna Janmbhoomi, 199
Shuja, Mirza, 134–5
Siberia, 151
Sichuan Province, 25
Sikhism, 190, 191, 194, 195
Silabhadra, 28, 237–8
silk, manufacture of, 315–16
Silk Road, 17, 24, 50, 60–2, 71, 84,
    145, 152, 305, 307, 312, 315, 321,
    328; beginnings of, 60
Sindhis, 171
Singapore, 119, 280
Singh, Harinder, 194
Singh, Tavleen, 207, 217, 257, 258, 259
Smith, John, 277, 278
Smith, Violet, 249–50
Snelling, John, 175
Sog, 163
Sogdia, 167
Sost, 287, 290, 291, 292
South Africa, 159, 256
South China Sea, 231
Soviet Union, former, 143–4, 151–4,
    169, 170, 171, 333; see also Russia
Spain, 253
Sri Lanka, 204, 234, 236, 254
Srinigar, 197
Stalin, Joseph, 152
Stein, Aurel, 24, 71–2, 74, 75, 283,
    307–9, 326, 328; Chinese
    expeditions and monument theft,
    71–3, 80, 85, 307–9, 314, 331; in
    Khotan, 307–9, 314
Stevenson, Robert Louis, 10
Sugong Tower, 84–5
Sui Dynasty, 23, 25, 29, 39–40, 88, 95
Suleiman, 84
sunyata, concept of, 95, 175–7, 240,
    246
Sun Yung, 37, 39
Sutra in Forty-two Sections, 3, 93
Swarnatep, King, 112–13
Swat River Valley, 111, 182–5, 188

Tai Tsung, Emperor, 23, 24, 34, 41,
    111, 149, 299, 301–2, 309, 311, 336

Taiwan, 12, 264
Taiyuan, 59
Tajikistan, 160
Tajiks, 134, 144, 163, 296
Takht-i-Bahi, 182, 184–5, 187, 314
Takla Makan Desert, 43, 53, 83, 90,
    92, 125, 135, 297–8
Taliban, 160, 168, 197
Talmud, 8, 32, 33, 147, 177, 247, 322
Tamerlane, 122, 144, 150, 163, 164, 166
Tang Dynasty, 19, 23, 24, 29, 34,
    40–1, 61, 66, 73–5, 77, 80, 95, 112,
    147, 149, 301–2, 313; poetry, 19,
    94, 147, 327
Tang Shu, 149
Taoism, 28, 93–5
Tao Te Ching, 94
Tarim Basin, 57, 59, 60, 81, 91, 92,
    149, 298, 302, 311, 313, 319, 320
Tashkent, 149, 154, 157, 159–62, 164,
    170, 171, 252
Tashkurgan, 296–300
Tash Rabat, 132, 145–50
Tata, 253
Tavajra, Ladi, 238, 246
Taxila, 181, 182, 185–8, 197, 201, 282,
    309
taxis, 51–2, 128, 131, 155, 157–9,
    164–5, 233, 269, 280, 336
Teheran, 252, 265
Temeudjin, 150
Teresa, Mother, 248
Termez, 160, 161, 162, 164–8, 171
terra-cotta soldiers, Qin, 19
terrorism, 137–8, 160, 162, 166, 170
Thailand, 204, 225
Thanesuar, 334
Tiananmen massacre (1989), 55, 115
Tianshan Mountains, 42, 60, 79, 80,
    97, 138, 152
Tinashui, 47
Tibet, 11, 62, 84, 137, 204, 225, 234,
    240, 246, 298, 330
Time magazine, 4, 64, 65, 118
Titianos, Maes, 60
Tokharians, 57–8, 111, 112, 149, 299,
    301–2

ALSO BY RICHARD BERNSTEIN

THE COMING CONFLICT WITH CHINA
with Ross H. Munro

From two former Beijing bureau chiefs with long experience in Asian affairs comes a clear-eyed and uncompromising look at the potentially disastrous collision course in the relations between the United States and China. Richard Bernstein and Ross H. Munro explain how the powerful new China lobby shapes U.S. policy with the support of American businesses eager for a share of its booming markets. *The Coming Conflict with China* is required reading for anyone who wishes to understand the tense global rivalry of the twenty-first century.

"A crucial contribution to the foreign policy debate."
—*Philadelphia Inquirer*
Current Affairs/Asian Studies/0-679-77662-1

DICTATORSHIP OF VIRTUE

*How the Battle Over Multiculturalism Is Reshaping
Our Schools, Our Country, Our Lives*

In *Dictatorship of Virtue*, Richard Bernstein examines multiculturalism, the movement that originated in a valid concern for the rights of the marginalized and oppressed but became a highly lucrative bureaucracy that shortchanged the very people it was meant to benefit. The result is an astute work of reportage that is as carefully researched as it is fearlessly provocative.

"Sometimes tart, sometimes eloquent, always graceful and lucid. [Bernstein's] reporting is fair and thorough. . . . Reading the book is arguably a civic duty."   —*Boston Globe*
Current Affairs/Politics/0-679-76398-8